M000281972

Contents

Contents

About the Author

Laura Hensley Choate, EdD, LPC, NCC, is an associate professor of counselor education in the Department of Educational Theory, Policy, and Practice at Louisiana State University in Baton Rouge. She received her EdD degree in counselor education from the College of William and Mary in 1997. Her research has focused on girls' and women's wellness issues and college student wellness. She has a particular interest in the promotion of body image resilience in adolescent girls and college women. She has published more than 20 refereed articles in the *Journal of Counseling & Development, Counselor Education and Supervision,* the *Journal of Mental Health Counseling,* and other journals. She is a past editor of the *Journal of College Counseling,* serving as editor during years 2004–2006 and as associate editor for years 2002–2004. She lives in Baton Rouge with her husband, Michael, and children, Benjamin and Abigail.

About the Contributors

Kimberly Anderson, PhD, Director of Psychology, Center for Eating Disorders at Sheppard Pratt Health System, Baltimore, MD

Catherine Clark, EdD, Associate Professor, Department of Human Development and Psychological Counseling, coordinator of the College Student Development program, Appalachian State University

Rita R. Culross, PhD, Jo Ellen Levy Yates Professor of Education, Louisiana State University

Marla J. Erwin, candidate for a doctoral degree in Educational Theory, Policy, and Practice, Louisiana State University

Susan K. Gardner, PhD, Assistant Professor, Higher Educational Administration, University of Maine

Gerri Miller, PhD, Diplomate in Counseling Psychology, ABPP, LPC, Professor in the Department of Human Development and Psychological Counseling, Appalachian State University

Jie Yu, candidate for a doctoral degree in Educational Theory, Policy, and Practice, Louisiana State University

Preface

Abigail's Future

I was 8-months pregnant with my daughter Abigail when I signed the contract to write this book. My husband Michael, my 2-year-old son Benjamin, and I were looking forward to welcoming a baby girl into our lives. Not long after her birth when I began to write these chapters concerning the current sociocultural climate for girls and women, I reflected on how these cultural trends might influence my daughter's life. As Abigail approaches her second birthday, I am aware that she will encounter many of the issues described in this book. I am both excited and apprehensive about what her future will bring.

I am excited for Abigail's future because girls and women are thriving as never before. Girls have high levels of academic success and are currently achieving higher grades and graduation rates when compared with boys (Halpern, 2006). Further, girls are becoming stronger and more physical; girls' sports participation is at the highest rate in history, with almost 3 million girls participating in sports at the high school level (National Federation of State High School Associations, 2006). They are also highly adept in the latest technological advances and know how to stay well connected with one another through various forms of technology.

Girls' progress extends well beyond the adolescent years. There are now more women than men enrolled in postsecondary institutions, and half of all medical and law school enrollments comprise women (National Center for Education Statistics, 2003; U.S. Census Bureau, 2001). Major social changes have led to increased opportunities and choices for women around work, motherhood, and household division of labor (Goodheart, 2006). More women are successfully working outside the home, owning their own businesses, and negotiating for better salaries. Employers are more supportive of women's desire to balance family and career by offering more flexible, family-friendly work environments. Today's women are encouraged to view their midlife years as a time for creativity, spiritual development, and psychological growth (Meyer, 2006). In addition, advances in women's health research have improved women's lives in their older years. These indicators are only a sample of the encouraging trends for today's girls and women.

However, other issues raise great concern for Abigail's future. One area is the clash between traditional and contemporary socialization processes for girls. Many of today's girls continue to be socialized according to traditional norms that encourage them to value themselves primarily for their appearance, to conform to a narrowly defined standard of beauty, and to be overly concerned with pleasing others (often at the expense of authentic self-development and self-expression). At the same time, they receive pressures to excel academically, engage in multiple extracurricular activities, and achieve equality with boys (Goodheart, 2006). Today's girls are struggling with how to best meet their needs for achievement while also meeting traditional cultural standards for femininity (Tryon & Winograd, 2003).

Further, while pressures for girls to be increasingly thin and beautiful are not new (particularly for White, middle-class girls), there is a contemporary cultural trend for girls also to appear "sexy" (American Psychological Association, Task Force on the Sexualization of Girls, 2007). From a young age, girls are exposed to highly sexualized merchandise, media, and advertising marketed to their age group. Among these items are Bratz dolls dressed in sexualized clothing such as miniskirts and fishnet stockings; thongs sized for 7- to 10-year-olds printed with slogans such as "Wink Wink" and "Eye Candy"; video games with sexy girls toting guns and wearing tight jumpsuits; and TV programs marketed to young adolescents like "The Pussycat Dolls Present: The Search for the Next Doll." These cultural pressures are confusing and damaging for girls as they navigate the complex waters of adolescence.

Other disturbing trends include various forms of violence involving women. Despite heightened public awareness around these issues, sexual assault and intimate partner violence remain threats for many women, and drug-facilitated sexual assault and cyberstalking create new challenges for women. Today's girls and women also are more likely to be perpetrators of violence than in previous years, with sharp increases in bullying and physical fighting in schools (Underwood, 2003).

Women are challenged by the multiple roles they manage in today's fast-paced society. Even though women have more technology available to them that is designed to make their lives more efficient, women spend much of their time multitasking and feel more rushed and stressed than in previous decades (Bianchi, Robinson, & Milkie, 2006). The time saved by technological advances is filled with more responsibilities and more role juggling. Even in midlife, when many women expect an easy transition into the retirement years, today's women find themselves in the "sandwich generation," called upon to care for children or grandchildren as well as aging parents (AARP, 2001). This trend is expected to increase exponentially in the near future as the baby boomer generation reaches old age (National Council on Aging, 2006).

After reflecting on cultural trends that represent both progress and problems, the questions remain: Are today's girls and women flourishing or are they floundering? Specifically, how do these trends affect the lives of girls and women? As a mother of a daughter, I am very interested in pursuing the answers to these questions. As a counselor and counselor educator, I am equally interested in uncovering the implications of these changes for counseling girls and women. It is clear that counselors need up-to-date resources to assist girls and women as they navigate these uncharted territories.

Counseling Girls and Women

I know from my own training and teaching experiences that many counselor education programs do not provide up-to-date information in this area. I became acutely aware of this gap several years ago when I had an opportunity to develop a course on girls' and women's issues in counseling. When I began my search for topics and readings to include in the course, I quickly recognized that few books addressed this specific area in our profession. Books in other mental health disciplines (most notably in psychology and psychiatry) focused on the mental health needs of women, but I found few books for counselors-in-training that reflected contemporary trends or that highlighted the profession's emphasis on developmental, wellness perspectives. Furthermore, I recognized that although theory-based books are necessary, today's practicing counselors need a current, accessible resource to guide them in their daily practice with girls and women.

This book focuses on relevant counseling issues and interventions for girls and women in contemporary society. In writing this book, I attempted to create a resource for counselors, regardless of their gender, that is different from many other texts in several ways. First, I draw upon the lived experiences of girls and women, noting the impact of sociocultural influences (including the experiences of women of color, lesbian/bisexual/transgendered women, and women living in poverty) on the current issues that they face. The chapter topics, ranging from childhood issues to older women's concerns, provide an in-depth journey through selected contemporary issues that many girls and women will encounter.

Second, I take a developmental, holistic perspective. Rather than assuming a pathology-driven model for working with women, I assume that clients are basically healthy people who are in need of support, empathy, and information to better navigate their lives. To this end, the book emphasizes client empowerment and focuses on their strengths and abilities to develop resilience for coping with current and future life transitions or obstacles. These approaches fit well with the counseling profession's emphasis on wellness models that encourage girls and women to develop and value their strengths in multiple life domains.

To this end, the wellness model of Myers and Sweeney (2005) is emphasized throughout this book. Each chapter adheres to a wellness philosophy and suggests prevention and intervention strategies that focus on more than merely resolving a particular client concern. The chapters emphasize the importance of enhancing multiple wellness dimensions in order to improve clients' overall life satisfaction. This focus helps clients to note their many strengths, work to develop life dimensions that have been neglected, and cope more effectively with future life demands.

Third, I believe counselors must go beyond knowledge of current research and implement these findings in their daily practice. Therefore, this book is designed to be as practical and detailed as possible. The chapters contain multiple examples, client handouts, workshop outlines, and strategies for both assessment and interventions. To enhance the readers' understanding of the material, each chapter contains at least one case example with study questions; additional activities, recommended readings, and Web site resources are provided at the end of each chapter. Further, because counselors' work begins with self-awareness, exercises to promote self-exploration are emphasized throughout the book.

Overview of the Journey: Girls' and Women's Counseling Issues

In Chapter 1, I begin by preparing readers for the journey that unfolds in the chapters to follow. I first introduce a sociocultural model for understanding girls' and women's socialization and life experiences. I then focus on counseling approaches, including Myers and Sweeney's (2005) model of wellness, which serves as a guide for informing counselors' work with girls and women. These approaches emphasize client empowerment and the importance of sociocultural influences in conceptualizing client concerns. The socialization processes and empowerment/wellness approaches described in this chapter provide the foundation for the topics explored throughout the book.

In early adolescence, a girl's physical appearance becomes increasingly important to her overall sense of self-worth. At the same time, her body begins to change in ways that are increasingly discrepant from the media-generated beauty ideal. As a result, it is not surprising that many adolescent girls are vulnerable to low self-esteem, body image dissatisfaction, and eating-related problems. I explore these issues in Chapter 2 by describing the process of body image development in girls. I then outline a theoretical model of body image resilience based on factors that can protect girls from body image dissatisfaction. I also provide specific prevention and counseling strategies that counselors can use to promote positive body image in adolescent girls and include a detailed outline of a workshop designed to promote body image resilience.

Girls also face challenges regarding their relationships with one another. Relational aggression (RA), or the act of hurting others through manipulating or harming their relationships, is explored in Chapter 3. I explore the socialization processes that drive RA, including the connection between RA and girls' pursuit of popularity. I also describe recent trends that indicate an increase in girls' relational and physical aggression. The chapter concludes with a tiered approach to the prevention of and interventions for reducing relational aggression, including (a) strategies for systemwide change in schools; (b) interventions for administrators, teachers, school staff, and parents; and (c) a guide for working directly with students.

To conclude the journey through girlhood and adolescent issues, a cognitive behavioral group model for building girls' self-esteem is described in Chapter 4. Kimberly Anderson and I emphasize the importance of enhancing self-esteem to assist girls in coping with the complex challenges of adolescence. Ideally, the group setting can become a natural learning environment for improving girls' self-esteem by assisting them to connect with others in healthy ways, to speak authentically about their thoughts and feelings, and to cope with life demands more effectively. We review developmental and cultural influences on adolescent girls' self-esteem and then describe a cognitive–behavioral model for understanding self-esteem development, maintenance, and change. Finally, a detailed 8-week group counseling protocol designed to enhance self-esteem in adolescent girls is outlined.

As adolescent girls reach late adolescence and early adulthood, many choose to enroll in postsecondary institutions, encountering new challenges to their growth and development. In Chapter 5, Susan K. Gardner and I focus on the changing campus climate for today's women. For the first time in U.S. history, women outnumber men on college and university campuses and receive more degrees than men. However, despite enormous gains, women experience significant challenges on campus, including current dating and relationship norms, sexual violence, and body image dissatisfaction. We provide prevention and intervention strategies for working with college women around these issues, including detailed resources for developing effective campus programs.

Many women graduate from college and begin their careers right away. Other women stay home to begin a family and return to the workforce when their children are older. Still others enter the workforce directly from high school. Regardless of their life situation, women are striving to find a balance between their work and family lives. In Chapter 6, Rita R. Culross, Marla J. Erwin, Jie Yu, and I first discuss issues important to working women, including gender discrimination in the workforce, opportunities for pregnant and working mothers, and sexual harassment. We then turn to some of the challenges that dual earner couples face, such as asynchrony in career development, caregiving concerns, and problems with the division of household tasks, and provide suggestions for counseling dual earner couples. Counseling issues specific to working mothers, including the benefits and challenges of managing both roles, are also explored. Finally, we discuss women's need for self-care, an aspect of life that is often sacrificed by women who are faced with the many demands of work and family. We conclude the chapter with counseling strategies for helping women to conceptualize self-care as an essential coping strategy for functioning optimally in relationships and work and for achieving a balance between the two.

While women are succeeding in the workforce in record numbers and have made great advances in changing social norms regarding women's equality, they are still disproportionately affected by the threat of sexual violence. There is a high probability that any woman will experience some type of violence in her lifetime, and the latest National Violence Against Women survey demonstrates that over half of all women report an experience of attempted or completed rape or physical assault. It is unfortunate that most mental health professionals report a lack of training in working with women survivors of violence in general and of sexual assault and intimate partner violence in particular. Chapters 7 and 8 are dedicated to bridging this training deficit by addressing contemporary issues and interventions. In Chapter 7, I discuss several treatment considerations that serve as a context for providing effective treatment for survivors of rape. I then describe a multimodal treatment approach for women who are experiencing chronic PTSD symptoms resulting from rape-related trauma.

In Chapter 8, I describe intimate partner violence (IPV), or violence perpetrated by a current or former intimate partner that is aimed at establishing control by one partner over the other. Women who are abused by an intimate partner are reluctant to seek counseling, and when they do they are often in crisis. Even then, IPV might go undetected if the counselor is not trained to properly assess for it and to work with these issues. In this chapter, I describe the various forms that IPV can take: physical abuse, sexual abuse, stalking, and psychological abuse. Because women do not intentionally enter into abusive relationships, I also explore the dynamics of abuse and how women can become entrapped in relationships characterized by this type of violence. Finally, I present a four-phase treatment model for working with women who experience IPV, including counselor preparation, strategies for engagement and assessment, interventions for working with women currently experiencing IPV, and approaches for working with postseparation issues such as stalking, safety planning, grieving, and eventual recovery.

Women across the life span are increasingly turning to spirituality as a resource for coping with many of the life transitions and obstacles described in this book. In Chapter 9, Gerri Miller, Catherine Clark, and I emphasize spirituality as a central component of optimal health and well-being. Because women are more likely than men to turn to spiritual practices to address life problems and to integrate spirituality into their daily life routines, we highlight the importance of counselors' openness to the spiritual dimension when working with women. We provide an overview of developmental theoretical models of spirituality that counselors may use in addressing counseling concerns and discuss sociocultural factors that may affect spiritual awareness and growth such as culture, sexual orientation, ethnicity, social location, and age. Finally, we provide counseling techniques that can enhance spiritual resilience.

The journey concludes with Chapter 10, in which I explore the lives of women as they reach midlife and their older years. As contemporary women approach midlife and beyond, they will become part of a diverse, rapidly growing group. Older persons are expected to increase to 20% of the total population by the year 2030 (National Council on Aging, 2006). Most counselors receive little information about the specific issues that women face as they age, so I provide an overview of significant counseling concerns for older women. The focus of the chapter is on assisting counselors' work with women in strengthening their coping resources for adjusting to new life roles in six areas: changes in appearance, changes in role status, adapting to the loss of significant others, transitioning to menopause, becoming a caregiver, and becoming a grandmother. The chapter concludes with a discussion of qualities women need to age optimally and ways in which counselors can promote these dimensions of wellness in older women clients.

It is my hope that readers will benefit both personally and professionally as they explore these selected counseling issues and interventions. In today's rapidly changing cultural climate, girls and women are often left without a roadmap for coping with emerging experiences and challenges. With support, I believe girls and women have the strengths and resilience to forge a new path through contemporary life demands. This book is designed to assist counselors as they accompany their clients on this journey.

References

AARP. (2001, June). *In the middle: A report on multicultural boomers coping with family and aging issues.* Washington, DC: Author.

American Psychological Association, Task Force on the Sexualization of Girls. (2007). *Report of the APA Task Force on the Sexualization of Girls.* Washington, DC: American Psychological Association. Retrieved April 5, 2007, from www.apa.org/pi/wpo/sexualization.html

Bianchi, S. M., Robinson, J. P., & Milkie, M. A. (2006). *Changing rhythms of American family life.* New York: Russell Sage Foundation.

Goodheart, C. D. (2006). An integrated view of girls' and women's health: Psychology, physiology, and society. In J. Worell & C. D. Goodheart (Eds.), *Handbook of girls' and women's psychological health* (pp. 3–14). Oxford: Oxford University Press.

Halpern, D. F. (2006). Girls and academic success: Changing patterns of academic achievement. In J. Worell & C. D. Goodheart (Eds.), *Handbook of girls' and women's psychological health* (pp. 272–282). New York: Oxford University Press.

Meyer, S. R. (2006, July 3). *Mapping midlife today—revisiting and re-visioning adulthood.* Retrieved April 23, 2007, from http://www.gather.com/

Myers, J. E., & Sweeney, T. J. (2005). *Counseling for wellness: Theory, research, and practice.* Alexandria, VA: American Counseling Association.

National Center for Education Statistics. (2003). *NCES fast facts.* Retrieved December 3, 2003, from http://nces.ed.gov/fastfacts

National Council on Aging. (2006). *Press room: Fact sheets.* Retrieved April 21, 2006, from http://www.ncoa.org/content.cfm?sectionID=103

National Federation of State High School Associations. (2006). *Participation in high school sports increases again.* Retrieved April 9, 2007, from www.nfsh.org

Tryon, G. S., & Winograd, G. (2003). Developing a healthy identity. In M. Kopala & M. A. Keitel (Eds.), *Handbook of counseling women* (pp. 185–192). Thousand Oaks, CA: Sage.

Underwood, M. K. (2003). *Social aggression among girls.* New York: Guilford Press.

U.S. Census Bureau. (2001). *Statistical abstract of the United States: 2001* (121st ed.). Washington, DC: Author.

Acknowledgments

First, I would like to extend my deepest gratitude to my family who supported me throughout this project. I would like to thank my two children, Benjamin and Abigail, now ages 4 and 2, who keep me on my toes and remind me daily of what is truly important. I am grateful for my husband, Michael, who is my life partner and strongest supporter. I also thank my parents, Judy and Lloyd Hensley, the most loyal grandparents a working mother could ask for.

Next, I would like to extend thanks to the students in my LSU ELRC 5300 Girls' and Women's Issues in Counseling course during the years 2003–2007, who helped to spark much of my thinking around these issues. I am especially indebted to the students in the 2007 class for reading a draft of the book and providing me with many examples and suggestions. The LSU Counselor Education program graduate assistants have been invaluable to me in completing the book. They have conducted countless literature searches, searched hundreds of Web sites to provide me with additional resources, and compiled all of the reference lists for the chapters. I would especially like to thank Michelle Roe, Adrienne Pizza, Jennifer Wale, and Melissa Doucet for their organizational skills and considerable effort in helping me to compile the book.

I would also like to thank my mentors, Becky Ropers-Huilman and Petra Hendry, who have taught me so much about writing and have provided me with invaluable feedback on many of these chapters.

Finally, I would like to thank the contributors to this book who helped to make this task much more realistic for me, including Kimberly Anderson, Susan K. Gardner, Rita R. Culross, Marla J. Erwin, Jie Yu, Gerri Miller, and Catherine Clark. I am also indebted to Carolyn Baker and her team at ACA for providing me with this exciting opportunity.

Chapter 1

Preparing for the Journey

The majority of clients who seek counseling services are women, yet most counselor education and other mental health preparation programs traditionally have paid little attention to the unique counseling issues of girls and women. Until the early 1970s, mental health professionals tended to perpetuate a gender bias in counseling by using male development and functioning as the models for normal human development. A classic study by Broverman, Broverman, Clarkson, Rosenkrantz, and Vogel (1970) revealed that when counselors were asked to describe a hypothetical female client, she was viewed as more unhealthy (e.g., submissive, less competitive, more easily influenced) than a hypothetical male. In another early study, counselors tended to rate any gender-role discrepant behaviors as characteristics of an "unhealthy" adult (Sherman, 1980). In other words, women in counseling historically have experienced a double bind; if they conformed to gender-role expectations, they were viewed as unhealthy or passive, but if they acted in ways that were discrepant from their expected roles, they were also viewed negatively.

In addition to counselors' use of a male model to assess normal human functioning, other biases of mental health professionals included the following: (a) Counselors tended to view women clients in terms of their symptoms rather than noting their many strengths; (b) counselors emphasized women's primary duty in terms of their roles as mothers, yet blamed mothers for all mental health problems that occurred in their children; and (c) counselors frequently engaged in victim-blaming; that is, victims of intimate partner violence, rape, and childhood sexual abuse were viewed as having somehow provoked the violence perpetrated against them (Chesler, 1972; Enns, 2004). Further, women of color were particularly underserved by mental health professionals, even while they frequently experience challenges related to racism, sexism, poverty, and value conflicts that emerged when trying to accommodate to two different cultures (Porter, 2000).

The feminist movement of the late 1960s brought significant attention to these biases, noting a need for a better understanding of gender differences in biology and socialization processes and how these differences call for necessary adaptations to traditional counseling approaches (Enns, 2004). Although tremendous advances have been made in the field, ongoing research to refine practices in this area continues to be emphasized. For example, the National Institute of Mental Health (NIMH) has called for a national focus on the mental health of women (Blehar, 2006), and several recently published volumes focused on women's issues in psychology (e.g., Kopala & Keitel, 2003; Worell & Goodheart, 2006). These recent issues and suggested interventions are highlighted throughout this book. In this chapter, I introduce a sociocultural approach for understanding women's development and life experiences to provide a background for the issues explored in this book. I also discuss ways in which traditional counseling approaches may be adapted to better meet the needs of girls and women clients. These tailored approaches are infused throughout each chapter.

Traditional Gender-Role Development

Any discussion of girls' development should begin with a distinction between "sex" and "gender," with *sex* referring to whether one is born biologically male or female. In contrast, *gender* refers to the psychological, social, and cultural characteristics that have become strongly associated with male or female in a particular society (Gilbert & Sher, 1999). *Gender-role conformity* refers to the extent to which an individual conforms to societal definitions of what traditionally is considered masculine or feminine (Basow, 2006).

According to Etaugh and Bridges (2004), traditional male qualities center around the concept of *agency* (e.g., achievement oriented, self-directed, competitive), whereas female qualities are grounded in *communion* (e.g., relatedness, other focused, warm, nurturing). While these stereotypes were more accepted by college students in the 1970s than they are in the 2000s, and are more frequently endorsed by Caucasians, Asian Americans, and Latinas than by African Americans (Worell, 2006), strict adherence to these gender-role expectations continues to be potentially limiting for both men and women.

On the other hand, there is evidence that a more fluid and flexible gender role (*androgyny*) is related to better mental health outcomes, including higher self-esteem and self-confidence (Worell, 2006). It makes sense that individuals who possess instrumental, active, and assertive traits, in addition to emotionally expressive, nurturing qualities, will be able to cope with a more diverse set of stressors and life experiences (Worell, 2006). As I explore later in the chapter, counselors can play a role in helping individuals express all aspects of themselves rather than being limited to traditionally held expectations for men and women. I also examine ways in which this process is more complex and problematic for women of color, who might hold traditional cultural values regarding gender roles.

How do girls develop their gender-role identity? The literature on this topic is extensive, and a detailed theoretical discussion is beyond the scope of this chapter. Here, I examine some of the major developmental milestones in childhood and adolescence.

Between 18 and 24 months, a child begins to have an understanding of gender but believes gender is something that could be changed with a change of clothing or hair. For example, if a child's favorite male doll is dressed in a skirt and a wig, the child will believe the "boy" has now become a "girl" doll. It is between the ages of 4 and 7 that *gender constancy* occurs, the belief that gender is constant, regardless of changes in appearance or behavior (Basow, 2006).

In middle childhood, girls tend to be confident, prefer to play in gender-segregated groups, and attend closely to other girls and women as role models. During this period, a girl's gender-role development is influenced by modeling (e.g., what she observes when significant people model gender-related values, attitudes, and behaviors), experience (e.g., whether or not her performance of gender-related behaviors is reinforced or punished), and direct instruction (e.g., what parents, siblings, peers, schools, and media directly say to her about what girls should do or should look like; Basow, 2006; Etaugh & Bridges, 2004).

Between the ages of 11 and 12, around the onset of puberty, girls develop *gender-role intensification*, a greater adherence to traditional gender-role expectations. Girls initially may have adopted gender-related behaviors and attitudes because they were reinforced by external influences, but at this time girls begin to develop a set of internal standards regarding what is appropriate for girls or for boys. They perceive that a limited range of

---

Self-Exploration Exercise

1. What is your first memory of noticing that adults held different expectations for boys and girls?
2. What did you learn from your mother about what it means to be a *female*?
    What did you learn from your father? From your siblings?
    What did you learn from your peer group?
3. As an adult, how do you self-define what it means to be a woman?
4. What did you learn from your mother about what it means to be a *male*?
    What did you learn from your father? From your siblings?
    What did you learn from your peer group?
5. As an adult, how do you self-define what it means to be a man?

Source: Adapted from Gilbert & Sher (1999).

behaviors are considered acceptable for girls and for boys. They also begin to focus intensely on how they appear to others and develop romantic attractions to peers (Basow, 2006).

The Crossroads

Just last year when I was in the 6th grade, everything was fine. Now in the 7th grade I don't feel too sure about anything. I don't like how my body is changing and how the girls at school are acting. Everyone is so into how they look and into trying to be popular. I want to be part of the popular group too, but do I have what it takes to get there? It seems like if I say the wrong thing, then no one will like me anymore. If I do too well in school, then the popular girls won't think I'm cool. Lately I just keep my mouth shut and don't really say what I want to do or what I really think about things. It's just not worth it. I don't really know what I think about all of this, but I do know that it sure would be nice to sit at the popular table at lunch every day.

—Ellyn, age 12

According to traditional theories of development (e.g., Erikson, 1963), adolescent identity development unfolds through separation and individuation, resulting in autonomy. Jean Baker Miller (1976), Carol Gilligan (1991), Judith Jordan (2003), and other feminist authors have critiqued traditional theories that tend to ignore the fact that women's development occurs through connection with others, not through separation. According to Gilligan and others, adolescent girls face a "crossroads" in their development; at this time, they receive cultural messages regarding the need for separation and autonomy (as is posited in traditional theories), yet they also are becoming increasingly concerned with maintaining their connections with others. If a girl wishes to gain and maintain acceptance by others, she receives the message that she must conform to traditional gender roles by becoming passive, quiet, attractive, and a caretaker, or in Carol Gilligan's (1991) words, "be nice and don't cause any problems" (p. 19).

At this time, a girl faces a conflict: If she does what is best for her by speaking openly about what she thinks and feels, she risks being criticized or abandoned by others she cares about. If she hides her true feelings, acquiescing to the opinions and needs of others, she maintains her relationships while failing to develop her identity (Stern, 1991). Because of these dynamics, many girls do not develop skills for asserting their own desires or for knowing how to face conflict directly or effectively (Brown, 1991). This is discussed further in Chapter 3. Many girls who struggle with these tensions experience negative outcomes in adolescence, including declines in self-esteem, self-image, and self-efficacy, in addition to an increased vulnerability to depression, body dissatisfaction, and eating disorders.

These adolescent struggles can lead to a double bind for women as they enter adulthood. If women adopt the traditional model of separation and individuation, preferring to be autonomous and high achieving at the expense of relationships, they may feel isolated from relationships with others, including their families of origin. If they try to conform to traditional expectations for women, placing their needs second to those of others, they may feel devalued and inauthentic in their relationships. In recent years, many women have tried to "do it all" (i.e., take on the superwoman role) by fulfilling others' expectations as a wife/mother/partner while also pursuing high aspirations at work (Tryon & Winograd, 2003). Many women have come to counseling because they struggle with these identity issues—value conflicts, problems expressing their own needs, difficulties fulfilling obligations to significant others at their own expense, or a lack of self-direction and confidence in their abilities to cope with stressors (Enns, 2004). Instead, the process of women's development may require a "different way of being in the world with others" (Brown, 1991, p. 83) that includes the development of a responsibility to both self and others.

It is important to note that the traditional socialization process as described here—which is more often the experience of middle-class, Caucasian girls—does not capture the lived experiences for girls from other social classes or cultural groups. For example, African American girls typically do not experience a loss of voice at adolescence; they maintain a sense of independence and ability to engage in "truth telling" by speaking their authentic thoughts and feelings (Basow & Rubin, 1999; see also Chapters 2 and 3). Historically, African American women have worked outside the home and have served as strong, independent role models within their families and communities (Porter, 2000). As such, African American girls often are socialized to receive both traditional messages of femininity, such as caretaking and nurturance, and nontraditional gender roles, adopting traits such as independence, self-reliance, resistance, worker role, and financial provider for the family (Buckley & Carter, 2005). In other words, African American girls' gender roles tend to be more flexible or androgynous, and these qualities are related to greater self-esteem (Buckley & Carter, 2005).

Latina women, on the other hand, traditionally have been socialized according to stringent rules about appropriate attitudes and behaviors for women. Historically, Latina women have been expected to adhere to *marianismo*, modeling the qualities of the Virgin Mary such as being passive, patient, obedient, possessing great endurance for suffering and hardship, accepting responsibility/blame for one's husband's problems, and being spiritually superior to men (Porter, 2000; Vasquez & De Las Fuentes, 1999). According to traditional gender roles, a Latina woman is responsible for her family and is expected to remain close to her family who will protect her (Vasquez & De Las Fuentes, 1999).

Asian American women also traditionally have been assigned inferior status to men. The women have been taught to be dutiful and to respect the needs of their husbands first, their children second, and themselves last (Porter, 2000). In traditional Asian cultures, adults teach their children the importance of filial piety (respect of elders and family and adherence to the wishes of family). Asian American women are socialized to prioritize community or family needs over their own needs, to avoid deviance from family customs and norms, and to solve emotional problems without outside help (Cummins & Lehman, 2007).

In contrast, American Indian women have a historical legacy of political and economic power, with many tribes adhering to matriarchal, matrilineal, or matrilocal customs, in which the husband moves into his wife's household and lives among her relatives. According to Dixon Rayle, Chee, and Sand (2006), American Indian traits are not as stringently characterized in a dichotomy as either "masculine" or "feminine," and children are socialized to become more androgynous. This process is considered a cultural strength of American Indian individuals (Dixon Rayle et al., 2006). A strong value of communalism, valuing tribal needs over individual needs, is also an important part of socialization for American Indian women.

Understanding these types of cultural influences on gender-role socialization is important, but it is equally vital to note that counselors cannot universalize girls' and women's life experiences because each individual's experience is complex and unique. It is helpful for counselors to balance their knowledge of traditional socialization processes for particular cultural groups with each client's particular life context. Because of these unique influences on women's socialization and life experiences, the mental health professions now recognize that traditional theories and techniques may need to be adapted to best meet the counseling needs of women clients. The counseling approaches outlined next provide flexible guidelines for informing our work with girls and women.

Counseling Approaches for Working With Girls and Women

Leaders in the early feminist movement were among the first to note the bias in traditional approaches to development and counseling based on male norms as the hallmarks of mental health (e.g., separation, autonomy, and independence). It also was recognized that this emphasis could serve to pathologize the worldviews of both women and members of racial/ethnic minority communities (Evans, Kincade, Marbley, & Seem, 2005). Feminist therapies emerged with a goal "to correct the negative effects of sexism and bias present in psychological theory, diagnosis and practice and to ensure that women gained access to gender-aware and gender sensitive mental health services" (Enns, 2004, p. 8).

Feminism and feminist therapies have had major influences on the mental health professions during the past several decades. The two central tenets of feminist therapy that have had a large impact on the ways that current counselors work with women are described here: the personal is political (i.e., paying attention to sociocultural context), and an emphasis on empowerment and a focus on client strengths.

The Personal Is Political

Women's counseling issues are seen through the lens of larger sociopolitical and cultural contexts, not solely as individual problems. For example, a woman who is experiencing emotional distress may not be manifesting inherent pathology; rather, her distress may be a result of larger oppressive forces such as sexism, racism, homophobia, or classism (Evans et al., 2005). Rather than women viewing themselves as victims of these larger sociocultural forces of oppression, women clients can be empowered to be active change agents in their lives. The "personal is political" tenet has been expanded today to encompass the experiences of all clients, including men and clients from diverse cultures (Enns, 2004), and is considered foundational to multicultural counseling competence.

Client Empowerment and Wellness

A second, related major theme of the feminist movement that has affected the mental health field is the empowerment of all individuals and a focus on client strengths. According to McWhirter (1991), empowerment is defined as

> the process by which people, organizations, or groups who are powerless or marginalized become aware of the power dynamics at work in their life context, develop the skills and capacity for gaining some reasonable control over their lives, which they exercise, without infringing upon the rights of others, and which coincides with actively supporting the empowerment of others in their community. (p. 224)

Instead of viewing clients as powerless and in need of an expert to tell them what to do, clients are empowered when counselors assist them in identifying strengths and in developing skills to cope more effectively with current and future life demands (Worell & Remer, 2002). As an example, Walker's (1994) survivor therapy approach for working with women survivors of violence focuses on women as survivors rather than victims, identifies strengths rather than focusing on injuries, and empowers clients to regain a sense of control and personal power (see Chapter 8). In sum, counselors view their clients basically as healthy people who are in need of support, empathy, and information to gain control in their lives. Developing a caring, nurturing connection with a counselor can create the foundation necessary to begin this transformation (Worell & Remer, 2002).

It is encouraging that a practice of building on client strengths rather than focusing on their deficits is now widely accepted within the mental health professions (Harris, Thoresen, & Lopez, 2007). Positive psychology—the study of human strengths and virtues—has generated a large body of research that has sparked public interest and influenced practice in this area. Rather than examining the factors that contribute to mental disorders, positive psychology examines qualities needed for optimal functioning, flourishing, thriving, and overall life satisfaction—qualities such as autonomy, environmental mastery, personal growth, positive relationships with others, purpose in life, and self-acceptance (Ryff & Keyes, 1995).

The counseling profession's emphasis on wellness and holistic approaches that build on the positive resources of clients has been informed by (and fits well with) these strengths-based approaches (Myers & Sweeney, 2005). Myers and Sweeney's model of wellness is the most researched and well-known wellness model in the counseling profession. As defined by Myers and Sweeney, wellness can be conceptualized as a "way of life oriented toward optimal health and well-being in which body, mind, and spirit are integrated by individuals to live life more fully within the human and natural community" (p. 252). Counseling for wellness (versus remediation of pathology) helps the client to improve her overall health, quality of life, and ability to cope effectively with life's demands.

The model was originally conceptualized as the Wheel of Wellness, with spirituality at the core of the wheel, surrounded by self-direction, which then responds to the life tasks of work and leisure, friendship, and love. (See Table 1.1 for a description of components.) Extensive research with the Wheel model led to development of a large database of wellness studies, which was recently analyzed through structural equation modeling to yield a new model, the Indivisible Self Model of Wellness (IS-Wel), which is illustrated in Figure 1.1.

The prevention and intervention strategies of this wellness philosophy are designed to help clients create balance in all life dimensions. When

Table 1.1
Components of the Individual Self

Factor	Definition of Wellness Factor
Wellness[a]	Higher order factor; sum of all other factors
Creative Self[b]	Combination of attributes that one forms to make a unique place among others in social interactions and to interpret the world. (What we think affects our emotions as well as our body. The ability to think clearly, perceive accurately, and respond appropriately can help decrease stress.)
Thinking[c]	Being mentally active, open minded; an ability and desire to be creative; curiosity, need to know, need to learn; capacity to collect data, analyze, synthesize, choose and value consequences of outcomes (divergent and convergent thinking); capacity to change one's thinking to manage stress (cognitive restructuring); capacity to apply these characteristics in resolving social conflicts.
Emotions[c]	Being in touch with feelings, being able to express/disclose feelings appropriately, ability to respond spontaneously and appropriately to life experiences from the full range of possible human emotional responses, enjoying positive emotion, coping with negative emotions, lack of chronic negative emotional states (such as anger), sense of energy (versus depression)

(Continued)

Table 1.1 (Continued)
Components of the Individual Self

Factor	Definition of Wellness Factor
Control[c]	Beliefs about mastery, competence, self-confidence, locus of control, self-efficacy, presentation of oneself as having influence through the exercise of imagination, knowledge, skill, and choice; sense of planfulness in life; ability to be direct in expressing one's needs (assertiveness).
Work[c]	Activity that contributes to the well-being of self and others: perception of adequacy of financial resources (financial freedom), job satisfaction, feeling that one's skills are used, perception of work overload, role conflict, role ambiguity (psychological job security), participation in decision making (feeling appreciated), satisfaction with relationships in the job setting.
Positive Humor[c]	Ability to laugh appropriately at oneself, ability to laugh appropriately at others, having the capacity to see contradictions and predicaments of life in an objective manner such that one can gain new perspectives, ability to use humor to cope with one's own difficulties, enjoying inconsistencies and idiosyncrasies of life.
Coping Self[b]	Combination of elements that regulate one's responses to life events and provide a means for transcending their negative effects.
Leisure[c]	Activities done in one's free time: satisfaction with one's leisure activities, importance of leisure, positive feelings associated with leisure, having at least one activity in which "I lose myself and time stands still," ability to approach tasks from a playful point of view, ability to put work aside for leisure without feeling guilty.
Stress Management[c]	General perception of one's own self-regulation, seeing change as an opportunity for growth rather than as a threat to one's security, ongoing self-monitoring and assessment of one's coping resources, structuring and an ability to organize and manage resources (time, energy, setting limits, scheduling), need for structure, satisfaction with one's stress management abilities.
Self-Worth[c]	Satisfaction with self, acceptance of self with one's imperfections; acceptance of one's physical appearance; valuing oneself as a unique, worthwhile person.

(Continued)

9

Table 1.1 (Continued)
Components of the Individual Self

Factor	Definition of Wellness Factor
Realistic Beliefs[c]	Ability to perceive truth/reality accurately (accurate information processing), lack of unrealistic expectations/wishful thinking.
Social Self[b]	Social support through connections with others in friendships and intimate relationships, including family ties. Friendships and intimate relationships enhance the quality and length of one's life. Mainstay of support is family, with healthier families providing the most positive sources of individual wellness.
Friendship[c]	Connectedness with others in a nonsexual manner; having social support when needed; having a confidant for tangible, emotional, and informational support; being able to give social support; not feeling lonely because of lack of friends; sense of comfort in social situations (social ease).
Love[c]	Concern for the life and growth of that which is loved; having faith that one's well-being will be respected; reciprocating by respecting the well-being of another (trust); ability to be intimate, trusting, self-disclosing with another person; ability to receive as well as express affection with a significant other; capacity to experience or convey nonpossessive caring that respects the uniqueness of another's presence of enduring, stable intimate relationship(s); recognition that others have concern for one's growth; physical satisfaction with sexual life/needs for touch are being met.
Essential Self[b]	One's essential meaning-making processes in relation to life, self, and others.
Spirituality[c]	Personal, private beliefs that enhance one's life; hope and optimism, purpose in life, moral values, transcendence, overall spiritual well-being.
Gender Identity[c]	Satisfaction with one's gender identity, feeling supported in one's gender, valuing relationships with people of both genders, transcendence of gender identity, competency to cope with stress of gender identity.
Cultural Identity[c]	Satisfaction with one's cultural identity, feeling supported in one's culture, valuing relationships with people of many cultures, transcendence of cultural identity, competency to cope with stress of cultural identity.

(Continued)

Table 1.1 (Continued)
Components of the Individual Self

Factor	Definition of Wellness Factor
Self-Care[c]	Not abusing substances, using seat belts, getting adequate sleep, obtaining preventative medical and dental care.
Physical Self[b]	The biological and physiological processes that comprise the physical aspects of one's development and functioning.
Nutrition[c]	Eating breakfast regularly, daily variety in diet of healthful foods, maintaining one's ideal weight.
Exercise[c]	Leading an active rather than sedentary lifestyle, exercising 20–30 minutes 3 times a week, stretching regularly.

[a]Single higher order factor. [b]Second order factor. [c]Third order factor.

counseling for wellness, not only will the client be assisted in resolving her presenting problem, she also will learn to note and draw on her strengths, work to improve life dimensions that have been neglected, and cope with future problems more effectively (Myers & Sweeney, 2005). This approach also is effective for working with women of color, who often value the need for interdependence and for maintaining balance (Lee, 2005). For example, for American Indian women, psychological distress indicates that one is out of balance and needs to work holistically to restore harmony between the physical, emotional, and spiritual aspects of the self (Dixon Rayle et al., 2006).

With these two broad themes as a foundation (the personal is political; empowerment and client wellness), in the following sections I outline four principles and interventions for counseling with girls and women. These principles are adapted from Worell and Remer's (2002) empowerment feminist therapy and Enns's (2004) feminist therapy approach.

Principle One: Understanding Intersecting Personal and Social Identities Is Important

I have designed my home life in such a way that I don't even have to think of myself as a woman with a disability. When I am at home with my family, I am a parent, a daughter, a spouse—my disability really isn't part of how I see myself at all. Then I go out into the world, and it hits me: People see me in terms of what I *can't* do. Even simple things like shopping for groceries become major sources of stress. I am either ignored or stared at with impatience. In those moments, I *am* my disability.

—Sherry, age 27

The Indivisible Self: *An Evidence-Based Model of Wellness*

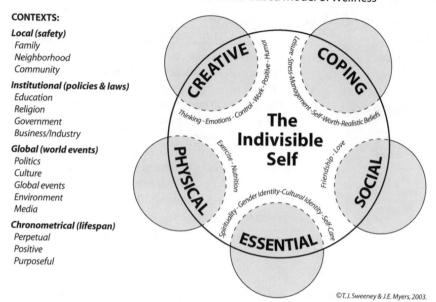

CONTEXTS:

Local (safety)
Family
Neighborhood
Community

Institutional (policies & laws)
Education
Religion
Government
Business/Industry

Global (world events)
Politics
Culture
Global events
Environment
Media

Chronometrical (lifespan)
Perpetual
Positive
Purposeful

©T.J. Sweeney & J.E. Myers, 2003.

Figure 1.1
Indivisible Self Model of Wellness

Note. From *Counseling for Wellness: Theory, Research, and Practice* (p. 32), edited by J. E. Myers and T. J. Sweeney, 2005, Alexandria, VA: American Counseling Association. Copyright 2005 by the American Counseling Association. Reprinted with permission of the authors.

All clients experience multiple identities (Enns, 2004). Such identities include our gender, ethnicity, social class, sexual orientation, age, and physical abilities. Different aspects of our identities come to the forefront in various social situations and counselors should refrain from making assumptions that race/ethnicity, for example, is the most salient source of oppression or distress for a client of color (Hansen et al., 2002).

It is important for women to become aware of how they define themselves in different situations and to understand how this process may influence their daily interactions with others (Enns, 2004). For example, a woman's race/ethnicity may not be in the forefront in her neighborhood where she is surrounded by others from her own culture, but her race may play a major role in how she views herself when she is in a counseling session with a counselor who is from a different race/ethnicity than her own. Women may need assistance in understanding and appreciating this ever-changing and shifting nature of their identities. Clients also may need to learn to accept themselves and the cultural groups to which they belong if they have not yet developed an appreciation of their multiple identities (Worell & Remer, 2002). For example, an Asian American woman may struggle with negative feelings about her physical appearance, particularly if she focuses on the ways in which her features differ from the Western thin and beautiful ideal (e.g., her eye and nose shape, skin color, or short stature). This comparison with an unattainable ideal can result in a negative body image and other psychological consequences for Asian American women (Grabe & Hyde, 2006). As discussed in Chapters 2 and 4, as women embrace their cultural identities as a source of pride and strength, they will be better able to resist negative media messages regarding how women should look.

Principle Two: The Personal Is Political

My 13-month-old daughter is sick a lot with ear infections, so of course lately I am up all night with her. I have to miss many hours at work to be with her and take her to the doctor. I think it's important that I spend as much time with her as possible, especially when she is sick. Unfortunately, no one else thinks so. My supervisor has made comments that I am missing too much work and that I might be let go. I am irritable from lack of sleep, and I feel so torn between my family and keeping a paycheck coming in. I am depressed, but no one seems to understand what I'm going through.

—Shanna, age 23

Counselors who work with women can acknowledge potential societal influences on women's individual problems, as personal distress is often connected to the political and social contexts within which women live (Worell & Remer, 2002). Enns (2004) stated it is critical to examine context when understanding women's problems because when external influences are not considered counselors will have a greater tendency to "define problems as a set of internal characteristics and to emphasize goals that overhaul internal deficiencies rather than promote healthy change and the alteration of oppressive environmental conditions" (p. 11).

Particularly for women of color, counselors should avoid assuming that a client's problems are due solely to intrapsychic difficulties (Constantine, Greer, & Kindaichi, 2003). When counselors conceptualize problems without examining the influence of external factors such as racism, poverty, or discrimination, clients often learn to blame themselves for causing their own difficulties (Constantine et al., 2003).

An important technique associated with this principle is the use of *reframing*. Instead of viewing an individual's symptoms as pathology, symptoms can be reframed as adaptive coping strategies, when they alert an individual to something that is in need of change. As Greenspan (1993) noted, "within every symptom, there is a strength that lies dormant" (p. 293). According to positive psychology, a client's distress can be viewed as a logical response to her developmental history (Harris et al., 2007).

When symptoms are viewed as coping strategies or as logical responses to distress, case conceptualization and assessment can be expanded to include a client's context in the following ways: (a) What myths exist in society about this issue? What is the source of the myth? Are there any labels or diagnoses associated with this issue? How do these myths serve to locate the problem within an individual? (b) What is the actual impact of societal factors on the client's personal experiences? What oppressive messages has the client internalized? How can the counselor and client work collaboratively to identify and change these messages? (c) What are some coping skills that need to be developed to enhance her functioning or to make changes to her environmental conditions? (d) What strengths or positive resources does this client already possess that should be supported? (Harris et al., 2007; Worell & Remer, 2002).

Implications of the personal is political tenet for understanding women's experiences with mental disorders are reviewed in the sections that follow. Although there is virtually no gender difference in the overall prevalence of mental disorders, there are distinct differences in the prevalence of specific disorders. For example, men are 2 times as likely as women to exhibit alcohol dependence and abuse, drug dependence, and antisocial personality disorder. However, 90% of individuals with eating disorders are women, and women are far more likely than men to experience panic, generalized anxiety disorders, social phobias, and posttraumatic stress disorder (PTSD; Burt & Hendrick, 2005). Another surprising gender difference is found in mood disorders; for example, depression is twice as common (a ratio of 1.96:1) in women as it is in men (NIMH, 2006a).

Women and Depression

Many researchers have looked at influences on gender differences in depression. Although biological differences play a role, sociocultural influences are strong contributing factors. For example, women have been traditionally devalued in society, and this contributes to lower wages, restricted upward mobility, and higher overall rates of poverty (Blehar, 2006; NIMH, 2006a). All of these stressors are linked with depression. Ethnicity and cultural background also can play a considerable role; for example, as a group, African American women may be less likely to experience major depression and dysthymia than Latina and Caucasian women (NIMH, 2006b). Women of color experience racism, sexism, poverty, and acculturation conflicts, which all contribute to depression (Porter, 2000). American Indian women, particularly those in urban environments, experience high rates of depression as they face acculturation difficulties and lack of support while away from family and tribe (Clark, 2006). Lesbian women also exhibit higher rates of depression, stress, and lower self-esteem than do heterosexual women (O'Hanlan, Dibble, Hagan, & Davids, 2004). O'Hanlan and colleagues cite recent national reports indicating that lesbian women report higher rates of depression and list contributing influences such as oppression in a heterosexist society, stress from isolation when they do not feel free to disclose their lesbian identity, and lack of support from family and community.

The socialization process described previously also contributes to depression. Girls who are encouraged to become passive and overinvolved with others at the expense of their own needs are more likely to become depressed (Whiffen & Demidenko, 2006). As adults, women who experience relational problems are more vulnerable to depression when they define themselves through a relationship and place extreme value on a single relationship to meet all of their needs. When they self-censor expression of their authentic thoughts, feelings, behaviors, or goals that might potentially threaten the relationship, they are more vulnerable to depression (Tryon & Winograd, 2003; Whiffen & Demidenko, 2006).

Women and Substance Abuse

Women's use and abuse of alcohol, tobacco, and other drugs (ATOD) is another notable example of the need to consider context when understanding client concerns. As noted previously, men are more likely than women to use and abuse substances, and alcoholism and substance abuse traditionally have been viewed as men's problems (Tait & Pergeroy, 2001). However, usage patterns have changed during the past 30 years, so lifetime prevalence rates do not reveal the true nature of these gender differences. For example, while the number of men who smoke has fallen substantially during recent years, the decrease in usage among women is much smaller. As described in Chapter 4, girls now outnumber boys in tobacco and prescription drug use and report trying alcohol, tobacco, and other drugs at higher rates than boys (Office of National Drug Control Policy, 2006). In examining specific age groups for abuse rates, women age 45–54 report higher lifetime prevalence of drug dependence, which reflects women's higher abuse rates of prescription drugs (Blume & Zilberman, 2005).

There are also gender differences in understanding risk factors for developing substance abuse disorders. Women age 21–34 report the highest problem rates, and those who are not married, are childless, and who are not employed are at highest risk. One of the most prominent risk factors for developing ATOD problems is a history of physical or sexual victimization/ abuse. Particularly at risk are women in the criminal justice system, lesbian women, and American Indian women (Blume & Zilberman, 2005).

There also are biological differences between men and women in the onset and progression of abuse/dependence. First, women process alcohol differently than men, so when given similar doses of alcohol, women reach higher blood alcohol levels more quickly than men and experience more intense and less predictable reactions to the same dosage of alcohol. Many of the serious medical problems that result from heavy alcohol use (such as cirrhosis and hypertension) develop earlier and progress much more rapidly in women. Further, women who are ATOD dependent have a higher mortality rate than men (Blume & Zilberman, 2005; Tait & Pergeroy, 2001).

Women also experience different psychological symptoms than men because women are more likely to link the onset of their ATOD disorder to a stressful event in their lives and to experience health and family problems, depression, low self-esteem, and suicide attempts (Blume & Zilberman, 2005). Women are more influenced by their relationships in developing a disorder, and they are more likely to have a significant other who also abuses ATOD. Significant others of women are likely to be the ones who introduced them to ATOD and who keep them supplied with substances (Blume & Zilberman, 2005; Tait & Pergeroy, 2001).

Finally, there are important sociocultural differences in men's and women's experience of ATOD disorders because cultural norms for substance use differ for males and females. According to Blume and Zilberman (2005), in U.S. culture, there is a greater stigma attached to female abusers of ATOD, and women who abuse substances are viewed less tolerantly than their male counterparts. Women who abuse ATOD are often viewed as being weak, immoral, deviant, promiscuous, and are treated in a sexually degrading manner. These social stereotypes can contribute to the belief that ATOD-addicted women are acceptable targets for sexual and physical violence, and alcoholic and drug-dependent women are more likely than other women to be victimized by violent crimes such as rape and intimate partner violence (Blume & Zilberman, 2005). Further, negative social stereotypes can contribute to the denial of the problem by women users and others in their lives. Women users appear to be more reluctant than men to admit they have a problem with ATOD (Blume & Zilberman, 2005; Tait & Pergeroy, 2001). Even when women do seek help, physicians and mental health professionals often fail to correctly diagnose and provide appropriate treatment when clients do not resemble the profile of a "typical" alcoholic or drug addict. There also may be no one in a woman's social support system able to recognize that she has a problem with ATOD and able to assist her in seeking treatment (Blume & Zilberman, 2005).

Drawing from these two examples, it is clear that counselors who view a client as a "depressed woman" or an "addicted woman" without taking into consideration some of these contributing external influences will be limited in their ability to understand and address her concerns effectively.

Principle Three: Relationships Are Egalitarian

> I have been to counseling before, and it wasn't so great for me. All my counselor did was tell me to dump my partner, and I didn't want to do that, so I quit going to my sessions. I guess I should have said something instead of just dropping out, but I didn't feel comfortable talking to her about it. I guess it's pretty typical of the way I usually handle things.
>
> —Marilyn, age 42

As much as possible, it is important to develop counselor–client relationships that are partnerships between equals. Unlike traditional models of counseling in which the counselor is viewed as the "expert" with "power over" a client, counseling relationships can be reconceptualized as egalitarian alliances based on "power with" the client (Cummings, 2000).

While egalitarian relationships are an aspirational goal, it is important to remember that a power differential exists even when a counselor makes an attempt to share power in the relationship. When counseling women clients, counselors should work to reduce power differentials while recognizing that they can never be eliminated entirely (Enns, 2004).

Counselors can strive to reduce the power differential in several ways. The first is the counselor's commitment to client empowerment, which was discussed previously. If counselors view clients as basically healthy, strong, and capable, with the ability to serve as their own best expert, clients will be empowered to find their own solutions to problems of daily living. Counselors will not need to tell their clients what to do but will assist clients in developing skills and accessing resources for finding their own answers. The counseling process will become a collaborative effort in which clients are able to openly question or even challenge the counselor regarding the direction of counseling sessions (Worell & Remer, 2002). In the previous example, the client might have been able to talk to her counselor about how she was feeling rather than dropping out of her counseling sessions. As another example, the client might feel free to say, "I don't like how we are spending so much time talking about my past relationships with my family. I really don't see how that helps me right now because I want to focus on how to make things better with my boss right away."

Another technique that helps to reduce the power differential is for the counselor to demystify the counseling process whenever possible. This can occur when clients are encouraged to become educated consumers of therapy (Worell & Remer, 2002). Worell and Remer recommend that counselors provide a free consultation session in which they provide clients with information that enables clients to make an informed decision about whether the counselor will be a good fit for them. As in the previous example, the client would be informed that the counselor would work with her in obtaining a referral for another counselor should the client become dissatisfied with the current counseling relationship. Clients can be encouraged to ask, "What are the counselor's values and beliefs? What is the counselor's theoretical orientation? What does the counselor believe about growth and change?" When clients are supplied with this information at the outset, they are better able to work collaboratively with a counselor throughout the process of counseling. Along these lines, counselors can strive to maintain a collaborative spirit even when working with formal assessments and diagnostic evaluations. Enns (2004) recommended that counselors fully disclose their rationale for administering assessments, explain results in jargon-free language, and always invite the client to agree or disagree with results. When working within the *DSM-IV-TR* diagnostic system, counselors can continue to respect the client as her own best expert by reviewing diagnostic criteria with the client, asking for feedback ("Does this criterion describe what you experience?"), and providing a clear rationale for how this particular diagnosis might be helpful to explain the client's current experience (Evans et al., 2005).

Finally, techniques such as selective self-disclosure are recommended as a way to facilitate an egalitarian counseling relationship. Counselor self-disclosure is often desired by women in general and women of color in particular in order to develop a trusting therapeutic relationship (Constantine et al., 2003). For women counselors, this disclosure might include issues that bond the counselor and client as women who share a similar cultural experience: "As women, these are issues we all share. . . . I experience this too" (Worell & Remer, 2002). Male counselors can disclose their desire to understand a woman's experiences as he recognizes that these experiences may be different from his own. Self-disclosure in the form of an immediacy response (i.e., responses that indicate how the counselor is affected by what the client just shared) can be effective as well, regardless of counselor gender. For example, the counselor may share, "When you talked about the struggles you experience as a Latina woman on a predominantly White campus, I was really moved. I was really affected by the sense of alienation you encounter on a daily basis." As the client learns that the counselor is actively working to understand and respect her experiences, she is better able to appreciate her own strengths and ways of approaching the world.

An egalitarian counseling relationship also serves as a model for relationships outside of the counseling relationship. Clients can learn skills for building healthy connections with others, such as assertiveness, dealing with conflict, and balancing dependence with independence. Because women have been socialized to suppress intense emotions, they often need assistance in learning to express negative emotions such as anger in healthy and appropriate ways. They may not believe that they have the right to express their authentic feelings to others out of fear of jeopardizing close relationships. Through the counseling relationship, clients can rehearse assertiveness skills and have opportunities for self-expression. They can also examine the difficulties they are likely to encounter if they develop new ways of relating with others.

Principle Four: Value the Female Perspective

I was hired at my company because I am a good leader and have strong technical skills, but it seems that no one appreciates those things about me. Whenever I speak up at meetings, I feel like people whisper behind my back about what a "witch" I am. I worry about this because I really value my friendships at work. If I just go with the flow and keep my mouth shut, then people think I am ineffective and unproductive.

—Kathy, age 38

Values that are traditionally associated with femininity, such as empathy, relationality, cooperation, intuitiveness, and affiliation, are generally devalued in our culture. Worell and Remer (2002) described women's double bind in this regard: They are socialized to adopt traditionally feminine qualities, but then are devalued for doing so (e.g., they are taught to be kind and nurturing at all costs, yet are then labeled as dependent and immature). Counselors can become more aware of ways in which they perpetuate this bias when they rely on an exclusive use of counseling approaches that privilege logic and independence over intuition and connections with others. Counselors can examine ways in which they can better respect the cultural worldviews of some Latina, African American, Asian American, and American Indian women who may value interdependence, communalism, and strong family ties (Constantine et al., 2003)

Counselors can challenge a client's internalized messages regarding any traits she possesses, helping her value aspects of herself that may be minimized by the larger culture. For example, she may have learned to view her experiences and intuition as invalid sources from which to base decisions, but she can learn to draw upon these qualities as strengths. She also may need assistance in owning all aspects of herself, regardless of whether or not these have been traditionally labeled as masculine or feminine. As discussed previously, women and men need both instrumental and expressive qualities to cope well with complex life demands. Clients may be limiting themselves when they hold onto ways of being that are based on others' expectations rather than their own personally derived belief and value systems. They can work to increase their awareness of the roles they have adopted and release aspects that are no longer congruent.

During counseling, some women might realize that they have no sense of self apart from others' definitions. Some clients may have few answers to the question, "Who am I really, apart from what others want from me?" Clients may have learned to fear that if they speak openly, or if they consider their own needs, they will place the security of significant relationships at risk: "Others may become angry with me or even leave me if I let them know how I really feel." This lack of emotional autonomy eventually leads to limited self-awareness and self-expression (McBride, 1990), and these clients will have great difficulty defining a sense of self not based on the approval of others. Before counselors can ask women to discard old roles and to embrace new ones, these concerns must be addressed so women can feel empowered to actively direct their own life path.

It also is helpful to note that this process may be particularly complex for many Asian American and Latina women. As previously discussed, multicultural research indicates that many Asian American and Latina women, in particular, have been socialized to define themselves in terms of connections to their social networks (family, extended family, and cultural communities) and to adhere to family or group priorities over asserting their own needs (Constantine et al., 2003). Consider the following case study that incorporates these complexities.

Case Study

Danita, a 25-year-old Latina woman, comes to counseling at a local agency to seek help for her two children, ages 5 and 3. She believes that they have "behavior problems" and that she is incompetent as a mother. The children's father is involved with the family, but Danita perceives that he is not very supportive of her. While her husband works on an as-needed basis as a contract laborer with several companies, Danita works full time as a managerial assistant. However, she feels unfulfilled with her role at work. She feels discouraged that without a college degree she will never be able to advance at her company, yet with two young children she believes she doesn't have time to return to college to finish her degree. She wants to be available for her children and for her husband as much as possible. Even though a management training program is available through her employer, she doesn't feel qualified or "together" enough to pursue this option. She also worries that her husband and extended family might not approve of this decision, although she has not discussed it with them directly. Her parents continually pressure her to quit her job and stay home more with her family. Her husband remains ambivalent because he knows her income is important to the family.

1. Consider Danita's social identities in understanding her problem. How can you help her view these as strengths?
2. How can you help Danita separate her external circumstances from her individual problems? How much of what she is experiencing might be due to gender-role socialization or internalized messages about gender, race/ethnicity, class, or sexual orientation?
3. How can you work to build an egalitarian relationship with Danita, and what skills does she need in order to construct more effective relationships in her life?
4. In what ways can you work to value the female perspective, which traditionally is devalued in mainstream culture? How can you help Danita increase her awareness of her gender role? Does she conform to traditional gender roles because they fit with who she is, or does she conform only to meet the expectations of others?

Women and Self-Care

Women who struggle with issues of self-definition can benefit from learning self-nurturance, a theme emphasized repeatedly throughout this book (see especially Chapter 6). Women who have learned to suppress their true thoughts and feelings for fear of jeopardizing relationships may have difficulty accessing their authentic thoughts, feelings, goals, and dreams. Carving out time for self-care helps women gain awareness of their own needs, devise alternatives for coping with life problems, and develop better ways of balancing self- and other-care (Enns, 2004). By using the wellness model developed by Myers and Sweeney (2005), self-care can be incorporated in the counseling process. As stated previously, when counseling for wellness, counselors help clients focus on overall life satisfaction and health rather than solely on remediation of the presenting problem. By collaborating with their clients, counselors can design individual wellness plans that help clients become more self-aware, be better able to cope with future problems, and able to relate to and provide care for others in healthy ways (McBride, 1990). Myers and Sweeney's process in formulating a personal wellness plan is shown in Table 1.2.

Conclusion

In the past several decades, counselors have developed an increased awareness of the limitations of traditional developmental theories and treatment approaches in their work with girls and women. Counselors will benefit from an understanding of girls' socialization experiences and

Table 1.2
Wellness Counseling Plan

1. Introduce the Wellness Model
   Describe the wellness concept to clients, inviting them to consider learning ways that they can more fully enjoy their lives. They can learn that changes in one area contribute to changes in other areas of wellness, thereby contributing to overall life satisfaction and quality of life.

2. Assessment
   Wellness can be assessed formally through the WEL-S (Myers, Sweeney, & Witmer, 2000), which is based on the Wheel of Wellness. The 5f-Wel (Myers & Sweeney, 2005) is the most current assessment to evaluate client wellness and is based on the indivisible self model. For counselors who prefer less formal methods of assessment, ask basic scaling questions such as "For each dimension of wellness, rate on a scale of 1–10 how well you feel on that dimension." Second, ask the client "How satisfied are you with your level of wellness in this area?" On the basis of these answers, clients can begin to choose several areas to target for improvement.

3. Develop a Personal Wellness Plan
   Design a plan based on the following components:
   • Definition of wellness dimension:
   • What are my personal strengths and limitations in this dimension?
   • What do I need to do to improve my wellness for this dimension?
     • Goals:
     • Methods:
     • Resources:
     • Timelines:

4. Evaluation and Follow-Up
   Client and counselor discuss the client's progress toward the chosen goals and develop maintenance plans for sustaining the changes in healthy living.

Note. Adapted from *Counseling for Wellness: Theory, Research, and Practice* (p. 178), edited by J. E. Myers and T. J. Sweeney, 2005, Alexandria, VA: American Counseling Association. Copyright 2005 by the American Counseling Association. Reprinted with permission.

the key role that relationships and connections may play in their lives. They will also be more effective as they adapt their practices to emphasize client empowerment and the importance of sociocultural influences in conceptualizing client concerns. These socialization issues, counseling principles, and wellness models serve as the foundation for the topics explored throughout this book.

Activities for Further Exploration

1. Reflect on a time in your own life when gender-role expectations (either pressures you experienced from others or from yourself) were an influence on a problem you experienced. How did you resolve these tensions?
2. Take a few minutes to brainstorm as many descriptors as possible for the word *male*; then do the same for the word *female*. Ask several peers to do the same. What do you notice about the two sets of lists? Did anything about this exercise surprise you?

Suggested Readings

Basow, S. A., & Rubin, L. R. (1999). Gender influences on adolescent development. In N. G. Johnson, M. C. Roberts, & J. Worell (Eds.), *Beyond appearance: A new look at adolescent girls* (pp. 25–52). Washington DC: American Psychological Association.

Cummings, A. L. (2000). Teaching feminist counselor responses to novice female counselors. *Counselor Education and Supervision, 40*, 47–57.

Enns, C. Z. (2004). *Feminist theories and feminist psychotherapies* (2nd ed.). Binghamton, NY: Haworth Press.

Evans, K. M., Kincade, E. A., Marbley, A. F., & Seem, S. R. (2005). Feminism and feminist therapy. *Journal of Counseling & Development, 83*, 269–277.

Kopala, M., & Keitel, M. A. (Eds.). (2003). *Handbook of counseling women.* Thousand Oaks, CA: Sage.

Myers, J. E., & Sweeney, T. S. (2005). *Counseling for wellness: Theory, research, and practice.* Alexandria, VA: American Counseling Association.

Worell, J. (2006). Pathways to healthy development: Sources of strength and empowerment. In J. Worell & C. D. Goodheart (Eds.), *Handbook of Girls' and Women's Psychological Health* (pp. 3–14). New York: Oxford University Press.Worell, J., & Remer, P. (2002). *Feminist perspectives in therapy.* Hoboken, NJ: Wiley.

Worell, J., & Remer, P. (2002). *Feminist perspectives in therapy.* Hoboken, NJ: Wiley.

Additional Resources

www.nimh.nih.gov
Information regarding current federal mental health initiatives on women.

www.wcwonline.org
   Information on feminist therapy and writings from women at the
   Wellesley Centers for Women.
www.apa.org/topics/topicwomenmen.html
   Current information on research regarding gender differences in mental health, including girls' and women's issues in psychology.
http://www.ppc.sas.upenn.edu/index
   Positive Psychology Center Web site contains information about positive psychology research, articles, and press releases. Also describes
   available questionnaires and research information and provides resources for teachers and researchers.
http://www.uncg.edu/~jemyers
   Jane E. Myers's home page contains descriptions of the Wheel of Wellness, the Indivisible Self Model, and information regarding the development of the Wel-S and 5f-Wel.

References

Basow, S. A. (2006). Gender and role development. In J. Worell & C. D.
   Goodheart (Eds.), *Handbook of girls' and women's psychological health*
   (pp. 242–251). New York: Oxford University Press.
Basow, S. A., & Rubin, L. R. (1999). Gender influences on adolescent de-
   velopment. In N. G. Johnson, M. C. Roberts, & J. Worell (Eds.), *Beyond
   appearance: A new look at adolescent girls* (pp. 25–52). Washington DC:
   American Psychological Association.
Blehar, M. C. (2006). Women's mental health research: The emergence of a
   biomedical field. *Annual Review of Clinical Psychology, 2*, 135–160.
Blume, S. B., & Zilberman, M. L. (2005). Addictive disorders in women. In
   R. J. Frances, S. I. Miller, & A. H. Mack (Eds.), *Clinical textbook of addictive disorders* (pp. 437–453). New York: Guilford Press.
Broverman, I. K., Broverman, D. M., Clarkson, F., Rosenkrantz, P., &
   Vogel, S. (1970). Sex-role stereotyping and clinical judgments of mental
   health. *Journal of Consulting and Clinical Psychology, 45*, 250–256.
Brown, L. M. (1991). Telling a girl's life: Self-authorization as a form of re-
   sistance. In C. Gilligan, A. Rogers, & D. Tolman (Eds.), *Women, girls, and
   psychotherapy: Reframing resistance* (pp. 71–86). Binghamton, NY:
   Haworth Press.
Buckley, T. R., & Carter, R. T. (2005). Black adolescent girls: Do gender role
   and racial identity impact their self-esteem? *Sex Roles, 53*, 647–661.
Burt, V. K., & Hendrick, V. C. (2005). *Clinical manual of women's mental
   health.* Washington DC: American Psychiatric Association.
Chesler, P. (1972). *Women and madness.* New York: Doubleday.
Clark, R. L. (2006). Healing the generations: Urban American Indians in
   recovery. In T. M. Witko (Ed.), *Mental health care for urban Indians:
   Clinical insights from Native practitioners* (pp. 83–99). Washington DC:
   American Psychological Association.

Constantine, M. G., Greer, T. W., & Kindaichi, M. M. (2003). Theoretical and cultural considerations in counseling women of color. In M. Kopala & M. A. Keitel (Eds.), *Handbook of counseling women* (pp. 40–52). Thousand Oaks, CA: Sage.

Cummings, A. L. (2000). Teaching feminist counselor responses to novice female counselors. *Counselor Education and Supervision, 40,* 47–57.

Cummins, L. H., & Lehman, J. (2007). Eating disorders and body image concerns in Asian American women: Assessment and treatment from a multicultural and feminist perspective. *Eating Disorders, 15,* 217–230.

Dixon Rayle, A. D., Chee, C., & Sand, J. K. (2006). Honoring their way: Counseling American Indian women. *Journal of Multicultural Counseling and Development, 34,* 66–79.

Enns, C. Z. (2004). *Feminist theories and feminist psychotherapies* (2nd ed.). Binghamton, NY: Haworth Press.

Erikson, E. H. (1963). *Childhood and society* (2nd ed.). New York: Norton.

Etaugh, C. A., & Bridges, J. S. (2004). *The psychology of women, a lifespan perspective* (2nd ed.). Boston, MA: Pearson Education.

Evans, K. M., Kincade, E. A., Marbley, A. F., & Seem, S. R. (2005). Feminism and feminist therapy. *Journal of Counseling & Development, 83,* 269–277.

Gilbert, L. A., & Sher, M. (1999). *Gender and sex in counseling and psychotherapy.* Needham Heights, MA: Allyn & Bacon.

Gilligan, C. (1991). Women's psychological development: Implications for psychotherapy. In C. Gilligan, A. Rogers, & D. Tolman (Eds.), *Women, girls, and psychotherapy: Reframing resistance* (pp. 5–32). Binghamton, NY: Haworth Press.

Grabe, S., & Hyde, J. S. (2006). Ethnicity and body dissatisfaction among women in the United States: A meta-analysis. *Psychological Bulletin, 132,* 622–640.

Greenspan, M. (1993). *A new approach to women and therapy.* Blue Ridge Summit, PA: Tab Books.

Hansen, L. S., Gama, E. M., & Harkins, A. K. (2002). Revisiting gender issues in multicultural counseling. In P. B. Pederson, J. G. Draguns, W. J. Lonner, & J. E. Trimble (Eds.), *Counseling across cultures* (pp. 163–184). Thousand Oaks, CA: Sage.

Harris, H. S., Thoresen, C. E., & Lopez, S. J. (2007). Integrating positive psychology into counseling: Why and (when appropriate) how. *Journal of Counseling & Development, 85,* 3–13.

Jordan, J. V. (2003). Relational-cultural therapy. In K. Kopala & M. A. Keitel (Eds.), *Handbook of counseling women* (pp. 22–30). Thousand Oaks, CA: Sage.

Kopala, M., & Keitel, M. A. (Eds.). (2003). *Handbook of counseling women.* Thousand Oaks, CA: Sage.

Lee, C. C. (2005). Ethnicity and wellness. In J. E. Myers & T. J. Sweeney (Eds.), *Counseling for wellness: Theory, research, and practice* (pp. 105–116). Alexandria, VA: American Counseling Association.

McBride, M. C. (1990). Autonomy and the struggle for female identity: Implications for counseling women. *Journal of Counseling & Development, 69,* 22–26.

McWhirter, E. H. (1991). Empowerment in counseling. *Journal of Counseling & Development, 69,* 222–227.

Miller, J. B. (1976). *Toward a new psychology of women.* Boston: Beacon.

Myers, J. E., & Sweeney, T. J. (Eds.). (2005). *Counseling for wellness: Theory, research, and practice.* Alexandria, VA: American Counseling Association.

Myers, J. E., Sweeney, T. J., & Witmer, J. M. (2000). Wheel of wellness counseling for wellness: A holistic model for treatment planning. *Journal of Counseling & Development, 78,* 251–266.

National Institute of Mental Health. (2006a). *Depression: What every woman should know.* Retrieved September 7, 2006, from http:// www. nimh. nig. gov/publicat/depwomenknows.cfm

National Institute of Mental Health. (2006b). *Women hold up half the sky.* Retrieved September 7, 2006, from http://www.nimh.nig.gov/publicat/womensoms.cfm

Office of National Drug Control Policy. (2006). *Girls and drugs.* Retrieved July 30, 2007, from www.mediacampaign.org/pdf/girls_and_drugs.pdf

O'Hanlan, K. A., Dibble, S. L., Hagan, H. J., & Davids, R. (2004). Advocacy for women's health should include lesbian health. *Journal of Women's Health, 13,* 227–234.

Porter, R. Y. (2000). Clinical issues and intervention with ethnic minority women. In J. F. Aponte & J. Wohl (Eds.), *Psychological intervention and cultural diversity* (pp. 183–199). Boston: Allyn & Bacon.

Ryff, C. D., & Keyes, C. L. (1995). The structure of psychological well-being revisited. *Journal of Personality and Social Psychology, 69,* 719–727.

Sherman, J. A. (1980). Therapist attitudes and sex-role stereotyping. In A. Brodsky & R. T. Hare-Mustin (Eds.), *Women and psychotherapy* (pp. 35–66). New York: Guilford Press.

Stern, L. (1991). Disavowing the self in female adolescence. In C. Gilligan, A. Rogers, & D. Tolman (Eds.), *Women, girls, and psychotherapy: Reframing resistance* (pp. 105–118). Binghamton, NY: Haworth Press.

Tait, C. S., & Pergeroy, J. J. (2001). Working with selected populations: Treatment issues and characteristics. In P. Stevens & R. L. Smith (Eds.), *Substance abuse counseling* (pp. 227–250). Columbus, OH: Merrill Prentice Hall.

Tryon, G. S., & Winograd, G. (2003). Developing a healthy identity. In M. Kopala & M. A. Keitel (Eds.), *Handbook of counseling women* (pp. 185–197). Thousand Oaks, CA: Sage.

Vasquez, M. J., & De Las Fuentes, C. D. (1999). American-born Asian, African, Latina, and American Indian adolescent girls: Challenges and strengths. In *Beyond appearance, a new look at adolescent girls* (pp. 151–174). Washington, DC: American Psychological Association.

Walker, L. E. (1994). *Abused women and survivor therapy: A practical guide for the psychotherapist.* Washington, DC: American Psychological Association.

Whiffen, V. E., & Demidenko, N. (2006). Mood disturbance across the life span. In J. Worell & C. D. Goodheart (Eds.), *Handbook of girls' and women's psychological health* (pp. 51–59). New York: Oxford University Press.

Worell, J. (2006). Pathways to healthy development: Sources of strength and empowerment. In J. Worell & C. D. Goodheart (Eds.), *Handbook of girls' and women's psychological health* (pp. 3–14). New York: Oxford University Press.

Worell, J., & Goodheart, C. D. (Eds.). (2006). *Handbook of girls' and women's psychological health*. New York: Oxford University Press.

Worell, J., & Remer, P. (2002). *Feminist perspectives in therapy* (pp. 173–202). Hoboken, NJ: Wiley.

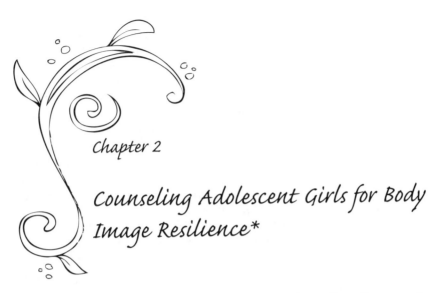

Chapter 2

Counseling Adolescent Girls for Body Image Resilience*

Growing up, I felt like the only way I could be happy with myself was if someone else loved me. I've got a lot of insecurities about the way I look. That's why I work out so much. And I'm always comparing myself to other people, wondering if I'm good enough.
—Pussycat Dolls' Nicole Scherzinger in *Vibe Magazine* interview, 2007

Early adolescence presents extensive developmental challenges for girls. As they face the onset of puberty and its associated psychological and physical changes, girls also confront the emergence of dating relationships, school transitions, and contradictory gender-role expectations. During early adolescence, girls also become more focused on their appearance, weight, and shape as key aspects of their identities. With the considerable weight gains that accompany puberty, girls become concerned about the discrepancy between their developing bodies and the societal ideal for female thinness that is portrayed in Western cultures (Thompson, Heinberg, Altabe, & Tantleff-Dunn, 1999). At a time when a girl's physical appearance is most important to her, her body is changing in ways that are increasingly discrepant from the thin ideal. These influences leave many girls vulnerable to body image dissatisfaction (BID) and eating-related problems (Levine & Smolak, 2002; Thompson et al., 1999).

According to Levine and Smolak (2002), between 40 and 70% of adolescent girls are dissatisfied with two or more aspects of their bodies, most generally with the hips, buttocks, stomach, and thighs. One study found that more than 80% of girls surveyed reported body dissatisfaction (Kostanski & Gullone, 1998), and another large-scale study revealed that

---

*Adapted from Choate, L. H. (2007). Counseling adolescent girls for body image resilience: Strategies for school counselors. *Professional School Counselor, 10,* 317–326; and Choate, L. H. (2005). Toward a theoretical model of women's body image resilience. *Journal of Counseling & Development, 83,* 320–330. Reprinted with permission.

42 to 45% of girls in grades 9–12 were dieting to lose weight (Thompson et al., 1999). With such large numbers of girls experiencing dissatisfaction with their bodies, it is important for counselors to note how body image experiences can adversely affect a girl's quality of life, as the amount of time, energy, and money she spends on beauty enhancement can restrict her opportunities to develop other aspects of her identity (Strachan & Cash, 2002; Striegel-Moore & Franko, 2002). There is a relationship between negative body image and a variety of psychosocial problems. First, body image dissatisfaction is among the most empirically supported risk factors for maladaptive eating practices (Cooley & Toray, 2001). Second, negative body image is associated with poor self-esteem, unnecessary elective cosmetic surgery, smoking onset, anxiety about social evaluation, public self-consciousness, depression, and sexual inhibition (Ackard, Kearney-Cooke, & Peterson, 2000; Lavin & Cash, 2000; Stice & Shaw, 2003; Stice & Whitenton, 2002; Wiederman & Pryor, 2000). Third, body image dissatisfaction also creates risks for mental health concerns, including higher levels of depression (Thompson et al., 1999). Finally, body image dissatisfaction is the primary precursor for the development of eating disorders such as anorexia nervosa and bulimia (Polivy & Herman, 2002), particularly during the adolescent period (Kalodner & DeLucia-Waak, 2003).

Because BID is such a pervasive problem in adolescent girls, counselors need to develop effective prevention and intervention programs in this area. Effective prevention programs focus beyond pathology-driven models, which emphasize treatment for the concerns of girls in clinical samples. The most promising approaches incorporate protective factors that build on girls' strengths, promote resilience, and buffer them from the development of body dissatisfaction and subsequent disordered eating practices (Cash, 2002; Crago, Shisslak, & Ruble, 2001; Irving, 1999; Piran, Levine, & Steiner-Adair, 1999; Striegel-Moore & Cachelin, 1999; Taylor & Altman, 1997).

Current research indicates that successful BID prevention programs incorporate two primary approaches: the social cognitive model (SCM) and the nonspecific vulnerability-stressor (NSVS) model (Levine & Piran, 2004). The SCM assists program participants in understanding the following body image issues: (a) how to change unrealistic and unhealthy attitudes about the importance of weight and shape; (b) the role of nutrition and exercise in maintaining a positive body image; (c) biological processes related to weight gains in puberty; and (d) strategies that enable participants to analyze and then resist persistent media messages about the importance of attaining the Western thin ideal. NSVS model programs, on the other hand, focus on general qualities that individuals need to cope well with life demands. According to Levine and Piran (2004), these include life skills such as stress management, decision making, and communication skills. Programs using this approach help girls to improve their negative-self-concept, develop coping skills for dealing with life stressors, and enhance social support. These qualities have been shown to protect against many emotional problems, including negative body image and eating disorders. These two approaches are explored throughout this chapter.

Cash (2002) argued for a paradigm shift away from the study of body image as pathology and proposed a move toward understanding "the trajectories whereby people create fulfilling experiences of embodiment" (p. 45). This shift examines the role of protective factors and resilience by exploring the life experiences and personality traits that build resistance to strong cultural pressures that influence girls to be dissatisfied with their bodies (Cash & Pruzinsky, 2002). The prevention literature also has called for research regarding body image resilience. According to the National Institute of Mental Health (Reiss & Price, 1996; Taylor & Altman, 1997), prevention initiatives in the area of eating disorders should devote a greater emphasis to the ways in which protective factors can be targeted and enhanced in girls and women. Promoting protective factors includes assisting all girls as they confront the multiple challenges of adolescence and helping them to define their identity and sense of worth apart from physical appearance (American Psychological Association [APA], 1999). This includes the wellness approaches describe in Chapter 1 in which counselors focus on helping clients enhance strengths in all life dimensions (Myers & Sweeney, 2005).

Researchers in this area have also called for holistic approaches that are focused on multiple dimensions of an individual's environment. Instead of an exclusive view of body image problems and eating disturbances as disorders that originate within an individual adolescent girl, counseling interventions also should target family, peers, schools, media, and other sociocultural influences (Barker & Galambos, 2003; Crago et al., 2001; Irving, 1999; Levine & Piran, 2001; Piran et al., 1999; Smolak & Murnen, 2001).

Because counselors possess a prevention focus and an orientation toward normal growth and development, they are well situated to take the lead in designing approaches that strengthen protective factors. The profession's emphasis on wellness and holistic approaches that build on the positive resources of clients (Gale & Austin, 2003; Myers & Sweeney, 2005; Myers, Sweeney, & White, 2002; Myers et al., 2000) can be aligned with research and interventions regarding resilience. Specifically, counselors need a prevention approach that identifies protective factors at the individual, family, peer, and school level and teaches girls how to challenge broader sociocultural influences. In this chapter, I first conduct a review of recent literature related to the development of body image in girls. I then redirect my focus to explore a proposed theoretical model of body image resilience based on factors that protect some girls from body image dissatisfaction and provide specific prevention and counseling strategies that can be used to promote positive body image in adolescent girls.

Girls' Body Image Development

Sociocultural theories explain the impact of social and cultural influences on the development of BID in Western societies (Heinberg, 1996; Stice &

Whitenton, 2002). These theorists assert that contemporary Western societies emphasize thinness as a central aspect of beauty for women (Mussell, Binford, & Fulkerson, 2000) and that pervasive social pressures to achieve extreme thinness result in women's "normative discontent" with their bodies (Rodin, Silberstein, & Streigel-Moore, 1985). Even as women have made great educational and vocational advances during the past several decades, increasing pressures have emerged for women to refocus their energies on achieving a largely unattainable ideal of beauty and thinness (Bordo, 1995; Thompson et al., 1999; Wolf, 1991). For example, in recent years the thin ideal has become progressively thinner while the average woman has become larger (Heinberg, 1996). Further, the beauty ideal encompasses often unattainable and frequently contradictory attributes including extreme thinness, white and flawless skin, thin waist, long legs, tall, young, physically fit, muscular, and angular while also espousing a curvaceous and full-breasted body type (Barber, 1998; Groesz, Levine, & Murnen, 2002; Heinberg, 1996; Levine & Smolak, 2002). Today's girls are socialized to appear as "sexy" as possible (APA, Task Force on the Sexualization of Girls, 2007). The pervasiveness of these messages leads researchers and practitioners to conclude that BID and even eating disorders are natural outcomes of extreme social pressures to achieve thinness (Attie & Brooks-Gunn, 1989; Thompson et al., 1999).

One of the strongest and most effective conveyors of these sociocultural messages is mass media. In early adolescence girls are especially likely to make social comparisons in forming a self-identity, and media images serve most often as their comparison standard. Research in social comparison theory demonstrates a consistent relationship between adolescent girls' BID and viewing media images promoting the thin ideal (Botta, 2000; Clay, Vignoles, & Dittmar, 2005; Cusumano & Thompson, 2000; Groesz et al., 2002; Hargraves & Tiggemann, 2003; Jones, 2001; Thompson et al., 1999). Girls themselves report the media as a strong influence on their negative attitudes toward their bodies (Tiggemann, 2006). In one study by Dunkley, Wertheim, and Paxton (2001), girls most often cited magazine advertisements as the source they turned to for information regarding how to achieve their ideal body size and shape. Further, Thomsen, Weber, and Brown (2001) found that high school girls who reported reading women's health and fitness magazines on a frequent basis were the most likely to engage in maladaptive dietary practices (such as taking laxatives and appetite suppressants, engaging in intentional vomiting, and restriction of calories) when compared with girls who were moderate or infrequent readers (Thomsen et al., 2001).

According to Haworth-Hoeppner (2000), pervasive media images are key influences on the development of body image, but these cultural pressures are mediated through the family. An important factor in the development of body image is the extent to which family members convey sociocultural pressures regarding the importance of thinness and beauty. Family characteristics that contribute to negative body image include the following: (a) negative family attitudes and behaviors regarding food, including parental modeling of the importance of thinness, weight, and shape issues (Haworth-Hoeppner, 2000; Mussell et al., 2000); (b) critical comments about an individual's weight, shape, or eating behaviors (Haworth-Hoeppner, 2000), including teasing by family members in general and brothers in particular (Levine & Smolak, 2002); (c) parental history of being overweight or dieting; (d) perceived parental pressure to be slender and to control weight and shape (Kichler & Crowther, 2001; Striegel-Moore & Cachelin, 1999; Phares, Steinberg, & Thompson, 2004); and (e) general family dysfunction, competitive family attitudes, and negative family communication (Haworth-Hoeppner, 2000; Kichler & Crowther, 2001).

Peers have a pronounced impact on the development of body image during adolescence. There is evidence that peer modeling influences body dissatisfaction in adolescent girls. Girls who are part of friendship groups share comparable levels of dieting behavior, drive for thinness, and overall body image concerns (Paxton, Schutz, Wertheim, & Muir, 1999), and girls are influenced by peer modeling of dieting and communication around weight loss (Phares et al., 2004). It is not surprising that peer teasing is related to body image dissatisfaction and dieting behavior. Although both male and female peers tease one other, boys are more likely to make critical comments about a girl's weight and shape than are other girls (Levine & Smolak, 2002). If girls place great importance on the opinions of others, particularly on the approval of males (Striegel-Moore & Cachelin, 1999), it is not surprising that male peer teasing results in body dissatisfaction and a focus on thinness as the key to social approval. Influenced by media messages and family or peer modeling of the importance of thinness, an adolescent is likely to engage in maladaptive weight control behaviors in an effort to lose weight (Stice, Presnell, & Spangler, 2002).

Self-Exploration Exercise

The following questions are designed to assist you in exploring the influences that had an impact on your body image development. An awareness of your personal journey will help you better understand the experiences of the girls with whom you currently work.

Family-of-Origin and Peer Influences

1. Overall, how did you feel about your body as a child? As an adolescent?
2. What are some things you remember about your mother's attitude toward her body? What were her eating habits like?
3. What messages did your mother give you about the importance of physical appearance and weight to a woman's worth? What messages did you receive from your father? How did these messages affect you? *(continued)*

Self-Exploration Exercise (Continued)

4. What messages did you receive from your siblings about your body shape, size, or physical appearance? How did these messages affect you?

5. Do you remember any comments about your body shape, size, or physical appearance made by male peers in childhood or adolescence? What about female peers? What effect did these comments have?

6. Do you remember any comments about your body made by teachers, coaches, or other significant adults in your life? What effects did these comments have?

Media and Other Influences

7. What are some movies or television programs you saw during your childhood or adolescent years that influenced your view of the importance of women's beauty?

8. What fashions were in style during your adolescent years? How interested were you in these styles? How did this interest influence what you thought you should look like?

9. What magazines did you read during your childhood and adolescent years? What messages did you receive from the magazines you chose to read? How did these messages affect your view of your body or appearance?

10. When you consider the variety of sociocultural influences on your development (e.g., ethnicity, culture, sexual orientation, disability status, spiritual/religious preferences, socioeconomic status), in what ways did these factors affect your view of your body? How did they influence your view of the importance of physical attractiveness for women?

   a. ethnicity and cultural community:
   b. sexual orientation:
   c. disability status:
   d. spiritual/religious preference:
   e. socioeconomic status:

Individual Differences in Body Image Development

All adolescent girls in Western societies are exposed to sociocultural pressures for thinness and beauty to some extent. Some girls are able to resist pressures to attain the thin ideal, and many others develop negative body image but not disordered eating. Some girls engage in unhealthy dieting and eating practices such as chronic dieting and purging, and a minority develop full-blown eating disorder syndromes.

There are two primary ways that body image development can lead to BID: girls' comparisons with the cultural ideal and girls' comparisons of themselves with others. When girls compare themselves against the cultural ideal, a discrepancy exists between the perceptions of their own bodies and the culturally defined standard. Girls grow increasingly aware of cultural standards for appearance as they reach adolescence, and many girls then internalize these attitudes as part of their personal belief systems. Research supports the idea that the thin-ideal internalization process increases for girls as they reach puberty (Bearman, Presnell, Martinez, & Stice, 2006). In fact, of the 16-year-old girls in one study, 65% endorsed overall acceptance of sociocultural attitudes toward appearance, a rate higher than that displayed by younger girls in the sample (Clay et al., 2005).

Girls who have internalized the thin ideal are also influenced by self-comparisons to other women. This practice may reinforce body dissatisfaction. Girls with negative body image engage in the process of body surveillance (McKinley, 2002), constantly watching themselves as though they are being observed, evaluating themselves against other girls, and paying a great deal of attention to others' perceptions of and reactions to their appearance. Tantleff-Dunn and Gokee (2002) concluded that a girl who is vigilant in comparing herself to others will be more vulnerable to the influences of cultural pressures and will have greater difficulties with body dissatisfaction. There is some evidence that Caucasian women have higher levels of this type of appearance surveillance than do Latina and African American women (Hrabosky & Grilo, 2007).

If a girl has internalized the thin ideal as the standard against which she evaluates herself, she may also subscribe to cultural messages conveying that thinness and beauty are the primary determinants of her self-worth. Girls who overvalue weight and shape as the basis for their sense of self tend to be heavily invested in their appearance and spend a great deal of time and effort in the pursuit of thinness. Many believe that regardless of their biological predispositions, with enough work and effort they can control their appearance (McKinley, 2002) and achieve the culturally defined ideal weight and shape.

For many girls in contemporary Western cultures, the process of body image development results in body dissatisfaction. However, the perceptions and experiences of girls who do not develop negative body image provide valuable information regarding protective factors that can serve to buffer girls against societal pressures to attain the thin ideal. I explore resilience and identify a theoretical model of body image protective factors in the sections that follow. First, read the case example and consider the time and energy that many girls spend on their physical appearance throughout adolescence.

Case Study: Part 1

Misty, a 14-year-old Caucasian girl, comes to counseling at the urging of her parents. She appears to be of normal weight for her height. She reports the onset of her menstrual cycle was at age 12. She says that all of her problems began at that time, as she gained 20 pounds and developed larger breasts, hips, and thighs than she had as a young girl. She reports feeling "ashamed" of these changes in her body and asserts that her parents treat her differently now that she is "fat." She claims that she now thinks about her body and appearance constantly, wondering why she can't look like the models she sees on television, on movies, and in magazines. If she were more attractive and thin, she believes she would be happier and more popular. When asked about her friends at school, she says her peers "feel the same way she does" and that they often encourage one another to diet and exercise excessively. She says that she has never had a boyfriend and is very concerned that boys will not find her attractive. Although she made excellent grades throughout elementary school, recently her schoolwork has started to suffer, and she seems to have lost interest in performing well in class. She also decided to quit the basketball team because she didn't want to be seen as a "jock." She claims that her primary goal is to lose 10 pounds, be a part of the "popular" group in her grade, and to have a boyfriend. Until she reaches this goal, she says, she will remain "miserable."

Cross-Cultural Contributions to Understanding Resilience

Body image development is highly influenced by lived experience, so cross-cultural literature is helpful in understanding the effects of cultural influences on resilience. Body dissatisfaction and its correlates initially were considered primarily to affect Caucasian girls and women, but research indicates that this problem has developed in any culture or ethnic group in which the Western thin ideal is adopted as the standard of beauty (Levine & Smolak, 2002). The extensive acceptance of the ideal means that no racial/ethnic or cultural group is immune to body image dissatisfaction or to the development of eating disorders. For example, a recent meta-analysis indicated no significant differences between Caucasian, Asian American, and Latina adolescents and women in terms of their level of body dissatisfaction (Grabe & Hyde, 2006). American Indian women were not studied due to lack of representation in the included studies.

Although Caucasian, Asian American, and Latina girls may have similar levels of dissatisfaction, Grabe and Hyde (2006) stated that these findings do not mean that their dissatisfaction reflects the same concerns (e.g., perhaps being dissatisfied with body type or racialized features) or that dissatisfaction results in the same type of psychological or behavioral consequences for women. However, a study of Caucasian, African American, Latina, and Asian American girls from an urban public school setting indicated no group differences between body image dissatisfaction and adjustment. In other words, regardless of racial/ethnic background, when girls experienced BID, they experienced similar levels of psychological and social consequences (Nishina, Ammon, Bellmore, & Graham, 2006). Another study found that Native American adolescent girls who had low levels of body satisfaction experienced anxiety, depression, social problems, and perceived nonacceptance by their peer group; these consequences are similar to those experienced by girls from other cultural groups (Newman, Sontag, & Salvato, 2006).

African American Women and Resilience

Few differences have been found in the rates of eating disorders when comparing Caucasian and African American women (Celio, Zabinski, & Wilfley, 2002), and some researchers explain any differences in eating disorder rates in terms of socioeconomic status or variability in body mass index (Polivy & Herman, 2002). Although this research indicates that rates of eating disorders may be more similar among African Americans and Caucasians than previously thought, membership in African American culture, which places less emphasis on thinness as the primary determinant of beauty, can provide protection from the development of negative body image (Grabe & Hyde, 2006; Levine & Smolak, 2002; Mussell et al., 2000; Paxton, Eisenberg, & Neumark-Sztainer, 2006; Striegel-Moore & Cachelin, 1999). In discussing these findings it is important to note that cultural factors do not necessarily lead to body satisfaction for all individuals of a specific group. Examining individual difference variables within cultural groups provides nuanced distinctions between factors that influence body image satisfaction (Falconer & Neville, 2000).

Within the African American community, the reduced cultural emphasis on weight appears to translate into a more positive body image for African American adolescents. Pedersen (2000) argued that because African American females are not part of mainstream culture, they are in a position to objectively view, evaluate, and interpret the messages of the dominant culture regarding definitions of beauty. Because of their vantage point outside the mainstream culture, African American women are able to question the thin ideal and are often able to resist the internalization of negative stereotypes, which they in turn are able to teach to their daughters. In general, African American girls report higher levels of self-esteem (Celio et al., 2002; Compitello, 2003), more body satisfaction even at higher weights (Harris, 1995; Molloy & Herzberger, 1998; Smolak, 2002), and more satisfaction with their overall appearance than Caucasian girls and women (Jaffee & Lutter, 1995; Smith, Thompson, Raczynski, & Hilner, 1999). In one study comparing Black and White adolescent girls, 40% of Black girls considered themselves to be attractive or very attractive, whereas only 9.1% of the White girls in the sample rated themselves positively (Jaffee & Lutter, 1995).

Several specific cultural factors have been identified as contributing to body image resilience and high self-esteem in African American girls and women. First, these girls do not limit their view of ideal body types to a narrow range of weights and shapes and often report larger ideal body shapes (Mussell et al., 2000). Additionally, they rate images of large, more buxom women more positively than do White girls (Celio et al., 2002). Part of the reason for these preferences may be attributed to their belief that Black men prefer larger women, and these perceptions appear to be accurate: Black men tend to prefer heavier women than do White men, reporting preferences for women with wide hips and round buttocks (Celio et al., 2002). Interestingly, Levine and Smolak (2002) reported that many African American girls say that they want to gain weight so that they will have bigger hips, thighs, and buttocks.

Second, family support contributes to the development of positive body image in African American girls. According to Celio et al. (2002), mothers convey messages to their daughters to be independent, strong, and to rely on themselves. These expectations are often supported through assigning daughters the responsibilities of household duties and caring for younger siblings or through making financial contributions to the family. Such responsibilities can provide girls with an enhanced sense of competence and independence (Pedersen, 2000). Girls who adopt these qualities are less vulnerable to low self-esteem and negative body image. In one study by Molloy and Herzberger (1998), African American college women who believed that men prefer larger body types and who had higher scores on measures of independence and assertiveness had higher levels of self-esteem and body satisfaction. These protective factors were less often present in Caucasian women, who are often encouraged to conform to stereotypical female gender roles such as being passive, nurturing, self-sacrificing, and dependent.

A third factor in the development of African American body image resilience is the presence of supportive peer and community relationships. Compared to White females, Black girls and women experience less pressure to achieve thinness and receive more support for resisting negative mainstream cultural images from their peers and significant others (Lovejoy, 2001). Rather than acting in a competitive manner, Black adolescents tend to compliment one another on their appearance (Celio et al., 2002). There is a tendency for African American girls to eschew beauty trends and to value the creation of a distinctive, individual style. Beauty is viewed as far more than thinness and encompasses other factors such as personal style, confidence, attitude, grooming, fit of clothes, hairstyle, skin tone/color satisfaction, and ethnic pride (Celio et al., 2002). Patton (2006) noted that taking the initiative to craft an individual style indicates creativity and is a way to design one's own beauty standard. According to Lovejoy (2001), these qualities lead to "a more egalitarian standard—one that is attainable by anyone with the use of imagination and self knowledge" (p. 250).

In sum, these three attitudes and behaviors, often present in the African American community, seem to serve to promote body satisfaction in girls. However, it is important to note that some of these values can lead to obesity, binge eating disorder, and other health-related problems such as diabetes and high blood pressure (Levine & Smolak, 2002; Lovejoy, 2001; Mussell et al., 2000). For example, there is evidence that the prevalence of overweight and obesity is higher for girls and women of color than for non-Hispanic Caucasian women (U.S. Department of Health and Human Services, 2001), which can lead to long-term health problems for these populations. Obesity among American Indian adolescents in particular is

even higher than that for the general population, and their obesity prevalence rates are higher than for all other races combined (Newman et al.,
2006). In sum, when working to improve body image satisfaction in all
girls, counselors can emphasize the enhancement of qualities found in
African American girls that contribute to positive body image (such as
self-esteem, family and peer support, fluid definitions of beauty, and individual style) while also promoting overall health and wellness.

Toward a Model of Resilience: Body Image Protective Factors

By exploring the experiences of girls who possess positive body image,
counselors can work with girls in building resistance to the strong cultural pressures that influence them to be dissatisfied with their bodies
(Cash & Pruzinsky, 2002). Five protective factors are components of a theoretical model of body image resilience: (a) family and peer support,
(b) gender-role satisfaction, (c) global and physical self-esteem, (d) effective coping strategies and critical thinking skills, and (e) holistic wellness
and balance. After discussion of each factor, prevention strategies based
on the SCM and NSVS approaches are provided, which counselors can
use in a variety of settings as part of their prevention and counseling work
with adolescent girls.

Protective Factor One: Family and Peer Support

Adolescent girls are confronted with cultural pressures regarding how
they should look and act, and for many girls these messages are strongly
reinforced by family and peers. Girls who develop secure attachments
(Striegel-Moore & Cachelin, 1999) and receive affirming reactions to their
bodies from parents throughout their childhood tend to develop body satisfaction (Kearney-Cooke, 2002). A girl's perception of her family's approval of her overall appearance is positively related to her body esteem
(McKinley, 1999). While body image is an aspect of a girl's developing
sense of identity, the emphasis that parents place on beauty and thinness
affects the importance she relegates to appearance as part of her overall
self-concept. Instead of an emphasis on appearance, parents of daughters
with positive body image provide them with positive comments regarding achievements in all areas of their lives (Jaffee & Lutter, 1995). Further,
girls who feel unconditional acceptance by their social support networks
may be less likely to embrace the thin ideal as a source of social validation
(Bearman et al., 2006).

Girls' sense of body satisfaction is strongly related to their mothers'
personal attitudes toward their own bodies (McKinley, 1999; Usmiani &
Daniluk, 1997). Daughters observe the ways in which their mothers cope
with cultural pressures and are highly influenced by such maternal modeling. Kearney-Cooke (2002) argued that mothers should become more
aware of their influence on daughters' body image and should model
positive attitudes regarding their own weight and shape. This can begin
with maintaining a weight within a realistic and medically sound range

and by adhering to healthful eating and exercise routines. Conversely, observing their mothers engaging in chronic dieting and excessive exercise regimens, and centering family discourse around the importance of thinness for success can have a negative effect on girls' body image development (Haworth-Hoeppner, 2000).

To develop positive body image, girls need family members who provide them with affirming messages about their bodies and who possess positive attitudes toward their own appearance, weight, and shape. As noted earlier, in comparison with Caucasian girls, African American girls receive maternal messages to be strong and self-reliant and are therefore less vulnerable to body image problems because these qualities lead to an enhanced sense of competence and independence (Celio et al., 2002; Pedersen, 2000). Further, general family qualities such as supportive parental relationships, open communication and expressiveness, and low family stress also protect against adolescent BID (Barker & Galambos, 2003; Graber, Archibald, & Brooks-Gunn, 1999; Haworth-Hoeppner, 2000; Kearney-Cooke, 2002; Striegel-Moore & Cachelin, 1999).

Peers have a significant impact on adolescent girls' body image development and serve as relevant sources of information regarding the culture of thinness. Paxton et al. (1999) found that girls share the attitudes and behaviors of their peer group regarding dieting, drive for thinness, and overall body image concerns. A girl's peer group negatively influences body image when her friends frequently discuss dieting and other weight loss behaviors or tease peers regarding their appearance (Smolak, 1999). Being the target of peer teasing is strongly related to BID (Paxton et al., 1999; Smolak, 1999). Negative body image is exacerbated as peer group discussions center around heightened interest in boys; research indicates that increases in girls' weight consciousness and dieting occur with the onset of dating (Graber et al., 1999). Counselors should note, however, that friends can serve as a protective factor in a girl's body image development when they are less invested in the achievement of appearance-oriented goals and are less competitive with one another regarding weight and shape (Paxton et al., 1999). Overall, the presence of a strong social support network comprised of both friends and family serves as a protective factor in body image development (Striegel-Moore & Cachelin, 1999) and is an essential element of wellness as defined by Myers and Sweeney's (2005) wellness model.

Prevention Strategies for Counselors

1. Educate parents regarding the impact of their weight, food, and appearance-related attitudes and behaviors on their children. Mothers in particular should be aware of the strong effects of modeling on their daughter's developing body image. Parents can change family discourse around the importance of weight and shape and can discourage daughters from evaluating themselves based on how they appear to others (McKinley, 1999). For those working in school settings, Graber et al. (1999) suggested that counselors create an infor-

mative newsletter regarding these issues for students to share with their parents. To aid in this initiative, counselors can draw from the specific prevention strategies and guidelines for parents available from the National Eating Disorders Association (NEDA, 2004a).

2. Inform clients and their parents (as well as teachers and school staff in school settings) of the negative effects of dieting (such as slowed metabolism, increased likelihood of binge eating, and eventual weight gain), how to discourage diet talk at school and home, and ways to take a nondieting approach to healthful eating. Programs should not focus on educating girls regarding the signs and symptoms of eating disorders, as this approach often results in girls' adopting these behaviors.

3. Encourage parents to display a low tolerance for peer teasing, particularly regarding weight and shape. Serve as a model by refusing to engage in "fat jokes" among faculty and staff in your own agency. Further, teach clients how to intervene to assist a teased peer and provide strategies for coping when a client is the victim of peer teasing.

4. Facilitate girls' development of friendship groups that provide support and help them to feel good about themselves (versus friends who are competitive or make them feel judged). Intervene with friendship groups to encourage them to adopt more positive attitudes toward body image (Paxton et al., 1999; Smolak, 1999).

Protective Factor Two: Gender-Role Satisfaction

In early adolescence, girls more than boys become increasingly dissatisfied with their bodies and overall physical appearance (Feingold & Mazzella, 1998). This discrepancy may be explained in part by two gender-role socialization processes that were introduced in Chapter 1. First, girls are taught the importance of attracting a dating partner and gaining popularity as a measure of their self-worth. They are socialized to take responsibility for establishing relationships and to sacrifice their own needs to maintain their social connections (Miller, 1990). This interpersonal orientation leaves girls vulnerable to others' opinions and motivates them to go to great lengths to achieve the approval of peers and potential dating partners. Girls receive the message that the best way to gain such approval is through conformity to the beauty ideal. Unfortunately, early adolescence is also a time in which the onset of puberty brings an average weight gain of 50 pounds in girls, with 20 to 30 pounds of fat deposited in the hips, waist, thighs, and buttocks; weight gains in these areas are in direct contradiction to the beauty ideal espoused in Western cultures (Levine & Smolak, 2002). Girls are better protected from BID when they begin to question the discrepancy between their changing bodies and how girls are represented in the media, and when they understand that achieving the beauty ideal is not the only avenue for achieving peer acceptance or popularity.

A second socialization process for girls occurs as they are confronted with societal messages regarding what it means to be successful as a woman: She is expected to fulfill the traditional female gender role by being nurturing, family- and relationship-oriented, and passive. At the same time she is expected to be independent, self-reliant, assertive, and high achieving in academic and career pursuits, while also achieving the cultural standard for thinness and attractiveness (Denmark, 1999; Hart & Kenny, 1997; Thompson et al., 1999). The message that "you can have it all," termed the *superwoman myth* by Steiner-Adair (1986), results in a sense of inadequacy, confusion, and frustration for all girls. For many adolescents, this gender-role discrepancy is manifested somatically as BID (Thompson et al., 1999).

Smolak and Murnen (2001) suggested that contradictory expectations are related to eating problems because thinness is valued in many of the roles to which girls aspire both in the workplace and in maintaining relationships. Further, girls who strive to be "superwomen" often do so at the expense of meaningful relationships, leaving them feeling disconnected and isolated. There is evidence that women of color experience difficulties when they attempt to meet the collectivistic beliefs of their families of origin while also adopting the individualistic values of mainstream culture. Especially for Asian American women, balancing these two cultural values may produce tension that is expressed as negative body image (Cummins & Lehman, 2007). To regain a sense of control, many girls learn to avoid facing contradictory pressures by refocusing their energies on trying to perfect their bodies (Friedman, 1999; Hensley, 2003). Many girls learn to believe that striving to achieve the thin ideal is a concrete, tangible strategy for attaining social approval and a sense of positive identity (Mussell et al., 2000).

As noted in Chapter 1, girls and women function optimally in the context of emotionally supportive relationships through which they can express these conflicted feelings. Counselors can help girls to acknowledge contradictory cultural expectations and, rather than internalizing their feelings, begin to address and understand these conflicts. Most women cannot thrive while being separate from or dependent upon others; rather, the hallmark of adaptive development for women is interdependence (Gilligan, 1982; Hart & Kenny, 1997). Girls who experience supportive networks that encourage them in their pursuits are less likely to be confused by gender-role conflicts or to develop negative body image. They can interpret contradictory cultural messages and define for themselves what it means to live an authentic life as a girl who is comfortable with her gender role and with her body. In following the example of African American women, who generally derive a greater sense of comfort, power, and prestige from their role as women than do Caucasian women (Lovejoy, 2001), all girls can learn to develop a strong, more positive gender identity that contributes to their overall wellness (Myers & Sweeney, 2005).

Prevention Strategies for Counselors

1. Provide girls in early adolescence with information regarding the physical and psychological changes that occur with the onset of puberty. Girls can learn of the normative nature of their weight gains and begin to challenge the inconsistencies between the thin ideal and their maturing bodies.

2. Because girls are being socialized to suppress their feelings in order to maintain relationships, assist girls in developing the skills to assertively express anger, conflict, and power in their relationships (Compitello, 2003).
3. Girls can be assisted in recognizing the effects of gender stereotyping and the harmful nature of the superwoman myth. Instead of avoiding their confusion and frustration, girls can begin to acknowledge and question the diverse roles they are expected to fulfill.
4. Rather than comparing their appearance to others in striving to achieve interpersonal success, counselors should reinforce girls' acceptance of each individual's unique body type. Expose girls to female role models representing a diversity of shapes and sizes who are praised for both their accomplishments and their appearances. Counselors can help girls recognize the importance of supportive relationships in their lives and encourage them to strengthen their relationships with friends and family.
5. Because boys are exposed to pervasive images regarding how women should look, they also need assistance in developing an appreciation for attractiveness that includes an array of body types (Halpern, Udry, Campbell, & Suchindran, 1999).

Protective Factor Three: Global and Physical Self-Esteem

In adolescence, body image becomes the most salient aspect of girls' global self-esteem, which may partially explain the significant decrease in girls' self-esteem during this period (Basow & Rubin, 1999). As noted previously, African American girls have higher levels of self-esteem than White girls do, in part because their self-esteem is not based on narrow definitions regarding what is considered attractive (Compitello, 2003). For all girls there is a strong relationship between high self-esteem, strong identity, and positive body image, suggesting that self-esteem and identity can play a role in the development of body satisfaction (Crago et al., 2001; Smolak & Murnen, 2001; Striegel-Moore & Cachelin, 1999).

One important aspect of global self-esteem that has direct implications for body image development is physical self-esteem, defined as one's attitudes toward physical activity, endurance, strength, coordination, flexibility, sports competence, body fat, appearance, and general health (Dunton, Jamner, & Cooper, 2003; James, Phelps, & Bross, 2001). Participation in physical activity is a central feature of physical self-esteem and is one of the dimensions of Myers and Sweeney's (2005) Indivisible Self Model of Wellness. When girls exercise to improve their overall fitness or health (versus working out to burn excess calories), they are more likely to possess positive body image. Further, physical activity leads to body satisfaction when girls develop an appreciation for what their bodies can do rather than how they appear to others (McKinley, 1999). Encouraging girls to engage in exercise is important, but counselors should be aware of the potential inadvertent negative effects of physical activity promotion. Zabinski, Calfas, Gehrman, Wifley, and Sallis (2001) found that a university program designed to teach students skills for enhancing their physical fitness actually increased women participants' drive for thinness and had no effect on changing their BID or body mass index. The authors noted that when girls are encouraged to become more engaged in physical activity, they also need assistance in setting realistic expectations for the effects of exercise on changing body shape or for improving other aspects of their lives.

Positive self-esteem and body image are associated with girls' and women's participation in organized athletic activities (Jaffee & Lutter, 1995; Mussell et al., 2000). Earlier research indicated that girls' sports participation was a risk factor for the development of BID, but such participation is a risk factor only for girls who participate in sports that emphasize leanness, who display high levels of perfectionism, and who possess beliefs that having a lower weight will enhance their athletic performance (Mussell et al., 2000). Another study indicated that girls' participation in refereed sports (such as basketball, tennis, volleyball, or track) versus judged sports (such as diving, cheerleading, or gymnastics) can serve as a protective factor against developing excessive concern with body size and shape (Zucker, Womble, Williamson, & Perrin, 1999). It is not sports participation per se that influences body satisfaction or dissatisfaction. Certain aspects of an athletic environment can contribute to protective effects for body image; these include the presence of supportive peer groups, emphasis on the body's physical competence rather than how it looks, and promotion of flexible gender-role attributes (Richman & Shaffer, 2000; Zucker et al., 1999).

Because of the relationship between exercise, healthful eating, and positive body image, researchers have consistently demonstrated the effectiveness of including healthy weight management information as part of BID prevention programs. As implemented by Stice, Presnell, Gau, and Shaw (2007), interventions to promote lasting changes to diet and exercise (including activities to ensure a balance between energy needs and energy intake, creation of individual lifestyle change plans to assist participants in the reduction of fat and sugar intake, and increases in physical activity) are effective in promoting healthier weights and body satisfaction. Girls also benefit from a home, school, and community environment that encourages healthful eating choices and exercise. One recent national study found that girls with the highest body satisfaction were those most likely to report parental and peer attitudes that encouraged them to eat healthfully and to exercise for fitness rather than for weight control (Kelly, Wall, Eisenberg, Story, & Neumark-Sztainer, 2005).

Prevention Strategies for Counselors

1. To help build girls' self-esteem in adolescence, encourage girls to become involved in a variety of school, volunteer, or work activities that are not focused on physical appearance or achievement of the thin ideal (Smolak & Murnen, 2001).

2. Develop mentoring programs between older and younger girls to discourage girls from overreliance on attractiveness as the only indicator of their self-worth (Crago et al., 2001; see Smolak, 1999).
3. Play an active role in promoting a broader, more fluid definition of beauty in your setting. This comprehensive view of beauty would include qualities unrelated to appearance such as self-respect, assertiveness, caring about others, wisdom, self-awareness, individuality, confidence, and motivation (NEDA, 2004b; Smolak, 1999).
4. Encourage girls to participate in a variety of physical activities that they enjoy; however, monitor girls' motivations so they learn to exercise for the purposes of health and improved fitness rather than for weight control or body shape change.
5. Work with parents and schools to implement healthy weight management programs for girls, and include individualized lifestyle change plans that incorporate healthy eating strategies and an emphasis on exercise for health and fitness (Stice et al., 2007).
6. Work with girls to focus on their positive physical attributes. For example, ask girls to list all aspects of their bodies that they appreciate and then help girls create a list of positive body affirmations to practice daily. An excellent resource for conducting this exercise can be obtained from the NEDA Web site (2004c).

Protective Factor Four: Coping Strategies and Critical Thinking Skills

As outlined previously, girls face many developmental transitions and challenges during the adolescent period. They need the internal resources to cope successfully with life demands (see emotions and thinking dimensions of wellness as described in Chapter 1). It is unfortunate that many girls focus on their weight and shape as a way of avoiding these complex issues. Steiner-Adair and Vorenberg (1999) noted, "Clearly dieting, eating, and shopping are not adequate skills for coping with life's ups and downs. . . yet it is not surprising that girls turn to these self-limiting behaviors in times of need" (p. 109). In response, prevention in the area of BID and eating disorders has increasingly emphasized nonspecific vulnerability stressor models including life skills training such as promoting problem-solving abilities, interpersonal competence/positive relationship development, assertive communication, stress management strategies, and internal locus of control as effective program components (Crago et al., 2001; Irving, 1999; McVey & Davis, 2002; McVey, Davis, Tweed, & Shaw, 2004).

Counselors can teach girls the critical thinking skills needed to question sociocultural norms, including the beauty ideal. Girls with this awareness are less likely to conform to limiting definitions of beauty and are more likely to hold favorable attitudes toward others whose bodies do not conform to the thin ideal (Cooley & Toray, 2001; Guinn, Semper, & Jorgensen, 1997). Just as African American girls emphasize style, confidence, and attitude in their evaluations of appearance, all adolescents can adopt flexible definitions of beauty that are attainable for any individual (Celio et al., 2002).

Another essential piece of life skills training is to foster media literacy: the ability to identify, evaluate, and resist media messages (Levine, Piran, & Stoddard, 1999). These promising approaches teach students how to become active consumers rather than passive victims of media influence (Levine & Piran, 2001; Levine et al., 1999). These skills can be taught to children in early adolescence, if not before, as increasing evidence points to the saturation of media images, stabilization of body image, and internalization of the thin ideal by the time a girl has reached puberty (Paxton et al., 2006; Tiggemann, 2006).

Media literacy can be conceptualized as a four-step process: (a) identifying harmful cultural images, (b) exploring and deconstructing their underlying messages, (c) resisting the message being sent, and (d) actively working to change these messages. These four components are reviewed in the following paragraphs.

As part of identifying and exploring harmful media messages, counselors can highlight the social construction of beauty in Western culture and the unrealistic, unattainable nature of the images girls see. For example, girls can learn how the majority of images that represent the beauty ideal are created through intricate strategies used to enhance models' appearances, including airbrushing, soft-focus cameras, digital editing, and cosmetic surgery (Botta, 2000; Groesz et al., 2002; Heinberg, 1996). It is powerful for adolescent girls to discover that even the models and celebrities that portray the beauty ideal don't meet these standards.

Once girls have identified the ways in which images are constructed, they must then begin to question the values embedded in these images. The Media Education Foundation (2004) has suggested that girls explore questions such as these:

- Do real women look like these models?
- What is the real purpose of this advertisement?
- Will buying this product help me look like this?
- If I did look like this, would my life really become like the life portrayed in this ad?
- Does this model really use this product to help her look like this?
- What are the consequences of these messages for girls?

Girls must also possess the skills to actively resist and challenge these messages and to generate positive alternatives to the messages conveyed through mass media. Rather than conforming to cultural norms, girls can learn to make informed choices regarding how they allow media messages to influence their personal lifestyles, beliefs, and values. Dissonance-based approaches promote girls' voluntary participation in verbal, written, and behavioral exercises in which they critique the thin ideal perpetuated by current cultural standards. According to Stice et al. (2007), when girls participate in these counterattitudinal activities, they experience discomfort that in turn motivates them to reduce their thin-ideal internalization in order to restore cognitive consistency. When they reduce thin-ideal internalization, they improve in BID (Stice et al., 2007). Such activities might include asking girls "What costs are associated with the thin ideal?" or "How can a younger girl not become affected by the ultra thin models in the media?" An older girl might compose a letter to a younger girl she cares about, trying to dissuade her from pursuing the thin ideal. An older girl also might benefit from generating recommendations to help a younger girl accept her own body. (Dissonance-based strategies are discussed in detail in Chapter 5.)

A final way to promote media literacy is to help girls learn media activism skills as they work to challenge the social status quo and shape healthier cultural norms. To this end, they can actively protest media products they identify as transmitting harmful messages to girls and praise advertisers when they portray women of varying ethnicities, ages, sizes, and shapes (Crago et al., 2001; Levine et al., 1999). Girls become empowered as they recognize themselves as citizens in a democracy who have the power to take collective action for change (Levine & Piran, 2001).

Prevention Strategies for Counselors

1. Reinforce girls' skills in developing an internally derived value system and an internal locus of control so they can begin to rely less on others' opinions about the importance of appearance. Girls can begin to explore what it would be like to trust their own values regarding how they should look and act.

2. To incorporate media literacy into prevention programs for girls, consult the Center for Media Literacy (www.medialit.org) and Media Education Foundation (www.mediaed.org) Web sites. Both Web sites contain excellent critical media viewing activities and resources, including downloadable handouts and study guides for students. Encourage the infusion of media literacy throughout the curriculum, as students benefit from repeated exposure to positive messages about self-esteem that are not based on achievement of the thin ideal (Steiner-Adair & Vorenberg, 1999).

3. Include education about the nature of the thin ideal and how it changes historically. Girls should learn to recognize the unrealistic images presented in the media, the methods used for altering and perfecting these images, and that these images do not represent the average woman. Excellent films by Kilbourne (1995, 2000) are helpful resources in this area. (For a description of two psychoeducational programs that use this approach, see Springer, Winzelberg, Perkins, & Barr Taylor, 1999, and Winzelberg, Abascal, & Barr Taylor, 2002.)

4. Teach girls critical thinking skills for deconstructing harmful media images. As an example, they can review popular magazines and collaboratively create a "wall of shame" and "rave wall" collage based on images that represent both negative and helpful messages to girls and women (Levine et al., 1999).

5. Girls can benefit from the use of cognitive–behavioral strategies to dispute any maladaptive beliefs regarding media portrayal of the thin

ideal (Strachan & Cash, 2002). For example, they can replace the thought "I must look like the model in this swimsuit ad in order to be popular" with the more rational belief that "This image is airbrushed. I don't have to look like this in order to feel good about myself. Others will be attracted to my positive attitude when I accept myself as I am."

6. Have older adolescent girls engage in dissonance-based activities such as designing workshops for younger girls to dissuade them from internalizing the thin ideal, or have participants create a compelling argument regarding the costs of a woman endorsing extreme cultural standards of beauty.

7. As suggested by prevention specialists, counselors can involve girls in a media activism project. For example, encouraging a girl to write a letter of support or protest to an advertiser can empower her to believe that she can make a difference in changing sociocultural norms. Examples of ongoing media activism campaigns in which girls may participate can be found through the Media Watchdog Program on the NEDA Web site (www.nationaleatingdisorders.org).

Protective Factor Five: Holistic Wellness and Balance

A review of the previous four factors of the resilience model—family and peer support, gender-role satisfaction, physical self-concept, and coping skills—demonstrates that adolescent girls need a broad foundation of internal resources and external support to develop body image resilience. When girls place an excessive emphasis on physical appearance, they may neglect the development of those supportive relationships and essential life skills needed for managing the challenges of adolescence (Striegel-Moore & Cachelin, 1999). The fifth protective factor, a sense of holistic wellness and balance, focuses on the importance of enhancing and balancing all life areas to foster body image resilience (see Figure 2.1). When girls are encouraged to develop and value their strengths in multiple life dimensions, including spiritual, intellectual,

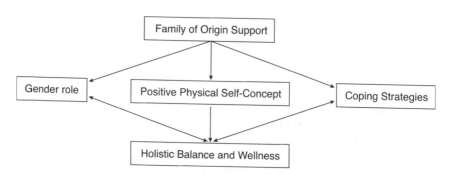

Figure 2.1
Theoretical Model of Body Image Resilience

social, emotional, and physical competence, they learn to view their identities as extending beyond their appearance. Unfortunately, an exclusive focus on one life area—physical appearance—is culturally reinforced for women. It is easy to see how a girl learns to perceive her body as a reflection of her total self; she believes that "who I am" is equated with how she appears to others.

To challenge these beliefs, counselors can introduce girls to the concept of holistic wellness, obtaining a balance between multiple life areas. An important aspect of this emphasis is the spiritual dimension of Myers and Sweeney's wellness model, or the "core characteristic of healthy people" that may be conceptualized as one's "awareness of a being or force that transcends the material aspects of life and gives a deep sense of wholeness or connectedness to the universe" (Myers et al., 2000, p. 253). A positive relationship exists between spirituality, mental and physical health, life satisfaction, and wellness (see also Chapter 9). If a girl draws her sense of meaning from a spiritual force that goes beyond herself and that provides coherence and purpose to the universe, she will find less need to focus on her weight, shape, and appearance in an attempt to find happiness or life satisfaction. Spirituality can serve as a buffer against sociocultural values espousing thinness as the only avenue through which happiness may be achieved. As girls decrease their emphasis on appearance and bolster their sense of self-worth not contingent on unattainable standards, they can dedicate their time and energy to the pursuit of goals in all areas of wellness.

Prevention Strategies for Counselors. Counselors can provide girls with some of specific strategies drawn from Myers, Sweeney, and Witmer (2000) and NEDA (2004b) to develop dimensions of wellness:

1. To develop their sense of spirituality, girls can spend more time with individuals whose spiritual lives they admire and relate to, and talk with their parents about their spiritual development.
2. Girls can practice keeping a gratitude journal, focusing on what is working well in their lives rather than focusing on their complaints.
3. Girls can learn to nurture their bodies, incorporating proper nutrition and sleep habits. They can create opportunities to move their bodies, exercising for pleasure rather than as a means to purge excess calories.
4. Through activities such as mentoring programs, girls can learn to view academics and work as activities that provide a sense of accomplishment, purpose, and competence.
5. To encourage the development of leisure as an important component of wellness, girls can find things that they like to do for fun that are congruent with their beliefs and values. They can engage in these activities on a regular basis as an expression of their creativity.
6. To develop social competence, girls can seek out a stable, supportive network of peers and adults who help them to feel good about themselves and their accomplishments.

Case Study: Part 2

Take a moment to reread the case study of Misty on pages 33–34, then answer the following discussion questions:

1. As a counselor, what are your initial reactions to Misty's story?
2. Although Misty's current goals are to lose weight, become popular, and attract a boyfriend, what might your overall counseling goals be?
3. Which aspects of the body image resilience model presented in this chapter seem particularly relevant to Misty's concerns?
4. How can you incorporate the concept of holistic balance and wellness with Misty to help her recognize and develop her strengths?
5. For each of the five factors of resilience, choose at least one of the counseling strategies listed that might be helpful to Misty. How, specifically, might you implement this strategy?

Conclusion

In adolescence, girls struggle to formulate an answer to the question "Who am I?" Girls are currently socialized to view their appearance as the most salient aspect of their identities, and their self-evaluation in this area becomes increasingly determined by comparisons with others. When girls base their identities on comparisons with the current standard for women's beauty as portrayed in mass media, it is not surprising that BID and low self-esteem are pervasive. When counselors work to prevent BID, they must recognize the difficulties inherent in asking a girl to challenge developmental gender norms and cultural standards at a time when she might not yet possess the skills to do so (Oliver, 2001). Counselors' goals in building girls' body image resilience are twofold: First, they must provide girls with the skills and support necessary to resist sociocultural pressures; and second, they must work tirelessly to reduce negative messages regarding the importance of the thin ideal that are present in their communities (Levine et al., 1999).

The body image resilience model gives counselors a framework within which they can begin to address these two objectives. Support from family and peers, gender-role satisfaction, global and physical self-esteem, and effective coping strategies and critical thinking skills are related to and are necessary for a girl to develop a sense of holistic wellness and balance, which is related to positive body image. The model provides conceptual and practical strategies for enhancing protective factors in multiple life dimensions and for working with clients and communities in changing the status quo. (A sample workshop outline for counselors is presented in the Appendix to this chapter.) While progress in creating this type of cultural shift might be slow, it is important for counselors to undertake this work because girls need help in recognizing the many ways in which they have value beyond their physical appearance. By reclaiming their strengths, girls can cultivate the resilience to navigate the complex sociocultural and developmental challenges of adolescence.

Activities for Further Exploration

1. Visit the National Eating Disorders Association Web site for information about their Media Watchdog program. Review the ongoing campaigns this organization has launched against certain print advertisements at www.nationaleatingdisorders.org/p.asp? WebPage_ID=300. Consider writing a letter to one of these advertisers. On the basis od what you read about becoming a critical media viewer, why might it be empowering for a girl to participate in such a campaign?

2. Visit Web sites listed in the Additional Resources section related to helping girls deconstruct ideal images and view photographs of models before and after the photographs were digitally altered. What surprised you about these images? Why might viewing these images be helpful for girls who are learning to refute the thin ideal espoused in popular culture?

3. View information and sample advertisements on the Media Education Foundation Web site under its study guide for the film *Killing Us Softly III* (www.mediaed.org/studyguides/pdf/KUS3handout.pdf). On the basis of what you have learned in this chapter, practice deconstructing these advertisements using the following steps:

   a. Make observations about the advertisement (e.g., people pictured, camera angle, lighting used)

   b. What is the purpose of the advertisement? What feelings is the ad intended to evoke?

   c. What assumptions are present in the message this advertisement intends to send? What assumptions are made about gender? Race? Class?

   d. What are the short- and long-term consequences of these messages? Are any unrealistic messages conveyed?

   Consider practicing these steps each time you view an advertisement, and teach them to your adolescent clients. (These steps are outlined in detail at www.mediaed.org/handouts/pdfs/DeconstructinganAd.pdf.)

4. Go to a bookstore and browse through popular girls' and women's magazines. What themes stood out for you? What messages are girls receiving about how they should look and act? Next, check out some popular media and Internet resources (e.g., *Mode* or *thebodypositive.com* or *teenvoices.org*) that have been developed to empower girls for positive body image. Are there any striking differences? Finally, consider why it might be important for counselors to be aware of the contents of popular media that their clients regularly consume.

Suggested Readings

American Psychological Association, Task Force on the Sexualization of Girls. (2001). *Report of the APA Task Force on the Sexualization of Girls.* Washington, DC: American Psychological Association. Retrieved from www.apa.org/pi/wpo/sexualization.html

American Psychological Association. (1999). American Psychological Association Task Force on Adolescent Girls: Strengths and stresses. In N. G. Johnson, M. C. Roberts, & J. Worell (Eds.), *Beyond appearance: A new look at adolescent girls* (pp. 405–432). Washington, DC: Author.

Basow, S. A., & Rubin, L. R. (1999). Gender influences on adolescent development. In N. G. Johnson, M. C. Roberts, & J. Worell (Eds.), *Beyond appearance: A new look at adolescent girls* (pp. 25–52). Washington, DC: American Psychological Association.

Compitello, V. (2003). Through the eye of the needle: The emerging adolescent. In M. Kopala & M. A. Keitel (Eds.), *Handbook of counseling women* (pp. 243–255). London: Sage.

Crago, M., Shisslak, C. M., & Ruble, A. (2001). Protective factors in the development of eating disorders. In R. H. Striegel-Moore & L. Smolak (Eds.), *Eating disorders: Innovative directions in research and practice* (pp. 233–254). Washington, DC: American Psychological Association.

Grabe, S., & Hyde, J. S. (2006). Ethnicity and body dissatisfaction among women in the United States: A meta-analysis. *Psychological Bulletin, 132,* 622–640.

Haworth-Hoeppner, S. (2000). The critical shapes of body image: The role of culture and family in the production of eating disorders. *Journal of Marriage and the Family, 62,* 212–227.

Kalodner, C. R., & DeLucia-Waack, J. L. (2003). Theory and research on eating disorders and disturbances in women: Suggestions for practice. In M. Kopala & M. A. Keitel (Eds.), *Handbook of counseling women* (pp. 506–532). London: Sage.

Kilbourne, J. (1995). *Slim hopes: Advertising and the obsession with thinness* [Video]. Media Education Foundation, 28 Center Street, Northhampton, MA 01060; www.mediaed.org.

Kilbourne, J. (2000). *Killing us softly III* [Video]. Media Education Foundation, 28 Center Street, Northhampton, MA 01060; www.mediaed.org.

Levine, M. P., & Smolak, L. (2002). Body image development in adolescence. In T. F. Cash & T. Pruzinsky (Eds.), *Body image: A handbook of theory, research, and clinical practice* (pp. 74–82). New York: Guilford Press.

Myers, J. E., Sweeney, T. J., & Witmer, J. M. (2000). Wheel of wellness counseling for wellness: A holistic model for treatment planning. *Journal of Counseling & Development, 78,* 251–266.

Pedersen, S. (2000). Multicultural perspective on middle-class women's identity development. *Journal of Counseling & Development, 78,* 63–71.

Piran, N., Levine, M. P., & Steiner-Adair, C. (Eds.). (1999). *Preventing eating disorders: A handbook of interventions and special challenges.* Philadelphia: Brunner/Mazel.

Steiner-Adair, C., & Vorenberg, A. P. (1999). Resisting weightism: Media literacy for elementary-school children. In N. Piran, M. P. Levine, & C. Steiner-Adair (Eds.), *Preventing eating disorders: A handbook of interventions and special challenges* (pp. 105–121). Philadelphia: Brunner/Mazel.

Striegel-Moore, R. H., & Cachelin, F. M. (1999). Body image concerns and disordered eating in adolescent girls: Risk and protective factors. In N. G. Johnson, M. C. Roberts, & J. Worell (Eds.), *Beyond appearance: A new look at adolescent girls* (pp. 85–108). Washington, DC: American Psychological Association.

Additional Resources

Web Sites to Help Girls and Women Deconstruct Ideal Images

www.homepage.mac.com/gapodaca/digital/digital.html
Features models before and after the photos have been digitally altered
www.deansplanet.com/nomakeup.html
Features celebrities with and without makeup
www.media-awareness.ca/english/resources/educational/teachable_moments/photo_truth.cfm
Features information and images about digital alterations of photographs used in print media
www.mediaed.org
Features information and educational materials for educating adolescents to become more critical viewers of the media

Web Sites Related to Positive Body Image and Prevention of Eating Disorders

www.something-fishy.org
www.mirror-mirror.org
www.eating.ucdavis.edu
www.hedc.org
www.nedic.on.ca
www.focusas.com/EatingDisorders.html
www.bibri.com/index.html
www.hugs.com

Web Sites of National Advocacy Groups

www.nationaleatingdisorders.org
www.eatingdisorderscoalition.org
www.anred.com
www.cswd.org
www.overeatersanonymous.org
www.eatingdisordersanonymous.org

Web Sites Dedicated to Empowering Girls

www.blackgirlmagazine.com
www.4girls.gov

www.girlpower.gov
www.thebodypositive.org
www.iemily.com
www.teenvoices.com

References

Ackard, D. M., Kearney-Cooke, A., & Peterson, C. B. (2000). Effect of body image and self-image on women's sexual behaviors. *International Journal of Eating Disorders, 28,* 422–429.

American Psychological Association, Task Force on the Sexualization of Girls. (2007). *Report of the APA Task Force on the Sexualization of Girls.* Washington, DC: Author. Retrieved from www.apa.org/pi/wpo/sexualization.html

American Psychological Association. (1999). American Psychological Association Task Force on Adolescent Girls: Strengths and stresses. In N. G. Johnson, M. C. Roberts, & J. Worell (Eds.), *Beyond appearance: A new look at adolescent girls.* (pp. 405–432). Washington, DC: Author.

Attie, I., & Brooks-Gunn, J. (1989). The development of eating problems in adolescent girls: A longitudinal study. *Developmental Psychology, 25*(1), 70–79.

Barber, N. (1998). The slender ideal and eating disorders: An interdisciplinary "telescope" model. *International Journal of Eating Disorders, 23,* 295–307.

Barker, E. T., & Galambos, N. L. (2003). Body dissatisfaction of adolescent girls and boys: Risk and resource factors. *Journal of Early Adolescence, 23,* 141–165.

Basow, S. A., & Rubin, L. R. (1999). Gender influences on adolescent development. In N. G. Johnson, M. C. Roberts, & J. Worell (Eds.), *Beyond appearance: A new look at adolescent girls* (pp. 25–52). Washington, DC: American Psychological Association.

Bearman, S. K., Presnell, K., Martinez, E., & Stice, E. (2006). The skinny on body dissatisfaction: A longitudinal study of adolescent girls and boys. *Journal of Youth and Adolescence, 35*(2), 229–241.

Bordo, S. (1995). *Unbearable weight: Feminism, Western culture, and the body.* Los Angeles: University of California Press.

Botta, R. A. (2000). The mirror of television: A comparison of Black and White adolescents' body image. *Journal of Communication, Summer,* 144–159.

Cash, T. F. (2002). Cognitive-behavioral perspectives on body image. In T. F. Cash & T. Pruzinsky (Eds.), *Body image: A handbook of theory, research, and clinical practice* (pp. 38–46). New York: Guilford Press.

Cash, T. F., & Pruzinsky, T. (2002). Future challenges for body image theory, research, and clinical practice. In T. F. Cash & T. Pruzinsky (Eds.), *Body image: A handbook of theory, research, and clinical practice* (pp. 509–516). New York: Guilford Press.

Celio, A. A., Zabinski, M. F., & Wilfley, D. E. (2002). African American body images. In T. F. Cash & T. Pruzinsky (Eds.), *Body image: A handbook of theory, research, and clinical practice* (pp. 234–242). New York: Guilford Press.

Choate, L. J. (2005). Toward a theoretical model of body image resilience. *Journal of Counseling & Development, 83*, 320–330.

Clay, D., Vignoles, V., & Dittmar, H. (2005). Body image and self-esteem among adolescent girls: Testing the influence of sociocultural factors. *Journal of Research on Adolescence, 15*(4), 451–477.

Compitello, V. (2003). Through the eye of the needle: The emerging adolescent. In M. Kopala & M. A. Keitel (Eds.), *Handbook of counseling women* (pp. 243–255). London: Sage.

Cooley, E. J., & Toray, T. (2001). Disordered eating in college freshman women: A prospective study. *Journal of American College Health, 49*, 229–235.

Crago, M., Shisslak, C. M., & Ruble, A. (2001). Protective factors in the development of eating disorders. In R. H. Striegel-Moore & L. Smolak (Eds.), *Eating disorders: Innovative directions in research and practice* (pp. 233–254). Washington, DC: American Psychological Association.

Cummins, L. H., & Lehman, J. (2007). Eating disorders and body image concerns in Asian American women: Assessment and treatment from a multicultural and feminist perspective. *Eating Disorders, 15*, 217–230.

Cusumano, D. L., & Thompson, J. K. (2000). Media influence and body image in 8–11 year old boys and girls: A preliminary report on the Multidimensional Media Influence Scale. *International Journal of Eating Disorders, 29*, 37–44.

Denmark, F. L. (1999). Enhancing the development of adolescent girls. In N. G. Johnson, M. C. Roberts, & J. Worell (Eds.), *Beyond appearance: A new look at adolescent girls* (pp. 337–404). Washington, DC: American Psychological Association.

Dunkley, T. L., Wertheim, E. H., & Paxton, S. J. (2001). Examination of a model of multiple sociocultural influences on adolescent girls' body dissatisfaction and dietary restraint. *Adolescence, 36*, 265–280.

Dunton, G. F., Jamner, M. S., & Cooper, D. M. (2003). Physical self-concept in adolescent girls: Behavioral and physiological correlates. *Research Quarterly for Exercise and Sport, 74*, 360–365.

Falconer, J. W., & Neville, H. A. (2000). African American college women's body image: An examination of body mass, African self-consciousness, and skin color satisfaction. *Psychology of Women Quarterly, 24*, 236–243.

Feingold, A., & Mazzella, R. (1998). Gender differences in body image are increasing. *Psychological Science, 9*, 190–196.

Friedman, S. S. (1999). Discussion groups for girls: Decoding the language of fat. In N. Piran, M. P. Levine, & C. Steiner-Adair (Eds.), *Preventing eating disorders: A handbook of interventions and special challenges* (pp. 122–133). Philadelphia: Brunner/Mazel.

Gale, A. U., & Austin, B. D. (2003). Professionalism's challenges to professional counselors' collective identity. *Journal of Counseling & Development, 81*, 3–9.

Gilligan, C. (1982). *In a different voice.* Cambridge: Harvard University Press.

Grabe, S., & Hyde, J. S. (2006). Ethnicity and body dissatisfaction among women in the United States: A meta-analysis. *Psychological Bulletin, 132,* 622–640.

Graber, J. A., Archibald, A. B., & Brooks-Gunn, J. (1999). The role of parents in the emergence, maintenance, and prevention of eating problems and disorders. In N. Piran, M. P. Levine, & C. Steiner-Adair (Eds.), *Preventing eating disorders: a handbook of interventions and special challenges* (pp. 44–62). Philadelphia: Brunner/Mazel.

Groesz, L. M., Levine, M. P., & Murnen, S. K. (2002). The effect of experimental presentation of thin media images on body satisfaction: A meta-analytic review. *International Journal of Eating Disorders, 31,* 1–16.

Guinn, B., Semper, T., & Jorgensen, L. (1997). Body image perception in female Mexican-American adolescents. *Journal of School Health, 67,* 112–115.

Halpern, C. T., Udry, J. R., Campbell, B., & Suchindran, C. (1999). Effects of body fat on weight concerns, dating, and sexual activity: A longitudinal analysis of Black and White adolescent girls. *Developmental Psychology, 35,* 721–736.

Hargraves, D., & Tiggemann, M. (2003). The effect of "thin ideal" television commercials on body dissatisfaction and schema activation during early adolescence. *Journal of Youth and Adolescence, 32,* 367–373.

Harris, S. M. (1995). Family, self, and sociocultural contributions to body image attitudes of African American women. *Psychology of Women Quarterly, 19,* 129–145.

Hart, K., & Kenny, M. E. (1997). Adherence to the superwoman ideal and eating disorder symptoms among college women. *Sex Roles: A Journal of Research, 36,* 461–479.

Haworth-Hoeppner, S. (2000). The critical shapes of body image: The role of culture and family in the production of eating disorders. *Journal of Marriage and the Family, 62,* 212–227.

Heinberg, L. J. (1996). Theories of body image: Perceptual, developmental, and sociocultural factors. In J. K. Thompson (Ed.), *Body image, eating disorders, and obesity: An integrative guide to assessment and treatment* (pp. 627–648). Washington, DC: American Psychological Association.

Hensley, L. G. (2003). Stepping off the scale. In B. Ropers-Huilman, (Ed.), *Gendered futures in higher education: Critical perspectives for change* (pp. 55–76). New York: SUNY Press.

Hrabosky, J. I., & Grilo, C. M. (2007). Body image and eating disordered behavior in a community sample of Black and Hispanic women. *Eating Behaviors, 8,* 106–114.

Irving, L. M. (1999). A bolder model of prevention: Science, practice, and activism. In N. Piran, M. P. Levine, & C. Steiner-Adair (Eds.), *Preventing eating disorders: A handbook of interventions and special challenges* (pp. 63–84). Philadelphia: Brunner/Mazel.

Jaffee, L., & Lutter. J. M. (1995). Adolescent girls: Factors influencing low and high body image. *Melpomene Journal, 14*, 14–22.

James, K. A., Phelps, L., & Bross, A. L. (2001). Body dissatisfaction, drive for thinness, and self-esteem in African American college females. *Psychology in the Schools, 38*, 491–496.

Jones, D. C. (2001). Social comparison and body image: Attractiveness comparisons to models and peers among adolescent girls and boys. *Sex Roles, 45*, 645–664.

Kalodner, C. R., & DeLucia-Waack, J. L. (2003). Theory and research on eating disorders and disturbances in women: Suggestions for practice. In M. Kopala & M. A. Keitel (Eds.), *Handbook of counseling women* (pp. 506–532). London: Sage.

Kearney-Cooke, A. (2002). Familial influences on body image development. In T. F. Cash & T. Pruzinsky (Eds.), *Body image: A handbook of theory, research, and clinical practice* (pp. 99–107). New York: Guilford Press.

Kelly, A. M., Wall, M., Eisenberg, M. E., Story, M., & Neumark-Sztainer, D. (2005). Adolescent girls with high body satisfaction: Who are they and what can they teach us? *Journal of Adolescent Health, 37*, 391–396.

Kichler, J. C., & Crowther, J. H. (2001). The effects of maternal modeling and negative familial communication on women's eating attitudes and body image. *Behavior Therapy, 32*, 443–457.

Kilbourne, J. (1995). *Slim hopes: Advertising and the obsession with thinness* [Video]. Media Education Foundation, 28 Center Street, Northhampton, MA 01060; www.mediaed.org

Kilbourne, J. (2000). *Killing us softly III* [Video]. Media Education Foundation, 28 Center Street, Northhampton, MA 01060; www.mediaed.org

Kostanski, M., & Gullone, E. (1998). Adolescent body image dissatisfaction: Relationships with self-esteem, anxiety, and depression controlling for body mass. *Journal of Child Psychology and Psychiatry, 39*, 255–262.

Lavin, M. A., & Cash, T. F. (2000). Effects of exposure to information about appearance stereotyping and discrimination on women's body images. *International Journal of Eating Disorders, 29*, 51–58.

Levine, M. P., & Piran, N. (2001). The prevention of eating disorders: Toward a participatory ecology of knowledge, action, and advocacy. In R. Striegel-Moore & L. Smolak (Eds.), *Eating disorders: Innovative directions in research and practice* (pp. 233–254). Washington, DC: American Psychological Association.

Levine, M. P., & Piran, N. (2004). The role of body image in the prevention of eating disorders. *Body Image, 1*, 57–70.

Levine, M. P., Piran, N., & Stoddard, C. (1999). Mission more probable: Media literacy, activism, and advocacy as primary intervention. In N. Piran, M. P. Levine, & C. Steiner-Adair (Eds.), *Preventing eating disorders: A handbook of interventions and special challenges* (pp. 1–25). Philadelphia: Brunner/Mazel.

Levine, M. P., & Smolak, L. (2002). Body image development in adolescence. In T. F. Cash & T. Pruzinsky (Eds.), *Body image: A handbook of theory, research, and clinical practice* (pp. 74–82). New York: Guilford Press.

Lovejoy, M. (2001). Disturbances in the social body: Differences in body image and eating problems among African American and White women. *Gender and Society, 15,* 239–261.

McKinley, N. M. (1999). Women and objectified body consciousness: Mothers' and daughters' body experience in cultural, developmental, and familial context. *Developmental Psychology, 35,* 760–769.

McKinley, N. M. (2002). Feminist perspectives and objectified body consciousness. In T. F. Cash & T. Pruzinsky (Eds.), *Body image: A handbook of theory, research, and clinical practice* (pp. 55–64). New York: Guilford Press.

McVey, G. L., & Davis R. (2002). A program to promote positive body image: A 1-year follow-up evaluation. *Journal of Early Adolescence, 22,* 96–108.

McVey, G. L, Davis, R., Tweed, S., & Shaw, B. F. (2004). Evaluation of a school-based program designed to improve body image satisfaction, global self-esteem, and eating attitudes and behaviors: A replication study. *International Journal of Eating Disorders, 36*(1), 1–11.

Media Education Foundation. (2004). Retrieved March 24, 2004, from www.mediaed.org

Miller, J. B. (1990). The development of women's sense of self. In C. Zanardi (Ed.), *Essential papers on the psychology of women* (pp. 437–454). New York: New York University Press.

Molloy, B. L., & Herzberger, S. D. (1998). Body image and self-esteem: A comparison of African-American and Caucasian women. *Sex Roles: A Journal of Research, 38,* 631–644.

Mussell, M. P., Binford, R. B., & Fulkerson, J. A. (2000). Eating disorders: Summary of risk factors, prevention programming, and prevention research. *The Counseling Psychologist, 28,* 764–796.

Myers, J. E., & Sweeney, T. J. (Eds.). (2005). *Counseling for wellness: Theory, research, and practice.* Alexandria, VA: American Counseling Association.

Myers, J. E., Sweeney, T. J., & White, V. E. (2002). Advocacy for counseling and counselors: A professional imperative. *Journal of Counseling & Development, 80,* 394–402.

Myers, J. E., Sweeney, T. J., & Witmer, J. M. (2000). Wheel of wellness counseling for wellness: A holistic model for treatment planning. *Journal of Counseling & Development, 78,* 251–266.

National Eating Disorders Association. (2004a). Retrieved March 24, 2004, from www.nationaleatingdisorders.org

National Eating Disorders Association. (2004b). *Fifty ways to lose the 3D's: Dieting, drive for thinness, and body dissatisfaction.* Retrieved May 15, 2007, from nationaleatingdisorders.org/p.asp?Webpage_ID=323& Profile_ID=41163

National Eating Disorders Association. (2004c). *No weigh.* Retrieved May 15, 2007, from http://nationaleatingdisorders.org/p.asp?WebPage_ID=325&Profile_ID=41164

Newman, D. L., Sontag, L. M., & Salvato, R. (2006). Psychosocial aspects of body mass and body image among rural American Indian adolescents. *Journal of Youth and Adolescence, 35,* 281–291.

Nishina, A., Ammon, N. Y., Bellmore, A. D., & Graham, S. (2006). Body dissatisfaction and physical development among ethnic minority students. *Journal of Youth and Adolescence, 25*, 179–191.

Oliver, K. L. (2001). Images of the body from popular culture: Engaging adolescent girls in critical inquiry. *Sport, Education, and Society, 6*, 143–164.

Patton, T. O. (2006). Hey girl, am I more than my hair? African American women and their struggles with beauty, body image, and hair. *NWSA Journal, 18*, 24–51.

Paxton, S. J., Eisenberg, M. E., & Neumark-Sztainer, D. (2006). Prospective predictors of body dissatisfaction in adolescent girls and boys: A five-year longitudinal study. *Developmental Psychology, 42*, 888–899.

Paxton, S. J., Schutz, H. K., Wertheim, E. H., & Muir, S. L. (1999). Friendship clique and peer influences on body image concerns, dietary restraint, extreme weight loss behaviors, and binge eating in adolescent girls. *Journal of Abnormal Psychology, 108*, 255–266.

Pedersen, S. (2000). Multicultural perspective on middle-class women's identity development. *Journal of Counseling & Development, 78*, 63–71.

Phares, V., Steinberg, A., & Thompson, J. (2004). Gender differences in peer and parental influences: Body image disturbance, self-worth, and psychological functioning in preadolescent children. *Journal of Youth and Adolescence, 33*(5), 421–429.

Piran, N., Levine, M. P., & Steiner-Adair, C. (Eds.). (1999). *Preventing eating disorders: A handbook of interventions and special challenges.* Philadelphia: Brunner/Mazel.

Polivy, J., & Herman, C. P. (2002). Causes of eating disorders. *Annual Review of Psychology, 53*, 187–213.

Reiss, D., & Price, R. H. (1996). National research agenda for prevention research: The National Institute of Mental Health report. *American Psychologist*, 1109–1115.

Richman, E. L., & Shaffer, D. R. (2000). "If you let me play sports": How might sport participation influence the self-esteem of adolescent females? *Psychology of Women Quarterly, 24*, 189–199.

Rodin, J., Silberstein, L. R., & Streigel-Moore, R. H. (1985). Women and weight: A normative discontent. In T. B. Sonderegger (Ed.), *Psychology and gender: Nebraska Symposium on Motivation, 1984* (pp. 267–307). Lincoln: University of Nebraska Press.

Smith, D. E., Thompson, J. K., Raczynski, J. M., & Hilner, J. E. (1999). Body image among men and women in a biracial cohort: The CARDIA study. *International Journal of Eating Disorders, 25*, 71–82.

Smolak, L. (1999). Elementary school curricula for the primary prevention of eating problems. In N. Piran, M. P. Levine, & C. Steiner-Adair (Eds.), *Preventing eating disorders: A handbook of interventions and special challenges* (pp. 85–104). Philadelphia: Brunner/Mazel.

Smolak, L. (2002). Body image development in children. In T. F. Cash & T. Pruzinsky (Eds.), *Body image: A handbook of theory, research, and clinical practice* (pp. 65–73). New York: Guilford Press.

Smolak, L., & Murnen, S. K. (2001). Gender and eating problems. In R. H. Streigel-Moore & L. Smolak (Eds.), *Eating disorders: Innovative directions in research and practice* (pp. 91–110). Washington, DC: American Psychological Association.

Springer, E. A., Winzelberg, A. J., Perkins, R., & Barr Taylor, C. (1999). Effects of a body image curriculum for college students on improved body image. *International Journal of Eating Disorders, 26,* 12–20.

Steiner-Adair, C. (1986). The body politic: Normative female adolescent development and the development of eating disorders. *Journal of the American Academy of Psychoanalysis, 14,* 95–114.

Steiner-Adair, C., & Vorenberg, A. P. (1999). Resisting weightism: Media literacy for elementary-school children. In N. Piran, M. P. Levine, & C. Steiner-Adair (Eds.), *Preventing eating disorders: A handbook of interventions and special challenges* (pp. 105–121). Philadelphia: Brunner/Mazel.

Stice, E., Presnell, K., Gau, J., & Shaw, H. (2007). Testing mediators of intervention effects in randomized controlled trials: An evaluation of two eating disorder prevention programs. *Journal of Consulting and Clinical Psychology, 75,* 20–32.

Stice, E., Presnell, K., & Spangler, D. (2002). Risk factors for binge eating onset in adolescent girls: A 2-year prospective investigation. *Health Psychology, 21,* 131–138.

Stice, E., & Shaw, H. (2003). Prospective relations of body image, eating, and affective disturbances to smoking onset in adolescent girls: How Virginia slims. *Journal of Consulting and Clinical Psychology, 71,* 129–135.

Stice, E., & Whitenton, K. (2002). Risk factors for body dissatisfaction in adolescent girls: A longitudinal investigation. *Developmental Psychology, 38,* 669–678.

Strachan, M. D., & Cash, T. F. (2002). Self-help for a negative body image: A comparison of components of a cognitive-behavioral program. *Behavior Therapy, 33,* 235–251.

Striegel-Moore, R. H., & Cachelin, F. M. (1999). Body image concerns and disordered eating in adolescent girls: Risk and protective factors. In N. G. Johnson, M. C. Roberts, & J. Worell (Eds.), *Beyond appearance: A new look at adolescent girls* (pp. 85–108). Washington, DC: American Psychological Association.

Striegel-Moore, R. H., & Franko, D. L. (2002). Body image issues among girls and women. In T. F. Cash & T. Pruzinsky (Eds.), *Body image: A handbook of theory, research, and clinical practice* (pp. 183–191). New York: Guilford Press.

Tantleff-Dunn, S., & Gokee, J. L. (2002). Interpersonal influences on body image development. In T. F. Cash & T. Pruzinsky (Eds.), *Body image: A handbook of theory, research, and clinical practice* (pp. 108–116). New York: Guilford Press.

Taylor, C. B., & Altman, T. (1997). Priorities in prevention research for eating disorders. *Psychopharmacology Bulletin, 33,* 413–417.

Thompson, J. K., Heinberg, L. J., Altabe, M., & Tantleff-Dunn, S. (1999). *Exacting beauty: Theory, assessment, and treatment of body image disturbance*. Washington, DC: American Psychological Association.

Thomsen, S. R., Weber, M. M., & Brown, L. B. (2001). The relationship between health and fitness magazine reading and eating disordered weight-loss methods among high school girls. *American Journal of Health Education, 32*, 133–138.

Tiggemann, M. (2006). The role of media exposure in adolescent girls' body dissatisfaction and drive for thinness: Prospective results. *Journal of Social and Clinical Psychology, 25*(5), 523–541.

U.S. Department of Health and Human Services. (2001). *2001 report on overweight and obesity, Section 1.5: Disparities in prevalence*. Retrieved July 12, 2007, from http://www.surgeongeneral.gov/topics/obesity/calltoaction/1_5.htm

Usmiani, S., & Daniluk, J. (1997). Mothers and their adolescent daughters: Relationship between self-esteem, gender role identity, and body image. *Journal of Youth and Adolescence, 26*, 45–62.

Wiederman, M. W., & Pryor, T. L. (2000). Body dissatisfaction, bulimia, and depression among women: The mediating role of drive for thinness. *International Journal of Eating Disorders, 27*, 90–95.

Winzelberg, A. J., Abascal, L., & Barr Taylor, C. (2002). Psychoeductional approaches to the prevention and change of negative body image. In T. F. Cash & T. Pruzinsky (Eds.), *Body image: A handbook of theory, research, and clinical practice* (pp. 497–508). New York: Guilford Press.

Wolf, N. (1991). *The beauty myth*. New York: William Morrow.

Zabinski, M. F., Calfas, K. J., Gehrman, C. A., Wilfley, D. E., & Sallis, J. F. (2001). Effects of activity intervention on body image. *Annals of Behavioral Medicine, 23*, 247–252.

Zucker, N. L., Womble, L. G., Williamson, D. A., & Perrin, L. A. (1999). Protective factors for eating disorders in college female athletes. *Eating Disorders, 7*, 207–218.

Appendix
Sample Workshop Outline: "Beyond the Mirror"

Objectives of Program:

By the end of the program, girls will have the resources to:

- Gain awareness of the unattainable body ideals conveyed through sociocultural influences (such as family, peers, media).
- Identify differences between what makes a girl beautiful on the "outside" and the "inside."
- Seek out strong and positive female role models.
- Understand their holistic nature and ways to develop the academic, social, spiritual, physical, and emotional aspects of themselves.
- Acknowledge their strengths, unique gifts, talents, dreams, and goals.

Materials Needed:

Handouts (Wheel of Wellness, other selected resources)
Advertisements from women's/girls' popular magazines
Flip chart or dry erase board
Internet connection and screen (optional)

Workshop Outline:

I. Introduction
   A. Hang poster collage of a diverse group of women (pictures collected and clipped from magazines). As participants gather around the poster, distribute written materials.
   B. Introduce the topic of how we feel about ourselves in general and our bodies in particular, the influences on our body image, and how we can begin to appreciate ourselves as being more than how we look to others.
II. "On the Surface": The Changing Nature of Cultural Beauty Ideals
   A. Ask participants, "What makes a girl or woman beautiful on the outside?" (Ask for physical characteristics; write responses on dry erase board.)
   B. Ask, "How did you learn that these features are important to a woman's beauty?" (Prompt: family, media, and so on)
   C. Assist participants in considering the specific influence of media on their self-images. "When you go to movies, watch television, look at magazines, who is considered to be beautiful?" (Prompt: Ask them to name celebrities, and so on.)
   D. Small Group Activity: Distribute magazines and ask participants to clip ads and images that seem unrealistic to them. (Alternatively, clip the ads prior to the presentation and distribute them to girls in groups of 2-3.) Assist girls in critiquing these images using the following prompts:
      1. What is the purpose of this ad?
      2. What are these advertisers trying to tell us?
      3. Will using this product actually help me look like this or have the lifestyle depicted in the advertisement?
      4. What do you notice about these faces?
      5. Is this really what girls look like? Think about the beautiful girls and women you know. What is different about the people you know versus these flawless faces?
   E. Explain to girls that even the models pictured in magazines don't look like the ideal; we often are expected to compare ourselves to media-generated ideals. To demonstrate how the pictures they see in magazines are altered through digital editing, airbrushing, and through lighting techniques, use before/after pictures found on the Web site www.homepage.mac.com/gapodaca/digital/digital.html. Ask girls to consider, "How do you feel that advertisers are showing you images that aren't even real?"

    F. Encourage girls to think about the consequences of these messages:
- 1. Seeing these images and believing that we must look this way in order to be happy or successful can lead to feeling that we are never good enough. Believing that you should try to look like these images can lead to:
  - a. Pressures to diet and overexercise (Presenter should mention the dangers and futility of dieting, diet myths, and the normative nature of weight gain during puberty.)

III. Redefining Beauty
    A. Ask the participants, "What makes someone beautiful on the inside?" (Write responses on board.) "Think of one person you know who is beautiful on the inside. How can you begin to surround yourself with more people with these qualities?"

> Message: When girls describe the girls and women they admire and like to be around, they generally describe individuals who are kind, compassionate, and fun. They do not usually describe those with only external beauty. Remind girls that they can develop these qualities in themselves instead of solely striving for improving their physical appearance.

    B. Discuss the concept of wellness: Spiritual wellness, Intellectual wellness, Social wellness, Emotional wellness, Physical wellness. (For example, appreciating your body for what it can DO, rather than how it LOOKS.)
- 1. Assist girls in identifying specific activities they can do to enhance their wellness in each area.
- 2. Emphasize that appearance is only one aspect of who we are. It is easy to believe that we have to look a certain way to be liked or accepted by others. Instead, it is helpful to focus on all life areas, not just physical appearance. If we feel good in all aspects of life, then we are truly beautiful."

    C. Distribute "I am Beautiful" worksheet. Ask participants to write
- 1. 3 things I appreciate about my body,
- 2. 3 things I appreciate about my personality,
- 3. 3 things I am grateful for,
- 4. 3 things I am proud of.

While girls are completing their worksheets, play the song "This One's for the Girls" by Martina McBride, or another popular song with an empowering message for girls. The classic song "Respect" by Aretha Franklin is fun to use with any age group.

    IV. Dissonance-Based Activity

Ask the participants: "Based on what we have discussed today, what are some things you might say to a person who looks at a magazine ad and exclaims, 'I'm so ugly . . . I will never look like her . . . maybe I need to go on a starvation diet so that I can look more like this!' How can you try to talk her out of feeling this way?"

"Now, imagine that your younger sister or cousin comes to you and says that she feels terrible about herself because she isn't thin and beautiful like the models in *YM*. What would you tell her to help her see herself differently? On the back of your worksheet, write a short paragraph about what you would say."

    V. Conclusions
- A. Ask girls to commit to the following:
  1. Refuse to engage in dieting, diet talk, and fat talk.
  2. Challenge the advertisements/images you see rather than feeling you must measure up to these images.
  3. Remember that you are much more than how you look.
- B. Ask participants to share some sample responses.
- C. Review additional handouts (or refer to additional materials to review on their own time).
- D. Complete evaluations.

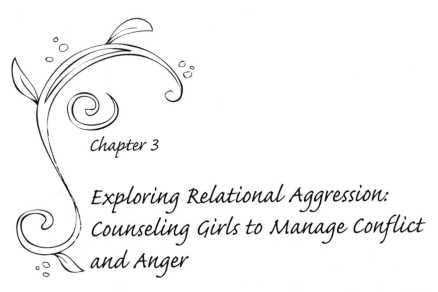

Chapter 3

Exploring Relational Aggression: Counseling Girls to Manage Conflict and Anger

As explored in Chapter 2, critical developmental issues surface for girls in early adolescence, including their rapidly changing bodies, emerging sexuality and relationships with/attention from potential romantic partners, and academic pressures. All of these changes result in a highly confusing time for girls. Whereas girls might have previously relied on parents for guidance around these issues, adolescents increasingly turn to their peer group as a primary source of information, validation, and support. Friendships can be a great resource for girls but often also serve as a source of hurt, betrayal, and bewilderment (Brown, Way, & Duff, 1999). Dara's story illustrates this time of transition:

> When I entered middle school, I was terrified. In elementary school, I had a group of friends, and I knew what was expected. I knew where to sit at lunch, who to sit with on the bus, and which parties I would be invited to. In middle school it was a whole new game. On the first day of school, I walked to lunch by myself and began to get worried. . . . Where were my friends from elementary school? I walked into the cafeteria after I got my food and stopped in terror: I had no idea where to sit! I felt that everyone was staring at me, the freak! I noticed that some of my former friends were sitting with the older, more popular girls, trying to be a part of the "popular" lunch table. When I walked by, they ignored me. I sat by myself that day, trying not to cry. What happened to my friends? I never wanted to go back to school again!
> —Dara, age 12

Girls value their friendships with other girls highly but often resort to hurtful and even cruel behaviors within their peer circles. During the past decade, a large body of research on *relational aggression* (RA) has centered on this aspect of girls' friendships. RA is the act of hurting others through manipulating or harming their relationships (Crick & Grotpeter, 1995;

Underwood, 2003). In this chapter, I explore the nature of RA, first describing the socialization processes that drive it. I then turn to the dynamics of RA and how it is related to girls' pursuit of popularity. Next I discuss the recent trend for increases in girls' physical aggression emerging in contemporary culture. Finally, I outline a tiered approach to the prevention of and interventions for reducing relational aggression and for enhancing wellness.

Socialization Processes

In early childhood, boys and girls display similar levels of aggression in that both sexes are equally likely to express their anger in a physical and overt way. However, by the preschool years, girls are less likely than boys to display physical aggression (Underwood, 2003). Girls learn that there are negative consequences for the overt expression of anger: Girls, but not boys, are more likely to be rejected by peers if they express angry feelings directly (Underwood, 2003). Why might this be the case? One reason might be related to biology: girls inherently possess more of a capacity to suppress negative feelings, to keep their composure when angry, and to mask negative emotions from others (Underwood, 2003). This does not mean that girls don't experience intense negative emotional reactions. Instead of expressing their feelings overtly, girls learn to retaliate against others through responses that are delayed, covert, and often involve manipulation of their relationships (Underwood, 2003).

Relationships

Girls are socialized to place a high value on their relationships with others. As girls enter early adolescence, they learn that developing friendships with other girls is a primary task in their development (Crothers, Field, & Kolbert, 2005; Pipher, 2002). Having a strong friendship group is a protective factor for at-risk girls (Bearman & Moody, 2004). In addition, girls are more likely than boys to value their relationships in several ways: girls expect and receive more kindness, loyalty, commitment, and empathy from friends than do boys (Parker, Walker, Low, & Gamm, 2005). Further, girls report spending more time thinking about friends, have more jealousy and exclusivity in friendships, and experience more negative emotions regarding exclusion by their friends than boys (Underwood, 2003). By the time they reach adolescence, girls' friendships feature high levels of intimacy, openness, and self-disclosure (Brown et al., 1999); this can lead to high-quality friendships, but this tendency also increases girls' vulnerability to relationship problems, particularly with close peers.

Another aspect of girls' socialization regarding friendships is learning to maintain these relationships at any price. Rather than drawing on an internally derived sense of self-worth, girls learn to look to others for reassurance (Garbarino, 2006) and are particularly susceptible to peers' impressions (Brown et al., 1999; Casey-Cannon, Hayward, & Gowen, 2001).

Girls may learn to do anything necessary in order to be accepted by their peer group, and usually this means to conform, blend in with the group, and follow others' lead (Brown, 2003; Dellasega & Nixon, 2003; Simmons, 2002; Tannenbaum, 2002).

Despite their learning about the importance of friendships, girls are socialized to value male approval over female approval, choose boyfriends over their girlfriends, and practice competition with one another for male attention (Brown, 2003; Dellasega & Nixon, 2003; Wiseman, 2002). Girls learn to evaluate one another using male standards, which often leads to jealousy and conflict between girls (Lamb, 2001). As they accept this norm, girls learn to value themselves and one another as being less than males (Wiseman, 2002). When girls value friendships but view each other as competitors for male attention, they remain confused about how to express their thoughts and feelings openly. Mariam's story illustrates the results of this competition for males:

> Upon turning eleven, I entreated my mother to purchase a subscription to Fashion Magazine X, believing that it would be a superb initiation into the sophisticated teenage world of which I was soon to become a member. I anxiously awaited its arrival in my mailbox each month, at which time I would assiduously labor at attempting to collect the pearls of wisdom encrypted in its pages. Eventually I had a proverbial necklace of knowledge, all acquired from the magazine. Among the pearls on the strand were articles like "How to Get Noticed at a Party" and "How to Get His Attention: 10 Great Beauty Tips That Really Work!" with the occasional "All About the Rivalry Between Generic Female Pop Star Y and Generic Female Pop Star Z" thrown in for variety. Whenever their contest comprised beauty tips relating to standing out or instructions on how to "walk sexy and get seen first," there was one key teenage girl concept I acquired an understanding of from reading the articles. The key concept was that, regardless of what else I would ever be occupied with, I would always inexorably be a contestant in a perpetual beauty contest, vying for the approval and attention of a male judge. As I understood it, this facet of female existence was inescapable, as it was the greatest determinant of one's worth. It therefore became necessary to do all I could, utilizing makeup, diet tips, and anything else which would aid my place as number one in the lifelong contest. I soon stumbled upon another invaluable piece of knowledge: if the postulate that life was a perpetual beauty contest was true, then it logically held true that every girl, everywhere, was my competitor. Every female I met was a prospective thief of my sash bearing the number one. This idea carried great significance because it meant that I could never have a truly profound relationship with any girl, no matter how lovely she, her slip dresses, or her makeup were. For regardless of how brightly they smiled at one another or how frequently they embraced, everyone knows that the contestants are all secretly plotting to procure the coveted tiara.
>
> —Mariam Firunts, age 15, California

Source: As cited in Dellasega & Nixon (2003, pp. 35–36).

Expression of Anger

Traditional gender-role prescriptions for girls teach them to limit their expression of anger in order to maintain their relationships (see Chapter 1). This restriction results in what Brown (2003) termed the "tyranny of kind and nice" (i.e., they are expected to please others), which translates into a strong message for girls to restrict their expression of anger and to consider others' feelings before their own. They learn that it is not okay to voice their true opinions or concerns if these might result in a disagreement with their peers. Girls prefer to avoid open expressions of anger, especially with close friends, and as a result, many girls lack the skills to address conflict directly.

These socialization processes most typically are seen in White, middle-class, heterosexual girls from mainstream culture in the United States. There are often distinctly different socialization practices for adolescent girls from other cultural groups. The ability to be assertive and to reject limiting gender stereotypes is a marker for positive mental health; however, this process is complex for girls and women of color who are socialized to emphasize community group needs over individual rights (Constantine, Greer, & Kindaichi, 2003).

The cultural practices that help African American girls cope with discrimination and oppression translate into the use of more direct approaches for handling anger and conflict. African American girls learn how to avoid internalizing negative societal messages and are taught to question and challenge these messages (Crothers et al., 2005). Instead of silencing their voices as many girls do, African American girls are more likely to use "truth telling"—the ability to speak one's thoughts and feelings directly—and to use assertiveness skills when problem solving with peers (Basow & Rubin, 1999).

However, it should be noted that African American girls who tend to speak freely are more likely than other girls to engage in physical violence (Jones-Bamman, 2004). Therefore, even when girls feel free to express

---

Self-Exploration Exercise

1. Do you remember your friendships from middle school? What are some positive memories? What are some moments that seem particularly hurtful?

2. As an adolescent, what did you learn from adults about the importance of relationships in your life?

3. What did you learn about communicating your thoughts and feelings with others? Were you taught to speak openly or to remain silent about your feelings? What cultural influences shaped what you learned about expressing negative feelings?

themselves openly, they may not possess the skills for expressing emotions and managing conflicts in healthy, productive ways. Further, physical aggression is becoming more common among girls from all races/ethnicities due to changing social norms (Garbarino, 2006). We return to the problem of physical aggression in girls later in this chapter.

Relational Aggression

If girls adopt traditional cultural standards, they have few available options for resolving conflict, so it makes sense that they might resort to using covert, manipulative means for dealing with anger. A recent study found that adolescent girls who identified with traditional gender roles were more likely to perceive themselves as having engaged in relational aggression (Crothers et al., 2005).

Since the inception of the term by Crick and her colleagues, researchers have demonstrated that RA is used significantly more by girls than boys and is a relatively normative conflict style in girls' peer groups (Crick & Grotpeter, 1995). In fact, Crick and Nelson (2001) found that 70% of third-through sixth-grade girls in their sample reported maltreatment by their friends. RA seems to become the most intensified in the middle school years (fifth to eighth grades). According to Underwood (2003), girls' use of RA is powerful because it threatens the asset girls' value most during this time: losing acceptance by significant others. It is important to note that boys are relationally aggressive too, but it is a far more common style of aggression in girls' friendship groups. Being a target of an RA episode is more distressing for girls than it is for boys (Crick & Nelson, 2001).

Girls who engage in RA tend to possess the following characteristics (as identified by Dellasega & Nixon, 2003):

1. They are more likely to use RA within their own friendship circles (Crick & Grotpeter, 1995; Yoon, Barton, & Taiariol, 2004), whereas boys who use RA tend to use it outside of their friendship circles.
2. They are less likely to show empathy to others than are other girls. Adolescent girls are cognitively able to understand another's perspective and incorporate it into their decision-making processes, but girls who use RA are less likely to have developed empathic skills.
3. They are more likely to use physical violence. There is a strong positive correlation between RA and physical aggression, with RA often preceding a physical altercation. Some girls become physically aggressive in retaliation after becoming the target of RA.
4. They are less likely to have a well-formed identity, including a strong belief and values set, and they are not likely to have well-defined values that guide their behavior.

All of these characteristics have strong implications for practice, as discussed later in the chapter.

The following list provides examples of relational and social aggression (Crick & Grotpeter, 1995):

1. Spreading rumors, gossiping
2. Writing notes with negative messages about another person
3. Making fun of someone's clothes, appearance, or weight
4. Eye rolling
5. Three-way phone calls
6. Cyberbullying: instant messaging rumors and gossip, stealing online identity
7. Getting friends to exclude someone one is angry with
8. Excluding someone from group ("You are not welcome")
9. Calling girls "ho's" "sluts," and "losers" or other names
10. Revealing someone's secrets
11. Talking behind others' backs
12. Making mean jokes and then saying "Just kidding"
13. Stealing friends or romantic partners
14. Threatening to withdraw emotional support or friendship
15. Deliberately ignoring someone
16. Manipulating or threatening a girl's romantic relationships (particularly in older adolescence)

Cyberbullying is a recent, rapidly developing phenomenon. According to a survey of middle schoolers, 18% said they had been cyberbullied at least once, and girls were twice as likely as boys to be victims of cyberbullying (Kowalski et al., 2005). This type of RA generally involves using e-mail, instant messaging, and Web pages, weblogs, text messages, and chat rooms to harm others (StopBullyingNow, 2006). For example, perpetrators use victims' personal Web pages (e.g., MySpace.com) to post negative gossip or use instant messaging to spread rumors about a particular girl. They might use victims' passwords to send out embarrassing e-mails that are presumably from the victim. Cyberbullying is becoming increasingly common because it is faster to use than other methods, reaches more people, and the bully never has to face the victim (Dellasega & Nixon, 2003; Simmons, 2002). Girls are more likely to use cyberbullying than are boys because girls are more likely to communicate with one another through technology on a regular basis (Blair, 2003; Kowalski et al., 2005). "Three-ways" (calling a girl on the phone and asking her to talk about a third party while that third party is listening in) are also common. All of these methods affect the responsibility and accountability an aggressor feels for her actions. It can free aggressors to say things they might not otherwise say, and victims are even more negatively affected because they don't know who the aggressors are (Blair, 2003).

Popularity and Relational Aggression

Any discussion of RA in adolescent girls must include the importance that the pursuit of popularity plays in perpetuating girls' aggression. In childhood, children look to adults for cues as to who among their peers is considered popular. At this stage, children who are well-behaved and kind to others are the most popular. Around age 10, however, children start to look to their peers instead of adults to determine who is popular. At this time, they learn that the popular kids are not necessarily those best liked by teachers or other adults. Instead, students' perceptions of each other splinter into two groups: those who are well-liked because they are kind, helpful, and trustworthy (termed *sociometric popularity*) and those who are popular because of other attributes, including glamour, social influence, or social prestige (termed *peer-perceived popularity*; Barasch, 1999; Cillessen & Mayeux, 2004; Rose, Swensen, & Waller, 2004; Underwood, 2003). In other words, in adolescence, the popular students are not necessarily well-liked and the well-liked students are not necessarily popular (Cillessen & Mayeux, 2004).

The role of aggression in popularity has been demonstrated in recent research. In early adolescence, the use of both physical and relational aggression is significantly and positively related to peer-perceived popularity (Cillessen & Mayeux, 2004; Rose et al., 2004). Further, both male and female adolescents who use RA experience high levels of popularity, but these popular students are not necessarily liked by their peers. When examining specific effects for girls, those girls who engaged in RA experienced increased popularity over time, and the more popular a girl becomes, the more likely she is to continue using RA because she learns it is effective. This particular finding did not hold true for boys (Rose et al., 2004). Rose and colleagues concluded that using RA gets girls what they want: popularity.

Queen Bees and Wannabes

The relationship between popularity and RA has gained a lot of attention in the popular press recently, with films like *Mean Girls, Odd Girl Out,* and *Thirteen* clearly demonstrating this destructive cycle. Rosalind Wiseman's (2002) widely read book, *Queen Bees and Wannabes* (also the basis for the *Mean Girls* movie) labels the leaders of popular circles as Queen Bees and describes the manipulation and mean behaviors that popular girls engage in to maintain their status as Queens.

According to Wiseman (2002), a Queen needs loyal followers in order to maintain her power, and these circles of friends emerge as the "popular clique." The goal of any clique is to keep outsiders out and for each member to work to stay within group boundaries. Being the leader of an exclusive clique helps the popular girl maintain her social position (e.g., she decides who is "in" or "out"). For many girls, being part of the "right" or "popular" clique is a primary aspiration, and girls who want to be popular work relentlessly to move toward this goal by employing many strategies that seem to work for the Queen Bee: manipulating and damaging the relationships around her. Wiseman (2002) refered to these girls as *Wannabes* or *Pleasers*—girls who are willing to try anything to be part of the elusive popular group. For example, a Wannabe will sacrifice her friendships if it will enhance her chances of attaining popularity. Many girls report tension between wanting to remain loyal to their former friends while knowing they must aspire to new friendships if they want to attain popularity (Merten, 2004). In many cases, a girl will betray a former friend by sharing her intimate secrets with others. For example, to win a more popular girl's favor, a girl might disclose a secret that she learned about another friend or even engage in bullying of her former friend. Crick and Grotpeter (1995) found that cliques with leaders who frequently use RA had the highest levels of intimacy and secret sharing. This puts girls who are in popular groups at high risk for betrayal by their own friends.

In the following case study, Candace experienced this type of betrayal.

Case Study

Candace is best friends with Jennifer, a girl she has known since she was in the second grade. Candace enjoys Jennifer's company, and they have a lot of fun going to the mall, looking at magazines, surfing the net, and watching MTV. Candace and Jennifer told each other everything—their crushes on older boys, their fights with their parents, their insecurities about their changing bodies. When they entered the eighth grade, Candace noticed that Jennifer gradually started avoiding her at school, although they still talked frequently on the phone and spent time together on the weekends. At school Jennifer began spending time between classes with Ashleigh and Rachel, two popular girls known for their cool clothes and for having lots of attention from guys. Jennifer felt it would be great to be part of their clique and to be like the popular girls. However, Ashleigh and Rachel didn't want to be friends with Jennifer, but they kept her around because she did whatever they said.

One day Candace noticed that girls at school looked at her strangely when she walked down the hall. Jennifer ignored her when she tried to ask her what was wrong. Ashleigh and Rachel whispered to each other when Candace walked into class. Finally, a girl told Candace, "Get away from me you slut!" and the whole class began laughing loudly. Candace ran to the bathroom, feeling horrified and confused: What had happened? From that point on, no one wanted to talk to Candace at school. Later, Candace found out that Jennifer had told Ashleigh and Rachel that Candace was having sex with various boys after school. Even though it was untrue, Ashleigh and Rachel loved this piece of gossip and included Jennifer in their friendship circle so they could learn more secrets about other girls. Candace and Jennifer were never friends again.

In her book *Odd Girl Out*, Rachel Simmons (2002) described many examples of conditional friendships in which friends are sacrificed as "tickets" or "tools" to gain popularity. With conditional friendships as the norm, girls often fear that they will be excluded from the popular clique at any given moment. Girls can be in the clique today and be the victim of teasing or gossip tomorrow. In this way, popularity remains elusive for every girl; even when she achieves her goal, she must remain vigilant for fear of losing her status.

Victims and Girls in the Middle

Any girl can become the target of RA; victims can be girls who are different in appearance or who differ from norms in any way such as not wearing the "right" clothes, having the "right" hairstyle, or attending the "right" activities. Dellasega and Nixon (2003) reported that girls who mature either early or late are particularly vulnerable to being bullied by other girls. Girls who are talented or confident, and therefore pose a threat to other girls, also are vulnerable to attack. As Simmons (2002) found, girls who possess self-confidence are labeled as someone who thinks she is "all that," a taboo in current adolescent girl culture. Finally, although girls might target victims outside of the clique, girls also frequently target those within their own cliques. This might happen when a girl knowingly or inadvertently challenges someone who is higher than she is in the current social structure of the group.

Consequences of Relational Aggression

Many girls have no real idea why they become victims, but the effects of being teased and excluded can be devastating. Children who are frequent victims experience social anxiety, social avoidance, depression, loneliness, and general psychological distress (Crick & Nelson, 2001). Victimized children may develop distorted perceptions of social relationships, be overly sensitive to negative evaluation, and tend to avoid social situations (Storch & Masia-Warner, 2004). In addition, they are more likely to feel they are to blame for their own victimization (Yoon et al., 2004). Victimization is related to poor overall self-concept, as well as to specific identity domains including poor physical appearance, romantic appeal, and athletic competence (Underwood, 2003).

Victims might cope with these situations in one of four ways: (a) try to escape the situation by being absent from school or avoiding activities with peers; (b) engage in active retaliation by fighting back through relational or physical aggression; (c) continue to remain in the friendship, accepting the abusive behavior in order to remain in the clique; or (d) ignore the bullying and choosing not to strive for the approval of more popular girls. Regardless of their coping strategy, girls are reluctant to report RA to educators or parents. In one study, Garbarino (2006) found that 67% of girls reported being humiliated by peers at school, but most (60%) didn't tell their parents. Girls may fear that because RA is generally undetected by adults, it will be dismissed as "normal" behavior for girls. They also believe that telling an adult about it won't improve the situation (Casey-Cannon et al., 2001). In fact, 71% of teachers believe that they always intervene in RA situations, but only 25% of girls believe that teachers will intervene in bullying situations (see Bullybeware.com, 2006). Later in this chapter, I explore detailed strategies for both counselors and parents in assisting victims to feel more confident in reporting these incidents and describe effective strategies for helping victims cope with the effects of RA.

Fortunately, there are girls outside of popular cliques who do not necessarily aspire to be part of this group, although they may float in and out of several friendship circles. These girls in the middle (Simmons, 2002) often do not meet the White, middle-class, heterosexual, physically able ideal for girls in U.S. culture. However, because of their position outside of mainstream pressures, they feel more empowered to voice their own opinions and needs (Brown, 2003).

Even though these girls are open to challenging the status quo they observe in their schools and communities, they often lack the skills for taking action (Brown, 2003). GIM—either within or outside of the clique—are the pivotal girls that are the most amenable to change, and they can actively choose to intervene on behalf of victims by standing up to girls who bully. According to Dellasega and Nixon (2003), GIM may be reluctant to interrupt RA when it occurs, but when they do, their interventions are likely to be successful. For example, when a girl gossips about a peer to a group of girls ("Cindy is a liar. She lies about all of you behind your backs."), the first response to the comment influences all of the comments to follow. If the initial response to the comment is supportive of the gossip ("Yeah, that's right! She said Jennifer was a backstabber!"), then other girls in the group are likely to join in with more gossip. If the initial response challenges the gossip ("That's not true. She's a good friend to me."), then the rest of the girls are more likely to be positive in their responses (Dellasega & Nixon, 2003). GIM can learn to challenge gossip when they hear it and to stand up for targets of RA when they see it occurring. This is where change is likely to begin. Interventions to embolden GIM to intervene are addressed later in the chapter.

Other Uses of Relational Aggression

In addition to helping a girl move ahead on the popularity treadmill (Simmons, 2002), RA is used by adolescent girls in a variety of ways:

1. *Expression of anger.* RA is an acceptable, traditionally feminine way to express strong negative feelings, particularly when girls don't have the words or skills to express negative feelings directly (Verlaan, 2005).
2. *Assertion of social dominance.* By asserting her power through threatening girls' relationships, a girl can increase her social status, feel powerful, and keep other girls from challenging her position in the social hierarchy (Verlaan, 2005).
3. *Compensation for a lack of self-esteem.* By excluding others from her clique, a girl can confirm her own sense of belongingness and acceptance (Underwood, 2003).
4. *Relief from boredom.* Girls often report that they use RA to create excitement or drama in their lives. For example, she might say, "If there

isn't something interesting going on, I will make something happen" (Jones-Bamman, 2004).

5. *Retaliation for jealousy or competition over romantic partners.* Girls often use male attention as a way to obtain power; therefore, when boys pay attention to another girl, a girl perceives this as a threat to her social standing. Girls who are relationally aggressive may feel justified in attacking other girls if they believe they pose a threat to their romantic relationships (Verlaan, 2005).

RA bears significant consequences for all girls, regardless of their role. However, the girls who strive to achieve and maintain popularity with the "right" clique are often the most at risk for negative consequences. One of the primary risks is that girls develop a lack of trust in relationships and are particularly wary of female friendships. Girls who are popular often lose their own identities as they strive to maintain the "right" image. Because RA often occurs within friendship circles, girls highly desire to stay in the group and are willing to tolerate abusive behavior from their friends. Their fear of being alone is greater than enduring abusive behavior, so they remain silent and often do not report the behavior to anyone. They learn that friendships are conditional ("I will stay friends with you only if nothing better comes along, or if you do as I say."). These dynamics are significant, and Simmons (2002) and Wiseman (2002) argued that this can lay the foundation for what a girl might tolerate in a romantic relationship in her adult years.

Second, girls learn to question their own experiences. A girl learns that she can't trust her own perceptions of how others feel about her ("She was my best friend yesterday, and now she is spreading rumors about me."). Because girls using RA often use humor to disguise their teasing—"I was only kidding"—girls learn to question whether they are being hypersensitive (as the bulliers often claim) or whether their feelings are legitimate.

A third consequence is that girls learn that it is not socially acceptable to be unique or different from the group in any way. They learn that to appear self-assured and confident will threaten their chances at popularity. Simmons (2002) described the name-calling that occurs in girls' friendship groups when they encounter a girl who is successful or confident ("She thinks she is *all that*."). The message girls receive is "Don't stand out or others will hate you" and "Girls don't want other girls to be confident" (Simmons, 2002). As girls become older and enter higher education and workforce settings, the damaging effects of these messages for women can be considerable (Simmons, 2002). If women feel that appearing self-assured or confident will result in social exclusion, how can they consistently perform at their optimal level of ability? It is of concern that girls and women might learn to hold themselves back instead of expressing their unique talents in personal and professional settings.

A fourth way that RA has a negative impact on girls is that they learn to limit their self-expression. In a recent study, Crothers et al. (2005) found that girls believe traditional femininity restricts their options for resolving conflict to two choices: either using RA or suppressing their wants and feelings. Both options are unhealthy for girls; they learn that to be accepted by their peers or romantic partners, they have to lose the right to voice their opinions, or that they have to resort to covert, manipulative ways to seek revenge against a perceived wrong. In this way, they do not engage in the process of developing an authentic self, living instead as if under constant surveillance and constantly seeking to maintain social approval.

Shifting Cultural Norms

The cultural norms for girls just described are beginning to change in contemporary society. Specifically, girls today do not feel as limited to conform to traditional notions of femininity in order to be accepted. In many ways today's girls are encouraged to be assertive, physical, and competitive. This newfound freedom has resulted in many positive developments for girls. For example, girls are learning martial arts, playing contact sports like rugby and hockey, exercising in group classes like kickboxing and Tae Bo, and participating in all sports at record levels. In 1970, only 1 in 27 high school girls played a varsity sport, whereas 1 in 3 girls participated in 2002 (Garbarino, 2006).

However, by-products of girls' socialization to be more physically aggressive might be the increase in physical fighting in schools and the sharp increase in girls' rates of violent offending in delinquent and criminal activities (Jones-Bamman, 2004). Between 1991 and 2000, girls' arrests increased by 25.3% whereas arrests declined by 3.2% for boys (Underwood, 2003). The increase in arrest rates is not distributed equally in the population; 50% of the girls in the juvenile justice system are African American (they comprise only 4.3% of the general female U.S. population) and 13% are Hispanic (Centers for Disease Control and Prevention, 2004). Girls who are physically aggressive are at risk for a plethora of negative outcomes: alcoholism, violent crime, unsafe sexual practices, risky driving, school drop out, unplanned pregnancy, STDs, and unresponsive parenting (Underwood, 2003). They also are more at risk for being in physically abusive relationships as adults and for becoming physically aggressive in these relationships (Underwood, 2003).

This shift toward female aggression is driven in part by cultural changes, resulting in a more "socially toxic" culture for girls (Garbarino, 2006). Physically aggressive women are glamorized in the entertainment industry through recent films (e.g., *Charlie's Angels*), music videos, television programs, teen magazines, and video games (e.g., Lara Croft in "Tomb Raiders"). These images result in a normalization of female physical aggression (Prothrow-Stithand & Spivak, 2005). According to Garbarino (2006), as girls grow up viewing television programs with aggressive female characters, they become desensitized to violence and begin to accept female aggression as normal and expected. He cited a direct connection between children's exposure to media violence and their own aggressive behaviors.

RA is also related to the rise of physical aggression in girls. Physical aggression often is preceded by an RA incident, so that girls feel they have a justification for fighting. Girls' increasing use of degrading and demeaning language both verbally and online creates a climate in which physical assault is more likely to occur (Garbarino, 2006). When girls compete with one another for male attention and call one another demeaning names, the conflict may escalate to a physical fight. For example, Gena might call Jackie a "bitch" or "slut" for flirting with her boyfriend. If Jackie responds by initiating a physical altercation, Gena then feels justified in her initial attack of Jackie.

The strong positive correlation between RA and physical aggression indicates that efforts to reduce female bullying must include interventions that address all forms of aggression. The increase in physical aggression also points to a need for interventions that address the confusing, contradictory messages that adolescent girls receive. When girls lack strong mentors to help them sort through these messages, they often turn to popular culture for guidance. As Dellasega and Nixon (2003) indicated:

> Role models for today's teens are not powerful women who have succeeded because of their persistence and kindness to others, but rather superstar singers acting like sexy schoolgirls and movie stars firing machine guns or using martial arts on opponents while wearing skintight jumpsuits. No wonder young women find themselves in a state of extreme confusion, unsure of how to relate to either themselves or others. (p. 3)

How can we assist adolescent girls to express themselves more effectively in relationships? Some prevention strategies are outlined next.

Prevention Strategies and Counseling Interventions

Girls' relational aggression is harmful to all girls. Rather than accepting it as a normative behavior, counselors can begin to address this issue directly in their schools and communities. This is difficult work because RA behaviors are resistant to change for several reasons. First, it is positively reinforced when it brings girls the social status they desire. Even though girls feel insecure in their relationships with other girls, they see no reason for changing these behaviors. Second, girls who do not hold power often are afraid to intervene on the behalf of victims, so they do nothing to stop the bullying behaviors. Third, victims often do not report the bullying because they fear that adults won't intervene or that it will make the situation worse. Finally, RA may go undetected by educators and parents, and even when it is noticed, RA may not be addressed because it is viewed as normal and accepted (Skowronski, Weaver, Wise, & Kelly, 2005). It is clear that RA won't be reduced without active, systemwide intervention (Vail, 2002).

Where to Begin: Preparation

Counselors can set the stage for reducing RA by examining their previous experiences with RA, their own current relationships, how they handle conflict, and their attitudes toward aggressive girls. Some important questions for self-exploration include the following:

- As a counselor committed to working with girls, am I prepared to examine my biases toward popular girls, GIM, and victims?
- What are my personal experiences as an adolescent, and how do these experiences influence my responses to girls' conflicts today? What role did I play in the social hierarchy in my school? Do I remember being teased or excluded? Did I engage in RA behaviors toward others?

It is also important to examine our current behaviors:

- What issues prevent me from standing up for myself during a conflict?
- Do I provide a positive model for girls by the way I respond to conflict?
- Do I engage in slander or gossip about women? Do I express myself assertively, clearly, and effectively?

A second area of preparation is to prevent RA in early childhood before it begins. Adults can work to replace a culture of aggression with a culture of kindness in their schools and communities. Children should be taught that relationally aggressive behaviors are hurtful and will not be tolerated. They can learn that teasing, gossiping, and ignoring others is not just a fun pastime but can be very damaging to others. If girls learn adult expectations early on and know that they will be consistently reinforced, girls will be less likely to resort to these behaviors.

Girls also need guidance in developing a strong belief and values set that guides their behavior. As they develop a strong moral identity (e.g., their decisions are based on their moral values), they can become more caring and supportive of others. As they intentionally choose to be kind, they will feel more secure and positive about themselves, what Dellasega and Nixon (2003) termed *confident kindness*. An example of promoting a culture of kindness might be the creation of a "Cool to Be Kind Day" in which students accumulate tokens whenever an adult notices them engaging in kind behavior. At the end of the day, students can trade in their tokens for prizes (Dellasega & Nixon, 2003). Students also benefit when they learn tolerance, acceptance, and respect for individual differences rather than valuing only those most like themselves (Yoon et al., 2004).

Systemwide Change in Schools

Most experts argue for a systemwide approach to preventing girl aggression (Dellasega & Nixon, 2003; Simmons, 2002; Underwood, 2003; Yoon et al., 2004). It is not enough to intervene directly with girls; counselors need to advocate for comprehensive intervention at several levels: (a) policy changes with clear expectations and consistent enforcement; (b) training for educators to sensitize them to the problem and to support them in enforcing antibullying policies, and training for parents to increase their awareness of the problem and how to intervene with their daughters; (c) prevention work in the form of curricular programs and prevention groups; and (d) specific interventions for perpetrators, GIM, and victims. These four areas are addressed in the sections that follow.

The first level of change is administrator attention to policy. Schools need to develop clear antibullying policies that incorporate RA and that do not tolerate these covert types of aggressive behaviors in girls (Dellasega & Nixon, 2003; Underwood, 2003). Many states now have antibullying legislation that can aid in forming an anti-RA/bullying policy (see www.stopbullyingnow.hrsa.gov). Underwood (2003) recommended that policies stipulate the behaviors that are or are not acceptable at school, articulate the procedures educators and students should follow when they suspect bullying, and include strong intervention programs that target bullies and victims.

At the second level of schoolwide change, teachers and all school staff should receive training about girls' aggression. Most of these behaviors are difficult to detect in the classroom; teachers know it occurs but often do not have direct evidence for accusing the perpetrators. Teachers should receive training to help them recognize the signs and effects of RA (Yoon et al., 2004). As stated earlier, when teachers are aware that RA is occurring, they should not dismiss these behaviors as "typical" of adolescents. If girls believe their teachers and other staff members will take these behaviors seriously by enforcing policy violations, their tendency to engage in RA will be reduced and victims will be more likely to report RA to adults. Teachers and coaches can make their expectations regarding behavior very clear at the beginning of each academic year. Students perform best when the rules are clear and they are aware of what will and will not be tolerated ("Teasing and gossip are not okay in this classroom, and if I see this occurring, I will report you to the disciplinarian immediately."). Encourage educators to spend time observing girls in nonstructured settings (cafeteria, recess). They can observe girls' nonverbal interactions, noting "Who is being excluded? Who is the leader? Who are the followers? How do the cliques keep nonmembers out?" (Davies, 2006).

Parents play an important role in the prevention of RA. Girls often do not feel comfortable approaching their parents when they are victims of RA. Counselors can provide educational sessions for parents about the harmfulness of RA and how children can learn these behaviors from observing their parents interactions at home (Underwood, 2003). For additional information, see the handout in the Appendix at the end of this chapter.

At the third level of change, a comprehensive prevention program for working directly with students is needed. General prevention strategies to include in any programmatic efforts include teaching the seven core anti-RA skills. This prevention model is based in the wellness approach, which emphasizes enhancement of multiple life areas to prevent RA as well as to increase girls' overall functioning and life satisfaction (Myers & Sweeney, 2005).

Core Anti-RA Prevention Skills

Provide education. Girls need education about the dynamics and effects of RA. They need to recognize that it is a form of bullying and that it does have significant and damaging effects on others (Vail, 2002). Underwood (2003) suggested that girls are more likely to refrain from using RA when they recognize how much they dislike it in others. An example of a helpful educational point is to ask girls to consider the following:

> Before you repeat a piece of information about someone you know, ask yourself: (1) Who will benefit if I repeat this gossip? Who will be hurt by this gossip? (2) How would I feel if this was said about me? (3) Would I repeat this gossip if the person were standing right here listening to me? After you have reflected on these three questions and are satisfied with the answers, you can make an informed decision about whether or not to repeat the information. (Dellasega & Nixon, 2003)

Underwood (2003) also encouraged girls to examine the long-term consequences of RA, such as inauthentic relationships, negative reputation, and eventual social rejection. As part of this education, girls can be encouraged to report RA behaviors to adults when they observe them.

Teach assertiveness skills. RA is highly related to girls' inability to express negative feelings directly. Counselors can provide girls with opportunities to become comfortable in voicing their concerns effectively through practicing assertiveness skills (Underwood, 2003). In this manner girls can learn to use more straightforward strategies in communicating their needs and wants. Many girls will have difficulty learning to face conflict directly, particularly if they have been socialized to value family and community wishes over their own needs. Brown (2003) suggested that adults help girls deal with conflict by noticing when a girl seems angry and then encouraging her to express her feelings. She might need help in developing the words needed to articulate what she is feeling. If adults notice a girl expressing her anger in an appropriate way, they can reinforce this action by telling her that they admire the way she handled the situation.

Further, girls need to learn that there are consequences for speaking the truth. When girls voice what they think and feel, others won't always appreciate what they have to say. Girls can learn that they don't always have to agree with their friends or be liked by everyone (Brown, 2003). This is not an easy task for an adolescent girl who is highly concerned with the opinions of others, but as she begins to practice it in her relationships, she can appreciate the freedom that comes with assertive communication.

Promote empathy-building skills. When girls reach adolescence, they have the developmental capacity to fully identify another's feelings and to attempt to understand his or her perspective. Although girls are capable of displaying empathy at this age, they aren't always skilled at using it. When a girl becomes angry with another girl, she can try to take her perspective to understand why the girl might be acting in this manner. For example, Maria can think about how hurt Carla might be if she isn't invited to Maria's party, even though Carla projects a tough exterior and acts as if she doesn't care about social events. GIM can also benefit from empathy skills as they learn to empathize with and potentially stand up for a victimized girl. Dellasega and Nixon (2003) recommended three strategies for empathy building: (a) present a scenario and help girls to identify the girl's feelings in the situation, (b) help girls take another girl's perspective in the situation, (c) encourage them to take an empathic action, such as sitting next to a victimized girl at lunch or in class.

Help her to view other girls as allies. Instead of encouraging the idea that girls are petty, mean, or backstabbing, help girls learn to defy these limiting stereotypes. Help them understand why it is important not to undermine one another. Teach girls to view each other as allies, not as enemies fighting one another for social status. Affirm girls' relational strengths, as "the greatest hope and the worst fear for interventions to reduce social aggression is that, for good or for ill, sisterhood is powerful" (Underwood, 2003, p. 230). Girls can develop these attitudes through frequent interactions with positive female role models. Instead of being angry with one another, help them rechannel their anger toward cultural forces that are degrading to girls, such as the media or advertising (Brown, 2003).

Facilitate leadership development. A girl who is aggressive needs to learn ways to redirect her aggressive energies. Counselors can help all girls to develop leadership skills in more productive ways. They can assist girls in gaining comfort with their leadership potential by supporting them in taking action on issues that matter most to them. For example, an aggressive girl can enact leadership by becoming involved in an activity to promote social justice in her community.

Help girls to engage in diverse activities, including sports. Participation in a variety of activities helps girls to become more resistant to aggression (both as perpetrators and as victims) because they become less focused on their social standing (Brown, 2003). If girls remain busy with positive activities, they will be less likely to engage in aggressive behavior and will develop a sense of self-esteem that is not based on peer approval. Counselors can help girls find more like-minded peers through their participation in activities such as athletics, arts programs, community organizations, school programs, or faith-based groups. Activities that promote a sense of personal accomplishment are especially effective. Brown (2003) recommended sports participation and free fighting classes (martial arts activities) through which girls can develop strength and courage.

Promote development of authentic friendships. Counselors can help girls to understand the difference between friendship and popularity. Girls can be encouraged to choose both girls and boys as friends who are affirming, supportive, and have mutual interests, regardless of their social status. It is helpful to ask girls to list the qualities they are looking for in a friendship and to evaluate their current relationships according to this standard (Skowronski et al., 2005).

Counseling Programs for Girls

Counselors can be creative in the ways that they implement the development of these skills in all girls at their schools. One general prevention strategy is to provide spaces for girls to have structured dialogue with one another. Girls can be empowered when they have safe places to talk openly about their concerns, express their feelings, and critique the culture and media messages about girls. Suggestions from Brown et al. (1999) included asking girls to openly discuss the nature and function of cliques, or how race/ethnicity, class, gender, sexual orientation, and differing abilities influence girls' relationships. Girls can honestly explore the ways in which current socialization processes cause declines in self-esteem for White, middle-class girls. Girls of color and White, working-class girls in particular can find support as they share their common experiences with social injustice and begin to work with one another (rather than against one another) in finding solutions that work effectively for them. Brown (2003) referred to these spaces as Hardiness Zones that can serve to protect girls from the many confusing messages they receive during adolescence. According to Jones-Bamman (2004), "To prevent aggression and violence, girls need safe spaces to be who they really are, not what they're expected to be" (p. 3). In Jones-Bamman's focus groups, girls reported the need for time in a structured setting to talk with their peers and to help them calm down after a conflict.

Several classroom programs have been developed to provide these kinds of opportunities for girls as a way to reduce aggression. The Ophelia Project uses high school students as mentors for younger girls. One of the program's primary tools uses role plays to help girls develop empathy and to practice how they might handle various RA situations (see Opheliaproject.org). Other examples include the Gen Austin Girls as Friends, Girls as Foes program (see GenAustin.org) and Rosalind Wiseman's Empower Program (see Empowered.org).

Small group formats are ideal for helping girls develop the skills they need to reduce RA. Because girls with high self-esteem are more likely to be kind and caring to one another, groups for girls that promote strong identity development are recommended. As an example, the Girl Power empowerment group developed by Fazio-Griffith (n.d.) promotes self-esteem in girls through the use of affirmative activities such as journaling, music, dialogue, and self-expression through art and images. To address RA directly, Cummings, Hoffman, and Leschied (2004) described a psychoeducational group for aggressive adolescent girls that includes the following components: (a) education about gender-role socialization, (b) forms of female aggression, (c) impact of violence in girls' lives, (d) nonaggressive coping strategies, (e) exploration of adolescent girl culture, and (f) facilitation of positive self-image. Further, Taylor (2006) recently published a group counseling curriculum for relationally aggressive girls in grades 5–12 titled *Salvaging Sisterhood*. Her detailed, 8-week curriculum includes activities that focus on the positives of sisterhood; explorations of authentic and inauthentic friendships; the sources/negative effects of cliques, popularity, and RA behaviors; empathy-building skills; communication and confrontation techniques; and positive affirmations.

Finally, the fourth level of change includes direct interventions with girls who comprise the three relational roles (perpetrators, victims, and GIM). When working directly with perpetrators of RA, counselors should remember that although typically popular in terms of being feared due to their social status, these girls are disliked by their peers. If they are popular, they generally are aware that their status is elusive and that their friendships are inauthentic. It is important to remember that most girls do not perceive the need to change their behaviors because they seem to work for them in their pursuit of social goals. Counselors should use strategies that are most effective with clients who are resistant to change such as reflective listening and empathic responses and use few confrontational techniques. Building a trusting, therapeutic alliance is critical to the success of any intervention. While working to help a girl understand that her behaviors have serious consequences, counselors can teach empathy and help her build the skills she needs to develop her leadership potential.

When working with victims, counselors can remain mindful that girls are reluctant to report these behaviors to professionals or parents. Girls who are victims are often in friendship groups with their perpetrators. They often choose to endure the abuse rather than to risk losing their membership in the friendship group. If they are concerned about pleasing others in order to maintain their social status, it is unlikely that they will choose to openly defy the leader of their group. However, girls might be more willing to stand up for themselves if they participate in settings in which anti-RA skills are emphasized. For example, if they learn to choose friends who treat them well and who have mutual interests, they will have an easier time removing themselves from harmful cliques. If they are valued for expressing their thoughts and feelings directly, they will be more likely to remove themselves from relationally aggressive episodes and to handle them more effectively. The following exercise is suggested as part of assertiveness training.

Simmons (2002) summarized her advice to girls who are experiencing RA as follows:

1. Get help. Don't do this alone.
2. Don't spend time with people who don't make you feel good about yourself.
3. Get it out: journal, paint, dance, run, bang on drums.
4. Do something: find a different community of people.
5. Believe that it will end.

Finally, GIM are the most amenable to change and can make a real difference in reducing RA behaviors because they are not generally as tied to one particular social circle. Interventions that encourage them to intervene on behalf of a victim when they see RA occurring can be particularly effective. If girls can learn to interrupt gossip by challenging a girl's initial piece of information with something positive rather than agreeing with the gossip, changing the subject, or directly asking the gossiper to stop, they can prevent the spread of harmful rumors. It is important that girls practice how they might stand up to a girl who has a higher social standing because this can be intimidating for many girls. When GIM recognize that they can be active agents in stopping these behaviors, they often are mobilized to take additional action (Dellasega & Nixon, 2003).

Revisit the case example of Candace and Jennifer on page 70. Based on the reccomendations presented in this chapter, answer the following questions.

1. Because Candace has been betrayed by her best friend and is also isolated from others at school, how might you assist Candace?
2. What might you do to intervene with Candace's friend Jennifer who is so desperately trying to enter the popular clique at her school? How open might she be to change?
3. What are some interventions for Ashleigh and Rachel, the leaders of the popular clique at this school? Would you work with them together? Alone?
4. How might you identify girls in the middle (or GIM) who might intervene on behalf of girls like Candace in the future? What kinds of skills do they need?

Confrontation Exercise: Confronting a Bully

1. Ask for a private discussion with the bully. Tell her what she is doing that bothers you using "I-statements" such as "I don't like it when you call me a fat cow behind my back and leave mean messages on my voice mail."
2. Tell her what you want her to do to stop the behavior: "I want you to stop saying these things and to stop calling my cell phone." The three-step sandwiching technique (Skowdowski et al., 2005) is recommended: (a) Say something positive, ("I value your friendship."), (b) then request that she stop the behavior ("I would like for you to stop."), and (c) end with something positive ("I do like how you stood up for me when the other girls were fighting last week.").
3. Even if the bullying doesn't stop, remind yourself that you feel good about yourself for having taken action.

Source: Adapted from Dellasega & Nixon (2003).

Conclusion

From an early age many girls are socialized to practice forms of traditional feminine behavior. They are taught to place high importance on the value of relationships in defining who they are, and they are subsequently discouraged from openly expressing their thoughts and feelings so they won't jeopardize their relationships. When girls perceive they are limited in their ways to express anger and address conflict, they often resort to RA. Further, even though more girls feel free to voice their negative emotions today, they are increasingly turning to physical violence rather than to healthy methods of self-expression. Counselors who work toward the prevention of these behaviors will be challenged because cultural norms serve to perpetuate the status quo ("Girls will be girls."). Rather than focusing only on girls and changing their individual behaviors, interventions require a systemic, tiered approach. When girls feel supported by one another when voicing their concerns directly, they will not have to resort to aggression to satisfy their need for self-expression.

Activities for Further Exploration

1. Describe the short- and long-term problems associated with the pursuit of popularity among adolescent girls, both to the girls in the "inner circle" of popularity and those who are on the outside. How might this pursuit affect girls' future relationships with both men and women? What role can counselors play in changing this problem?

2. To increase your understanding of RA, interview a middle school girl (preferably in grades 6–8). Ask her some questions about how girls handle conflict and anger. Ask her to explain relational aggression in her school ("When girls want to be mean in your class, what kinds of things do they do?"). What has the interviewee observed regarding cliques, popularity, and the various roles girls play in their friendship circles? How does she think parents or teachers should help?

3. To further increase your understanding of the popular media's representation of RA in middle school, watch a film like *Odd Girl Out* or *Mean Girls* and become familiar with the books *Odd Girl Out* (Simmons, 2002), *Queen Bees and Wannabes* (Wiseman, 2002), and *12 Strategies That Will End Female Bullying: Girl Wars* (Dellasega & Nixon, 2003). How do these films and books relate to your experiences both personally and professionally? In what ways do they differ? Would you recommend that girls watch these movies or read these books? Why or why not?

4. Design a workshop for middle-school girls regarding the prevention of RA. On the basis of the recommendations in this chapter, what components might you want to include?

Suggested Readings

Basow, S. A., & Rubin, L. R. (1999). Gender influences and adolescent development. In N. G. Johnson, M. C. Roberts, & J. Worell (Eds.), *Beyond appearance: A new look at adolescent girls* (pp. 25–52). Washington DC: American Psychological Association.

Brown, L. M., Way, N., & Duff, J. L. (1999). The others in my I: Adolescent girls' friendships and peer relations. In N. G. Johnson, M. C. Roberts, & J. Worell (Eds.), *Beyond appearance: A new look at adolescent girls* (pp. 205–225). Washington DC: American Psychological Association.

Crick, N. R., & Nelson, D. A. (2001). Relational and physical victimization within friendships: Nobody told me there'd be friends like these. *Journal of Abnormal Child Psychology, 30*(6), 599–607.

Dellasega, C., & Nixon, C. (2003). *12 strategies that will end female bullying: Girl wars.* New York: Simon & Schuster.

Lamb, S. (2001). *The secret lives of girls: What good girls really do—sex play, aggression, and their guilt.* New York: Free Press.

Rose, A., Swenson, L. P., & Waller, E. M. (2004). Overt and relational aggression and perceived popularity: Developmental differences in concurrent and prospective relations. *Developmental Psychology, 40*(3), 378–387.

Simmons, R. (2002). *Odd girl out.* Orlando, FL: Harcourt.

Underwood, M. K. (2003). *Social aggression among girls.* New York: Guilford Press.

Wiseman, R. (2002). *Queen Bees and Wannabes.* New York: Three Rivers Press.

Additional Resources

http://www.empowerprogram.org
Information about the Empower Program for girls.
http://www.genaustin.org
Gen Austin's Girls as Friends, Girls as Foes program.
http://stopbullyingnow.org
Of particular interest, see What Adults Can Do: Cyberbullying.
http://www.empowered.org/svpi.htm
Information about the Empower Training Institute, which has been effective in decreasing physical and verbal aggression
http://www.opheliaproject.org
Information about RA, current research on RA, and information about RA programs for schools, parents, and professionals
http://www.tolerance.org
Information on bullying, aggression, and hate, with sections for parents, teachers, teens and children

References

Barasch, D. S. (1999). Dealing with cliques. *Family Life,* 37–38.

Basow, S. A., & Rubin, L. R. (1999). Gender influences and adolescent development. In N. G. Johnson, M. C. Roberts, & J. Worell (Eds.), *Beyond appearance: A new look at adolescent girls* (pp. 25–52). Washington DC: American Psychological Association.

Bearman, P. S., & Moody, J. (2004). Suicide and friendships among American adolescents. *American Journal of Public Health, 94,* 89–96.

Blair, J. (2003). New breed of bullies torment their peers on the Internet. *Education Week, 22*(21), 6–8.

Brown, L. M. (2003). *Girlfighting: Betrayal and rejection among girls.* New York: New York University Press.

Brown, L. M., Way, N., & Duff, J. L. (1999). The others in my I: Adolescent girls' friendships and peer relations. In N. G. Johnson, M. C. Roberts, & J. Worell (Eds.), *Beyond appearance: A new look at adolescent girls* (pp. 205–225). Washington DC: American Psychological Association.

Bullybeware.com. (2006). *More information on bullying.* Retrieved November 12, 2006, from www.bullybeware.com

Casey-Cannon, S., Hayward, C., & Gowen, K. (2001). Middle-school girls' reports of peer victimization: Concerns, consequences, and implications. *Professional School Counseling, 5*(2), 138–147.

Centers for Disease Control and Prevention. (2004). Violence-related behaviors among high school students, 1991–2003. *Morbidity and mortality weekly report* [Electronic version]. Washington, DC: Author. Retrieved April 26, 2006, from http://www.cdc.gov/mmwr/preview/mmwrhtml/mm5329a1.htm

Constantine, M. G., Greer, T. W., & Kindaichi, M. M. (2003). Theoretical and cultural considerations in counseling women of color. In M. Kopala & M. A. Keitel (Eds.), *Handbook of counseling women* (pp. 40–52). Thousand Oaks, CA: Sage.

Cillessen, A. H. N., & Mayeux, L. (2004). From censure to reinforcement: Developmental changes in the association between aggression and social status. *Child Development, 75*(1), 147–163.

Crick, N. R., & Grotpeter, J. K. (1995). Relational aggression, gender, and social-psychological adjustment. *Child Development, 66,* 710–722.

Crick, N. R., & Nelson, D. A. (2001). Relational and physical victimization within friendships: Nobody told me there'd be friends like these. *Journal of Abnormal Child Psychology, 30*(6), 599–607.

Crothers, L. M., Field, J. E., & Kolbert, J. B. (2005). Navigating power, control, and being nice: Aggression in adolescent girls' friendships. *Journal of Counseling & Development, 83,* 349–354.

Cummings, A. L., Hoffman, S., & Leschied, A. W. (2004). A psychoeducational group for aggressive adolescent girls. *Journal of Specialists in Group Work, 29,* 285–299.

Davies, L. (2006). *Aggressive girls.* Retrieved January 2007 from www.guidancechannel.com/default.aspx?index=1298&cat=13

Dellasega, C., & Nixon, C. (2003). *12 strategies that will end female bullying: Girl wars.* New York: Simon & Schuster.

Fazio-Griffith, L. (n.d.). *Girl power: An eight week empowerment group for adolescent girls.* Unpublished manuscript.

Garbarino, J. (2006). *See Jane hit.* New York: Penguin Press.

Jones-Bamman, L. (2004). *Preventing girls' aggression and violence: A report of the Girls and Violence Task Force.* The Governor's Prevention Partnership. Retrieved from www.preventionworksct.org

Kowalski, R., Limber, S. P., Scheck, A., Redfearn, M., Allen, J., Calloway, A., Farris, J. Finnegan, K., Keith, M., Kerr, S., Singer, L., Spearman, J., Tripp, L., & Vernon, L. (2005, August). *Electronic bullying among school-aged children and youth.* Paper presented at the annual meeting of the American Psychological Association, Washington, DC.

Lamb, S. (2001). *The secret lives of girls: What good girls really do—sex play, aggression, and their guilt.* New York: Free Press.

Merten, D. E. (2004). Securing her experience: Friendship versus popularity. *Feminism & Psychology, 14*(3), 361–365.

Myers, J. E., & Sweeney, T. J. (Eds.). (2005). *Counseling for wellness: Theory, research, and practice.* Alexandria, VA: American Counseling Association.

Parker, J. G., Walker, A. R., Low, C. M., & Gamm, B. K. (2005). Friendship jealousy in young adolescents: Individual differences and links to sex, self-esteem, aggression, and social adjustment. *Developmental Psychology, 41,* 235–250.

Pipher, M. (2002). *Reviving Ophelia: Saving the selves of adolescent girls.* New York: Ballantine Books.

Prothrow-Stithand, D., & Spivak, H. (2005, November 20). Beyond mean girls: Why young females are fighting more. *The Boston Globe.* Retrieved from www.boston.com.

Rose, A., Swenson, L. P., & Waller, E. M. (2004). Overt and relational aggression and perceived popularity: Developmental differences in concurrent and prospective relations. *Developmental Psychology, 40,* 378–387.

Simmons, R. (2002). *Odd girl out.* Orlando, FL: Harcourt.

Skowronski, M., Weaver, N. J., Wise, P. S., & Kelly, R. M. (2005). Helping girls combat relational aggression. *Communique, 33*(6).

StopBullyingNow. (2006). *Stop bullying now: What adults can do: Cyberbullying.* Retrieved May 5, 2006, from www.stopbullyingnow.hrsa.gov.

Storch, E. A., & Masia-Warner, C. (2004). The relationship of peer victimization to social anxiety and loneliness in adolescent females. *Journal of Adolescence, 27*(3), 351–362.

Tannenbaum, L. (2002). *Slut! Growing up female with a bad reputation.* New York: Seven Stories Press.

Taylor, J. V. (2006). *Salvaging sisterhood.* Chapin, SC: Youthlight.

Underwood, M. K. (2003). *Social aggression among girls.* New York: Guilford Press.

Vail, K. (2002). Relational aggression in girls. *Education Digest, 68*(2), 7–14.

Verlaan, P. (2005). The importance of social context and relationships in female aggression. In D. J. Pepler, K. C. Madsen, C. Webster, & K. S. Levene (Eds.), *The development and treatment of girlhood aggression* (pp.161–165). Mahwah, NJ: Erlbaum.

Wiseman, R. (2002). *Queen bees and wannabes.* New York: Three Rivers Press.

Yoon, J. S., Barton, E., & Taiariol, J. (2004). Relational aggression in middle school: Educational implications of developmental research. *Journal of Early Adolescence, 24*, 303–318.

Appendix
Handout for Parents: How to Help Your Daughter Navigate the Experience of Girls' Aggression

- *Understand the dynamics of girls' aggression,* including the role of cliques in the school environment. What is your daughter's position in the social hierarchy at her school?
- *Be willing to admit that your daughter can be aggressive* (both overtly and indirectly), and help her to channel her anger in more appropriate ways.
- *Provide a positive role model.* Remember that your daughter is watching you as you interact with others. Do you ever slander or gossip about other women? Do you stand up for yourself in conflicts? Express your feelings directly? View other women as allies rather than competitors? Does she regularly see adults treat one another with love and respect in her home?
- *Prepare your daughter.* Girl aggression is common at every school, so girls can't avoid it entirely. Let her know that she will probably lose a friend at school through no fault of her own. Help her understand that even though there is conflict in the world, she can learn how to deal with it effectively.
- *Help your daughter to express her feelings appropriately.* Don't force her to "make nice" just to end a conflict with another girl. Help her to understand she doesn't have to like or agree with everyone, but she does need to learn how to work through conflict in healthy ways.
- *Help your daughter develop empathy and give her moral guidance.* Help her define her beliefs and values. Teach her to display empathy in the following three ways: (a) identify another's feelings; (b) take another's perspective; and (c) show empathic behavior, such as sending a friendly note to another person (see *12 Strategies That Will End Female Bullying: Girl Wars* by Dellasega & Nixon, 2003, for more suggestions).
- *Be involved but unobtrusive.* Be an active part of her life while giving her freedom. Let her know that you are interested in her day. Establish one routine that you and she engage in together that is a nonnegotiable part of your weekly schedules.
- *Don't hesitate to call your daughter on behaviors that are relationally aggressive.* When it occurs, start a dialogue about what you observed. For example, how might the outcome be changed if she responded in a more direct manner? Girls need guidance in helping them challenge social norms that encourage them to use relational aggression instead of using direct and assertive communication.

- *Monitor your daughter's use of the Internet.* Learn the technology your daughter uses and know what she is doing on the computer. Discuss with her your expectations regarding the safe use of the Internet. Print out the downloadable version of "My Online Safety Pledge" published by the Girls Scouts and sign it with your daughter (see jfg.girlscouts.org). Contact these helpful resources, wiredsafety.org and wiredkids.org, for more information.

If you suspect that your child is a victim of girl aggression:

- *Be an active and patient listener.* If she is reluctant to share her experiences with you, remember that she might find it humiliating to admit her problem to you. Ask some leading questions to help her open up. Simmons (2002) suggested the following questions: "When girls want to be mean in your class, what kinds of things do they do?" "Are some girls more secret than others about their meanness? How?" "Can friends be mean to each other? How?"
- *Empathize with what she is going through,* but don't relive your experiences through your daughter. She doesn't want to worry you, and this will only make the experience worse for her.
- *Make your home a sanctuary.* The most important thing that helps girls get through difficult times at school is the "refuge" of home and family. Create a home that is "the place where she can fill herself up with unconditional love and support" (Simmons, 2002, p. 232).
- *Get your daughter's opinion before taking action.* Help her to feel empowered by respecting her wishes about what you can do. It is generally not helpful to call the bully's parents. Listen, reflect, and validate her story *first*, then ask your daughter to think of what she would like to say to the girl who is bullying her.

Some action steps you can consider:

1. Listen to the whole story and get the facts: "Who is doing this to you? When does it occur?" Paraphrase and reflect what you heard. Validate and give her praise where appropriate.
2. Find out what she wants you to do: "Do you want me to talk to the teacher or someone at the school?"
3. Help her to plan her day to minimize the effects of the bullying.
4. Encourage her to role-play how she will respond to bullies in various situations at school.

References

Simmons, R. (2002). *Odd girl out.* Orlando, FL: Harcourt.

Dellasega, C., & Nixon, C. (2003). *12 strategies that will end female bullying: Girl wars.* New York: Simon & Schuster.

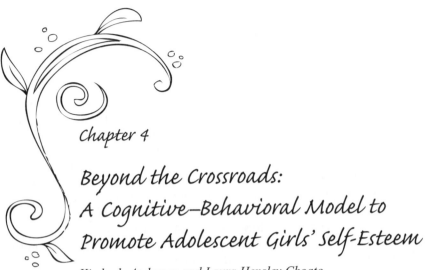

Chapter 4

Beyond the Crossroads: A Cognitive–Behavioral Model to Promote Adolescent Girls' Self-Esteem

Kimberly Anderson and Laura Hensley Choate

Positive self-esteem is one of the best predictors of adolescent mental health and life satisfaction. Specifically, adolescents with positive self-esteem report effective personal coping resources, autonomy, and confidence in their abilities, peer-related social skills, and appearance (Eccles, Barber, Jozefowicz, Malenchuk, & Vida, 1999). Further, high levels of self-esteem serve as a buffer or defense against stressful life transitions. Building self-esteem is a particularly important task for adolescents as they manage the many challenges that arise during this developmental period, including those described in Chapters 2 and 3 (Eccles et al., 1999; Malanchuk & Eccles, 2006). The following example illustrates how self-esteem can play a role in a girl's response to a typical adolescent dilemma.

A girl in a middle-school class is having a birthday party. All of the girls in her class are talking about the party and how much fun they're going to have. They're talking about what they will wear and who is going. One girl does not get an invitation, however. How will she feel? How will she respond? Her reaction to not being included may depend, in part, on her self-esteem. If she possesses a positive self-image, she may think to herself, "That's weird that I'm the only one not included." She might try to find out what happened or she may make other plans for that night so that she will have something to do. But, if she's not very secure in herself, and if her self-esteem is low, she might be very hurt, even devastated. She may tell herself, "I'm never going to be as good as the rest of the girls. They don't like me anyway." She may react by withdrawing from the girls, shutting down, and ultimately losing friends.

Due to the importance of self-esteem in enhancing resilience, a group model for promoting adolescent girls' self-esteem is the focus of this chapter. To provide a context for the group design, we first review developmental and cultural influences on adolescent girls' self-esteem. Next, we describe a cognitive-behavioral model for self-esteem development. Finally, we present a detailed, 8-week group counseling protocol designed to enhance self-esteem in adolescent girls.

Understanding Adolescent Girls' Self-Esteem

There are unique developmental, gendered, and cultural differences in self-esteem, and a large body of research indicates that levels of self-esteem tend to vary by age, gender, and ethnicity (Malanchuk & Eccles, 2006). Self-esteem is highest in early childhood (ages 9–11), drops sharply during adolescence (12–17), and continues to decline into the young adult years (18–22). The age range of 12–17 is a period of rapid physical, social, and cognitive growth (Biro, Striegel-Moore, Franko, Padgett, & Bean, 2006), so it is not surprising that both adolescent boys and girls tend to experience decreases in self-esteem as a result of these changes.

Self-esteem decreases more for girls than it does for boys during the adolescent period, although this gender difference is not true for African American girls. They report higher levels of self-esteem than Caucasians or other minority groups and do not experience significant decreases in self-esteem over the adolescent years (Malanchuk & Eccles, 2006). Specifically, African American girls report greater confidence in their assertiveness skills, physical attractiveness, and popularity, and hold a more positive view of themselves than do Caucasian girls (Biro et al., 2006).

So why might adolescent girls in general, and Caucasian girls in particular, experience declines in self-esteem during this period of their lives? Three processes operate during this period that are strongly related to changes in girls' self-esteem: (a) Girls are faced with multiple changes simultaneously (such as pubertal changes, school transitions, peer pressures); (b) girls increasingly seek validation by others through their appearance and through attracting a romantic partner; and (c) girls experience pressures to fulfill contradictory societal expectations regarding their relationships and connections with others.

First, it is understandable that adolescent girls who cope with numerous stressors simultaneously will be at greater risk for experiencing problems that might result in decreased self-esteem. Girls who transition from elementary to middle school at the same time that they reach puberty have more difficulties than do girls who experience these transitions one at a time (Malanchuk & Eccles, 2006). For Caucasian girls, pubertal timing is particularly important to their self-esteem, as those who mature early report lower self-esteem and mental health outcomes. However, maturational rate is not related to self-esteem in African American girls (Michael & Eccles, 2004).

Second, as was discussed extensively in Chapter 2, a girl's perception of her physical appearance is an important factor in predicting her self-esteem. This is not the case for boys (Malanchuk & Eccles, 2006). It is also interesting to note that African American girls' self-esteem is not as tied to their physical appearance as it is for girls from other cultural groups. As noted in Chapter 2, even at higher weights, African American girls are more likely than White girls to be satisfied with their bodies and with their overall appearance (Jaffee & Lutter, 1995), which contributes to their higher levels of self-esteem.

In adolescence, many girls grow increasingly concerned with how they appear to others and look to external sources for approval. As a way to gain validation, they become highly concerned with social presentation, with popularity with same-sex peers, and with attracting a dating partner. As an avenue for obtaining feedback, they often compare themselves to unrealistic media images of thin and beautiful women, which can have a direct and negative impact on their self-esteem. At the same time that girls are striving to meet societal standards for appearance, their bodies are changing in ways that are increasingly discrepant from media-generated thin ideals. If they have learned to overly value their appearance as central to their sense of self-worth, these changes will have damaging effects on overall self-esteem. This puts some girls at risk for developing negative body image, maladaptive eating practices such as excessive dieting or overexercising, or clinical eating disorders.

Other problems, such as experimentation with alcohol, tobacco, and other drugs (ATOD), can emerge when girls seek validation from others or have difficulties coping with multiple stressors during the adolescent period. For example, in 2005 girls were more likely than boys to report that they used alcohol or drugs to improve their mood, to increase confidence, to reduce tension, to cope with problems, or to lose inhibitions (Office of National Drug Control Policy [ONDCP], 2006). This is alarming in that girls are now trying ATOD at higher rates than boys; for the first time, more teenage girls than boys started using marijuana, alcohol, and cigarettes (ONDCP, 2006). In the past boys surpassed girls in all categories of ATOD use, but girls are now using illicit drugs and alcohol at the same rate as boys and have actually surpassed males in cigarette and prescription drug use.

These statistics are also of concern because of the mental and physical complications that can emerge from girls' substance use. For example, girls who consume even moderate amounts of ATOD substances can experience disruptions in their growth and pubertal development. Further, early substance use puts girls at risk for mental health problems such as depression in their early adult years (ONDCP, 2006).

A third process that is related to changes in girls' self-esteem is tied to a girl's relationships and connections with others. As was described in Chapter 3, relationships with others are central to a girl's sense of self, and perceived success or failure in obtaining or maintaining relationships becomes increasingly important to her self-esteem (Malanchuk & Eccles, 2006). As girls reach adolescence, they obtain the cognitive ability to think more abstractly and to better understand their larger social contexts. Many adolescent girls become attuned to societal messages regarding the importance of establishing and maintaining relationships (even if this means disconnecting from one's authentic self by suppressing one's true thoughts and feelings). At the same time, they experience social pressures to individuate and become increasingly autonomous by disconnecting from their significant relationships with family and peers. A girl becomes aware that she is facing a double bind: If she disconnects from her authentic self in pursuit of connections with others, she experiences a loss of self-esteem; if she attempts to disconnect from others in pursuit of autonomy, she also experiences declines in self-esteem if she does not feel supported by others. It is understandable that girls become confused when they internalize contradictory social pressures for women and feel unsure of how to meet these demands (Tolman & Brown, 2001).

In addition to receiving these messages, girls of color are often further confused by cultural values conflicts in this area. Girls of color are often socialized by their communities to adhere to their traditional cultural values, which often clash with the values of dominant U.S. culture. As a result, girls may feel that in order to accommodate to the dominant culture they must separate from their communities and deny their cultural identities (e.g., "I can't be who I am if I am going to fit in with the mainstream cultural expectations."). Denying aspects of their cultural heritage can have a negative influence on girls' developing sense of identity, as this process can lead to decreases in self-esteem for girls who need supportive relationships and a sense of belongingness to navigate adolescent challenges (Constantine, Greer, & Kindaichi, 2003). To develop positive self-esteem as well as a sense of belonging, girls can learn to appreciate and connect with their cultural identity while also learning how to identify with the macroculture (Lee, 2005). As will be discussed later in the chapter, helping girls to develop a strong cultural identity is a key dimension of wellness and positive self-esteem (Myers & Sweeney, 2005).

Many of problems associated with low self-esteem can be ameliorated through promoting a girl's connection to her authentic self (e.g., respecting, accepting, and valuing her identity by expressing her own beliefs and values) and by providing her with ample opportunities for balancing a sense of autonomy (e.g., developing confidence in handling life demands) with communion (e.g., cultivating connections with others). As noted previously, African American girls tend to possess these qualities—an ability to engage in truth telling and assertiveness, strong community and family ties, a sense of independence, and the skills to reject harmful social stereotypes about the importance of physical appearance—all of which serve as protective factors for maintaining high levels of self-esteem. Through the cognitive behavioral group model described in this chapter, all girls can develop these skills as they learn to better identify negative internalized messages and to replace them with more empowering, positive thoughts that enhance authenticity, autonomy, and communion.

A Cognitive–Behavioral Model of Self-Esteem

Counselors working with all varieties of psychological disturbance and distress commonly direct their treatment toward building self-esteem. In fact, it has been suggested that low self-esteem represents a common denominator in most, if not all, varieties of problems seen by counselors (Branden, 1997). For example, self-esteem building is an important component of the prevention and treatment of negative body image and relational aggression (see Chapters 2 and 3). Cognitive behavioral therapy (CBT) stands out as one treatment model that is particularly well suited to this task. In fact, CBT emphasizes self-esteem building as an essential element of the treatment process for a wide variety of psychological difficulties (Beck, 1995; Beck, Freeman, Davis, & Associates, 2003; Young, Klosko, & Weishaar, 2003). Because cognitive behavior theory is based on the idea that emotional and behavioral reactions are a result of clients' thoughts about themselves, self-esteem building (i.e., improving one's thoughts and image of oneself) is a natural part of the treatment process for virtually all problems. Further, researchers and clinicians have developed specific, manualized, and highly effective approaches for improving self-esteem (e.g., Burns, 1993; Fennell & Jenkins, 2004).

According to the cognitive model of low self-esteem (Fennell, 1998), an individual's life experience can lead to negative core beliefs about herself, others, and the world (e.g., "I'm not lovable."). On the basis of these beliefs, she develops a set of guidelines or rules for living (e.g., "I must look perfect in order for people to like me."). The presenting cycle of maladaptive thoughts, actions, and feelings (presenting problems and symptoms) is ultimately a reflection of negative core beliefs and associated dysfunctional rules. In other words, an individual's negative assessment of her own worth leads to the development of certain standards or guidelines that she uses as a measure of her own personal value. For example, if a girl believes that she is "unworthy" or "damaged" because of an early traumatic experience, she may develop an extensive self-evaluation system consisting of a set of rules that she must follow (such as "I must earn good grades." "I must please everyone." "I must look a certain way."). She then judges herself according to how well she follows the rules. The symptoms and problems (e.g., anger, anxiety, depression, interpersonal difficulties) that ensue can be a result of her efforts at meeting the standards or preoccupation with fear of not meeting the standards. For instance, if a girl believes she must lose weight in order to be "acceptable," she might engage in a restrictive eating pattern. If she does not lose weight despite her efforts, a maladaptive cycle of negative thinking, mood, and behaviors will be triggered. Her thoughts become intensely critical and harsh ("I'm disgusting. I'm such a loser."). Her anxiety and depression may escalate because of these thoughts. She may react by increasing her attempts at restrictive eating or some other form of weight control such as exercise, which may cause her to withdraw socially. This then becomes a self-maintaining, maladaptive cycle that ultimately serves only to further reduce her self-esteem.

Case Study
Margaret's Internal Dialogue

Waking up at 5 a.m.: I have to get moving. I have to make sure I study the math problems again before I can exercise. Then, I need to get in early to ask Coach how I can work on my serve. I really should get up earlier because now I'm only going to have an hour to work out. I'm getting so fat. I can't believe I got that 85% on the science test. I'm so stupid. If I would just focus more. . . .

Lunch time at school: I am having salad and nothing else. That should be enough. If I want to look good for the weekend, I can't be eating so much. Oh, gosh, I hope I get to sit with the "popular group" today. Why didn't I wear something cooler? They're not going to like my new haircut. Why did I listen to my mother?????

Math class: Okay, I'm in trouble. I really should have gotten up at 4 a.m. I did not study enough. If I don't get an *A* on this test, my average could drop. I only have 5 more years before I have to apply to college. If I want to get into the right school, I can't let my grades slip. I know dad really wants me to go to his school, and he'll be so disappointed in me if my grades aren't good enough. . . .

Tennis practice: Oh, there's dad talking to the coach. They're probably talking about how I stunk up at the last match. I wish I could tell dad I really don't love tennis that much. Maybe if I work harder, I'll get better. Then, maybe I'd like it more and Coach and Dad will be happy. . . .

At home in the evening: I really want to call Mary to see what she's doing this weekend, but she was quiet today. I bet she's mad at me for something. I wonder what I did. Maybe I'll make her a bracelet with my new beads. . . .

1. What are the cognitive distortions that are particularly relevant in this case?
2. How would you work with Margaret in replacing some of her negative thoughts with more rational, positive self-talk?
3. How do Margaret's concerns mirror the three themes introduced at the beginning of the chapter: managing multiple demands simultaneously, the importance of physical appearance, and the importance of maintaining relationships? Which of these might be a particular area of counseling focus?

Margaret is a 13-year-old girl who is struggling with symptoms of anxiety and depression. Her system for self-evaluation is highly perfectionistic. Although she is able to achieve a lot, she is never satisfied. She can never relax or enjoy her successes. She is plagued by self-doubt, intensely concerned about what others think, and fearful of failure. Further, she is limited in her ability to fully express her thoughts or feelings to others and is vulnerable to the development of inauthentic relationships. In sum, her self-esteem is low because she does not see herself as "good enough," and she continually attempts to earn her sense of worth. She judges herself and her acceptability by her grades, what her parents and friends think, and her appearance. According to the cognitive model of low self-esteem, Margaret's inferior sense of self led her to develop a perfectionistic set of standards. The constant pressure to meet these expectations ultimately affects her mood, increasing her feelings of anxiety, and her actions, as can be seen in her people pleasing, lack of assertiveness, and overachievement.

Self-Esteem Building Group

In this section, we present a self-esteem building group designed for adolescent girls that draws on the wellness dimensions of self-worth, realistic beliefs, and self-control. This group format may be tailored to work with a variety of adolescent girls with an array of self-esteem concerns including compulsivity, lack of achievement, relationship problems, substance abuse, antisocial behavior, depression, or anxiety (Biro et al., 2006; Eccles et al., 1999). This group design originated as a critical element in working with individuals with eating disorders.

It has become clear to me (Kimberly Anderson) that low self-esteem plays a central role in both understanding and treating these multidetermined disorders. For several decades, low self-esteem has been considered a primary factor in the clinically derived theories of eating disorders (Bruch, 1973; Fairburn, 1981). More recently, research has identified low self-esteem as a major determinant, or risk factor, in the development of eating problems (Cervera et al., 2003; Ghaderi & Scott, 2001). Often, clients will describe a sense of accomplishment and pride associated with controlling their weight and appearance. This temporary boost in self-confidence

Self-Exploration Exercise

1. Complete the self-esteem timeline activity (Appendix A). What significant events occurred for you around the time of adolescence? How did these experiences affect your self-esteem during that period, and how do they continue to affect you today?
2. What are your rules or standards for being an "acceptable" or "worthwhile" person? How might your current responses be different from those you might have listed when you were an adolescent?
3. As an adolescent, how would you have described yourself in terms of your strengths and weaknesses? How is this description different from the way you describe yourself now?

can be a significant factor in the development and maintenance of the eating disorder. Moreover, clients often view the eating disorder itself as a way of being "special." Thus, they describe that the eating disorder becomes a basis for their identity, which helps them to feel better about themselves. Nevertheless, with assistance, clients usually realize that no matter how much they control their eating and weight, they still feel "worthless," "like a failure," and generally "not good enough." With intervention, this negative view can be challenged and new methods for self-evaluation developed.

The group we describe here is designed to be effective for girls who are already experiencing interpersonal problems or eating disorders as a result of low self-esteem. However, it is also a helpful intervention for promoting resilience in all girls in an effort to prevent future problems. As such, it can be implemented as a prevention strategy for girls in almost any setting. The group provides adolescent girls with an opportunity to discuss their thoughts openly with others who not only understand but have shared many of their experiences. Although the interventions presented in the group protocol can be applied individually, the group modality is more powerful. Group members may benefit from processes not available during individual counseling such as positive peer pressure, models of coping, universality, interpersonal feedback, and the opportunity for group experiential activities. Further, clients often report an increase in self-efficacy associated with helping others along with themselves. This, of course, would be a benefit for any group participant, but it is especially relevant for those working on increasing self-esteem. For each session in the protocol, we describe the main focus of the session and provide suggested group activities, discussion topics, and homework.

Building Self-Esteem:
A Guide to an 8-Week Group Counseling Protocol

Group selection. Group selection will vary depending on the setting. Although the group protocol is designed to be suitable for most types of problems and for girls ages 12–17, group leaders will want to put together a group that is fairly homogeneous in terms of age, diagnoses (if applicable), motivation level, and life experiences. For example, it would be a challenge to facilitate discussion around dating and intimacy issues with younger adolescents present. Likewise, the older girls may have difficulty relating to some younger adolescents' concerns regarding puberty. For inpatient settings, groups will be established based on admission to the hospital. Given the acute nature of an inpatient unit, group leaders may need to exclude patients who are actively psychotic, dissociative, suicidal, or aggressive. In such cases, these patients may join the group once they are stabilized. Otherwise, inclusion in the group is fairly unrestricted given that all girls, whether they are currently experiencing problems or not, can benefit from self-esteem building.

Group design. The self-esteem group is a highly structured, CBT-based, 8-week group with a specific agenda for each session. Because it is time limited, a closed group format is preferable. It is recommended that the group remain fairly small in size, ranging from 6–10 group members. This will allow for full member participation.

Group rules. At the start of each session, group rules should be discussed. Of course, each counselor will have his or her own set of rules depending on the setting. Rules commonly discussed include the importance of maintaining confidentiality, completing homework, respecting group members by not starting side conversations or doing something else during group or talking over each other, and attending all sessions or giving notice of an absence.

Group agenda. The agenda is the same for each group session and consists of the following parts:

1. Review of group rules,
2. Review of homework,
3. Presentation of new topic and activity,
4. Discussion, and
5. Homework assignment.

The group leader determines how much time to allow for each segment of the group, but the leader should remain flexible to respect member needs. The new topic/activity and discussion usually assume a primary role in each session. The psychoeducational format may be modified for counselors to use in groups or in classroom guidance activities with students.

Session 1: Defining Self-Esteem
Goals and Interventions

Goals:
- Set the agenda for the group protocol.
- Engage group members.
- Define self-esteem and assess members' current self-image.
- Set a positive expectancy regarding self-esteem building.

Interventions:
- Begin with introductions that engage each group member in the process.
- Provide education regarding meaning of self-esteem.
- Orient group members to process and structure of group.
- Assign homework: Self-esteem timeline.

During the initial group session, members spend a few minutes introducing themselves and getting to know each other. During this time, members usually describe why they are attending the group. They may discuss their personal goals for the group and how they are feeling about being in a group. It is important to address each group member. Although only lasting 10 to 15 minutes, this allows the group a chance to "warm-up."

Focus. Session 1 focuses on the meaning of self-esteem. Because this is the first session, it may be helpful to go around the group asking each member what self-esteem means to them. Ultimately, the group leader facilitates a discussion including the definition of self-esteem, the impact of low self-esteem on the girls' lives, and ways to cultivate self-esteem. Often during this session, the leader will get a general sense about how each group member evaluates herself as well as her current level of self-esteem. When discussing the meaning of self-esteem, it is not uncommon for someone to suggest that self-esteem is the feeling you get when you achieve something or when you are proud of yourself for doing something. Also, self-esteem can be confused with self-confidence. It is not necessarily helpful to point out the inaccuracies in their definitions, but it would be helpful to explain to the group that their definitions might be incomplete. In this regard, it would be appropriate for the leader to provide a definition of self-esteem: for example, self-esteem is the tendency to experience oneself as being competent to cope with life and as worthy of happiness. Further, a discussion of the two main elements of self-esteem (self-efficacy and self-worth) is helpful. It should be explained that in order to develop healthy self-esteem, an individual must believe in her worth as a person (self-worth) as well as her competence to function and succeed in life (self-efficacy). This will most likely lead into a dialogue about the fact that self-esteem is not conditional. That is, self-esteem is not something that has to be earned, and it is not temporary. Rather, self-esteem is related to a sense of self-awareness, self-respect, self-responsibility, and purposeful living. To help girls explore these ideas, the leader might ask, "How do you know when someone has high self-esteem? How do they act? How do they talk about themselves? How do they interact with others?" The girls can learn to recognize the connection between self-esteem and the ability to openly express thoughts and feelings to others. These can be difficult concepts for many members and will require repetition throughout the group.

Homework. For homework, the girls will work on understanding their self-esteem and how it developed. Often a self-esteem timeline is assigned as homework for Week 1 (see Appendix A). This allows the opportunity for a historical review of events that may have contributed to the development of their current negative self-images.

Session 2: Understanding the Cognitive–Behavioral Model and Developing Realistic Beliefs

Goals and Interventions

Goals:
- Develop an understanding of CBT and its role in self-esteem.
- Provide an opportunity for group members to identify automatic thoughts related to their self-images.

Interventions:

- Provide education regarding CBT.
- Demonstrate cognitive–behavioral principles using specific examples from the group.
- Assist group members in identifying automatic thoughts using experiential activity (automatic thought game).
- Assign homework: Thought log.

Weekly review. The second session begins with a thorough review of the homework. This provides an opportunity for the group to discuss the historical events that members believe may have contributed to their low self-esteem. Often, group members are surprised at the similarities in experiences. Beginning the session this way is very important for several reasons. First, the group will realize that the homework is critical to the session and that a significant amount of discussion will be focused around the previous week's assignment. If homework is not done, the group cannot proceed. And, of course, practice (working between sessions) is essential to change. This point should be emphasized early on and will most likely require repetition throughout. If, despite efforts at motivation, group members did not complete their homework, it is recommended that this become a focus of the group. For instance, part of the session will then be spent discussing what the obstacles were that got in the way of completing the homework. Advantages and disadvantages of doing homework can be discussed. Finally, homework should be completed in session before moving on to the next topic. In some cases, it may be helpful to collect homework, provide written feedback, and then return it to the girls. Again, this reinforces the importance of their between-group practice.

Focus. Session 2 focuses on the relationship between thoughts, feelings, and behaviors. Group members are taught basic CBT. In a very straightforward way, the counselor explains that individuals' reactions (feelings and actions) to events or situations are a result of their interpretation of the situation (thoughts). Education regarding the method of change based on a cognitive–behavioral model is provided as well. Many examples should be provided and discussed until there is a sense that the group has a general understanding of the model. At first, the most basic examples (such as reactions to a traffic jam or fire alarm) typically are effective ways to introduce the idea that thoughts mediate emotional and behavioral reactions. Examples involving self-esteem, such as situations that result in feelings of inferiority, can be provided as well. For instance, most girls can relate to the situation in which they have called or e-mailed a friend but received no timely response. They may describe feeling hurt, rejected, or angry. They believe they are feeling rejected because their friend did not reply. However, the group leader will explain that the feelings of anger and hurt are actually a result of the girl's thoughts about what happened. In this case, if the girl thinks that her friend is ignoring her and doesn't like her anymore, she may feel hurt. But, if she were to assume that her friend did not get the message or that there is some other explanation, she might not feel upset at all.

In addition to providing prepared examples, it is helpful to have a few group members provide their own personal examples of situations in which they recently felt upset. For instance, one group member described how she had tried out for the school play. She was not selected for the starring role and felt extremely upset. She reported that she felt sad, hopeless, and then decided not to be in the play at all (even though she did earn a fairly substantial supporting role). With discussion, she was able to identify her thoughts about not being chosen for the starring role. To this adolescent, it meant she was "no good" and "a failure." The group suggested that perhaps it was her thoughts about not getting the role that were causing her to feel so sad, not the situation per se. Other ways of thinking about this situation were generated by members. One alternative suggested was to think, "This is perfect. Now, I can be in the play, but I won't have too many lines to learn." Another group member suggested that she might have the thought, "Oh, good, I really don't want to be in the play anyway; I was just doing it because my parents wanted me to." The goal is to help the girls see that their various reactions to different situations will depend on their thoughts. In this example, through the group discussion, this adolescent recognized that her extreme, negative thinking was the problem, not the fact that she didn't get the role she wanted. Further, if she could look at it another way, she might feel better. When group members give one another helpful feedback and support, they are empowered to generate their own future solutions as well.

The activity included during this session is designed to facilitate practice with identifying automatic thoughts and self-talk in general. The leader explains that automatic thoughts are the running internal dialogue that each of us has throughout the day. These thoughts are spontaneous, habitual, influential, and problematic when they are distorted, negative, and self-critical. Members learn that if they are interested in making changes in the way they feel and behave, it is important for them to become aware of their automatic thoughts. To illustrate this idea, the leader has group members play the "automatic thought game." In this activity, each member takes a turn standing in the center of the group with a word or phrase taped to her back. The group member in the center does not know what is written on the paper. As she turns around so that all other members can see the writing, the rest of the group states their automatic thoughts. The written prompts usually include issues or events related to self-esteem in some way such as "giving a presentation," "wearing a bathing suit," or "going to a party." Each girl in the group will take a turn in the center. The girls usually have fun trying to "guess" what the word or phrase is while they practice identifying their automatic thoughts.

Homework. Group members are asked to complete at least one thought log during the week. To complete the form, members pick an event or situation in which they feel low in self-esteem. They then record the upsetting event while identifying and sorting out their thoughts, feelings, and behaviors. They will be prompted to provide an alternative, perhaps more realistic or less negative, thought as well. For girls who have access to electronic devices, it may be helpful to suggest that the self-monitoring be done on palm pilots. This is very convenient for the girls who have access to these and is often less cumbersome and less noticeable than monitoring sheets. Keeping thought logs will be a consistent part of the groups' homework throughout.

Thought Log:
- Record Upsetting Event.
- Identify Thoughts,
- Feelings, and
- Actions.
- Challenge negative thoughts.

Session 3: Challenging the Negative and Building the Positive

Goals and Interventions

Goals:
- Promote understanding of cognitive distortions and impact on self-esteem.
- Assist clients with recognition of distorted, negative thinking.
- Begin to challenge/modify distorted thoughts.

Interventions:
- Provide education regarding distorted thinking.
- Review list of cognitive distortions.
- Discuss specific examples of cognitive distortion with each group member.
- Assign homework: Affirmation box.

Weekly review. Session 3 begins with a review of thought logs. This may be a week in which the homework review requires more time than other sessions because it is important to provide members with the opportunity to share their thought logs. The group can work together to differentiate thoughts from feelings and generate possible alternative perspectives. Many will have difficulty identifying thoughts, recognizing emotions, and then distinguishing feelings from thoughts. The counselor will need to provide feedback, education, and facilitate in-session practice of this skill. This process should be reinforced throughout the entire group protocol.

Focus. During the third session, group members will begin to challenge some of their automatic self-talk. They will be educated about the ways that people can distort their thinking and how that can affect their self-esteem. A portion of the session will focus on cognitive distortions and recognition of group members' tendencies for distorted thinking. Part of the session may be spent reviewing a list of distortions (Burns, 1993) and discussing how this kind of negative thinking perpetuates their negative self-images.

Examples of Cognitive Distortions:
- *All-or-Nothing Thinking*: You look at things in absolute, black-and-white categories.
- *Overgeneralization*: You view a negative event as a never-ending pattern of defeat.
- *Mental Filter*: You dwell on the negatives and ignore the positives.
- *Discounting the Positives*: You insist that your positive qualities and accomplishments don't count.
- *Jumping to Conclusions*: You assume things are bad without any evidence.
- *Mind-reading:* You assume that people are reacting negatively to you.
- *Fortune-telling:* You predict that things will turn out badly.
- *Magnification/Minimization*: You blow things way out of proportion or shrink their importance.
- *Should Statements*: You criticize yourself or others with "shoulds," "shouldn'ts," "musts," and "oughts."
- *Labeling*: Instead of saying "I made a mistake," you tell yourself "I'm a jerk" or "I'm a loser."
- *Blame*: You blame yourself for things you were not responsible for, or you blame others and overlook ways that you may have contributed to a problem.

The group leader may have group members take turns reading the definitions. It is helpful to ask several group members to choose one cognitive distortion and describe a recent situation in which they felt they had engaged in the distortion. Such personal examples allow for more meaningful processing and learning. For instance, one adolescent described a situation in which her teacher had called her to the front of the class and asked if she could stay late to meet with her that day after school. The client became extremely anxious, couldn't eat lunch, and was in tears by the end of the day. She was convinced that her teacher wanted to meet with her to talk about how her performance in class had been slipping. She had assumed that the teacher was unhappy with her. When she finally spoke with her teacher, she learned that the teacher wanted to ask her to join the school newspaper because she was such a talented writer. The client had not even considered that the teacher might have something positive to discuss. Because of her distorted, negative focus, she spent her day worrying.

Challenging negative thoughts takes practice. Group leaders will assist members in developing ways to challenge their automatic thoughts and to consider that there might be another perspective. Group leaders may provide some specific suggestions in this regard. It is helpful to give the girls a set of questions such as these to ask themselves when they are beginning to recognize and challenge their self-talk: "Is there another way of thinking about this?" "What is the evidence to support this thought?" "How is this thought helping/hurting me?" "What would my friend say to me now?" "Even if this were true, what are the worst and best things that can happen?" "Are my thoughts extreme, rational, self-critical?"

As the girls begin to recognize their tendency for negative thinking, they will practice challenging their negative self-talk. At the same time, they will begin to substitute more positive and realistic thoughts for the negative. Often, girls have difficulty incorporating the positive. It should be emphasized, however, that it is not enough to challenge the irrational thought. To build self-esteem, increasing the frequency and intensity of positive thinking is just as important as eliminating the negative thoughts and attitudes. During group wrap-up, ask each girl to state a positive about herself.

Homework. For homework, in addition to completing one thought log, group members will create an "affirmation box" to decorate and bring to the next session. This box provides a special place for the girls to collect thoughts and images related to positive aspects of themselves that can assist them in challenging some of their negative self-talk. These positive aspects can include their personality, things they like to do, accomplishments, and so forth.

Session 4: Defining Self-Worth
Goals and Interventions

Goals:
- Increase group members' understanding of their own self-worth.
- Evaluate group members' current system for measuring worth.

Interventions:
- Provide education regarding self-worth (definition, link between worth and self-esteem, introduce idea of unconditional self-worth).
- Discuss "what makes a person worthy."
- Develop and review members' lists of criteria for how worth is measured.
- Assign homework: Test validity of self-worth evaluation system.

Weekly review. During the first portion of Session 4, group members share their affirmation boxes. They can discuss what it was like to spend time thinking about themselves in a positive way. They can share some of the content of the box and discuss how it feels to talk about their positives. It is helpful and fun for the girls to write messages to one another that can be included in their boxes. These messages can be read later at home. The idea is for the girls to keep the box in a place where they review it, add to it, and reflect on the positives about themselves. Often, this becomes a very helpful coping tool during difficult times.

Focus. As discussed during Session 1, self-worth is a critical element to self-esteem. A sense of being worthy and valuable plays a significant role in one's overall sense of identity. It is also a dimension of overall wellness and life satisfaction (Myers & Sweeney, 2005). Within that context, Session 4 focuses on the groups' ideas about what makes a person worthy and how that affects her self-esteem. The group leader may begin by asking the following questions: "What makes a person worthy?" "Is it a person's achievements that make her worthy?" "Is it the fact that she doesn't make mistakes?" "Is it that everyone likes her?" "Is it that she looks a certain way?" After a discussion on the general meaning of worth, each member creates her own list of criteria for being worthy. As part of the activity, members are asked about the rules they have created regarding what they believe it takes for them to be a worthwhile person. These lists are shared with the group. Typically, there is a difference in the general idea about what makes a person worthy and each individual's idea about the criteria for her own self-worth. Thus, most girls will recognize that all humans have worth and that it is not a matter of proving it or earning it. When they judge themselves, however, they are much less forgiving. For example, one girl stated that in order to be "good enough" she must be an excellent student, earning *As* only. She must be nice to everyone all the time. She must weigh a certain amount and follow her eating and exercise plan carefully. She must never waste time and always be productive.

The group spends the rest of the session evaluating these lists and considering the problems associated with this kind of thinking. Often, they quickly recognize that it is impossible to ever feel worthy or good enough if it is measured in this way. One client stated, "because even if you do manage to follow all those rules, you still have to worry about messing up and losing it all." Members also begin to recognize that while they are judging themselves according to their rules, they also become reliant on the judgments of others. When they are overly concerned with pleasing others, they lose the ability to stay connected to what they truly think and feel, which negatively affects their overall self-esteem.

Homework. In addition to thought logs, group members are asked to choose one item from their list of criteria for being worthy. They will then design a plan (or behavioral experiment) for evaluating the validity of the statement. For example, an adolescent girl might believe that in order to be worthy she must be liked by everyone. For this homework assignment, she will need to check out the accuracy of this statement by talking to others, observing various situations, and ultimately identifying situations in which this belief does or does not seem to be true. The group typically enjoys helping one another in creating ways to test out these beliefs.

Session 5: Acceptance: Acknowledging Strengths and Weaknesses
Goals and Interventions

Goals:
- Promote self-acceptance and cultural identity.
- Identify perceived personal strengths and weaknesses.

Interventions:
- Focus discussion on acceptance of both achievements and mistakes.
- Elicit specific examples of perceived mistakes and weaknesses from group members.
- Assist group members with restating weaknesses in less judgmental way.
- Assign homework: Monitor mistakes and practice finding the positive.

Weekly review. Session 5 begins with a review of the experiments from the previous session. Participants often are anxious to learn the outcome for each of their peers. Frequently, group members will describe taking risks with this assignment. For example, one group member described how she decided that she was not going to study all night for her weekly math test. She studied for a few hours, went to bed, and took the test. She did not get 100% (her typical score) but still got an A. She was a little anxious but overall was pleased with challenging her belief that she must be perfect (make perfect grades in school) to be worthy. She was surprised to see that her teacher, her parents, and especially her friends didn't really even seem to notice.

Focus. Self-acceptance, the willingness to experience and recognize all aspects of oneself, is the focus of Session 5. The session focuses on accepting the reality of each group member's situation. The counselor begins the discussion by pointing out how people with low self-esteem often have difficulties describing themselves accurately. They tend to focus too much on weaknesses and mistakes, ignore strengths and successes, and strive for perfection. During the group activity, the girls will identify strengths and weaknesses in themselves. Equal time will be given to both. Thus, the group will spend a good deal of time acknowledging their mistakes and weaknesses and considering them in a new, less judgmental way. The goal is not to dwell on the negative but to recognize that there may be positives associated with a weakness. Overall, the discussion supports the idea that weaknesses are not something to be feared but to be accepted.

Group members will complete an activity in which they describe themselves in terms of perceived positives and negatives. Additionally, they are asked to restate the weaknesses and to look for strengths within the weakness. For example, one group member described hating herself because of her shyness. She viewed herself as boring, no fun, stupid, and invisible. She stated that she alternates from trying to pretend she's outgoing (forcing herself to "act" more social) to isolating herself and avoiding social situations altogether. During this activity, the group was able to help her see that maybe there are some advantages to being shy and quiet. Maybe she is a really good listener. Although she doesn't have large numbers of acquaintances, she may have several very close friends. It was also suggested that maybe there was a gentler, less judgmental way of thinking about her shyness. Instead of thinking "I'm so shy, stupid, and boring," she might say to herself something like "Yes, it's true that I'm quiet around new people and I can get uncomfortable in certain situations, but I can open up with people I trust and know well." When she can learn to reframe her thoughts in a less judgmental way, she can begin to accept all aspects of herself.

Part of this process of identifying strengths might include a focus on ways to incorporate a girl's unique cultural identity into her overall self-concept. If she lacks a connection with her cultural community or denigrates aspects of her cultural self, she may need to develop a better appreciation for her cultural heritage and learn to view it as a coping resource. A girl may benefit from asking family members about her cultural traditions, or from studying the literature, music, and family history that connects her to her larger cultural community (Dixon Rayle, Chee, & Sand, 2006). She may want to explore ways in which she can develop stronger connections with extended and immediate kinship networks, which can serve as a source of support (Lee, 2005).

Homework. In addition to thought logs, group members will monitor mistakes made during the week. As part of this assignment, they will practice describing the mistake in a realistic, nonjudgmental way. They will evaluate whether the mistake represents an overall personal weakness and, if so, attempt to identify the strengths within the weakness. Behavioral experiments may be utilized as well. For example, group members may be asked to carefully observe people throughout the week to see how frequently others make mistakes. Further, they may be assigned to deliberately make a mistake and observe others' reactions.

Session 6: Behaviors That Enhance Self-Esteem: Purpose and Reward

Goals and Interventions

Goals:
- Understand the role of behavior in the maintenance of low self-esteem.
- Understand the role of behavior in building self-esteem.
- Recognize specific behaviors to be modified or developed.

Interventions:
- Focus discussion on identification of behaviors that lower self-esteem and on those that may increase self-esteem.
- Elicit specific examples of self-defeating and self-enhancing behaviors from group.
- Assign homework: Pleasurable/rewarding behavioral experiment.

Weekly review. During the homework review, the group will discuss the behavioral experiments and self-monitoring. Group members are frequently surprised to learn how common mistakes are and how little attention others pay to their mistakes.

Focus. The focus of Session 6 shifts from cognitions to behaviors. The counselor explains that decreasing negative behaviors and increasing positive behaviors is another important element of self-esteem building, as these activities can enhance girls' confidence in their ability to effectively manage new tasks and situations. Again, it is helpful to provide specific examples. For instance, the counselor may describe to the group how some individuals with low self-esteem may withdraw from others. Because of their sense of inferiority, they may believe that others would not be interested in spending time with them, so they avoid social situations. Then, as a result of the avoidance, they may have fewer friends and fewer invitations. This then leads to negative and critical thoughts such as, "I'm a complete loser. I don't have any friends," which only reinforces their reason for withdrawing. In this example, the isolation and withdrawal perpetuate the negative thinking, decrease the likelihood of developing relationships, and make it difficult to develop a new perspective. Other examples of behaviors that can contribute to low self-esteem include people pleasing, perfectionism, self-destructive behaviors, and self-punishing behaviors.

The group discussion should also focus on positive behaviors that could enhance self-esteem. The counselor may point out how individuals with low self-esteem tend to neglect pleasurable or rewarding activities. For example, when self-esteem is impaired, the thoughts "I don't deserve . . . to take a break . . . to take guitar lessons . . . to try out for basketball" are not uncommon. During the group activity, the counselor will ask each group member to identify at least one negative behavior that she feels might be self-defeating (such as drinking, dieting, gossiping) and that she would like to eliminate. Members will then identify one positive behavior that they believe could be rewarding but that they have avoided because of their low self-esteem (such as attending a social event, joining a club, engaging in a new hobby). They will then predict the degree of satisfaction they would expect to feel from engaging in both the positive and negative activities.

Homework. In addition to the thought logs, group members will follow through with their pleasurable/rewarding activity and complete the associated monitoring form. If they engage in their identified negative behavior during the week, they will record that as well.

Pleasurable Activities Monitoring Form:
- Activity Planned:
- Alone or with others?
- Predicted satisfaction rating (0–100%)
- Actual satisfaction rating (0–100%)
- What I learned from this activity:

Session 7: Relationships and Low Self-Esteem

Goals and Interventions

Goals:
- Develop an understanding of the impact of low self-esteem on relationships.
- Identify specific interpersonal problems and possible solutions.

Interventions:
- Focus discussion on relationships and self-esteem using question/answer activity.
- Educate group regarding common interpersonal problems associated with low self-esteem, including assertiveness problems, dependency, and competitiveness.
- Assign homework: Develop interpersonal experiment for addressing specific relationship problems.

Weekly review. Group members share stories about their pleasurable activities during the week. Throughout the review, it is a good idea to remind each member of her initial thoughts and reasons for not engaging in the particular activity. This provides an opportunity to compare those thoughts to her current beliefs, after the actual experience. For instance, individuals frequently state that their reason for avoiding certain activities stems from thoughts like, "Why bother, I'm not going to be good at it anyway." This kind of thinking keeps them from trying out new things and helps maintain the idea that they are unworthy, inferior, and undeserving. On one occasion, a group member had expressed interest in photography but felt that she shouldn't bother with it because she wasn't very talented. With some support from the group, she found a photography class for beginners and attended. She had predicted that she would be very anxious and uncomfortable with the class full of strangers and embarrassed about her lack of knowledge. After attending the class, this member returned to Session 7 group feeling very surprised and excited about the nice people she met. She stated that she felt proud of herself for trying something new. She did admit to feeling very nervous for the first 15 minutes, but she became more and more relaxed and distracted with the lecture. When reminded of her initial thought, "Why should I go? I won't be any good," she stated, "Well, after going, I realized that no one else was really any good either, and it didn't matter."

Focus. Session 7 includes a general discussion about the girls' social functioning including friendships, dating, and family. The leader assists group members in exploring the connection between their low self-esteem and relationship problems. Often, it is useful to ask more specific questions like these that may advance the discussion:

"Do you have problems asserting yourself or standing up for yourself?"
"Do you put others first most of the time?"
"What is it like to speak up for yourself, even when you know others might not like it?"
"How do you handle rejection?"
"Do you approach or avoid new relationships?"
"Do you constantly question your current relationships?"

"Do you 'test' the commitment of those with whom you do have relationships?"
"How do you respond to compliments?"

For the group activity, these and other questions can be written on a piece of paper and placed in a box. Each group member will take a turn drawing a question from the box and answering. During the discussion, girls can consider the importance of relationships in their lives and explore the ways in which being overly concerned with trying to please others might lead to decreases in their own self-esteem. They can also discuss ways in which they can develop healthy relationships that allow them the freedom to be themselves. Following the discussion, each girl is asked to think about one area of difficulty in particular that she believes is negatively affecting her relationships. In session, members complete an activity in which they complete a Relationships and Self-Esteem Planning Form. For example, one group member believed that if she were to ask for what she wanted, others would refuse and think less of her. As a result, she had a very hard time giving her opinion with friends or saying "no" to them. During this exercise, she decided to tell her girlfriends that she would like to make the plans for the weekend (decide what movie to see, what time, and so on) and that she would not be the driver, as she usually was. Although the plan caused her a good deal of anxiety, this member realized that if she continued with her current lack of assertiveness, she would always feel inferior and dissatisfied. So, she decided that the plan would be worth trying.

Relationships and Self-Esteem Planning Form:
- Describe a current relational problem that might be linked to low self-esteem and that you would like to change.
- Develop a plan for addressing the problem (short-term, long-term goals).
- What is the first step needed for making a change?
- What are the obstacles that might get in the way of making this change? How will you manage these obstacles?

Homework. In addition to the thought logs, group members are asked to follow through with their interpersonal experiments. Although these trials typically go very well, every once in a while the experiment backfires. For example, one girl had developed a plan to ask her boyfriend to come to a family party rather than playing basketball with his friends on Saturday (as he always did). The group member had been feeling like the relationship was not well balanced and that she had consistently been making most of the compromises. Unfortunately, the boyfriend refused, got angry, and did not understand her perspective. Although this was not the intended outcome, the group was very helpful in providing support and feedback. They decided that she had done the right thing for herself. They were able to help her to see that "sometimes you have to stand up for yourself even if someone else doesn't like it." They also discussed the idea that sometimes, because of low self-esteem, people stay in relationships that are not healthy or well balanced.

Because the next session is the final group meeting, members are asked to identify changes that they have made since beginning the group. This can be done in the form of a collage, drawing, or some artwork that represents their progress.

Session 8: Group Conclusion

Goals and Interventions

Goals:
- Terminate group.
- Motivate group members to continue to develop self-esteem.

Interventions:
- Review progress with each group member.
- Facilitate peer feedback regarding progress.
- Emphasize need for continued work on self-esteem building skills.
- Present and describe coping cards.

Weekly review. Group begins with members sharing their interpersonal experiments. Because this is the last session, the leader may choose to go over only one or two, allowing adequate time to conclude the group.

Focus. The majority of group time will be spent on wrapping-up, with each member sharing her before/after project and describing the changes she has made. Members should have an opportunity to provide feedback to one another regarding positive changes that they have observed in their peers. The group leader will review the topics covered throughout the group and highlight the importance of continued focus and practice. It should be explained that the group has just touched upon each of these important areas and that to continue to improve self-esteem, ongoing application and practice is necessary. The group leader will present sample "coping cards" (see Appendix B) to assist the girls with practicing their self-esteem building skills. Group members, if interested, can expand on the coping cards, creating their own, personalized cards. Often, group members keep the cards with them as a reference and reminder during difficult situations. Finally, each group member completes a brief (3 or 4 questions) survey. Counselors may develop their own set of questions, depending on the context of the group. This provides useful feedback for the group leader and gives group members a chance to identify the major take-home messages from their experience. Sample items for the final session survey include the following: (a) Briefly summarize the main things you have gained from this group; (b) List five things you will take away and apply in your life; (c) Identify one thing you would like to share with a friend about self-esteem; and (d) List any suggestions for future groups.

Conclusion

This group protocol is intended to guide counselors in their important work with adolescent girls as they face developmental challenges and changes. Although the group is meant to be a foundation or starting point for building self-esteem, many girls do experience significant improvement during the 8-week time period. Often, they make changes in how they spend their time. They begin to question belief systems and self-imposed rules. Some even begin to modify relationships. In addition, they develop meaningful relationships with one another. In this way, the group process adds to the learning experience and serves as a built-in opportunity for behavioral and interpersonal experiments.

In addition to learning the skills necessary for positive self-esteem, the group provides a natural learning environment for girls to establish connections with others, to speak authentically about their thoughts and feelings, and to practice coping with life demands in more autonomous ways.

Activities for Further Exploration

1. Complete a thought log (as described in this chapter) for 24 hours. What did you learn about how your thoughts affect your feelings and reactions? What practical strategies did you use in recording your thoughts that you might be able to share with your clients?
2. Complete the "Mistake Monitoring" activity described in this chapter. Describe a recent mistake you made, then practice describing it in a more compassionate, less judgmental way. Attempt to identify strengths within any perceived weaknesses. What are your reactions to this activity?
3. Complete the relationship activity described in Session 7. How easy or difficult is it to formulate a plan and to identify obstacles that might get in your way of implementing the plan? How might this be useful for clients?
4. Review the Coping Cards in Appendix B. How might you use these in your own life or with particular client concerns? Create an original coping card tailored to your individual needs at this time.

Suggested Readings

Resources for the Counselor

Beck, A., Freeman, A., Davis, D., & Associates. (2003). *Cognitive therapy of personality disorders* (2nd ed.). New York: Guilford Press.

Beck, J. (1995). *Cognitive therapy: Basics and beyond.* New York: Guilford Press.

Fennell, M. (1997). Cognitive therapy in the treatment of low self-esteem. *Advances in Psychiatric Treatment, 4,* 296–304.

Fennell, M. (1998). Low self-esteem. In N. Tarrier, A. Wells, & G. Haddock (Eds.), *Cognitive-behavioral therapy for complex cases: An advanced guidebook for the practitioner.* Chichester, England: Wiley.

Fennell, M. (2004). Low self-esteem. In J. Bennett-Levy, G. Butler, M. Fennell, A. Hackmann, M. Mueller, & D. Westbrook (Eds.), *The Oxford guide to behavioral experiments in cognitive therapy.* Oxford, England: Oxford University Press.

Young, J, Klosko, J., & Weishaar, M. (2003). *Schema therapy: A practitioners' guide.* New York: Guilford Press.

Resources for the Client

Burns, D. (1989). *The feeling good handbook.* New York: William Morrow.

Burns, D. (1993). *10 days to self-esteem.* New York: William Morrow.

Fennell, M. (2006). *Overcoming low self-esteem: A self-help guide using cognitive behavioral techniques.* London: Robinson.

Greenberger, K., & Padesky, C. (1995). *Mind over mood: A cognitive therapy treatment manual for clients.* New York: Guilford Press.

Young, J., & Klosko, J. (1993). *Reinventing your life: How to break free from negative life patterns.* New York: Dutton.

Additional Resources

http://www.girlsinc.org/
Girls Incorporated is a national nonprofit youth organization dedicated to inspiring all girls to be strong, smart, and bold. The site provides resources and tips for adults and girls.

http://www.newmoon.org/
Edited by and for girls ages 8 to 14, *New Moon* is an international, multicultural magazine that connects girls so they can express themselves and communicate with other girls around the world.

http://www.academic.org/
The Women's College Coalition provides information regarding parental influence on girls' involvement in science and math and has tips for parents on encouraging their daughters to succeed academically.

http://www.dadsanddaughters.org/
Dads and Daughters is an organization dedicated to maximizing the power and potential of father–daughter relationships.

http://www.girlscouts.org/
Girl Scouts of the USA is the world's preeminent organization dedicated solely to providing girls with an accepting and nurturing environment in which they can build character and skills for success in the real world.

http://girlstart.org/
Girlstart, a nonprofit organization created to empower girls to excel in math, science, and technology, has quickly established itself as a best-

case practices leader in empowering, educating, and motivating girls to enjoy and become more proficient in math, science, and technology.
http://www.glsen.org/
The Gay, Lesbian & Straight Education Network strives to assure that each member of every school community is valued and respected regardless of sexual orientation or gender identity/expression.
http://www.self-esteem-nase.org/
The purpose of the National Association for Self-Esteem is to fully integrate self-esteem into the fabric of American society so that every individual, no matter what his or her age or background, experiences personal worth and happiness.
http://www.teenvoices.com/
This is the Web site for the magazine *Teen Voices,* which is about teen women being themselves. *Teen Voices* challenges the mainstream media's harmful images of girls and women by providing an intelligent alternative.
http://www.youthventure.org/
Youth Venture helps to empower young people ages 12–20 by providing all the tools necessary to create civic-minded organizations, clubs or businesses.

References

Beck, A. (1995). *Cognitive therapy: Basics and beyond.* New York: Guilford Press.

Beck, A. T., Freeman, A., Davis, D., & Associates. (2003). *Cognitive therapy of personality disorders* (2nd ed.). New York: Guilford Press.

Biro, F. M., Striegel-Moore, R. H., Franko, D. L., Padgett, J., & Bean, J. A. (2006). Self-esteem in adolescent females. *Journal of Adolescent Health, 39,* 501–507.

Branden, N. (1997). *The six pillars of self-esteem.* New York: Bantam Books.

Bruch, H. (1973). *Eating disorders: Obesity, anorexia nervosa and the person within.* New York: Basic Books.

Burns, D. (1993). *Ten days to self-esteem: The leaders' manual.* New York: Quill Morrow.

Cervera, S., Lahortiga, F., Martinez-Gonzalez, M., Gual, P., Irala-Estevez, J., & Alonso, Y. (2003). Neuroticism and low self-esteem as risk factors for incident eating disorders in a prospective cohort study. *International Journal of Eating Disorders, 33,* 271–280.

Constantine, M. G., Greer, T. W., & Kindaichi, M. M. (2003). Theoretical and cultural considerations in counseling women of color. In M. Kopala & M. A. Keitel (Eds.), *Handbook of counseling women* (pp. 40–52). Thousand Oaks, CA: Sage.

Dixon Rayle, A., Chee, C., & Sand, J. (2006). Honoring their way: Counseling American Indian women. *Journal of Multicultural Counseling and Development, 34,* 66–79.

Eccles, J., Barber, B., Jozefowicz, D., Malenchuk, O., & Vida, M. (1999). Self-evaluations of competence, task value, and self-esteem. In N. G. Johnson, M. C. Roberts, & J. Worell (Eds.), *Beyond appearance, a new look at adolescent girls* (pp. 53–84). Washington, DC: American Psychological Association.

Fairburn, C. (1981). A cognitive behavioral approach to the management of bulimia. *Psychological Medicine, 11,* 707–711.

Fennell, M. (1998). Low self-esteem. In N. Tarrier, A. Wells, & G. Haddock (Eds.), *Treating complex cases: The cognitive behavior therapy approach.* Chichester, England: Wiley.

Fennell, M., & Jenkins, H. (2004). Low self-esteem. In J. Bennett-Levy, G. Butler, M. Fennell, A. Hackman, M. Mueller, & D. Westbrook (Eds.), *Oxford guide to behavioral experiments in cognitive theory* (pp. 413–430). New York: Oxford University Press.

Ghaderi, A., & Scott, B. (2001). Prevalence, incidence and prospective risk factors for eating disorders. *Acta Psychiatrica Scandinavica, 104,* 122–130.

Jaffee, L., & Lutter, J. M. (1995). Adolescent girls: Factors influencing low and high body image. *Melpomene Journal, 14,* 14–22.

Lee, C. (2005). Ethnicity and wellness. In J. E. Myers & T. J. Sweeney (Eds.), *Counseling for wellness: Theory, research, and practice* (pp. 105–116). Alexandria, VA: American Counseling Association.

Malanchuk, O., & Eccles, J. S. (2006). Self-esteem. In J. Worell & C. D. Goodheart (Eds.), *Handbook of girls' and women's psychological health* (pp. 149–156). New York: Oxford University Press.

Michael, A., & Eccles, J. S. (2004). When coming of age means coming undone: Links between puberty and psychosocial adjustment among European American and African American girls. In C. Hayward (Ed.), *Gender differences at puberty* (pp. 277–307). New York: Cambridge University Press.

Myers, J. E., & Sweeney, T. J. (Eds.). (2005). *Counseling for wellness: Theory, research, and practice.* Alexandria, VA: American Counseling Association.

Office of National Drug Control Policy. (2006). *Girls and drugs.* Retrieved July 30, 2007, from www.mediacampaign.org/pdf/girls_and_drugs.pdf

Tolman, D. L., & Brown, L. M. (2001). Adolescent girls' voices: Resonating resistance in body and soul. In R. K. Unger (Ed.), *Handbook of the psychology of women and gender* (pp. 133–155). New York: Wiley.

Young, J., Klosko, J., & Weishaar, M. (2003). *Schema therapy: a practitioner's guide.* New York: Guilford Press.

Appendix A
Self-Esteem Timeline

Think about events in your life that may have contributed to your current self-image. Try to identify events that have both helped and hindered the development of your self-esteem. List all events that *you* believe are important.

Example:

Age 5	Age 7	Age 10
Won art contest in kindergarten. Felt very proud of myself. Helped self-esteem	Needed glasses. Kids teased me. Hurt self-esteem	Did not make the soccer team. All my friends did. Hurt self-esteem

                       *   *

Appendix B
Sample Coping Cards

Coping Card 1

Situation: Automatic Thought: I'm so fat, stupid, etc.
Coping response: Ask myself . . .
 Is my thinking extreme?
 What's the evidence that this is true?
 Is there another way of thinking about this?
 What would a friend say to me right now?

Coping Card 2

Situation: When I am feeling low, insecure, lacking self-esteem . . .
Coping response:
 Call _____ (list of support people).
 Practice positive self-talk/affirm self.
 Remember self-worth is unconditional.
 Review my meaning of worth.
 Use affirmation jar/box.

Coping Card 3

Situation: Feeling uncomfortable in social situations
Coping response:
 Identify my feelings and needs.
 Ask myself
  Do I need to assert myself?
  Do I need to set a limit?
  Am I just trying to please everyone?
  Am I thinking negatively about myself?
 Stop comparing myself to others.

Coping Card 4

Situation: Thoughts of being ineffective, unproductive, worthless, etc. . . . .
Coping response:
 Plan a daily fun activity.
 Plan a daily mastery activity.
 Ask myself . . . Am I spending my time in a way that is rewarding?

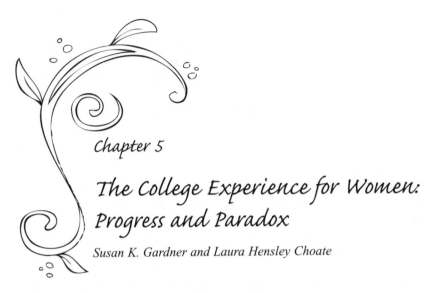

Chapter 5

The College Experience for Women: Progress and Paradox

Susan K. Gardner and Laura Hensley Choate

> *I read today on the Internet that women now outnumber men on college campuses.*
> *I guess this a good year to start college in terms of finding friends, but maybe not so*
> *much in terms of finding a boyfriend. Oh well, I am still excited to begin my college*
> *experience and look forward to the challenges and excitement that lie ahead of me.*
> *Of course I have worries—Will I do well in my classes? Will I meet people like me?*
> *Will I fit in? I guess we'll just wait and see, but anyway, here I am world!*
> —College Girl 08 Blog Entry, September 1, 2006

An interesting shift in the past several years is reflected in these newspaper headlines: "Men Dwindling on College Campuses" (Durhams, 2000), "Where Are the Boys?" (Hodges, 2005), and "College Gender Gap Widens: 57% Are Women" (Marklein, 2005). For the first time in U.S. history, women outnumber men on college and university campuses. Also, for the first time, women have received more degrees than men in every degree category: associate through doctorate. Considering that men make up a larger percentage of the U.S. population (U.S. Census Bureau, 2000), the growing numbers of women in college and earning degrees has prompted many to ask, "Isn't this a sign of women's progress?" (Marklein, 2005).

Despite the increasing number of women on campuses and leaving with degrees, gender inequity still exists in higher education and, most certainly, in society. For example, today women earn 76 cents for each dollar a man earns in the United States (National Organization for Women, 2006), and on college and university campuses women comprise only 39% of all faculty members and less than 24% of tenured, full professors (National Center for Education Statistics, 2003), and only 21% of all college and university presidents (*The Chronicle of Higher Education*, 2005). Growing enrollment and degree attainment numbers may point to a changing culture and climate for women, but a gap remains between college women's achievement and status.

In the early 1980s, Hall and Sandler (1982, 1984) completed a series of reports on behalf of the Association of American Colleges and Universities on the status of women in U.S. colleges and universities, reporting on the "chilly climate" that existed for women. On the basis of a measure of many items, including being singled out for their gender in class, being treated differently by faculty because they are women, or observing discrimination of other women on the campus, Hall and Sandler demonstrated a distinctly different environment for women that hindered their intellectual and personal development. Many scholars have tested Hall and Sandler's hypothesis about the existence of the chilly climate for women in higher education, but the growing numbers of women in today's colleges and universities lead many to wonder if the climate is indeed changing for women.

A new generation of women is walking onto campuses each day. Referred to as the Millennial Generation by many scholars, this generation of students was born between 1982 and 2002 and has been characterized as made to feel special by the society that has reared them. These young women were sheltered by parents and society throughout their childhood and are confident, conventional in their politics, and team-oriented in their approach to work. They are high achieving but at the same time feel pressured to be successful (DeBard, 2004). Millennial women have been exposed to positive and strong images of women throughout their youth and development. DeBard commented, "Girls, for the first time in American history, wield tangible power in dictating popular culture, and they are confident consumers, secure in their opinions" (p. 27). In the same work, Broido (2004) remarked, "This generation holds attitudes about appropriate roles for women that are much more egalitarian than in earlier generations . . . as these women enter the university, however, they are likely to notice that women are less evident in the leadership of college campuses" (p. 78). Furthermore, the racial and ethnic demographics are changing. In 2002–2003, 67% of the degrees conferred among African Americans went to women, 63% to Native American women, 61% to Latina women, 58% of all degrees to Whites went to women, and 55% to Asian American women (National Center for Education Statistics, 2003). These demographics point to growth not only in enrollment among women but in degree attainment for women across all racial groups.

In this chapter we examine the current climate in higher education in relation to women. What issues do today's college women face, and how can counselors assist them in navigating these challenges? These questions are examined through the literature that exists about women in today's colleges and universities as well as through a composite of online diary, or blog, entries of actual college women across the United States. The hope is to paint a picture of both progress and challenge for these women as well as to ways to assist them through the issues they face.

The Current Status of U.S. College Women

Am I alone here? I often feel that way. Even though there must be 30,000 other students walking around this campus every day, I don't feel a connection with any of them. I feel like, if anything, I stick out like a sore thumb. I just feel lonely.

What is it about me that makes me so different from everyone else? I joined a sorority this year hoping to find some connection on this campus, but I even feel an outcast within this group of women who are supposed to be my sisters for life. I often feel left out of conversations, left out of plans to hang out, and just left out in general. This sucks. Maybe I should transfer.

—Band Chick 09 Blog Entry, November 12, 2006

More than 9.4 million women can be found on college and university campuses today, including 100,200 Native American women, 570,200 Asian American women, 1.27 million African American women, 962,700 Latina women, 6.24 million White women, and nearly 264,000 international women (National Center for Education Statistics, 2003). Women in higher education include older women, women with children, first generation women (i.e., women who are the first in their family to attend college), women who work full-time while pursuing their degrees, women with disabilities, and women of every size, shape, color, and creed. Furthermore, women participate in multiple forms of higher education, including community or technical colleges, private liberal arts institutions, regional institutions, research universities, tribal colleges, women's colleges, and historically Black colleges and universities, and they matriculate at the associate, bachelor's, master's, professional, or doctoral levels. We need to recognize the diversity within our institutions today and discuss and attend to issues of diversity among women. However, that topic is beyond the scope of this chapter; our discussion here focuses on women in the traditional 4-year college setting, within the "traditional" age group of 18–22 years, with the recognition that the diversity of women on college campuses today goes far beyond this segment of the population.

Women face many obstacles in today's higher education environment. The historical underpinnings that surround women's participation in U.S. colleges and universities—a history that summarily excluded women from higher education until the mid-1850s (Thelin, 2004)—have left lasting impressions on women's attainment and status in both the higher education environment and in society at large. As Jana Nidiffer (2003) aptly stated, "Higher education has become a national stage on which social attitudes about women and gender are dramatized" (p. 15). The social attitudes to which Nidiffer referred include challenges to the role of women in society and subsequently in education, sexual objectification of women, issues of safety, and enduring beliefs that women somehow are intellectually inferior to men. These attitudes play out in many ways that result in contradictions for today's college women. For example, while women earned more degrees than men in the past several years, women were still underpaid in relation to men. While women earned nearly 80% of the associate and bachelor's degrees in legal studies in 2003 (National Center for Education Statistics, 2003), every year 132,000 women reported being victims of rape or attempted rape (National Organization for Women, n.d.). And while nearly 6 times more women than men earned degrees in health professions in 2003 (National Center for Education Statistics, 2003), more than half of all college women were regularly dieting and engaging in unhealthy eating practices (Thombs, Rosenberg, Mahoney, & Daniel, 1996).

It is important for counselors to understand these experiences and to develop ways to assist college women with their complex academic and social experiences. In this chapter, we look first at an overview of college women's development, and then explore some of the most pressing contemporary issues college women face, including dating and relationships, sexual violence, and women's body image dissatisfaction.

Becoming a Woman: Development of Women in College

I got into a total fight in my poli sci class today. I feel really weird about it. It started with this class discussion we were having about women's rights and it somehow got onto the topic of abortion. I know what you're thinking—duh, Kim, of course this was going to get ugly. But how I was raised and my church have told me it is wrong. I guess you all know this—but where it got weird was when one of the other students in class started questioning me about other things—like what do I think about whose right it is to tell me to have sex or to use birth control or other things. Some of the questions I felt were totally out of line and none of her business, but I have to tell you, some of them have really made me think. Maybe I need to rethink some of this stuff. And in a way, that really scares me.

—AKO Lady Blog Entry, February 20, 2007

The literature regarding personal, interpersonal, and cognitive development of college students has a rich and diverse place in the research on higher education. However, it was not until the 1980s that literature regarding the developmental issues related to college women in particular was seen. The early studies used to guide counseling and student affairs programs on college and university campuses were often based on studies conducted with men (e.g., Chickering, McDowell, & Campagna, 1969; Erikson, 1980). Scholars such as Gilligan, Josselson, Belenky, Clinchy, Goldberger, and Tarule all have made considerable contributions to the understanding of the development experienced by women throughout the college years and beyond. The development that occurs throughout the college experience, or student development, is defined by Rodgers (1990) as the way "that a student grows, progresses, or increases his or her developmental capabilities as a result of enrollment in an institution of higher education" (p. 27). Student development theories, as they relate to college students, are generally divided into several different categories, including psychosocial theories, cognitive–structural theories, typology theories, and person-in-environment theories (Evans, Forney, & Guido-DiBrito, 1998). Our discussion focuses on women's development in terms of the psychosocial and cognitive theories and women's relationship to appropriate counseling and programmatic interventions.

Psychosocial Development in College Women

Women's development occurs quite differently from men's during the college experience and beyond. For example, the role of positive interpersonal relationships plays an integral role in the development of women (Evans et al., 1998). Ruthann Josselson's (1973) theory of identity development in women demonstrates the role of relationships in women's development, wherein women relate to one of four identity categories: Foreclosure, Identity Achievement, Moratorium, and Identity Diffusion. For example, Foreclosing women tend to be single-minded in their purposes in life and rarely question the messages they received from parents and from childhood, thereby never trying to disappoint their parents. These women are rarely pushed out of the security of this identity and show few signs of psychological growth, often relying on others to validate their identity. Identity Achievement women break from their childhood experiences to form individual identities that allow them to be open to new experiences and ideas in the world around them. Identity Achieving women feel pride in themselves rather than seeking others' approval but will often seek out their identity through their work rather than through relationships, as the Foreclosing women often do. As Evans et al. (1998) stated, "Identity Achievement women are forever becoming" (p. 60). Moratorium women exhibit instability and experimentation with their identities as they wrestle with the concept that multiple truths do exist in the world around them. This uncertain identity has been linked with overprotective mothers. Moratorium women often struggle to mold their identities in a form that is completely opposite from how they viewed their mothers' identities. These women, like Identity Achievers, seek validation and affirmation through others, but rarely through their parents, which may result in a continual feeling of guilt and uncertainty. Finally, Identity Diffusion women often have a difficult period of identity formation. Many of these women may abuse substances while they work toward understanding the world around them or may endlessly search for meaning and identity in life. Identity Diffusion women often lack control in their lives, rank lowest in ego development, have difficulty establishing relationships, and tend to make decisions based on external pressures rather than on internal drive and motivation. These women have an overall tendency to withdraw from situations and therefore may be difficult to assist through traditional counseling methods.

Identity development for college women has been shown to be important in several realms. For example, participation in college activities is related to identity achievement (Weston & Stein, 1977), and we already know that involvement and engagement in campus activities and organization is related to success and retention of college students (Astin,

1984; Tinto, 1993). Political and religious attitudes and beliefs as well as cognitive development have been shown to relate to identity status (Evans et al., 1998), demonstrating the need to nurture the development of women in all spheres of the campus environment.

Cognitive and Moral Development of College Women

Women's Ways of Knowing (Belenky, Clinchy, Goldberger, & Tarule, 1986) offered the world a new view of women's cognitive development. Unlike other cognitive development models and theories, Belenky et al. (1986) premised their model on the importance of the relationships women have with others. Five "epistemological perspectives from which women know and view the world" (p. 15) emerged from their model: silence, received knowledge, subjective knowledge, procedural knowledge, and constructed knowledge. Evans et al. (1998) described these perspectives:

- *Silence* "is characterized as mindless, voiceless, and obedient. Access to language is limited and silence represents powerlessness" (p. 147). Women in this perspective are subject to the control and whims of others and are often younger, less educated, and from less affluent backgrounds.
- *Received knowledge* "consists of listening to others, and truth resides in others, not in the self" (p. 148). Women in this perspective lack self-confidence and look to others for understanding the world and for direction from authority figures around them.
- *Subjective knowledge* is a perspective in which "truth is now seen as residing in the self. One's own inner knowledge is considered superior to the knowledge of others" (p. 148). Women in this perspective often are seeking out themselves, which may stem from a disappointment in their youth by a male adult or role model.
- *Procedural knowledge* "involves learning and applying objective procedures for receiving and conveying knowledge"(p. 149). Procedural knowledge can be divided into separate knowing, such as critical thinking, listening to reason, and self-extrication from decision making and thought creation, and connected knowing, in which knowledge is thought to be produced from personal experience instead of from external authority figures (p. 149).
- *Constructed knowledge* "involves the integration of subjective and objective knowledge, with both feeling and thought present in ways of knowing"(p. 149). Women who are constructed knowers are generally described as "articulate, reflective, caring, self-aware, concerned with separation and connection, engaged in a struggle to balance the extremes in their lives, and fighting to find their own voices" (pp. 149–150).

Understanding how college women think and view the world is important for working with them, counseling them, and understanding the developmental issues they may be facing. Class discussions, interactions with peers and mentors, and formal interactions in counseling situations should all be structured to facilitate growth in women's cognitive development and to challenge these women to think about the world in multiple ways and through multiple lenses.

Counseling Interventions and Campus Prevention Programs

Many counseling efforts have been implemented to assist women through their developmental issues and challenges. Constructivist counseling approaches are particularly recommended for college women who are struggling with identity concerns. According to Vinson and Griffin (1999), constructivist counseling helps clients have a successful college experience by providing both a place of safety and a bridge to a more autonomous adulthood. Specifically, constructivist counseling places a primary emphasis on the therapeutic relationship as a safe and caring base from which clients can experience new ways of knowing themselves and the world (Mahoney, 1996). From the secure base of the therapeutic relationship, clients may begin to reexamine their personal beliefs and values, asking themselves such questions as, "Who am I apart from my peers? My parents? My relationships?" or "What do I believe? Think? Value?" Through this process, women may become aware that they are "living in stories in which choice is restricted and options are painful and unfulfilling" (Vinson & Griffin, 1999, p. 70).

Many women of color recognize the need to come to terms with cultural value conflicts. Gloria, Castellanos, and Orozco (2005) described the frustrations that Latina college women feel when striving to balance their community values of family and interdependence with the individualistic values of the academic setting. Women in their study felt a constant tension between pursuing their own academic goals and remaining close to their families. Counseling can be a place where women clients begin to identify the conflict they experience between their growing sense of autonomy and their continued desire for connection. Women can explore ways in which they can find the supportive relationships they need on campus while still striving for achievement. In this way, counseling can serve as an exciting transition, providing opportunity for a joint reconstruction of the ways in which women view the world, with clients as authors of their new stories.

Programmatic interventions and campus environments can "offer safety, structure, facilitation, and guidance while students experiment with their choices of becoming" (Evans et al., 1998, p. 67). Staffing classrooms and offices with those who are responsible and understanding about the needs of women and the challenges they need to overcome to achieve positive identity formation is an integral part of providing the nurturing environment needed for development (Evans et al., 1998). In addition, training for faculty and staff in how to understand the multiple dimensions of women's identity and to best work with women at all stages of development is integral to meeting these individuals' needs.

What's Love Got to Do With It? Hooking Up and Relationships in College Women

Mark still hasn't called! He said he would call when he got home from class and it's now 10 o'clock at night and I still haven't heard from him. I am starting to get really aggravated. He acted so interested at first, but now it's like I can't read him. I'm so tired of the games!

We hooked up about two months ago and we've been dating pretty consistently for about a month now, but Karen told me she just saw him getting coffee with some other girl! What is that? I know he has a test coming up . . . maybe he was studying?? I don't know. I just wish I knew where we stand rather than just having to wonder. Well, it has been about 2 months; maybe it's time for the dreaded DTR. (For those of you who don't know, DTR stands for Defining the Relationship, a little acronym my friends and I made up). Anyway, I just get so sick of always having to be the one to bring it up! Why does the girl always have to define the relationship? Why can't guys just grow up and commit! Well I guess I can't really expect too much from him. After all, his Facebook profile still says he's "single" . . .

—FacebookGirl86

More than 15 years ago, Dorothy Holland and Margaret Eisenhart (1990) set out to study women in the collegiate setting to better understand why more women were not entering science and mathematics fields. What they found in these higher education settings was a culture that promoted romance and attractiveness as important factors to the women's success in college, where "the women found constant evaluations of their worth on the basis of their sexual appeal to men," and even more disturbing, that the women they studied "made life 'decisions' in the shadow of that reality" (p. 21).

But that was 15 years ago. What does the contemporary college culture hold for its women and the decisions they make about themselves and their future? One way to answer this question is to examine the changes that have occurred in collegiate dating and relationships. Once upon a time, dating tended to include dinner and a movie, but today's college students are involved in a culture of "hanging" out" and "hooking up." Today's college women report that it is rare for them to be asked on planned dates; rather, they hang out at group activities such as parties (Glenn & Marquardt, 2001). Hookups often occur while students are hanging out. In a 2001 national survey of college students, 75% agreed that a hookup occurs "when a girl and a guy get together for a physical encounter and don't necessarily expect anything further" (Glenn & Marquardt, 2001, p. 1). This type of behavior is common on campus: 40% of college women report that they have experienced a hookup, and 10% say they have hooked up six or more times (Glenn & Marquardt, 2001).

Even though campus norms promote the idea that a hookup is a one-time encounter, women often report feeling awkward after a hookup and hope that it will lead to a relationship. Even if they hang out and continue to hook up with the same partner over a period of time, women remain confused as to whether they are in a committed relationship. The woman and her partner may remain in this ambiguous state until she initiates what is termed "the talk" (Glenn & Marquardt, 2001). During this conversation, the woman asks her partner if he considers them to be in a relationship. The male is then in a position of deciding the answer to her question, which clearly gives him more power in the relationship. Men report that they are very comfortable with this power and like the fact that they can be passive in pursuing relationships with women (Glenn & Marquardt, 2001). As indicated in the blog example cited earlier, MySpace and Facebook add to the confusion as couples can determine and make public the status of their relationship with a click on their computer.

In today's college environment, where women outnumber men and have made advances in so many academic and professional arenas, it is interesting that men still maintain control in this common type of college relationship. It is also paradoxical that in the midst of a culture in which hookups are the norm, college women still say that they are looking for long-term commitments while enrolled in college. In Glenn and Marquardt's (2001) national survey, marriage was a major goal for an overwhelming majority of the college women surveyed (83%), and 63% stated they would like to meet a spouse while attending college. This is in contrast with national data showing the marriage rate for women has been on a steady decline since 1970, decreasing from 76.5 to 39.9 per 1,000 women (Whitehead & Popenoe, 2005).

In their work with college women, counselors will likely encounter women who are dissatisfied with their involvement in the hookup culture. It is helpful to remember that most college women are uncomfortable with the current dating culture but may feel that this is the only avenue available for pursuing the long-term commitments that they truly desire. Counselors can assist them in examining how their current behaviors might hinder or enhance the achievement of this goal. They can help their clients explore the ways in which women can respond differently to a culture in which their male partners maintain the power in relationships.

College Women and Sexual Assault

I can't believe I am now one of THOSE women. I have always read about this stuff happening to women, but you always think—oh, that will never happen to ME. I'm smart, I'm tough, I'm not some dim-witted bimbo or anything. But he hurt me, he really hurt me. And I think what's worse than the pain caused by him forcing himself on me is the pain he caused by betraying me the way he did. This was my friend. I trusted him.

What was I thinking? How could I have been stupid?!?! I should have read the signals a little bit better and I certainly should have gone home with the girls when they all left last night. But, I thought I can trust him—he's my friend, right? What am I going to tell my mom?

—Annie Mae 85 Blog Entry, December 2, 2006

If women are immersed in a culture in which alcohol consumption is prevalent and hookups are common, the following statistics are not surprising:

- 62% of college women were sexually harassed, and 66% of these women were harassed in their first year of college (Hill & Silva, 2005)
- 90% of attempted or completed campus rapes were committed by an acquaintance (Fisher, Cullen, & Turner, 2000)
- 27% of women surveyed in a 2006 study reported being sexually assaulted or raped during their college experience (Gross, Winslett, Roberts, & Gohm, 2006)
- 13% of college women have reported being stalked, most often by someone they knew (Fisher et al., 2000)

The prevalence of sexual assault on the college campus has been an ongoing concern for many years that does not seem to have diminished despite changes in women's status in society. Even though newspapers report an apparent decline in rape and sexual violence across the general population of U.S. women (Martinez & Greve, 2006), college women are still faced with overwhelming statistics in regard to nonconsensual sex and rape. In addition, stalking of college women has increased throughout the past several years, now taking the form of "cyberstalking" as more students engage in online social environments such as Facebook and MySpace (Alexy, Burgess, Baker, & Smoyak, 2005). Because most campus sexual assaults and stalking are committed by someone the victim knows, statistics are likely to be underreported because women are reluctant to label their experiences as rape, may fear retaliation, or may be concerned that their claims will not be taken seriously by administrators or legal officials (Fisher et al., 2000).

Prevention Strategies

Many prevention programs have begun to spring up on college campuses nationwide, and most of these are targeted at women. Programs include risk reduction and self-defense classes, environmental changes to promote increased campus safety, and victim-advocacy programs (Hong, 2000). Several authors, however, have recently called for an approach to prevention that focuses on men, the perpetrators of most campus sexual violence (Foubert, 2005; Choate, 2003). One well-researched program directed explicitly at men to educate them about sexual assault behaviors and warning signs is *The Men's Program* (Foubert, 2005), which uses empathy strategies to educate about the effects of rape.

Given the shifts in today's campus social climate, two major areas of emphasis should be highlighted in sexual assault prevention programs for all students: (a) education regarding the use of alcohol in the hang out/hookup culture, and (b) discussions around the ambiguity of hook-ups and the increased importance of open communication about sexual behaviors.

The prevalence of alcohol use prior to sexual activity should be addressed in all prevention programs. Many campus acquaintance rapes

occur when men have sexual intercourse with women who are too intoxicated to give consent for sexual activity. This type of incident meets the
criteria of a felony crime, yet many men and women do not define these
instances as rape (Schwartz & Legett, 1999). There is a need for counselors
to raise men's and women's awareness of legal definitions of rape as they
apply to alcohol and other drugs. In most legal jurisdictions, simple rape
is committed when sexual intercourse occurs without the victim's lawful
consent under the following condition: The victim is incapable of resisting by reason of intoxication produced by an agent (alcohol or other
drugs) not administered by the offender, but the offender knew or should
have known of the victim's incapacity.

As reported in a study conducted by Choate (2003), male fraternity
members who were participants in a date rape prevention program
seemed surprised to learn that engaging in sexual activity with a woman
who is too intoxicated to give consent is considered rape, according to
legal definitions. During program discussions, participants seemed quite
concerned about the fairness of these definitions to men and felt that
"rape can occur without even knowing it." Many men described a perceived vulnerability to rape charges from any woman with whom they
have sexual contact when under the influence of alcohol (as one male
stated, "A drunk couple can have sex and the man can be charged with
rape"). Women may also have trouble understanding the intent of these
laws. Presentation programs should balance a review of specific legal definitions with an open discussion of concerns and confusion.

Second, prevention programs need to address the importance of clear
and direct communication regarding hookups. Both women and men can
benefit from education about obtaining and giving consent for sexual activity. When discussed in an open, nondefensive manner, students may be
more open to learning essential communication skills. In the Choate
(2003) program, male participants indicated that as a result of the program they now recognized a need for clear, sober communication with
their partners to avoid misinterpretation of a woman's sexual intentions.
As one man stated, "I found you have to hear 'yes' not just imply it."
College women can also benefit from basic assertiveness training that will
help them express their sexual limits clearly.

A full discussion of counseling strategies for working with women who
are survivors of sexual assault or rape is provided in Chapter 7. College
women also commonly experience intimate partner violence as part of
their romantic relationships, these issues are discussed in Chapter 8.

Body Image Dissatisfaction in College Women

I stepped on the scale this morning. Another pound gained. Why did I
agree to go out with my roommate for pizza last night? Looks like I'll have
to starve myself again today. I'll go to the gym too—no, wait, I don't want
guys to see me looking like this! I can't stand the way guys in there are always checking girls out. What will they think when they see my huge

stomach and thighs? I have a study group this afternoon that I should skip too. I really like Chris but I want to lose some weight before he sees me again. Oh no . . . I just remembered that I have to give a speech in my public speaking class next week! I know I'm a good speaker, but I am sure that everyone in there will be staring at the fat bulges hanging over my pants. I know this is ridiculous and that I shouldn't feel this way—after all, I have a 3.5 GPA and I want to go to law school, but it seems like all anyone cares about on this campus is how other people look!

—BrownEyedGirl 19 Blog Entry, January 12, 2007

Issues of body image and disordered eating behaviors are prevalent on college campuses, and large numbers of women are engaging in these behaviors (Thombs et al., 1996). This type of body image dissatisfaction, weight preoccupation, and unhealthy weight management are prevalent among college women of normal weight (Schwitzer, Bergholz, Dore, & Salimi, 1998; Springer, Wilzelberg, Perkins, & Barr Taylor, 1999). This is of concern because negative body image can adversely affect a college woman's quality of life. The amount of time, energy, and resources she spends on beauty enhancement can restrict her opportunities to develop other aspects of her identity or to engage in more empowering activities such as academic and professional pursuits (Engeln-Maddox, 2005; Strachan & Cash, 2002; Striegel-Moore & Franko, 2002).

Furthermore, there is a relationship between negative body image and a variety of psychosocial problems including poor self-esteem, anxiety about social evaluation, public self-consciousness, depression, and sexual inhibition (see Chapter 2). Negative body image also is associated with early smoking onset, maintenance of high levels of smoking, and unnecessary elective cosmetic surgery (Ackard, Kearney-Cooke, & Peterson, 2000; Lavin & Cash, 2000; Stice & Shaw, 2003; Stice & Whitenton, 2002; Wiederman & Pryor, 2000). Body image dissatisfaction is the primary precursor for the development of eating disorders such as anorexia nervosa and bulimia (Polivy & Herman, 2002).

The sociocultural model of body image development (see Chapter 2) describes how today's women are expected to be extremely thin in order to be considered beautiful, and how beauty is equated with success and happiness for women. This message is perpetuated through the media, and a cursory glance at current media images indicates the promise that beauty and extreme thinness will bring happiness, success, and popularity. College women may accept these beliefs; in one study, a majority of college women in the sample believed that thinness is associated with greater attractiveness, social success, and acceptance (Brazelton, Greene, Gynther, & O'Mell, 1998). Another study that examined the weight loss expectancies of college women found those who had the highest expectations for the effects of weight loss (i.e., increased social confidence and sense of self-worth, positive performance, and social approval) were more likely to binge, purge, have body image concerns, and experience a perceived lack of control of eating (Thombs et al., 1996).

Pressures for women to be thin and beautiful can be conveyed through the family and peers, but college women seem to be most influenced by media sources (Coughlin & Kalodner, 2006). There is a considerable body of evidence documenting the direct negative impact of exposure to thin-and-beautiful media images on women's body image (see the meta-analysis by Groesz, Levine, & Murnen, 2002). College women do compare themselves with the media images they view, resulting in appearance-related dissatisfaction. One study randomly assigned college women to two groups: one group read news magazines and the other read women's fashion magazines. After only 10 minutes of reading the magazines, the women who read the fashion magazines reported a lower ideal body weight and had greater body dissatisfaction than did women who read the news magazines (Turner, Hamilton, Jacobs, Angood, & Dwyer, 1997). Fashion magazines are an obvious source of media-generated, thin, ideal images, but there is growing evidence that fitness and health magazines can be just as damaging or more damaging to body satisfaction, especially for college women who are already dissatisfied with their bodies (Cameron & Ferraro, 2004).

Sociocultural influences can be mediated by two important aspects of an individual college woman's belief and value system: the extent to which she compares herself with the cultural ideal, and the importance she places on how she is evaluated by others, particularly men. When women are bombarded with images of beauty and thinness, many internalize the cultural ideal as the standard against which they evaluate themselves, resulting in an acceptance and even an endorsement of societal standards. For these women, there exists a discrepancy between their mental representation of their bodies and their image of the ideal. When they do not measure up to the culturally defined standard, they evaluate themselves negatively. Because the ideal is unattainable for the vast majority of women, it is not surprising that the extent to which women internalize societal standards for thinness is a strong predictor of body dissatisfaction, tendency to overestimate body size, negative affect, depression, and disordered eating behaviors (Levine & Smolak, 2002; Monteah & McCabe, 1997; Mussell, Binford, & Fulkerson, 2000; Polivy & Herman, 2002; Tsiantas & King, 2001).

Women are not only highly influenced by media images but also by their beliefs about how they are evaluated by others. According to self-objectification theory (Frederickson, Roberts, Noll, Quinn, & Twenge, 1998, p. 270), many women have learned to think about themselves and their bodies from a third-person perspective, focusing on observable body attributes ("How do I look?"), rather than from a first-person perspective ("What am I capable of?" or "How do I feel?"). Women who self-objectify chronically monitor themselves in anticipation of how others might perceive them. This phenomenon causes women to be preoccupied with their own physical appearance and creates feelings of constantly being "checked out" by others, particularly by males. This constant self-monitoring can lead to self-consciousness, body shame, and a decreased ability to experience pleasure from activities, and it eventually leads to a decrease in available mental resources. In one study of college students, among participants who were asked to try on either a swimsuit or a sweater with no observers present, the women in the swimsuit condition subsequently performed worse on an advanced math test (Frederickson et al., 1998). In another study, Calogero (2004) found that for college women, merely anticipating a male entering the room (versus anticipating a woman entering the room) caused greater body shame and anxiety. If women are using valuable mental resources to evaluate themselves, particularly in anticipation of what men are thinking about their bodies, it is reasonable to assume that they will not perform to their fullest potential in academic or professional settings. As college women attempt to advance professionally, it is important that counselors work with them to remove these significant obstacles to their growth.

Prevention Strategies for Promoting Positive Body Image

Most campuses have incorporated eating disorder prevention programs into their counseling or wellness education-based services. For counselors who wish to develop strong prevention and intervention services on their campuses, excellent resources are available online. Many of these programs can be accessed through the counseling center village clearinghouse at http://ccvillage.buffalo.edu/ (see also Additional Resources at the end of this chapter). Most empirically supported components of college programs are based on sociocultural theory and incorporate a psychoeducational approach that includes (a) media literacy and psychoeducation about the impact of the thin ideal and (b) dissonance-based strategies. For a detailed description of program components that can be used for prevention work with college women, see the Appendix at the end of this chapter.

Media literacy approaches that promote critical thinking and help participants become more conscientious consumers have considerable support for preventing body dissatisfaction, particularly among those women most at risk for eating disorders (Coughlin & Kalodner, 2006). Even briefly reminding women that media images are inappropriate standards of comparison because the images are digitally altered, or providing education that the vast majority of women are genetically predisposed to be heavier than models, can buffer the damaging effects of exposure to thin-and-beautiful media images. Yamamiya, Cash, Melnyk, Posavac, and Posavac (2005) experimentally demonstrated the effectiveness of a brief 7-minute media literacy presentation in preventing the negative effects of exposure to thin-and-beautiful media images. When women viewed the 7-minute presentation, they were not negatively affected by a presentation of media slides depicting fashion models (compared with women who did not view the media literacy presentation). Some examples of brief, empirically supported programs for college women include ARMED (Acknowledging and Rejecting the Media's Influence on Eating and Body Image Dissatisfaction; see Coughlin & Kalodner, 2006) and Body Traps (see Springer et al., 1999).

Dissonance-based strategies are also effective components of prevention programs for college women. The approach initially developed by Stice, Chase, Stormer, and Appel (2001; see also Stice, Trost, & Chase, 2002) helps college women to voluntarily take a stance against the pressures for women to be extremely thin and beautiful. The conflict between participants' internalized acceptance of the thin ideal and the stance they choose to take during the intervention creates a dissonance that serves to alter their beliefs in this area. For example, during these workshops college women are asked to create a body acceptance program for high school girls. During the preparation of the high school program, women explore the costs of the thin ideal to themselves and others. Another strategy used by Yamamiya et al. (2005) is to ask participants to write a persuasive argument to help a girl they know to not become affected by the ultra-thin models in the media. These findings underscore the importance of infusing media literacy information and including women in body acceptance advocacy projects throughout their collegiate activities as a way to promote more body acceptance among college women.

One final note: There is some evidence that a positive trend is occurring in the area of college women's body image. Counselors should be aware that despite the negative impact that media and other influences can have on women's body image, recent research indicates that college women's body image has improved for non-Black women and has remained stable for Black women. In a major review, Cash, Morrow, Perry, and Hrabosky (2004) examined cohorts of college students between 1983 and 2001. They found a reversal in the 1980s to early to mid-1990s trend of increased negative evaluation of appearance, more overweight preoccupation, and diminished satisfaction with overall appearance that was evident among non-Black college women. From the early to mid-1990s through 2001, college women unexpectedly reported a more favorable overall body image and less overweight preoccupation, along with improved lower torso satisfaction. This finding was surprising to the authors given that the later cohorts of college women were significantly heavier than the 1980s cohort. Interestingly, no changes were found in men or in Black women during this time.

Cash et al. (2004) provided some tentative hypotheses to explain these promising findings. First, they speculated that because today's college women have more professional opportunities available to them perhaps they are able to focus more on their achievements and less on appearance as the primary criterion for self-evaluation. Second, college women overall seem to engage in fewer appearance-managing behaviors such as spending excessive time on grooming, which leads to greater body satisfaction. Third, college women overall are heavier now than in recent years, so when women compare themselves with one another, they regularly encounter individuals who weigh as much as or even more than they do.

Finally, perhaps the growing attention to this area is having a small impact. Media literacy education and body image awareness campaigns (see Dove campaign for Real Beauty, 2006, and programs by the National

Eating Disorder Association, 2006, for examples) are making incremental shifts that can promote body acceptance in college women. Counselors should continue their efforts to promote body image resilience whenever they find the opportunity.

In the following case study, consider your reactions and how you would work with a client who is frustrated by the relationship and body image trends that affect her everyday life.

Case Study

Angela, a 20-year-old college junior, comes to the university counseling center because of frustration with her dating relationships. She reports that her most recent relationship with a senior, Tim, turned out not to be a monogamous relationship as she had believed. When she confronted Tim after she learned that he was romantically involved with other women, he told her that he had never thought of her as his "girlfriend" and didn't understand why she had to be so "serious." Because this pattern had occurred many times throughout her college career (hooking up at a party, hanging out together for several months, and eventually drifting apart), Angela is ready to "give up on herself" as a dating partner and reports depressed mood, low energy, and an erratic appetite. She occasionally goes through periods of fasting, binging, and purging. She has become intensely focused on finding out what is so wrong with her appearance (especially her weight), personality, or intelligence that no man wants to be in a real relationship with her. Because she blames herself and feels deficient in all life areas, she believes she has nowhere to turn except for expert advice from a counselor.

1. After reviewing the theories of college women's development, which may be particularly relevant to working with Angela's identity development?
2. As a counselor, where do you begin when working with Angela? What kinds of myths might you need to dispel? What counseling approach might you take?
3. In reviewing the section on dating relationships in this chapter, how does Angela's experience fit with current campus trends, and how can you use this information in your work with Angela?
4. What body image concerns might be relevant in this case? How might you work with these issues?
5. How might a wellness approach be relevant when working with this client?

Conclusion

I am graduating in two weeks! I cannot wait! It's weird to look back now at my experience in college and see all the changes that have happened. Caitlyn and I were talking the other day about our freshman year and realizing how much we have changed since then. Not only do we see ourselves differently, but we really see the world differently.

College has been a blast. Don't get me wrong—there were still some things about it that I absolutely hated—but overall, I feel like I have learned a lot and am ready to take on the world . . . so the world better watch out because here I come!

—Blogger Babe Blog Entry, April 25, 2007

College women today face both progress and paradox. As illustrated in this chapter, today women have more opportunities in society and on college campuses than ever before, but they also face multiple obstacles. Indeed, a recent study by Kelly and Torres (2006) extended the research by Hall and Sandler (1982) and their "chilly" campus climate and its effects on college women's learning and development. Kelly and Torres (2006) found that despite the gains in representation, women still experience fear and concern about their safety on the college campus. Further, women's body image concerns affect classroom performance, and dating norms have shifted toward women voluntarily allowing men to have power in relationships.

Women must struggle against the rigid, societally bound constructions of who they can and should be, while at the same time they face greater gains in the higher education setting, in the workplace, and in society in general. We know that women are resilient; time and history have shown us this. But college women, especially those of traditional age, are still in need of assistance to overcome the obstacles put before them. Purposefully structuring educational opportunities, cocurricular programs, and counseling interventions will go far in assisting them in dealing with issues such as cognitive and psychosocial development, sexual development, learning about the dangers of alcohol, and understanding healthy dating relationships and positive body image. Ensuring support for college women is paramount to ensuring success in the college experience.

Activities for Further Exploration

1. Spend some time browsing the Web site of your local campus or university. What unit handles sexual assault policies and procedures? How comprehensive are the sexual assault policies? How easy are they for students to access?

2. In your review of a local college or university Web site, what types of services does the counseling center provide around body image concerns? What types of prevention services are provided to student groups? How aware are students of these services?

3. Interview a college student about the dating culture for heterosexual relationships on campus. Do the interviewee's responses correspond with the information presented in this chapter? In what ways?

4. How might you use the psychosocial theories of college women's development in your counseling work with women? What counseling implications do they suggest? Which theory seemed particularly relevant for you?

Suggested Readings

Belenky, M. F., Clinchy, B. M., Goldberger, N. R., & Tarule, J. M. (1986). *Women's ways of knowing: The development of self, voice, and mind.* New York: Basic Books.

Coughlin, J., & Kalodner, C. (2006). Media literacy as a prevention intervention for college women at low- or high-risk for eating disorders. *Body Image, 3,* 35–43.

DeBard, R. (2004). Millennials coming to college. In M. D. Coomes & R. DeBard (Eds.), *Serving the millennial generation* (pp. 33–45). San Francisco: Jossey-Bass.

Evans, N. J., Forney, D. S., & Guido-DiBrito, F. (1998). *Student development in college: Theory, research, and practice.* San Francisco: Jossey-Bass.

Fisher, B. S., Cullen, F. T., & Turner, M. G. (2000). *Sexual victimization of college women.* Washington, DC: U.S. Department of Justice, National Institute of Justice.

Frederickson, B. L., Roberts, T. A., Noll, S. M., Quinn, D. M., & Twenge, J. M. (1998). That swimsuit becomes you: Sex differences in self-objectification, restrained eating, and math performance. *Journal of Personality and Social Psychology, 75,* 269–284.

Josselson, R. (1973). Psychodynamic aspects of identity formation in college women. *Journal of Youth and Adolescence, 2,* 3–52.

Kalodner, C. R., & DeLucia-Waack, J. L. (2003). Theory and research on eating disorders and disturbances in women: Suggestions for practice. In M. Kopala & M. A. Keitel (Eds.), *Handbook of counseling women* (pp. 506–532). London: Sage.

Kilbourne, J. (2000). *Killing us softly III* [Video]. Media Education Foundation, 28 Center Street, Northhampton, MA 01060; www.mediaed.org.

Mahoney, M. J. (1996). Connected knowing in constructive psychotherapy. In N. Goldberger, J. Tarule, B. Clinchy, & M. Belenky (Eds.), *Knowledge, difference, and power: Essays inspired by women's ways of knowing* (pp. 126–147). New York: Basic Books.

Schwitzer, A. M, Bergholz, K., Dore, T., & Salimi, L. (1998). Eating disorders among college women: Prevention, education, and treatment responses. *Journal of American College Health, 46*(5), 199–208.

Additional Resources

http://ccvillage.buffalo.edu/vpc.html

The Counseling Center Village provides home pages and other Web resources created by college and university counseling centers around the world. There is a category called "virtual pamphlets" and a subcategory called "eating disorders" that link to various resources colleges offer for body image and eating disorder issues.

http://www.health.umd.edu/programs/eatingdisorders.html

The University of Maryland has an impressive Web site with information about eating disorders and negative body image. Group therapy regarding body image and self-esteem is offered during the semester. Individual therapy for the treatment of eating disorders is available on campus with a professional. Students can request an eating disorder workshop to be presented by a professional. The university has a program called SEEDS (students educating about eating disorders).

http://www.usc.edu/student-affairs/Health_Center/cs.eating.disorders.shtml
The University of Southern California offers students a group for body image and eating disorder issues called "Peace with Food and Body Image." The UPHC has an Eating Disorder Treatment Team, individual counseling, group counseling, psychiatric consultations, medical services, nutritional counseling, community referrals, and off-campus treatment for eating disorders.

http://www.utexas.edu/student/cmhc/booklets/eating/eating.html
The University of Texas has an impressive Web site with resources, links, and recommended readings about body image issues and eating disorders. The counseling center also offers outreach programs about Body Image and Media Influence, Understanding Eating Disorders, and Emotional Eating (New You) Parts 1 & 2. The site also has an extensive list of links to online brochures and pamphlets about body image and eating issues.

http://www.uhs.umich.edu/wellness/edbi/
http://www.uhs.umich.edu/wellness/edbi/care.html
The University of Michigan health service offers an extensive list of resources for eating disorders and body image issues. The university health service also has an interesting program called CARE, the Coalition for Action Regarding Eating and Body Image Issues.

http://vaden.stanford.edu/topics_resources/nutrition/index.html
Stanford University's Vaden Health Center offers many services for students struggling with negative body image or eating disorders. A support group sponsored by the counseling and psychological center (CAPS) is called Image and Identity: Women's Body Image Group. The health center provides workshops and outreach presentations on campus related to body image and eating concerns and has a page devoted to nutrition, body image, and disordered eating.

References

Ackard, D. M., Kearney-Cooke, A., & Peterson, C. B. (2000). Effect of body image and self-image on women's sexual behaviors. *International Journal of Eating Disorders, 28,* 422–429.

Alexy, E. M., Burgess, A. W., Baker, T., & Smoyak, S. A. (2005). Perceptions of cyberstalking among college students. *Brief Treatment and Crisis Intervention, 5*(3), 279–289.

Astin, A. W. (1984). Student involvement: A developmental theory for higher education. *Journal of College Student Personnel, 25,* 297–308.

Belenky, M. F., Clinchy, B. M., Goldberger, N. R., & Tarule, J. M. (1986). *Women's ways of knowing: The development of self, voice, and mind.* New York: Basic Books.

Brazelton, E. W., Greene, K. S., Gynther, M., & O'Mell, J. (1998). Femininity, bulimia, and distress in college women. *Psychological Reports, 83,* 355–363.

Broido, E. M. (2004). Understanding diversity in millennial students. In M. D. Coomes & R. DeBard (Eds.), *Serving the millennial generation* (pp. 73–85). San Francisco: Jossey-Bass.

Cameron, E. M. & Ferraro, F. R. (2004). Body satisfaction in college women after brief exposure to magazine images. *Perceptual and Motor Skills, 98*(3, Pt1), 1093–1099.

Calogero, R. (2004). A test of objectification theory: The effect of the male gaze on appearance concerns in college women. *Psychology of Women Quarterly, 28,* 16–21.

Cash, T. F., Morrow, J. A., Perry, A. A., & Hrabosky, J. I. (2004). How has body image changed? A cross-sectional investigation of college women and men from 1983 to 2001. *Journal of Consulting and Clinical Psychology, 72,* 1081–1089.

Chickering, A. W., McDowell, J., & Campagna, D. (1969). Institutional differences and student development. *Journal of Educational Psychology, 60,* 315–326.

Choate, L. H. (2003). Sexual assault prevention programs for college men: An exploratory evaluation of the men against violence model. *Journal of College Counseling, 6*(2), 166–176.

Chronicle of Higher Education, The. (2005). Almanac issue 2005–2006. *The Chronicle of Higher Education.*

Coughlin, J., & Kalodner, C. (2006). Media literacy as a prevention intervention for college women at low- or high-risk for eating disorders. *Body Image, 3,* 35–43.

DeBard, R. (2004). Millennials coming to college. In M. D. Coomes & R. DeBard (Eds.), *Serving the millennial generation* (pp. 33–45). San Francisco: Jossey-Bass.

Dove Campaign for Real Beauty. (2006). Retrieved November 13, 2006, from http://www.campaignforrealbeauty.com

Durhams, S. (2000, October 15). Men dwindling on college campuses. *Milwaukee Journal Sentinel.*

Dunlap, L. (2006). *Media and me: Media literacy workshop for college women.* Unpublished manuscript.

Engeln-Maddox, R. (2005). Cognitive responses to idealized media images of women: The relationship of social comparison and critical processing to body image disturbance in college women. *Journal of Social and Clinical Psychology, 24*(8), 1114–1138.

Erikson, E. H. (1980). *Identity and the life cycle.* New York: Norton.

Evans, N. J., Forney, D. S., & Guido-DiBrito, F. (1998). *Student development in college: Theory, research, and practice.* San Francisco: Jossey-Bass.

Fisher, B. S., Cullen, F. T., & Turner, M. G. (2000). *Sexual victimization of college women.* Washington, DC: U.S. Department of Justice, National Institute of Justice.

Foubert, J. D. (2005). *The men's program: A peer education guide to rape prevention* (3rd ed.). New York: Routledge.

Frederickson, B. L, Roberts, T. A., Noll, S. M., Quinn, D. M., & Twenge, J. M. (1998). That swimsuit becomes you: Sex differences in self-objectification, restrained eating, and math performance. *Journal of Personality and Social Psychology, 75*, 269–284.

Glenn, N., & Marquardt, E. (2001). *Hooking up, hanging out, and hoping for Mr. Right: College women on dating and mating today.* New York: Institute for American Values.

Gloria, A., Castellanos, J., & Orozco, V. (2005). Perceived educational barriers, cultural fit, coping responses, and psychological well-being of Latina undergraduates. *Hispanic Journal of Behavioral Sciences, 27,* 161–183.

Groesz, L. M., Levine, M. P., & Murnen, S. K. (2002). The effect of experimental presentation of thin media images on body satisfaction: A meta-analytic review. *International Journal of Eating Disorders, 31*, 1–16.

Gross, A. M., Winslett, A., Roberts, M., & Gohm, C. L. (2006). An examination of sexual violence against college women. *Violence Against Women, 12*(3), 288–300.

Hall, R., & Sandler, B. (1982). *The campus climate: A chilly one for women?* Washington, DC: Association of American Colleges.

Hall, R., & Sandler, B. (1984). *Out of the classroom: A chilly campus climate for women?* Washington, DC: Association of American Colleges.

Hill, C., & Silva, E. (2005). *Drawing the line: Sexual harassment on campus.* Washington, DC: AAUW Educational Foundation.

Hodges, M. H. (2005, December 4). Where are the boys? *The Detroit News.*

Holland, D. C., & Eisenhart, M. A. (1990). *Educated in romance: Women, achievement, and college culture.* Chicago: The University of Chicago Press.

Hong, L. (2000). Toward a transformed approach to prevention: Breaking the link between hegemonic masculinity and violence. *Journal of American College Health, 48*(6), 269–280.

Josselson, R. (1973). Psychodynamic aspects of identity formation in college women. *Journal of Youth and Adolescence, 2*, 3–52.

Kelly, B. T., & Torres, A. (2006). Campus safety: Perceptions and experiences of women students. *Journal of College Student Development, 47*(1), 20–36.

Kilbourne, J. (2000). *Killing us softly III* [Video]. Media Education Foundation, 28 Center Street, Northhampton, MA 01060; www.mediaed.org.

Lavin, M. A., & Cash, T. F. (2000). Effects of exposure to information about appearance stereotyping and discrimination on women's body images. *International Journal of Eating Disorders, 29*, 51–58.

Levine, M. P., & Smolak, L. (2002). Body image development in adolescence. In T. F. Cash & T. Pruzinsky (Eds.), *Body image: A handbook of theory, research, and clinical practice* (pp. 74–82). New York: Guilford Press.

Mahoney, M. J. (1996). Connected knowing in constructive psychotherapy. In N. Goldberger, J. Tarule, B. Clinchy, & M. Belenky (Eds.), *Knowledge, difference, and power: Essays inspired by women's ways of knowing* (pp. 126–147). New York: Basic Books.

Marklein, M. B. (2005, October 19). College gender gap widens: 57% are women. *USA Today.*

Martinez, J., & Greve, F. (2006, May 14). Rape, sexual violence seem to be on decline. *The Advocate,* p. 25A.

Monteah, S. A., & McCabe, M. P. (1997). The influence of societal factors on female body image. *Journal of Social Psychology, 137,* 708–728.

Mussell, M. P., Binford, R. B., & Fulkerson, J. A. (2000). Eating disorders: Summary of risk factors, prevention programming, and prevention research. *The Counseling Psychologist, 28,* 764–796.

National Center for Education Statistics. (2003). *NCES Fast Facts.* Retrieved December 3, 2003, from http://nces.ed.gov/fastfacts

National Eating Disorders Association. (2006). Retrieved November 14, 2006, from http://www.nationaleatingdisorders.org

National Organization for Women. (2006). *Facts about pay equity.* Retrieved May 5, 2006, from http://www.now.org/issues/economic/factsheet.html

National Organization for Women. (n.d.). *Violence against women in the United States.* Retrieved May 6, 2006, from http://www.now.org/issues/violence/stats.html

Nidiffer, J. (2003). From whence they came. In B. Ropers-Huilman (Ed.), *Gendered futures in higher education: Critical perspectives for change* (pp. 15–34). Albany: State University of New York Press.

Polivy, J., & Herman, C. P. (2002). Causes of eating disorders. *Annual Review of Psychology, 53,* 187–213.

Rodgers, R. F. (1990). Recent theories and research underlying student development. In D. Creamer & Associates (Eds.), *College student development: Theory and practice for the 1990s* (pp. 27–79). Alexandria, VA: American College Personnel Association.

Schwartz, M. D., & Legett, M. S. (1999). Bad dates or emotional trauma? The aftermath of campus sexual assault. *Violence Against Women, 5,* 251–271.

Schwitzer, A. M., Bergholz, K., Dore, T., & Salimi, L. (1998). Eating disorders among college women: Prevention, education, and treatment responses. *Journal of American College Health, 46*(5), 199–208.

Springer, E. A., Winzelberg, A. J., Perkins, R., & Barr Taylor, C. (1999). Effects of a body image curriculum for college students on improved body image. *International Journal of Eating Disorders, 26,* 12–20.

Stice, E., Chase, A., Stormer, S., & Appel, A. (2001). A randomized trial of a dissonance-based eating disorder prevention program. *International Journal of Eating Disorders, 29,* 247–262.

Stice, E., & Shaw, H. (2003). Prospective relations of body image, eating, and affective disturbances to smoking onset in adolescent girls: How Virginia slims. *Journal of Consulting and Clinical Psychology, 71,* 129–135.

Stice, E., Trost, A., & Chase, A. (2002). Healthy weight control and dissonance-based eating disorder prevention programs. Results from a controlled trial. *International Journal of Eating Disorders, 33,* 10–21.

Stice, E., & Whitenton, K. (2002). Risk factors for body dissatisfaction in adolescent girls: A longitudinal investigation. *Developmental Psychology, 38,* 669–678.

Strachan, M. D., & Cash, T. F. (2002). Self-help for a negative body image: A comparison of components of a cognitive–behavioral program. *Behavior Therapy, 33*, 235–251.

Striegel-Moore, R. H., & Franko, D. L. (2002). Body image issues among girls and women. In T. F. Cash & T. Pruzinsky (Eds.), *Body image: A handbook of theory, research, and clinical practice* (pp. 183–191). New York: Guilford Press.

Thelin, J. R. (2004). *A history of American higher education.* Baltimore: Johns Hopkins University Press.

Thombs, D. L., Rosenberg, J. M., Mahoney, C. A., & Daniel, E. L. (1996). Weight-loss expectancies, relative weight, and symptoms of bulimia in young women. *Journal of College Student Development, 37*(4), 405–413.

Tinto, V. (1993). *Leaving college: Rethinking the causes and cures of student attrition* (2nd ed.). Chicago: University of Chicago Press.

Tsiantas, G., & King, R. M. (2001). Similarities in body image in sisters: The role of sociocultural internalization and social comparison. *Eating Disorders, 9*, 141–158.

Turner, S. L., Hamilton, H., Jacobs, M., Angood, L. M., & Dwyer, D. H. (1997). The influence of fashion magazines on the body image satisfaction of college women: An exploratory analysis. *Adolescence, 32*(127), 603–615.

U.S. Census Bureau. (2000). *United States Census 2000.* Retrieved February 18, 2004, from http://www.census.gov/main/www/cen2000.html

Vinson, M. L., & Griffin, B. L. (1999). Using a constructivist approach to counseling in the university counseling center. *Journal of College Counseling, 2*, 66–75.

Weston, L. C., & Stein, S. L. (1977). The relationship of identity achievement of college women and campus participation. *Journal of College Student Personnel, 18*, 21–24.

Whitehead, B. D., & Popenoe, D. (2005). *The state of our unions.* Piscataway, NJ: National Marriage Project.

Wiederman, M. W., & Pryor, T. L. (2000). Body dissatisfaction, bulimia, and depression among women: The mediating role of drive for thinness. *International Journal of Eating Disorders, 27*, 90–95.

Yamamiya, Y., Cash, T. F., Melnyk, S. E., Posavac, H. D., & Posavac, S. S. (2005). Women's exposure to thin-and-beautiful media images: Body image effects of media-ideal internalization and impact-reduction interventions. *Body Image, 2*, 74–80.

Appendix
Evidence-Based Workshop Components for Promoting Positive Body Image in College Women

Note: These components can be divided into several sessions to compose a small-group workshop or can be presented as a longer single-session workshop to accommodate larger audiences.

1. What is body image? Review components of body image, including how we evaluate ourselves, the feelings this invokes in us, and how much importance we place on our appearance. Review the prevalence of negative body image in college women and provide statistics.

2. Define the thin ideal. Ask participants to describe the current media-generated thin ideal. Who represents the ideal in today's culture? How is this ideal reinforced by the media? Does the thin ideal represent the average woman in U.S. culture? (An average woman in the United States is 5'4" and weighs 142 pounds.)

3. Describe the historical context of the thin ideal. How has it changed over time? Did anyone know what size dress Marilyn Monroe wore (size 12) versus the models of today (size 0)?

4. Describe the direct negative impact exposure to media images has on women over time. Describe studies reviewed in this chapter.

5. Introduce the idea of the advertising industry and its motives for designing media images, such as to keep women dissatisfied with themselves so they will continue to buy products.

6. Help participants understand that models used in media images are inappropriate standards for comparison because (a) the images are digitally altered so that even the models themselves do not look like this; (b) the vast majority of women are genetically predisposed to be heavier than the models represented in the media. To emphasize this point, refer to the before/after pictures on the Web site www.homepage.mac.com/gapodaca/digital/digital.html.

7. To emphasize the power of advertising, use film clips from Kilbourne (2000, *Still Killing Us Softly*).

8. Help participants process the following questions: What are the messages we receive from viewing these images? What are the consequences to women (low self-esteem, extreme dieting, overexercising, competition with other women)?

9. Review cognitive strategies for challenging messages, e.g., "These images aren't real. I need to accept myself for who I am." Include media literacy strategies for deconstructing an advertisement (see mediaed.org; also Chapter 4).

10. Incorporate exercises that can enhance appreciation of self. What are nonappearance-related aspects of yourself that you appreciate in yourself or in someone you admire? What are things you appreciate about what your body can do rather than how it looks?

11. Provide participants with information about healthy weight management, including the dangers of dieting and the importance of long-term approaches to health, nutrition, and exercise.

12. Incorporate dissonance-based strategies such as the following:
    a. Conduct a counterattitudinal role play with two participants (e.g., role play what you might say to a girl who is engaging in fat talk and who is comparing herself to unrealistic thin ideal standards).

b. Write a persuasive argument that might dissuade a teenage girl you care about from accepting the thin ideal as her social comparison standard.

c. Write an essay exploring "Who benefits from me believing the messages that are implied in these ads and images?"

d. Ask participants to create a body acceptance program for high school girls. What do girls need to hear in order to resist negative cultural messages?

Source: Program components are based on programs conducted by Dunlap (2006), Stice et al. (2002), and Yamamiya et al. (2005).

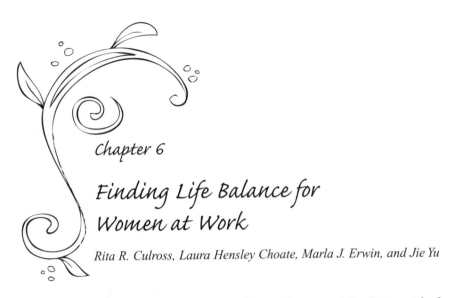

Chapter 6

Finding Life Balance for Women at Work

Rita R. Culross, Laura Hensley Choate, Marla J. Erwin, and Jie Yu

During spring 2006 Purdue University honored some of its distinguished alumni, including Dr. Rena Khator, currently provost and vice president for academic affairs at the University of South Florida (USF). Among Dr. Khator's many distinguished accomplishments are being the first female provost at USF, being the first Indian-born immigrant administrator at a Florida university, publishing five books and 50 articles or book chapters, and being a wife and mother of two daughters, both of whom are ophthalmologists. In an article highlighting her accomplishments in *The Purdue Alumnus* (Gasper, 2006), Khator raved about the work she has been fortunate to do, saying "I usually work until midnight each night and pull an all-nighter at least once a week."

That comment sparked a letter to the editor in the following issue from another alumna, Natalie Wisniewski, a 1994 chemical engineering graduate. Ms. Wisniewski (2006) wrote: "I understand that one path to career success is to work more hours than the people around you, but I would hope people who would be rounded models for success would find some balance in life. This article sends the message that what it takes to be successful is sacrificing a balanced life" (p. 5).

Work–life balance is an important issue for women in today's world and a likely topic that women clients will bring to counseling. The focus of this chapter is to inform counselors about gender differences in career advancement and salary, issues related to working mothers and dual-earner couples, and the benefits of enhancing wellness and self-care for women. In addition, prevention and counseling interventions are offered for helping women cope with the many issues presented by work–life conflicts.

Gender Differences in Career Advancement and Salary

Women constitute almost half of the current labor force. According to data from the U.S. Bureau of Labor Statistics (2005), the workforce participation rate for women has risen dramatically from about 43% in the 1970s to 68% at the beginning of this century. These changes are the result of social transformations in the last hundred years, yet women have not completely achieved equal working opportunities and situations with men. In fact, women still face explicit and implicit problems of gender discrimination at work.

First, we focus on gender discrimination in women's career advancement and explore three questions: What is gender discrimination in the workplace? Why does it occur? and, How can women struggle against it? We explore workforce gender segregation, wage discrimination, discrimination of pregnant and working mothers, and sexual harassment. By critically analyzing the phenomena of career gender discrimination, counselors can be more aware of and help advocate for possible solutions to workplace discrimination.

Gender Segregation in the Workplace

Although the labor force participation of women and men is seemingly equal, underlying vocational gender segregation inhibits women's career advancement and contributes to the wage gap between women and men (Betz & Fitzgerald, 1987; Fitzsimons, 2002; Gregory, 2003; Hesse-Biber & Carter, 2000). Fitzsimons (2002) lists two types of occupational segregation: horizontal and vertical. Horizontal segregation refers to concentrations of males or females in different types of occupations. As data from the U.S. Bureau of Labor Statistics (2005) indicate, occupations that had the highest percentage of women's participation included preschool and kindergarten teachers (97.7%), secretaries and administrative assistants (97.3%), licensed practical and licensed vocational nurses (93.4%), tellers (91.4%), and housekeeping cleaners (89.5%). Occupations with the lowest percentages of women included mechanical engineering (5.8%), construction management (6.3%), transportation and material moving (14.8%), and network and computer systems administrators (18.4%).

Vertical segregation also exists in these same occupations; that is, men are generally employed at the top of the career hierarchy, doing more skilled and highly paid jobs than women. Women who attempt to advance in their careers often encounter what is referred to as the *glass ceiling*, "those artificial barriers based on attitudinal or organizational bias that prevent qualified individuals from advancing upward in their organization into management-level positions" (Martin, 1991, p. 1). Even at advanced professional levels, it can be more difficult for women than men to get promotions in careers. For example, in 2002 women represented 15.7% of executive officers in the United States. Further, there were only 11 women CEOs in *Fortune* 1000 companies and only 6 represented in *Fortune* 500 companies ("Break the Glass Ceiling," n.d.).

Wage Discrimination

With the increasing participation of women in the labor force, the wage difference between men and women has become a long-term public concern. Three pieces of legislation enacted in the early 1960s greatly helped women to make more money by prohibiting wage discrimination on the basis of sex. In 1963 President John F. Kennedy signed the Equal Pay Act, considered to be landmark legislation guaranteeing equal pay for women and men who held the same job (Herman & Castro, 1998). Title VII of the Civil Rights Act of 1964 prohibits discrimination on the basis of sex as well as race, religion, and national origin. President Kennedy also signed the Equal Employment Opportunity Commission (EEOC) into law. The EEOC investigates claims of discrimination against employers under Title VII.

Because of these changes, the absolute amount of women's earnings to men's has increased sharply in recent decades, but women still receive relatively lower pay than men. In the second quarter of 2006, full-time working women had median earnings of $593 per week—81.1% of the $731 earned by men (U.S. Bureau of Labor Statistics, 2006).

Evelyn Murphy (2005) use the term *wage discrimination* to remind women that discrimination costs them money when they do not receive equal pay for equal work—"all women lose," for the more women are paid, the more they lose (p. 14). In Murphy's review of the AFL-CIO survey of working women in 2002, 92% of women marked "equal pay" as the top priority above all of the other collective concerns such as health insurance, pensions, and child care (p. 24). A consequence of earning less money than men is that women become less able to provide for themselves and their families and lack enough money for their own development and self-care.

Working Opportunities for Pregnant Women and Working Mothers

After passage of the Civil Rights Act of 1964, Congress passed the Pregnancy Discrimination Act (PDA) as an amendment to Title VII of the Civil Rights Act. PDA aims to protect women from discrimination on the basis of pregnancy, childbirth, or related medical conditions in hiring, pregnancy and maternity leave, health insurance, and fringe benefits.

The courts receive increasingly frequent claims of discrimination against pregnant employees; in most of those cases the employers could not justify their different treatment toward pregnant women with reasonable causes (EEOC, 2006a). Gregory (2003) pointed out that even the rising number of lawsuits understates the problem because many new mothers are reluctant to file suit as a result of the discrimination they received during pregnancy. Therefore, it is difficult to know the full extent of discrimination encountered by pregnant employees. Balancing work and family while fighting a claim of discrimination requires more energy than most working mothers have available.

Working mothers are also disadvantaged in career advancement, both from external pressures and from personal choices. About 70.5% of all mothers participated in the labor force in 2005 (U.S. Bureau of Labor Statistics, 2006), but the labor force participation rate of married mothers, which had increased steadily in previous decades, stopped its advance and has even decreased since 1997. The biggest declines are among mothers of infants. Participation rates of mothers of children under the age of 1 year fell from 59% in 1997 to 51% in 2007 (Cohany & Sok, 2007). The largest declines in workforce participation were among highly educated mothers with bachelor's degrees or more, but declines were seen in all demographic categories. Participation rates were down among all ethnic groups, with the exception of African American mothers whose workforce participation trends have not changed. (Cohony & Sok, 2007).

This reversal of workforce participation rate gains by mothers, and particularly by mothers of young children, may reflect a trend among new mothers to leave the workforce temporarily (between 1 and 3 years) to care for their children full-time. There are many reasons more women are choosing to leave today's workforce. Many mothers are older, have college degrees, and have husbands whose earnings can support their households. Women with less education leave the workforce because they cannot afford child care. Still others find that balancing work and family is increasingly difficult when faced with longer work hours, so they choose to leave the workforce temporarily (Cohany & Sok, 2007).

Because of these demands, many mothers who continue to work or who return to the workforce after a temporary leave prefer part-time work. In a recent national survey by the Pew Research Center (2007), when full-time working mothers were asked to describe their ideal working situation (to work full-time, part-time, or not at all outside the home), 60% said they would prefer to work part-time (an increase of 12 percentage points from 1997), and 19% reported that they would like not to work at all.

Recognizing this need for more flexible options for women, many employers have created "mommy tracks"—a special career path designed by employers with "flex-time, part-time, extended maternity leaves, and job sharing" (Gregory, 2003, p. 106). These tracks may reflect a changing attitude among corporations that more flexible, family-friendly policies may benefit all workers and enhance workplace effectiveness (Lewis & Cooper, 2005). Job sharing, flexible hours, telecommuting, and onsite child care are some of the innovations now in place in the world of work. Working families have become more demanding of alternative models of work, and companies now appear more willing to balance personal quality-of-life issues with workplace demands.

Gregory (2003) and Murphy (2005) described the disadvantages mothers receive from the mommy track: It supports the stereotypes that working mothers are less committed to their jobs and less efficient. Thus, mothers are withdrawn from more competitive, prestigious, and rewarding positions and are assigned lower-level positions from which they are less likely to be considered for promotions. Murphy (2005) gave the example of an employer's differential reaction to men and women with children: "He just had a baby; give him that big project, since he'll be working harder now that he has to support a family. She just had a baby; don't give her that big project, she won't be able to travel or even get here on time anymore" (p. 202). In sum, motherhood, in combination with stereotypical biases in the workplace, can constitute a heavy barrier working women with children must overcome in the development of their vocations, but today's women are searching for options that allow them to balance both family and career.

Sexual Harassment at Work

Shortly after I began working with my boss, he asked if I could give him a ride home from work. He said he and his wife only had one car and his house was on the way to mine. Over time his requests became more frequent, and one night he reached over while I was driving and slid his hand up my thigh. I was scared, but I didn't want to lose my job. I really didn't know what to do.

—Andrea, age 24

Hesse-Biber and Carter (2000) found that sexual harassment, especially toward women, is present in every field in the workplace. The EEOC (2006b) defined sexual harassment as "unwelcome sexual advances, requests for sexual favors, and other verbal or physical conduct of a sexual nature . . . which explicitly or implicitly affects an individual's employment, unreasonably interferes with an individual's work performance, or creates an intimidating, hostile, or offensive work environment." The number of harassment charges filed with the EEOC has risen sharply, from 19,434 in the 1980s to 109,472 in the 1990s. In 2005 more than 90% of harassment charges were filed by women (EEOC, 2006b). However, this rising trend fails to depict the broad extent of workplace sexual harassment. Gregory (2003) cited findings from a survey that showed that 60% of women in management positions experienced various forms of sexual harassment at work, but only 14% of the women reported it and less than 1% filed a charge or took legal action. Gregory pointed out that most women choose to keep silent rather than confront harassers or report the harassment to others. Many women are embarrassed to tell the details of their harassment to others or fear retaliation or other repercussions. For working women, the "filing of a sexual harassment complaint often is a form of career suicide" (Avner, as quoted in Hesse-Biber & Carter, 2000, p. 121). Murphy (2005) described the danger as one exclusively for women; women often lose their jobs for reporting sexual harassment, whereas the men usually keep their positions.

Furthermore, when employers try to avoid charges of sexual harassment by not hiring women, women's employment choices are restricted. This unpromising prospect of career advancement keeps women reluctant to disclose the sexual harassment they encounter in the workplace. Both overt and subtle forms of harassment serve to reinforce vertical and horizontal gender segregation in occupations.

Models for Understanding Workplace Gender Discrimination

The key questions for counselors and their clients to understand are, Why does sex discrimination occur? and, Why does it persist? Here we focus on some primary sources for workplace sex discrimination: stereotypes of gendered work roles for men and women; the influence of education in general and postsecondary education in particular on women's career choices and advancement; and the influences of women's socialization.

Stereotypes of Gendered Work Roles

The foundations for learning gendered work roles begin very early in girls' lives. Betz and Fitzgerald (1987) demonstrated that traditional gender-role stereotypes are transferred to and are reinforced in children through the influences of parents, teachers, and mass media. Betz and Fitzgerald found that as young girls learn culturally based stereotypes that their future roles should include good wife and mother, they also learn occupational stereotypes regarding the difference between traditionally labeled "men's jobs/positions" and "women's jobs/positions." Girls' career development is therefore highly influenced by social learning and exposure to same-sex models. In one study of African American women who were successful in their careers, the women participants cited several factors that were critical to their success: a strong family emphasis on the importance of education, family resources allocated to exposing them to a variety of career and academic role models, and family members being highly involved in their decisions regarding career development (Pearson & Bieschke, 2001). Family influences can strongly influence girls in their pursuit of academic goals and in developing a strong career orientation toward a variety of vocations.

Education

I was salutatorian of my high school class, receiving all *A*s and only one *B*. When I applied for admission to our state university, I was admitted "on probation" because I lacked the required core courses in math and science from high school. I felt really dumb; no one had ever encouraged me to take these classes.

—Morgan, age 21

Girls and women are doing well academically, making better grades in school, graduating at higher rates, and entering college at higher rates than are males (Halpern, 2006; also see Chapter 5). However, girls continue to opt out of core courses in mathematics in high school, limiting their ability to pursue scientific and technical careers in college. Further, even among the few girls who pursue higher level math or science courses in high school and who are successful as science and technology majors in college, many do not go on to pursue advanced degrees in these fields (Betz, 2006). Instead, the majors of women at both the graduate and undergraduate levels are concentrated in the health professions and education; far fewer women chose science and engineering as their majors (National Center for Education Statistics, 1996).

Extracurricular activities also reinforce gendered roles. According to Meece and Scantlebury (2006), girls are likely to work on student publications, perform community service, or participate in musical activities, whereas boys gravitate to computer and science clubs. The number of girls who participate in varsity sports has increased substantially during the past several decades (from a ratio of 35:1 in 1970 to a ratio of 1:1.33 in 2002), and was at an all-time high in 2006, but boys still outnumber girls in sports participation with 4 million boys and only 3 million girls participating (National Federation of State High School Associations, 2006).

Women's Socialization

When I was offered my job, I happily accepted what I thought was a good salary. In talking with my (male) officemates, it was clear that they were much more aggressive in negotiating their offers. One of them asked for and got six weeks vacation for the first year (three weeks is the norm), and another was given new furniture and a new computer at his request. It never occurred to me that I was in the position to ask for anything.

—Jackie, age 26

Throughout the life span women are more oriented toward an "ethic of caring" and are more relationally oriented than men (e.g., Gilligan, 1982; see also Chapter 1). When moral issues arise, Gilligan theorized, women are grounded by their concerns for others, whereas men generally respond in terms of their individual welfare. When work and family conflicts develop, women often place the welfare of their family and children above their own needs. For example, women may choose to leave work to attend a child's soccer game rather than work overtime. They give up paid employment to care for a chronically ill parent. They choose to put a career on hold while their children are young. Cultural influences reinforce this socialization; for example, an Asian American woman may choose to observe filial piety, putting the needs of the extended family over the pursuit of a career of her own choosing (Ali, Lewis, & Sandil, 2006).

When women consistently put the needs of others first, it places them at a disadvantage in negotiating on the job. Women often don't ask for what they deserve (Hymowitz, 2004) in terms of pay, responsibilities, and rewards. Babcock and Laschever (2003) reported that women often take the first salary offer made without attempting to negotiate for a better one. The socialization that women receive as girls in elementary school to be quiet, follow directions, and do what the teacher wants is at odds with a corporate workplace that rewards assertive behavior.

The world of work relies heavily on the relationships individual workers can build both within a company and with suppliers, clients, and vendors with whom a company does business. Although women are good at building relationships, they have less success in networking. Women with families might have less time for informal corporate networks. Moreover, the lack of women in higher-level positions within a company means fewer available mentors to nurture their careers and provide assignments that reward their talents and skills (Babcock & Laschever, 2003).

Addressing Workplace Discrimination

After analyzing reasons for gender discrimination in the workplace, several suggestions for addressing the problem emerge. First, counselors can take actions to advocate for clients by working to change harmful social stereotypes and to reshape traditional women's roles in line with current reality. They should certainly be aware of any biases they hold that might perpetuate cultural stereotypes that are potentially damaging to women (Chae, 2002) while at the same time remaining respectful of each client's cultural values.

Hesse-Biber and Carter (2000) suggested women should work not only at the individual level to create change but also at the organizational level to ally with others for institutional transformation. Women have begun to work together in establishing and developing their organizations such as the Institute for Women in Trades, Technology, and Science, the Institute for Women's Policy Research, the National Association of Working Women, 9 to 5, and the National Women's Law Center (Giele & Stebbins, 2003). Encouraging women to participate in professional organizations allows them opportunities to network with other women, seek support, and advocate for change.

The educational system is another important avenue toward change. Betz and Fitzgerald (1987) argued that education can have a very negative influence in promoting social stereotypes of gender roles, but it also can serve as a powerful force in facilitating sex fairness and individual potential. For example, school counselors can work to create a school culture in which girls are encouraged to explore all career paths, to pursue advanced math and science courses, and to provide positive role models of women who have pursued nontraditional careers.

Self-Exploration Exercise

1. In what ways have you (or someone you know well) experienced gender discrimination at work or in pursuing your career? How have horizontal and vertical segregation, wage discrimination, or sexual harassment played a role in your life?
2. Traditionally, work–family balance challenges have been viewed as the responsibility for the woman in the couple to address. Why is there a need for both partners to address these issues? How do you currently manage to share household responsibilities in an equitable way?
3. Who was your role model for what it means to be a woman? A mother? How has this affected you in your choices as an adult? How has it affected your expectations for yourself (or your partner) in terms of household management? Child care? Work?

Counseling Issues for Dual-Earner Couples

Gender differences in pay and career advancement affect all women, but women in dual-earner couples face unique challenges. We have purposefully selected the term *dual-earner* rather than *dual-career* couples for this chapter because it is the more inclusive term. Dual-earner couples now constitute the majority family type (Haddock, 2002), and we address three primary areas of concern: (a) asynchrony in career development, (b) caregiving, and (c) problems with division of household tasks.

Career Asynchrony

I just got promoted at work and was offered a new title. I should be happy but now my husband has been offered his "dream job" in another state. There are few opportunities for me there. I feel like just when I'm getting somewhere, our careers collide. How do we compromise? How do we decide if we should move or not?

—Joyce, age 36

Many couples do not make conscious decisions about coordinating their job or career paths, and even when they do, it is women who generally alter their career aspirations for the good of their partners or to care for young children (Kaltreider, Gracie, & Sirulnick, 1997). Further, even when couples attempt to coordinate their separate careers with the family's life phase, most dual-earner couples' careers do not develop in tandem. One partner's career may remain stagnant while the other partner unpredictably experiences rapid growth, and the pattern may be reversed with sudden changes in the economy. Moving up the corporate ladder often entails physical moves to other locations for the purpose of gaining more diverse experience. Such a move, while a clear advancement for one partner, can be a disruption in career for the second partner.

Many dual-earner couples, however, live paycheck to paycheck with little thought of career advancement. Women in such relationships may be more concerned with the "sticky floor" (Barnett & Rivers, 1999) than with the "glass ceiling." For those women, the struggle is to get beyond a low-level, low-wage job rather than worrying about bumping up against the top levels of promotion.

Caregiving Concerns

Dual-earner couples with children face challenges in finding adequate child care, with the major issues being quality and affordability. With some families working long hours at two or three jobs to sustain a living, child care may be shared among families or neighbors (Newman, 2000). Most families with young children participate in child-care arrangements by grandparents and other relatives (Overturf Johnson, 2005). Others must seek formal child-care services. These are difficult decisions for parents, as research on the effects of children's participation in child-care centers is still emerging (see Belsky et al., 2007, for a recent review by the National Institute of Child Health and Human Development Study of Early Child Care and Youth Development). Unlike the K–12 school environment, the qualifications of teachers and child-care workers is largely unregulated, and centers need meet only minimal health standards to operate.

Further, parents who seek high-quality child care must be able to pay large tuition costs. Child care for one child for one year can easily exceed the cost of a year's college tuition (Shulman, 2000), yet financial aid is extremely limited for child care. After-school care is also a concern both for parents with children in child-care settings and for parents whose school-age children come home to an empty house.

Finally, care of family members extends not only to minor children but also to elderly or sick adult family members who are dependent on their adult children or partners for assistance with daily living, transportation to medical appointments, and companionship. According to Barnett and Hyde (2001), it is women who are most likely to assume the responsibility for elder care. The term "sandwich generation" has been coined to describe women caring for both parents or grandparents and their own children (see also Chapter 10).

Division of Household Labor

Another area of concern for dual-earner couples is the division of household labor. Unless the family is one of some means, with the capacity to hire a housekeeper or cleaning service, the domestic chores of cleaning, cooking, laundry, and child care remain to be done after a couple's day at work. Women, on average, spend twice as much time on family work as men, although current research indicates that fathers are spending far more time engaged in child care than in the past. According to a national study, fathers now spend approximately 6.5 hours per week on child care, a 153% increase since 1965 (Bianchi, Robinson, & Milkie, 2006). Even though this is a sharp increase in time for fathers, it comprises only half of the hours that mothers spend in child care (12.9 hours per week; Bianchi et al., 2006). Further, while dads have become more involved in child care, their participation in other household tasks is relatively unchanged. Women still do 66% of all routine, household work (Coltrane, 1996) and 90% of the planning, supervising, and scheduling of children's activities (Steil, 2000).

When a woman enters the labor force or returns to the labor force after the birth of a child, the amount of "home" work does not go down; it is merely added onto the work time on the job. This phenomenon led Arlie Hochschild (1989) to coin the term "second shift" to describe the work that women do at home after work. Early speculation that the amount of domestic work would decrease with the advent of new technologies and would lead to more leisure time has not come to pass (Stratton, 2003). Instead, family work has increased with the addition of strong societal expectations regarding the need for "intensive parenting" (including more outside activities for children), increasing use of cell phones and computers, and lives that are fuller than ever before (Bianchi et al., 2006).

Prevention Strategies for Dual-Earner Couples

Women place a high value on relationships and connections with others, but they also derive satisfaction from pursuit of their individual goals. For most women, optimal mental health results from having ample opportunities for both meaningful achievements outside the home and quality relationships with others (Betz, 2006). Because most women experience conflicts between these life dimensions, it is important for counselors to assist dual-earner couples around issues of work–family balance.

Traditionally the challenges of work–family balance were viewed solely as a problem for women to address—"If she just manages her time better, then the couple's problems will be resolved," or "Why doesn't she just cut back on her hours at work?"—but current research indicates the need for addressing these issues with both partners (Crosby & Sabattini, 2006; Zimmerman, Haddock, Current, & Ziemba, 2003). Through couples counseling, dual-earner couples can benefit from modifying current beliefs about the partnership or marriage, from strengthening communication and negotiation skills, and from making active efforts to promote overall marital satisfaction. Addressing these concerns through premarital counseling can prevent future problems from developing. The following areas of counseling focus are suggested: creating a vision for the relationship, communication and negotiation about household management, and shared commitment to the relationship (Gilbert & Kearney, 2006; Zimmerman et al., 2003).

Creating a Vision for the Relationship

It is important for both partners to clarify their roles and their expectations for personal, family, and career development. Some sample questions for a dual-earner couple might include the following:

- What are their priorities and overall life goals? What are their career aspirations?
- What do they feel they need from their partner to achieve their goals? What are their expectations of one another?
- What are their views about gender roles, and how do these affect the relationship? What are potential areas of conflict? How flexible is each partner willing to be in modifying traditional gender-role attitudes and behaviors?
- What are the couple's plans for setting boundaries around work and family so that work does not unnecessarily intrude on home life?

In addition to communication regarding each partner's priorities and values, couples must spend time communicating about the process of managing family and work responsibilities.

- How will they make decisions together?
- How will they make short- and long-term plans?
- How will the couple recognize and renegotiate when their plans are no longer efficient or effective?

If couples do not communicate openly about these larger issues, it will be much more difficult for them to manage day-to-day tasks effectively.

Communication and Negotiation About Household Management

As traditional gender norms are changing in current society, male partners are less likely to view household management as "women's work" and are more likely to be involved in these tasks than in the past. As described earlier, however, women still tend to do much more of the household and child-care duties than their partners, and women tend to feel that they are always in a rush because there are always more tasks to be completed (Bianchi et al., 2006). Although sharing these tasks is important, Kaltreider et al. (1997) suggested that it is generally unhealthy (if not impossible) for couples to strive for an equal distribution of tasks. Instead, they recommended that couples seek equity; that is, each of the two partners should perceive the overall balance between rewards and costs in the relationship to be relatively equal for both individuals. Instead of dividing a list of duties into equal halves, a couple who experiences equity assumes that the good of the overall relationship is more important than the individual's needs or wants at a particular time. It is not the actual division of tasks but each partner's satisfaction with the arrangement that contributes to marital satisfaction (Gilbert & Kearney, 2006). This attitude can help either partner tolerate a temporary imbalance in the workload if he or she believes a balance will resume over a period of time. For example, a male partner might take on more home responsibilities while his partner faces a complex project at work, and his partner might manage the majority of household duties while he is preparing for a promotion. It is clear that open communication regarding perceived equity is important throughout a relationship as circumstances change. Counselors can assess whether couples have discussed questions such as these:

- How do they share responsibility for aspects of family life such as housework, child care, or financial management?
- What aspect of household management does each partner prefer? How can the household management system better reflect each partner's preferences (perhaps one partner dislikes doing laundry, but prefers washing dishes)?
- What strategies do they use for household organization (e.g., family calendars, schedules for completing tasks)? Who manages impending due dates, deadlines, and appointments (Zimmerman et al., 2003)?
- What is their support system like, and how can they build stronger social support networks comprising of family members, community resources, and employers?

Shared Commitment to the Relationship

According to Gilbert and Kearney (2006), marital satisfaction is enhanced when there is agreement on household tasks, emotion work (e.g., warmth and family cohesiveness), and status enhancement work—the things each partner does that express respect and appreciation for their partner's family contributions and careers. The importance of status enhancement was evident in Zimmerman et al.'s (2003) study of successful dual earners as well. Couples in their study displayed strong positive regard for one another. Not only did they appreciate their spouse as a life partner, they openly expressed respect for their partner's competence as a working professional. Each couple discussed the importance of making time and effort to keep the relationship a priority, despite their busy schedules. To this end, counselors can encourage couples to plan for uninterrupted time together. For example, does the couple have a daily time to reconnect with one another? Do they make time for intimacy? Do they regularly spend time as a couple?

Further, an important way that partners can support the relationship is to support their partner's need to engage in personally meaningful activities outside of work (Zimmerman et al., 2003). Counselors can assist each partner in identifying pleasurable leisure activities that support positive physical and mental health. As discussed in the following two sections, finding time for self-care is generally more difficult for women than it is for men.

Counseling Issues Specific to Working Mothers

It was originally assumed that maternal employment would result in negative outcomes for families, but research has demonstrated that this is not the case. Maternal employment in and of itself seems to have little affect on the overall quality of family relationships. Rather, quality is more determined by such factors as parental attitudes about maternal employment, income derived, mother's warmth and sensitivity, quality of both parent's jobs, and the quality of child care (Haddock, 2002). As Haddock explained, it is not *whether* a mother works, but *how* she and her partner work that affects the quality of family relationships.

For example, women who possess multiple roles (wife, mother, employee) can reap positive mental and physical health benefits (Crosby & Sabattini, 2006). Occupying more than one role appears to buffer women from the stress within each role. According to Barnett and Rivers (1999), work or home can balance the stressors of the other sphere, as each role provides a woman with alternative perspectives through which to view her experiences and allows for temporary distance from difficult situations. Working at a job that one finds meaningful can mediate difficulties with children or conflicts within a dysfunctional marriage. Likewise, the support of loved ones and the reciprocal bonding between mother and child may provide a source of resilience in the face of a long commute, an angry boss, or encountering other problems on the job (Arkin, 1995). In addition, working outside the home helps to reduce financial stress and can result in increased social support by providing increased opportunities for meeting new people (Barnett & Hyde, 2001).

In addition to these potential positive outcomes, women in dual-earner relationships face significant challenges in managing multiple roles. *Role strain* involves the conflicts that occur between and within the demands emerging from multiple life roles (Kaltreider et al., 1997). Role strain can occur when roles are ambiguously defined, causing one to be uncertain as to what is expected for each life role. This can result in feelings of confusion and guilt over not meeting others' perceived expectations. Many women internalize cultural myths regarding the "ideal" mother and the "superwoman" ("I must do it all, do it all perfectly, and never ask for help."), thereby placing pressure on themselves to achieve unrealistic standards. For example, if a dual-earner couple does not communicate about how they will manage the household tasks that accumulate after the arrival of an infant, the woman might assume that she is expected to provide all child care and complete all of her previous household duties. At the same time, she might be working late at night to complete the tasks assigned to her by her employer, even though her boss has not explicitly stated when he or she expects the work to be done. This woman will experience the stress and strain of struggling to meet others' demands even though the nature of their expectations for her in her new roles is unclear.

Role overload occurs when the demands of multiple roles exceed one's resources (Kaltreider et al., 1997). Role overload can result in extreme fatigue, time pressures, and problems in the marital relationship, particularly in families with preschool children when attending to children's needs often exceeds a mother's time and energy reserves. The type of work in which a woman is employed also has an impact on role overload. Women who work in low-wage or low-quality jobs are particularly vulnerable to role overload (Crosby & Sabattini, 2006).

Role underload can occur in working women when they decrease their role at either work or home. When this shift in roles leaves a woman feeling that she is disconnected from both working life and home life, role underload becomes a new source of stress (Kaltreider et al., 1997). For example, a woman who decides to work part-time so that she can spend more time with her children might feel diminished in her capacity at the office but also feel that she is not accepted or understood by the stay-at-home mothers in her community.

Prevention Strategies: Preparing First-Time Parents for the Challenges of Work–Family Balance

Most couples are unprepared for and don't have a realistic picture of the challenges of balancing work and family life (Jackson, Tal, & Sullivan, 2003). Counselors can consider offering psychoeducational workshops for couples about the transition to parenthood for both partners. Areas of focus can include (a) training in basic communication skills to assist couples in keeping lines of communication open during this stressful period in their relationship; (b) comparing commonly held myths and unrealistic expectations with the reality of parenthood to help both partners plan for the changes that will likely occur in their lives; and (c) helping couples to develop coping strategies for effectively dealing with the stressors of parenting and balancing work and family commitments (such as those suggested throughout this chapter).

First-time mothers may need specific preparation for the challenges of motherhood. This type of information would be extremely effective when presented in a support group format. Jackson et al. (2003) suggested addressing the following topics:

- First-time mothers may not be prepared for the physical pain and discomfort of delivery and recovery, nor are most expecting the intense emotional changes that occur during the first 6 weeks postpartum. To normalize these motherhood experiences, counselors can remind women that up to 80% of women experience "baby blues" (mild depressive symptoms) after delivery (Burt & Hendrick, 2005).
- Many first-time mothers hold the expectation that mothering will come naturally and is a purely joyful experience. Counselors can help to reassure women that it is normal to feel overwhelmed at the barrage of tasks and the all-consuming nature of caring for an infant, thus alleviating some of their guilt and anxiety around these concerns.
- Counselors can help first-time mothers understand the concepts of equity versus equality (as previously described). They can be reminded that at first there may seem to be an inequitable division of household tasks, as she may feel she is doing more of the parenting tasks during the baby's first months of life.
- Counselors can provide parenting and self-care information, as most first-time mothers desire information about the actual delivery process, caring for a newborn, and creative ways of finding time to care for themselves.
- Counselors can assist mothers in anticipating and managing their fears around body image, their competence as mothers, how parenthood will affect their marriage, and how parenthood will affect their career.

Counseling Interventions With Working Mothers

The best intervention is to work with couples toward preventing the onset of work–family conflicts, but working mothers currently coping with these concerns may need additional support. As described previously, despite the potential benefits that multiple roles can provide, working mothers often experience stress, pressure, guilt, and exhaustion when they try to meet unrealistic standards in all life areas. It is clear that working mothers can benefit from counseling approaches that (a) provide psychoeducation about the effects of maternal employment on families; (b) employ cognitive restructuring to dispel myths about meeting the standards of the ideal mother or superwoman; (c) help clients to develop coping resources such as time management and priority setting skills, stress management techniques, and strategies for self-care; and (d) emphasize the development of strong social support networks. An example of this type of approach is presented here.

A Multimodal Psychoeducational Group for Working Mothers

Barbara Morgan and Laura Hensley Choate developed a 6-week group for working mothers as an outreach service to the community. Child care and an evening meal were provided as part of the 2-hour sessions. For a complete description of the group format, see Morgan and Hensley (1998). Core components and specific techniques are described here.

1. Psychoeducational component: Women were provided with education about the effects of maternal employment on their families and how managing multiple roles can potentially contribute to positive mental health for many women (Barnett & Hyde, 2001). To identify their current beliefs, participants in the group examined the impact of cultural messages and stereotypes on their own role expectations. They explored questions such as, Who was your role model for what it means to be a woman? How has this affected you in your jobs and families? What are some of the feelings you experience as you balance your roles as career woman and mother?

2. Cognitive restructuring component: After their current beliefs were identified, participants were taught how to dispute irrational beliefs regarding their roles. They were asked to challenge their assumptions about their views of the "ideal" mother and their beliefs that they were to always put others' needs above their own. To directly address the guilt they experienced, participants learned to practice thought stopping and to replace negative thoughts with positive affirmations (e.g., "I am still a good mother even if my house isn't perfectly neat and I don't enroll my child in every extracurricular activity available at his school," or simply "It is okay to ask for help!").

3. Coping resources component: Participants were encouraged to develop a repertoire of coping resources. They were assisted in assessing their strengths in both motherhood and work domains and identified the aspects from both roles from which they derived satisfaction. During group sessions, the women were introduced to stress management and relaxation techniques such as daily meditations, relaxing music, and deep breathing exercises. A self-care focus was emphasized throughout the group. When discussing self-care, many of the participants became aware that they no longer pursued individual goals or hobbies. To emphasize the importance of self-care, we asked participants to make a list of five changes they could make in their approach to self-care. Participants were encouraged to implement at least one of these self-care activities and to explore what the process was like for them.

4. Social support component: While women were encouraged to develop strong social support networks with family, friends, coworkers, employers, and community resources (Jackson et al., 2003), the support group consisting of other working mothers also grew to become an important source of support. Women in the group reported that they need a space in which they can voice their concerns and truly feel heard. They felt the group was a place in which they experienced trust and nurturance from other women, which in turn gave them strength to better cope with the stressors of their daily lives.

Consider the following case study and your responses to a new mother who is struggling to "get everything right" both at home and at work.

Case Study

Mary is a 30-year-old married Caucasian woman who works as a salesperson at a marketing firm. She has been employed with the same company for the past 7 years and is one of the firm's top salespersons. She recently gave birth to her first child, who is now 4 months old. Mary was able to take 3 months of maternity leave and has now been back at work for 1 month.

After returning to work, Mary is experiencing a great deal of fatigue, tension, and guilt. At work, Mary is trying to put in extra effort to make up for the time lost during maternity leave and to prove to her boss that she is still a top salesperson. However, when Mary drops her child off at her child-care center each morning, Mary is flooded with guilt. She manages to push these feelings aside during the workday, but after picking her daughter up from day care in the evening and returning home to face household responsibilities like laundry, cooking, and dishes, she becomes discouraged. She feels guilty if she does not hold and play with her daughter in the evenings because she has not seen her all day, yet she also wants some down time for herself. Her husband is helping with some of the household tasks, but she feels guilty that he has to do these things when she views them as her responsibility. In sum, Mary says that between her boss, husband, and child, she can't make anyone happy and feels like she is failing in all of her relationships.

1. Where would you begin in your work with Mary?
2. What myths about being a woman, a mother, and a working mother might you need to dispel for Mary?
3. How can you assist Mary in easing her transition to becoming a working mother?
4. According to strategies outlined in the chapter, how can Mary and her husband become a more effective dual-earner couple?

Promoting Women's Wellness

I make time for my family and my work, but there is very little time left for me. I feel guilty when I do take time to go for a walk or even to sit for ten minutes and enjoy my morning coffee because I feel I "should" be playing with the kids, doing the laundry, or catching up on my work. I know I need "me" time, but I can't enjoy it when I have it because I feel that others are missing out because of my self-indulgence.

—Carla, age 29

Women recognize the need for self-care, yet they often sacrifice self-care when faced with prioritizing the many demands of daily life (Williams-Nickelson, 2006). According to Williams-Nickelson (2006), self-care can be defined as "activities women undertake with intention to promote, ensure, or restore psychological and physical health; to prevent, manage or recover from disease, injury, or trauma; or to achieve a sense of well-being" (p. 183). This definition is compatible with the concept of wellness described in Chapter 1, which also encourages optimal health and well-being (Myers & Sweeney, 2005). Research has shown that qualitative differences exist in how men and women experience self-care activities (Mattingly & Bianchi, 2003). Some of the social forces that affect women's experience of self-care include inequalities in time use between men and women, changes in the cultural context of childhood, and the expectation for women to be continually available to care for others. These issues are explored next.

Self-care has been described as a context in which to find and care for the self away from the demands of work and family, but women often experience barriers in access to free time and constraints on their use of free time. Iwasaki, MacKay, and Mactavish (2005) suggested that compared with men, women are much more likely to experience free time that is fragmented or contaminated by nonleisure activities, such as child care and household chores. When they do engage in self-care, women may not experience the same level of relief from time pressures due to feelings of guilt associated with viewing themselves as less deserving of free time, feelings of pressure to get on with other responsibilities, or the motivation to choose leisure activities that promote family cohesion rather than activities that promote personal relaxation and rejuvenation (Mattingly & Bianchi, 2003).

Women who feel pressured to combine a high level of paid work with a high level of home work can experience feelings of being rushed, even when increased free time is available to them (Mattingly & Sayer, 2006). One national study indicated that today's mothers feel pressure to complete their paid work, finish home-related tasks, and spend quality time with their children. To accomplish these things, they tend to multitask; most parents say that they spend about half of their waking hours doing two or more things at once (Bianchi et al., 2006).

In addition, the changing nature of childhood contributes to difficulties for women in taking the time for quality self-care (Mattingly &

Sayer, 2006). Children of the mid- to late-20th century typically spent after-school and weekend time engaged in free play, either with siblings or neighborhood friends. In contrast, today's children's lives are highly structured with organized sports teams, artistic or music lessons, and special events. In line with today's cultural trend of intensive parenting, the expectation remains that women will develop time-intensive strategies to provide structured activities for children, even after a full day of paid work. For many women, free time has been consumed with planning, attending, and supervising this type of child-oriented leisure rather than focusing on adult-oriented leisure that might be personally refreshing.

Counseling Interventions That Promote Women's Wellness

As described throughout this book, counseling for wellness involves a focus beyond remediation of the presenting problem and that promotes overall well-being and life satisfaction (Myers & Sweeney, 2005). A counselor using a wellness approach assists clients in examining all life dimensions to discern existing strengths, to explore areas that have been neglected, and to develop an action plan for enhancing wellness. As women often have a difficult time accepting the need to incorporate these types of self-care activities into their daily lives, counselors may need to spend some time educating women about the importance of self-care for overall life satisfaction. Counselors can also assist women in viewing self-care as a coping strategy necessary to function effectively in relationships, work, and in achieving balance between the two. It is helpful to remember that "balance is not achieved by trying to handle more or work faster and harder. In general, it is achieved through meaningful work (paid and unpaid), satisfying relationships, and personal rejuvenation" (Williams-Nickelson, 2006, p. 183). As suggested by Tryon and Winograd (2003), women can graph their daily and weekly activities, noting how much time they devote to promoting personal wellness. They can explore the reasons that keep them from doing more things to care for themselves.

Women may need to be reminded that although their time for wellness activities is often fragmented, they can nevertheless practice these strategies in small increments of time (Simpson, 2006). Counselors can support women in creating a "personal wellness calendar" on which they schedule brief daily rituals and short weekly blocks of time set aside for personal rejuvenation. They can also be reminded of the following basic principles of balanced living as identified by Williams-Nickelson (2006): focus, delegate, consolidate and use technology, and simplify.

Focus. Multitasking can work in the short run, but over long periods of time, juggling multiple tasks becomes ineffective. Encourage women to give their undivided attention to each task they undertake (including self-care activities).

Delegate. Women often resume primary responsibilities for household management in addition to paid work duties and subsequently have difficulty relinquishing control of these responsibilities even when they need help from their partners and families (Jackson et al., 2003). Encourage women to build strong support systems, access them when necessary, and to say no to opportunities that are not priorities.

Consolidate and Use Technology. Women can explore the use of technology and innovative services that might add flexibility to their schedules e.g., paying bills or filing taxes online.

Simplify. Women can identify time wasters and eliminate nonessential activities from their schedules. They can ask themselves, "What is truly most important to me?" and begin to say no to activities that are not in line with these goals.

Conclusion

In this chapter we have reviewed the literature related to women's work and career advancement, issues in maternal employment and dual-earner couples, and women and self-care. As the chapter's four authors—a young wife and mother enrolled full-time as a doctoral student; a married graduate student with a full-time job; a married, newly tenured professor with two toddler-age children; and a married professor nearing the end of her career—we each reflect some of the life situations described in the text. What is striking is not the different issues that we face day to day but the common bond we share in our struggles to achieve work–life balance.

Activities for Further Exploration

1. How do traditional socialization processes affect women on the job? Are traditional conceptualizations of gendered work roles changing in contemporary culture?
2. If adults have more technology available to assist with household tasks than ever before, why are so many women still overburdened with the "second shift"?
3. How might balancing multiple roles provide a positive benefit to working women?
4. In the chapter, what is meant by the "changing nature of childhood"? How might this create new pressures for working mothers?
5. How is it possible for women to learn the value of self-care? How will you go about promoting this strategy in your counseling work with women?

Suggested Readings

Barnett, R. C., & Hyde, S. J. (2001). Women, men, work, and family: An expansionist theory. *American Psychologist, 56,* 781–796.

Barnett, R. C., & Rivers, C. (1999). *She works/he works: How two income families are happy, healthy and thriving.* Cambridge, MA: Harvard University Press.

Betz, N. E. (2006). Women's career development. In J. Worell & C. D. Goodheart (Eds.), *Handbook of girls' and women's psychological health: Gender and well-being across the life span* (pp. 312–320). New York: Oxford University Press.

Bianchi, S. M., Robinson, J. P., & Milkie, M. A. (2006). *Changing rhythms of American family life.* New York: Russell Sage Foundation.

Crosby, F. J., & Sabattini, L. (2006). Family and work balance. In J. Worell & C. D. Goodheart (Eds.), *Handbook of girls' and women's psychological health: Gender and well-being across the life span* (pp. 350–358). New York: Oxford University Press.

Giele, J. Z., & Stebbins, L. F. (2003). *Women and equality in the workplace: A reference handbook.* Santa Barbara: ABC-CLIO, Inc.

Gregory, F. R. (2003). *Women and workplace discrimination: Overcoming barriers to gender equality.* New Brunswick: Rutgers University Press.

Hesse-Biber, S., & Carter, G. L. (2000). *Working women in America: Split dreams.* New York: Oxford University Press.

Hochschild, A. (1989). *The second shift: Working parents and the revolution at home.* New York: Viking Press.

Kaltreider, N. B., Gracie, C., & Sirulnick, C. (1997). Love in the trenches: Dual-career relationships. In N. B. Kaltreider (Ed.), *Dilemmas of a double life: Women balancing careers and relationships* (pp. 121–139). Northvale, NJ: Jason Aronson.

Mattingly, M. J., & Sayer, L. C. (2006). Under pressure: Gender differences in the relationship between free time and feeling rushed. *Journal of Marriage and Family, 68,* 205–221.

Morgan, B., & Hensley, L. (1998). Supporting working mothers through group work: A multimodal psychoeducational approach. *Journal for Specialists in Group Work, 23,* 298–311.

Williams-Nickelson, C. (2006). Balanced living through self-care. In J. Worrell & C. D. Goodheart (Eds.), *Handbook of girls' and women's psychological health: Gender and well-being across the life span* (pp. 183–191). New York: Oxford University Press.

Additional Resources

Resources for Working Mothers

http://www.bluesuitmom.com/career/
This Web site provides resources for working women on finding balance, changing jobs, women-owned businesses, special topics including maternity leave, and an online job center.

http://life.familyeducation.com/parenting/working-parents/34415.html
This Web site offers pros and cons on deciding to work or stay home, tips on balancing work outside the home, stress relief, and pregnancy and working. Message boards are available that allow moms to chat with each other and also receive expert advice.

http://www.momsrefuge.com/
This Web site provides information on a variety of subjects for mothers, including family, career, single moms, dads, recipes, and the art of juggling work and motherhood.

http://www.workingmother.com/?service=vpage/106
The Web site for *Working Mother* magazine is dedicated to serving the personal, professional, and family needs of all women. The site includes resources from *Working Mother* magazine, the National Association of Female Executives (NAFE), the Working Mother 100 Best Companies for Working Mothers, the Working Mother Best Companies for Women of Color, and has information on conferences and events.

http://www.singlemom.com/career/careerhtm.
This Web site, designed specifically for the single mom, provides information on financial aid and scholarships, education, employment, strategies and tips, and other information for working moms.

Resources for Working Women

http://www.womenworking2000.com/
This Web site provides resources for empowering women at the office and at home. It has business skills, networking, and advancement and leadership tips from top professionals.

http://www.career-intelligence.com/
This is a for-women career resource that includes tips for career planning and assessment, transition, management, small business services, and therapy.

http://www.careerjournal.com/specialreports/specialwomen_index/
This is part of the *Wall Street Journal* Web site and provides articles on women's career choices and challenges, job search hurdles, opportunities, employer selection, minority women, and balancing multiple roles.

http://www.womensmedia.com/
This Web site for working women provides articles on a diverse set of topics including career advancement, self-employment, simplifying life, working mothers, financial success, and more.

http://www.aaup.org/AAUP/issuesed/WF/resources.htm
This article on work and family for academics provides resources on balancing family and academic work, including gender discrimination, motherhood, balancing work and family for faculty, developing work and family policies for faculty, risks of taking time for family, and working part-time after tenure.

References

Ali, S. R., Lewis, S. Z., & Sandil, R. (2006). Career counseling for Asian women. In B. Walsh & M. J. Heppner (Eds.), *Handbook of career counseling for women* (2nd ed., pp. 241–270). Mahwah, NJ: Erlbaum.

Arkin, C. F. (1995). Multiple roles and women's mental health. *Human Development and Family Life Bulletin, 1.* Retrieved February 12, 2002, from http://www.hec.ohio-state.edu/famlife/bulletin/volume.1/bull13a.htm

Babcock, L., & Laschever, S. (2003). *Women don't ask: Negotiations and the gender divide.* Princeton, NJ: Princeton University Press.

Barnett, R. C., & Hyde, S. J. (2001). Women, men, work, and family: An expansionist theory. *American Psychologist, 56,* 781–796.

Barnett, R. C., & Rivers, C. (1999). *She works/he works: How two income families are happy, healthy and thriving.* Cambridge, MA: Harvard University Press.

Belsky, J., Burchinal, M., McCartney, K., Vandell, D. L., Clarke-Stewart, K. A., & Owen, M. T. (2007). Are there long-term effects of early child care? *Child Development, 78,* 681–701.

Betz, N. E. (2006). Women's career development. In J. Worrell & C. D. Goodheart (Eds.), *Handbook of girls' and women's psychological health: Gender and well-being across the life span* (pp. 312–320). New York: Oxford University Press.

Betz, N. E., & Fitzgerald, L. F. (1987). *The career psychology of women.* Orlando, FL: Academic Press.

Bianchi, S. M., Robinson, J. P., & Milkie, M. A. (2006). *Changing rhythms of American family life.* New York: Russell Sage Foundation.

Break the glass ceiling: Equal opportunity for women and minorities. (n.d.). Retrieved February 16, 2007, from http://www.breaktheglassceiling.com/statistics-women.htm

Burt, V. K., & Hendrick, V. C. (2005). *Clinical manual of women's mental health.* Washington DC: American Psychiatric Association.

Chae, M. H. (2002). Counseling reentry women: An overview. *Journal of Employment Counseling, 39,* 146–152.

Cohany, S. R., & Sok, E. (2007, February). Trends in labor force participation of married mothers of infants. *Monthly Labor Review,* 9–16.

Coltrane, S. (1996). *Family man: Fatherhood, housework, and gender equality.* New York: Oxford University Press.

Crosby, F. J., & Sabattini, L. (2006). Family and work balance. In J. Worrell & C. D. Goodheart (Eds.), *Handbook of girls' and women's psychological health: Gender and well-being across the life span* (pp. 350–358). New York: Oxford University Press.

Equal Employment Opportunity Commission. (2006a). *Pregnancy changes from fiscal years 1992-2005.* Retrieved November 2, 2006, from http://www.eeoc.gov/stats/pregnanc.html

Equal Employment Opportunity Commission. (2006b). *Sexual harassment.* Retrieved November 2, 2006, from http://www.eeoc.gov/types/sexual_harassment.html

Fitzsimons, A. (2002). *Gender as a verb: Gender segregation at work.* Burlington: Ashgate Publishing Limited.

Gasper, S. (2006, May/June). At the top of their game. *The Purdue Alumnus,* 17–20.

Giele, J. Z., & Stebbins, L. F. (2003). *Women and equality in the workplace: A reference handbook.* Santa Barbara: ABC-CLIO, Inc.

Gilbert, L. A., & Kearney, L. K. (2006). Sex, gender, and dual-career families: Implications and applications for career counseling for women. In B. Walsh & M. J. Heppner (Eds.), *Handbook of counseling for women* (2nd ed., pp. 193–217). Mahwah, NJ: Erlbaum.

Gilligan, C. (1982). *In a different voice: Psychological theory and women's development.* Cambridge, MA: Harvard University Press.

Gregory, F. R. (2003). *Women and workplace discrimination: Overcoming barriers to gender equality.* New Brunswick: Rutgers University Press.

Haddock, S. A. (2002). A content analysis of articles pertaining to therapeutic considerations for dual income couples (1979–1999). *The American Journal of Family Therapy, 30,* 141–156.

Halpern, D. F. (2006). Girls and academic success: Changing patterns of academic achievement. In J. Worell & C. D. Goodheart (Eds.), *Handbook of Girls' and Women's Psychological Health* (pp.272–282). New York: Oxford University Press.

Herman, A. M., & Castro, I. L. (1998). *Equal pay: A thirty-five year perspective.* Washington, DC: U.S. Department of Labor and Women's Bureau.

Hesse-Biber, S., & Carter, G. L. (2000). *Working women in America: Split dreams.* New York: Oxford University Press.

Hochschild, A. (1989). *The second shift: Working parents and the revolution at home.* New York: Viking Press.

Hymowitz, C. (2004). Women put noses to the grindstone, and miss opportunities. *Wall Street Journal,* p. 243.

Iwasaki, Y., MacKay, K., & Mactavish, J. (2005). Gender-based analysis of coping with stress among professional managers: Leisure coping and non-leisure coping. *Journal of Leisure Research, 37,* 1–28.

Jackson, M. A., Tal, A. I., & Sullivan, T. R. (2003). Hidden biases in counseling women: Balancing work and family concerns. In M. Kopala & M. Keitel (Eds.), *Handbook of counseling women* (pp. 152–172). Thousand Oaks, CA: Sage.

Kaltreider, N. B., Gracie, C., & Sirulnick, C. (1997). Love in the trenches: Dual-career relationships. In N. B. Kaltreider (Ed.), *Dilemmas of a double life: Women balancing careers and relationships* (pp. 121–139). Northvale, NJ: Jason Aronson.

Lewis, S., & Cooper, C. L. (2005). *Work-life integration: Case studies of organizational change.* Hoboken, NJ: Wiley.

Martin, L. (1991). *Report on the glass ceiling initiative.* Washington, DC: U.S. Department of Labor.

Mattingly, M. J., & Bianchi, S. M. (2003). Gender differences in the quantity and quality of free time: The U.S. experience. *Social Forces, 81,* 999–1030.

Mattingly, M. J., & Sayer, L. C. (2006). Under pressure: Gender differences in the relationship between free time and feeling rushed. *Journal of Marriage and Family, 68,* 205–221.

Meece, J. L., & Scantlebury, K. (2006). Gender and schooling: Progress and persistent barriers. In J. Worrell & C. D. Goodheart (Eds.), *Handbook of* girls' and women's psychological health (pp. 283–291). New York: Oxford University Press.

Morgan, B., & Hensley, L. (1998). Supporting working mothers through group work: A multimodal psychoeducational approach. *Journal for Specialists in Group Work, 23,* 298–311.

Murphy, E. F. (2005). *Getting even: Why women don't get paid like men and what to do about it.* New York: Simon & Schuster.

Myers, J. E., & Sweeney, T. J. (Eds.). (2005). *Counseling for wellness: Theory, research and practice.* Alexandria, VA: American Counseling Association.

National Center for Education Statistics. (1996). *Child care and early child education: Program participation of infants, toddlers, and preschoolers.* Washington, DC: U.S. Department of Education.

National Federation of State High School Associations. (2006). *Participation in high school sports increases again.* Retrieved April 9, 2007, from www.nfhs.org

Newman, K. (2000). On the high wire: How the working poor juggle job and family responsibilities. In E. Appelbaum (Ed.), *Balancing acts: Easing the burdens and improving the options for working families* (pp. 85–94). Washington, DC: Economic Policy Institute.

Overturf Johnson, J. (2005). Who's minding the kids? Child care arrangements: Winter 2002. In *Current Population Reports* (pp. 70–101). Washington, DC: U.S. Census Bureau.

Pew Research Center. (2007). *Fewer mothers prefer full-time work.* Retrieved July 15, 2007, from http://pewresearch.org/pubs/536/working-women

Pearson, S. M., & Bieschke, K. J. (2001). Succeeding against the odds: An examination of familial influences on the career development of professional African American women. *Journal of Counseling Psychology, 48,* 301–310.

Shulman, K. (2000). *The high cost of childcare puts quality care out of reach for many families.* Washington, DC: Children's Defense Fund. Retrieved November 2, 2006, from http://childrensdefensefund.org/pdf/highcost.pdf

Simpson, C. (2006). *Ten minute stress zappers.* Retrieved February 5, 2007, from http://www.coachingsolutionsforwomen.com

Steil, J. M. (2000). Contemporary marriage: Still an unequal partnership. In C. Hendrick & S. S. Hendrick (Eds.), *Close relationships: A sourcebook* (pp. 125–152). Thousand Oaks, CA: Sage.

Stratton, L. S. (2003). Gains from trade and specialization: The division of work in married couple households. In S. Moe (Ed.), *Women, family, and work* (pp. 65–84). Malden, MA: Blackwell.

Tryon, G. S., & Winograd, G. (2003). Developing a healthy identity. In M. Kopala & M. Keitel (Eds.), *Handbook of counseling women* (pp. 185–197). Thousand Oaks, CA: Sage.

U.S. Bureau of Labor Statistics. (2005). *Women in a labor force: A databook.* Retrieved November 2, 2006, from http://www.bls.gov/cps/wlf-databook2005.htm

U.S. Bureau of Labor Statistics. (2006). *Employment characteristics of families in 2005*. Retrieved August 10, 2007, from http://www.bls.gov/news.release/famee.nr0.htm

Williams-Nickelson, C. (2006). Balanced living through self-care. In J. Worrell & C. D. Goodheart (Eds.), *Handbook of girls' and women's psychological health: Gender and well-being across the life span* (pp. 183–191). New York: Oxford University Press.

Wisniewski, N. (2006, July/August). Concerned with work/life balance. *The Purdue Alumnus*, 5.

Zimmerman, T. S., Haddock, S. A., Current, L. R., & Ziemba, S. (2003). Intimate partnership: Foundation to the successful balance of family and work. *American Journal of Family Therapy, 31*, 107–124.

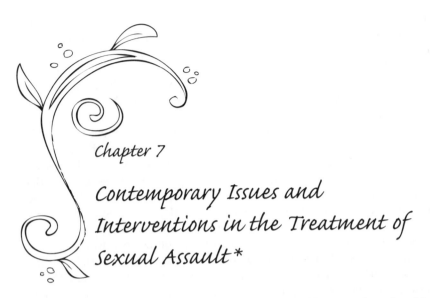

Chapter 7

Contemporary Issues and Interventions in the Treatment of Sexual Assault *

Violence against women is a significant social problem, as there is a high probability that any woman will experience some type of violence in her lifetime. According to the National Violence Against Women (NVAW), more than half of all women surveyed reported an experience of attempted or completed rape or physical assault. Of these, 17.6% were forcible rapes (Tjaden & Thoennes, 2006). Women of all cultural backgrounds experience rape, and there are no significant differences between the reported rape prevalence rates when comparing minority and non-minority women. However, prevalence rates do vary significantly by specific racial and ethnic groups. For example, American Indian women experience significantly higher rates of rape than do women from all other racial/ethnic backgrounds (Tjaden & Thoennes, 2006).

Further, although both men and women are victims of rape, women are disproportionately affected by this crime: 1 in 6 women compared with 1 in 33 men reported having experienced an attempted or completed rape in their lifetimes (Tjaden & Thoennes, 2006). The focus of this chapter is on women's experiences and treatment needs following sexual assault and rape.

A significant proportion of women who are sexually assaulted or raped experience symptoms of posttraumatic stress disorder (PTSD) within 2 weeks following the assault (Resnick, Acierno, Holmes, Kilpatrick, & Jager, 1999). The *Diagnostic and Statistical Manual of Mental Disorders* (*DSM-IV-TR*; American Psychiatric Association, 2000) groups PTSD symptoms into three clusters: intrusion (reexperiencing the trauma, including nightmares,

---

* This chapter is adapted from Hensley, L. G. (2002). Treatment for survivors of rape: Current issues and interventions. *Journal of Mental Health Counseling, 24,* 330–347. Reprinted with the approval of the American Mental Health Counseling Association.

flashbacks, and recurrent thoughts), avoidance (avoiding trauma-related stimuli, social withdrawal, and emotional numbing), and hyperarousal (increased emotional arousal, exaggerated startle response, and irritability). Most women experience these symptoms in the immediate aftermath of rape, but PTSD continues to persist in survivors at lifetime rates between 30 and 50% (Foa, Hearst-Ikeda, & Perry, 1995; Meadows & Foa, 1998; Resnick et al., 1999).

When symptoms persist for 3 months or longer and meet *DSM-IV-TR* diagnostic criteria for chronic PTSD, there is a likelihood that survivors will also experience comorbid disorders including anxiety, depression, and substance abuse (Foa, Davidson, & Frances, 1999; Koss & Kilpatrick, 2001; Resnick, Acierno, Holmes, Dammeyer, & Kilpatrick, 2000). Further, they are likely to experience greater physical distress (such as chronic pain, sexual dysfunction, headaches, upset stomach, back pains, acne, indigestion) in the year following rape and to utilize medical services at higher rates than do women who have not been raped (Clum, Nishith, & Resick, 2001). Women who are particularly at risk for chronic PTSD include those who were injured during the attack, were threatened by the perpetrator that they may be hurt or killed, have a history of prior assault, or have experienced negative interactions with family, peers, or law enforcement systems (Regehr, Cadell, & Jansen, 1999; Ullman, Filipas, Townsend, & Starzynski, 2006).

Survivors typically do not seek formal mental health services in the year following rape (Kimerling & Calhoun, 1994). Despite their initial hesitancy, survivors may seek counseling when their symptoms become intensified or chronic (Draucker, 1999). Counselors need expertise in providing treatment for survivors whose symptoms are both persistent and severe. Mental health professionals can serve as a primary source of support in a survivor's recovery, yet many practitioners report a lack of training in this area during their programs of study (Campbell, Raja, & Grining, 1999). Campbell et al. (1999) also found that when training does occur, it takes place through continuing education and does not include information regarding the significant legal and medical issues that can affect a woman's recovery. Counselors' lack of training may become particularly problematic if they are not adequately prepared to assist survivors of rape who are experiencing chronic PTSD symptoms and comorbid disorders.

The aim of the discussion in this chapter is twofold: (a) to provide an overview of treatment considerations for survivors of rape, and (b) to describe a multimodal treatment approach for women who are experiencing chronic PTSD symptoms resulting from rape-related trauma. The model incorporates four empirically supported techniques based on expert consensus guidelines for treating survivors of trauma: psychoeducation, exposure therapy, cognitive therapy, and anxiety management (Foa et al., 1999). The chapter concludes with a discussion of counseling survivors for wellness and resilience.

Self-Exploration Exercise

1. Reflect on joking comments you have heard about sexual assault, movies you have seen that portray rape, and victim-blaming comments you have made or have heard from others. How do these three influences reflect societal myths about rape? How have you internalized societal myths regarding victim blame?
2. What are some behaviors or actions you take (or do not take) as a precaution against being raped? Reflect on how much the threat of rape influences your actions. If you are male, how have the women in your life been influenced by their fear of rape?
3. Was there ever a time in your life when you experienced any of the following?
   a. A time you were alone and began to experience fear that you could be raped.
   b. Someone you were dating became overly sexually aggressive (e.g., discounting or ignoring your opposition to becoming sexually involved).
   c. Sexual and verbal abuses you have encountered on the street, at parties, at work, or other places that have caused you to feel violated.
   d. Physical abuses (even minor ones) that made you feel sexually violated.
4. After reflecting on questions 1–3, do you have any unresolved feelings that might interfere with your ability to effectively counsel a survivor of sexual assault? What do you need to do to resolve these issues?
5. In what way can your own life experiences assist you in being a more compassionate, empathic counselor for women survivors of sexual assault?

Source: Adapted from Worell & Remer (2002).

Treatment Issues in Counseling Survivors of Rape

There are four important issues for counselors to explore when counseling a survivor of rape: (a) sociocultural influences on a woman's response to rape, (b) her history of victimization, (c) the specific nature of her assault, and (d) her experiences with victim-blame.

Sociocultural Influences

Counselors who work with survivors of rape should consider a woman's reaction to rape within a sociocultural context. Early feminist scholars (e.g., Brownmiller, 1975) argued that rape is not a crime of sex but should be conceptualized as a crime of power. Brownmiller asserted that rape is a tool of a patriarchal system that serves to perpetuate gender inequality and the devaluation of women. According to this theory, fear of rape limits women's freedom and use of power. This pervasive fear operates to maintain gender inequality, as women's "actions and movements, self-expression, self-presentation, and agency within relationships are constrained by the fear of sexual assault" (Low & Organista, 2000, p. 132).

While feminists have examined rape through the lens of gender and power, cultural variables such as ethnicity and class also affect women's responses to and recovery from rape-related trauma. (Low & Organista, 2000). Counselors can remain sensitive to cultural differences in a survivor's access to services, her feelings of safety when reporting crimes, or how disclosures following rape may be received in her community. For example, it is important that counselors not assume that they understand a woman's reasons for not reporting a rape. Only 1 in 5 women in the NVAW survey reported their rape to the police, citing reasons such as fear of the rapist, embarrassment, or not considering it a crime or a police matter (Tjaden & Thoennes, 2006).

Further, counselors should consider how cultural factors shape a survivor's view of gender roles, which in turn influence the meaning she imparts to the rape experience. Latina women, for example, may be more likely to blame themselves for causing a rape if they subscribe to the cultural belief that women invite rape by their behavior and dress and are responsible for controlling male sexuality as well as their own (Littleton, Breitkopf, & Berenson, 2007; Low & Organista, 2000). It is critical that counselors assess for cultural influences in their conceptualization of a survivor's rape experience and choose strategies that are appropriate for use with clients from diverse cultural groups (Hansen, Gama, & Harkins, 2002).

History of Victimization

Counselors providing treatment for survivors of sexual assault and rape should be aware of a client's history of victimization. Early sexual abuse and maltreatment are significant risk factors for rape as an adult (Kessler & Bieschke, 1999; Koss & Kilpatrick, 2001; Sanders & Moore, 1999; Tjaden & Thoennes, 2006), as women who are raped before the age of 18 are twice as likely to be raped as adults (Tjaden & Thoennes, 2006). One explanation for these findings is that rape in childhood or adolescence can lead to the experience of low self-worth and powerlessness, resulting in poorer general functioning, lack of protection against high-risk situations, and greater risk of multiple victimization (Breitenbecher & Gidycz, 1998). In one study with a national sample of female college students, women who had been raped in adolescence or early in college were more likely to report engaging in high-risk health-related behaviors (e.g., physical fights, smoking, binge drinking, two or more current sexual partners) than were college women in general; these behaviors may also put them at risk for multiple victimization (Brener, McMahon, Warren, & Douglas, 1999).

Women who have a history of abuse or maltreatment will likely have different treatment needs than other survivors, and mental health counselors should assess for prior victimization in an effort to understand these needs. It is important for counselors to reassure survivors that while they are not to blame for the current rape, they can benefit from examining their current patterns of high-risk behavior. As part of this process, survivors can gain insight into how the effects of past victimization experiences are influencing their decisions and actions in the present.

Specific Nature of the Assault

A third treatment issue is related to the specific nature of the assault. As rapes are generally classified as stranger, acquaintance, date, partner, or marital rapes, counselors need to understand a client's response to rape in the context of her prior relationship to the perpetrator. Women perceive their risk of being raped by a stranger as much higher than by an acquaintance, date, or partner (Nurius, Norris, Dimeff, & Graham, 1996), yet there is a much greater likelihood of a woman being raped by someone she knows (Tjaden & Thoennes, 1998). Despite the fact that women fear stranger rapes more than acquaintance or date rapes, the effects of both crimes in terms of negative psychological effects are similar (Cowan, 2000; Shapiro & Schwartz, 1998), although there is some recent evidence that survivors of stranger rapes experience more PTSD symptoms than do acquaintance or romantic partner survivors (Ullman et al., 2006). Women survivors of acquaintance, date, or partner rapes tend to engage in more self-blame and are less likely to label their experiences as rape when compared with those who experienced stranger rapes (Koss & Kilpatrick, 2001). When working with survivors of rape perpetrated by someone they know, counselors can validate clients' fears and reactions and assist them in challenging their self-blaming tendencies regarding their role in the rape.

Counselors must further consider issues specific to women who were sexually assaulted while under the influence of alcohol or other drugs. Rape is highly associated with alcohol use by both perpetrator and victim; this finding is particularly robust for college students. In a recent national survey of college students conducted by Ullman, Karabatsos, and Koss (1999), half of all women had experienced some type of sexual victimization. During these incidences, 53% of perpetrators and 42% of victims reported using alcohol at the time of the assault. In many alcohol-related cases, women are raped while they are too intoxicated to give consent for sexual activity. In a study by Schwartz and Leggett (1999), women who reported being raped when they were too intoxicated to give consent tended to blame themselves, questioned their role in the assault, and did not label the attack as rape even when the incident clearly met the criteria of a felony crime. Many women who are raped while intoxicated may not be aware that most legal jurisdictions define rape as sexual acts committed without a woman's consent, including when she is incapable of giving consent due to intoxication. Counselors can educate women who are raped while intoxicated regarding the legal definitions of rape so that they can appropriately label their experiences and make informed decisions regarding the initiation of legal proceedings.

Women may also experience intoxication by substances administered to them without their knowledge. Recently, drug-facilitated sexual assaults, including those involving gamma-hydroxybutyrate (GHB), have increased both on college campuses and in rural communities. GHB is preferred by perpetrators due to ease of use, rapid effects (within 10 to 15 minutes), and its ability to produce permanent anterograde amnesia (Donovan, 2000: Shwartz, Milteer, & LeBeau, 2000). Because the GHB liquid is odorless, colorless, and has a low dosage threshold (approximately one teaspoon), the substance is easily poured into a victim's drink without her knowledge. A victim generally awakens spontaneously from a GHB-induced coma after approximately 5 hours and may subsequently realize she was raped but have no memory of the perpetrator nor of the events surrounding the rape. Women may be hesitant to label the event as rape or to report the crime to the police due to their memory impairments. On the occasions when such rapes are reported, prosecutors may be reluctant to pursue these cases since the legal system requires evidence of a struggle to prove that sexual activity was nonconsensual (Easton, Summers, Tribble, Wallace, & Lock, 1997). It is important for mental health counselors to consider the multiple violations that a survivor of drug-facilitated sexual assault has experienced: She was drugged against her will, forced into sexual activity without her consent, has no memory of the rape, may receive skeptical reactions from law enforcement, and may receive limited support from prosecutors in pursuing legal recourse (see the chapter Appendix on strategies for prevention of drug-facilitated rape).

Victim-Blame

Mental health counselors can increase their awareness of the societal tendency toward victim-blame. Many survivors experience negative reactions from others and are often blamed for causing the rape. Termed a *secondary victimization* (P. J. Feldman, Ullman, & Dunkel-Schetter, 1998), the experience of insensitivity and minimization by others can have a considerable effect on a woman's recovery. Victim-blaming and negative social reactions are common for all rape survivors, but they are particularly pronounced for women who are raped by someone with whom they had a prior intimate relationship. In comparing social reactions to survivors of the four types of rape, Cowan (2000) found that victim-blame was most likely to occur in cases of partner and date rape. Even though these survivors are similarly affected despite their relationship to the perpetrator (Cowan, 2000; Resnick et al., 2000; Schwartz & Leggett, 1999), they receive more blame and less support than survivors of stranger rapes. Women who are survivors of rape committed by someone they know and trust may be particularly at risk for negative social, medical, or legal reactions (P. J. Feldman et al., 1998). This is significant in that a survivor's experience of negative social reactions is related to greater PTSD symptom severity (Ullman et al., 2006).

Women may be significantly affected by the reactions of others, yet these negative effects can be buffered by the availability of social support. Kimerling and Calhoun (1994) reported that survivors who confide in one or more friends or family members after a rape were less likely to experience increased physical symptoms than were those women with no such support. Unfortunately, many survivors never tell anyone about the event, or choose to delay disclosures for long periods of time. This is particularly true for survivors of acquaintance or date rape (Ahrens & Campbell, 2000; Dunn, Vail-Smith, & Knight, 1998). In one study of disclosures to friends, survivors of date rape waited an average of 7 months prior to telling a friend about the experience (Ahrens & Campbell, 2000). In a more recent national survey of 1,000 sexual assault survivors, 37.3% waited a year or more before telling anyone about the rape (Ullman et al., 2006)

Because survivors of rape may experience a lack of validation from significant others, it is understandable that they are subsequently reluctant to disclose their experiences to mental health professionals. Counselors who anticipate and explore this hesitancy with clients will be more successful in developing trust and in building working alliances with survivors of rape-related trauma (Marotta, 2000).

As noted previously, a counselor's knowledge of the treatment issues related to sociocultural differences, the client's prior abuse history, and the specific nature of the assault also will foster trust in the therapeutic relationship. With these issues and considerations in mind, mental health counselors can more effectively incorporate interventions that target PTSD symptoms commonly experienced following rape. In the case study that follows, consider your work with Alaina and the messages she sends you regarding her experiences and feelings after being sexually assaulted.

Case Study: Part 1

Alaina is a 23-year-old single White female who recently graduated from a local university. She is currently employed as an assistant bank branch manager. She comes to you, a mental health counselor, because she is having trouble concentrating at work and finds that she is increasingly irritable with coworkers and customers. When you ask about her past treatment history, you find out that she went to a counselor at the University Mental Health Center after she was sexually assaulted during her senior year of college. She only attended one counseling session but seems vague about the reasons she never returned to counseling.

After asking about her symptoms, you recognize the need to find out more about the sexual assault. When asked about the incident, she says that she was very intoxicated at the time of the assault, and she blames herself for being at a party too late after her friends had already gone home for the evening. Because she chose to stay and agreed to go to a man's apartment with him, she believes she deserved what happened.

When asked to describe the incident in more detail, she becomes very uncomfortable and answers your questions with only one or two words. It is evident that her memories of the incident are vague. She says that after the assault she began to consume more alcohol, mostly to avoid thinking about the attack. Whenever she does think about it, she gets highly anxious and has trouble breathing. She also currently tends to avoid getting close to people, claiming that she doesn't want to deal with "complicated relationships." She does not want to date anyone, mostly because she claims that "men are scum and only want to hook up anyway," but she frequently engages in sexual activity with men during her drinking episodes. She says that she is ashamed of this behavior, yet she does not know what to do to prevent it from happening.

Now that she has graduated and is working full-time, she still frequents the same bars from her college days and spends most of her time with other people who are into the "party scene." She feels that she is drifting and has no purpose in her life. It is increasingly hard for her to perform her job duties. She doesn't like how her anxiety, irritability, and her daily alcohol consumption seem to be worsening.

1. Which of the issues reviewed previously are particularly pertinent to Alaina's experiences?
2. What questions would you want to ask to gain additional information about Alaina's experiences?
3. What stands out for you about Alaina's experiences? What feelings emerged for you as you read this case study?

Multimodal Treatment Approach for Rape Survivors

The treatment approach described in the paragraphs that follow was drawn from best practice guidelines for the treatment of PTSD (Foa et al., 1999). The multimodal format for rape survivors encompasses four treatment strategies designed to address specific PTSD symptoms (a) to provide education about commonly experienced PTSD symptoms through psychoeducation, (b) to facilitate the client's retelling of the event through exposure-based techniques, (c) to challenge the client's maladaptive beliefs about her role in the event through cognitive restructuring, and (d) to enhance her coping skills through anxiety management techniques.

Modality One: Psychoeducation

All supported treatments for rape-related trauma include an educational component (Foa et al., 1999; Marotta, 2000). While this approach alone does not reduce symptoms in the long term (Rauch, Hembree, & Foa, 2001), it has been demonstrated to be most effective when combined with exposure-based techniques, cognitive therapy, and anxiety management. Early in treatment, clients can be provided with education about PTSD symptoms. Clients experience relief as they recognize they are not "crazy" but are experiencing manifestations of PTSD, a reaction to trauma experienced by most women who are raped (Rauch et al., 2001). Counselors can also provide clients with written materials outlining rape survivors' commonly experienced thoughts and feelings (fear, guilt, anger, shame, embarrassment, betrayal, powerlessness, depression) to review as homework.

As clients view their symptoms as a response to trauma rather than as pathology (Bratton, 1999; Lubin & Johnson, 1997), they can strengthen esteem and a sense of self-worth. To this end, counselors can teach the client to separate her PTSD symptoms and reactions from her view of herself as an individual. Through psychoeducation, clients can identify strengths that the trauma did not disrupt, including intellect, perseverance, and coping skills (Lubin & Johnson, 1997). Clients may also be empowered through education regarding the impact of sociocultural processes that perpetuate rape. Further, they can discuss and dispel commonly accepted rape myths including the belief that the survivor somehow invited the rape and is responsible for the crime. These psychoeducational segments can be structured in the form of minilectures at the beginning and end of the session to balance the intensity of each session (Williams & Sommer, 1994).

Modality Two: Exposure Therapy

The goal of this phase of treatment is to assist the survivor in working through painful memories by confronting specific situations, emotions, and thoughts that have become associated with the rape and currently evoke intense anxiety and fear. As survivors recount thoughts, feelings, and memories surrounding the rape, a highly formalized, structured approach is needed to help them face this emotionally charged material (Johnson & Lubin, 2000). Prolonged exposure (PE) incorporates imaginal and in vivo exposure and is particularly well suited to address the PTSD symptoms of intrusive thoughts, flashbacks, and trauma-related fears (Foa et al., 1999).

When survivors are asked to confront their fears, it is understandable that they will be resistant to this strategy. Counselors can express empathy by acknowledging a survivor's fears and conveying positive expectations for her recovery (Draucker, 1999). Counselors also need to spend adequate time educating clients about the rationale for this phase of treatment. As suggested by Foa, Rothbaum, and Steketee (1993), counselors can explain the use of PE to clients in the following way:

1. Memories, people, places, and activities now associated with the rape make you highly anxious, so you avoid them.
2. Each time you avoid them, you do not finish the process of digesting the painful experience, and so it returns in the form of nightmares, flashbacks, and intrusive thoughts.
3. You can begin to digest the experience by gradually exposing yourself to the rape in your imagination and by holding the memory without pushing it away.
4. You will also practice facing those activities, places, and situations that currently evoke fear.

5. Eventually, you will be able to think about the rape and resume your normal activities without experiencing intense fear.

After explaining the rationale for the use of these techniques, counselors can utilize imaginal exposure to assist clients in repeatedly recounting the memories associated with the rape until the thoughts no longer induce intense fear and anxiety (Foa et al., 1999). As clients close their eyes, they are asked to describe the rape as if it were happening in the present, including all details, feelings, thoughts, and behaviors. They are asked to visualize and describe the rape as vividly as possible. As part of this process, mental health counselors often instruct clients to select a number ranging from 0 to 100 that best represents their current level of anxiety or discomfort. Termed *subjective units of distress* (SUD), these self-ratings are elicited prior to, during, and after the rape description as a method for assessing progress in reducing anxiety over time (Meadows & Foa, 1998). The rape scenario is repeated several times per session, long enough for the discomfort and anxiety to be experienced and then decreased. Meadows and Foa (1998) recommended that these descriptions be audiotaped, as clients may then listen to the tapes as daily homework assignments. Writing about the event in a journal is also recommended (Harris, 1998; Resick & Schnicke, 1993). Through the use of journaling, clients can recount the details and emotions associated with the event, and then read these entries aloud in session. As this exercise is completed over the course of several weeks, clients are asked to increase the level of detail and emotion with each repetition (Harris, 1998). Counselors should assist clients in processing their emotions following the use of imaginal exposure to decrease intensity prior to the end of the session. They can also acknowledge the difficulty of this phase of treatment and can reinforce a client's willingness to face and work through her fears. According to Foa, Hearst-Ikeda, and Perry (1995), clients are empowered when they recognize their successes in confronting anxiety-producing memories and in tolerating the resulting emotions.

The third component of PE is the use of in vivo exposure. As described by Meadows and Foa (1998), the survivor is asked to focus on those activities and situations associated with the rape that are now safe but that she currently fears or avoids, thus causing significant disruptions in her daily functioning. Mental health counselors can assist survivors in creating a list of avoided situations and then in hierarchically ordering these items so that they range from least to most distressing. An SUD rating is assigned to each situation. Starting with the situation that causes the least distress, the client remains in that situation for a minimum of 30 minutes. This time period is deemed long enough for her to experience anxiety, challenge and evaluate her ideas about the actual danger present in the situation, and let the anxiety decrease. She is asked to rate her anxiety through SUD ratings and to note reductions in these ratings as she experiences these feared situations and activities. For example, a college student who refuses to attend classes due to her fear of all men who resemble her perpetrator can practice studying in the library with a friend as a step toward resuming class attendance. Over the course of several sessions, she can progress through the hierarchy until she is able to resume her normal activities and routines.

The use of PE is effective for women survivors of rape who have intact memory of the attack, but these techniques need to be modified for use with women who experience memory impairment. A survivor can be reassured that she does not have to access and reexperience the rape in order for recovery to occur, but she does need to recognize the significance and the impact of the rape in her life (Williams & Sommer, 1994). Clients who cannot recall the actual rape will not be able to recount or journal about the concrete details surrounding the event. While writing in a journal is a helpful way for clients whose memories are intact to process their experiences, writing is not a recommended strategy for survivors in accessing memories of trauma (S. C. Feldman, Johnson, & Ollayos, 1994). However, survivors may benefit from reexperiencing the emotions and thoughts that occurred immediately prior to and following the memory loss. In vivo exposure also may be helpful for clients who avoid feared cues associated with the rape, regardless of their memory impairment of details of the actual event.

If a survivor has no verbal memories of the rape, emotions associated with the event may be accessed through nonverbal means. As suggested by Harris (1998), "the body remembers what the mind forgets" (p. 96). Techniques for use with survivors of drug-facilitated sexual assault or alcohol-induced memory impairment can, therefore, include alternative, experiential approaches drawn from art, music, or dance/movement therapies (see Johnson, 2000, for a review). The use of art has been recommended for survivors of rape as a means to access emotions that have been visually encoded (Backos & Pagon, 1999; Hargrave-Nyakaza, 1994). Art, described as a visual dialogue (Spring, 1994), can give the survivor with no verbal memory something tangible to hold onto during the counseling process and can also represent a survivor's progress in counseling. Further, Stuhlmiller (1994) suggested that survivors with memory impairment may benefit from movement and activity to rebuild body awareness and access imagery and emotions related to the rape.

Modality Three: Cognitive Therapy

Cognitive approaches have demonstrated efficacy in treating survivors of rape (Foa et al., 1993; Meadows & Foa, 1998; Resick & Schnicke, 1993), and they are particularly recommended for addressing symptoms of numbing, detachment, loss of interest in activities, irritability, guilt, and shame (Foa et al., 1999). In cognitive therapy, clients are taught to identify the thoughts or beliefs they experience during negative emotional states. The counselor and client then collaboratively evaluate the validity and challenge the helpfulness of these ideas, and subsequently replace irrational beliefs with rational or beneficial thoughts (Meadows & Foa, 1998). This process can be incorporated with thought stopping, in which maladaptive beliefs are stopped and replaced with positive thoughts (Muran & DiGiuseppe, 2000). Resick and Schnicke (1993) used cognitive restructuring principles in their cognitive processing therapy (CPT) designed for rape victims. As part of the CPT approach, survivors are assisted in identifying and then challenging maladaptive beliefs and "stuck points" related to five areas: self-blame, power, esteem, trust, and intimacy.

Self-Blame and guilt. Mental health counselors can play a critical role in assisting survivors in challenging self-blame, even when victim-blame is perpetuated by society and significant others in their lives. In one study of survivors of rape, all women experienced victim-blame from their support systems, but the women who experienced the highest distress and greatest PTSD symptom severity following rape were those who incorporated these negative reactions into their views of themselves (Regehr, Marziali, & Jansen, 1999; Ullman et al., 2006). Of women who blamed themselves for the crime, some survivors assigned blame to their behavior, others attributed blame to their character (Muran & DiGiuseppe, 2000). Those who attributed blame to their behavior ("I could have gone home earlier that night.") experienced fewer symptoms than those who blamed their character ("I deserved this," or "I am a bad person.").

The issue of guilt is often related to self-blame. Trauma-related guilt issues can include perceived responsibility for causing the rape, beliefs that decisions made and actions taken during the rape were not justified, or the belief that one knew what was going to happen and did not do enough to prevent the crime (Kubany, 1998). As clients can examine their decisions at the time of the rape, they can begin to explore the ways in which the perpetrator's actions were not justified, no matter what decisions the woman made at the time. As self-blaming and guilt-related beliefs are reviewed during counseling sessions, these thoughts can be replaced with more logical self-statements that reflect the client's strengths and power (Kubany, 1998). For example, she can replace the thought "I made a stupid decision to go to my date's apartment, and since I could have prevented it, I deserved what happened to me" with "I may have made a decision I wouldn't make now, but the rapist is responsible for this crime. I will do everything I can now to regain the power he took away from me." As part of reducing self-blame and guilt, survivors can continue to examine the sociocultural forces that perpetuate victim-blame, and they can use this knowledge in restructuring their beliefs about their role in the rape. This type of cognitive restructuring also can help to assuage the negative effects of victim-blame frequently encountered by survivors of rape.

Power and control. Treatment should be designed to assist survivors in restoring personal power that was temporarily disrupted during the assault. Due to the perpetrator's violent use of power and control, women may initially view all issues related to power as negative and may attempt to avoid regaining personal power (Carey, 1998). Through cognitive restructuring, clients' negative views of power and control can be replaced with empowering beliefs that equate power with recovery. While the client was indeed powerless at the time of the rape, she can learn to make the distinction between this temporary lack of control and her ability to make decisions in the present regarding the direction of her recovery. Survivors who develop a sense of agency have more positive treatment outcomes; Regehr, Marziali, and Jansen (1999) found that rape survivors who were able to view themselves as active agents in determining the results of events in their lives experienced fewer symptoms of PTSD and depression than did women with an external locus of control. As an important part of regaining a sense of power, counselors can encourage clients to take an active role in treatment by providing choices and flexibility regarding counseling goals and in the timing and pacing of sessions. Clients who claim the direction of their treatment are empowered to be the "authors and arbiters of their own recovery" (Draucker, 1999, p. 18).

Self-esteem, intimacy, and trust. It is important to explore the impact of rape on a survivor's self-image. Resick and Schnicke (1993) recommended asking clients to examine their meanings of the rape, and what effect it has had on their view of themselves. Clients' answers to these questions can reveal a pattern of stuck points (e.g., "I am unlovable because this happened to me") that can be challenged and reframed. Survivors' difficulties with self-esteem are interconnected with issues of trust and intimacy. If a survivor questions her judgment, engages in self-blame, and experiences victim-blame following rape, she may experience problems in trusting both herself and others. As rape is a trauma intentionally inflicted upon a woman by another individual, critical issues to explore in counseling will include disruptions in her capacity for intimacy and her ability to trust others (Draucker, 1999).

As clients challenge maladaptive beliefs in recovery, they can eventually learn to view the rape and its aftermath as a traumatic but growth-enhancing experience (Williams & Sommer, 1994) that provides them with a more flexible worldview (Koss & Kilpatrick, 2001). According to Frazier and Burnett (1994), 57% of adult rape survivors in their sample cited positive changes that resulted from their rape experience (e.g., improved interpersonal relationships, enhanced self-awareness, and spiritual growth). Studies in resilience theory demonstrate that resilient individuals grow and develop as a result of trauma; rather than being stunted by life difficulties, they recover from traumatic events with an increased sense of empathy, enhanced coping skills, and greater capacity for intimacy (Young-Eisendrath, 1996). Regehr, Cadell, and Jansen (1999) found similar qualities in a study of survivors of sexual assault who displayed the most resilience in recovery. These women possessed a sense of safety and trust, a positive view of self, a sense of power, positive relationships, the ability to employ cognitive reframing, and a refusal to engage in self-blame.

As has been suggested throughout this book, counselors can use a wellness approach to help build client resilience. When counseling rape survivors from a wellness perspective, counselors can design treatment goals that extend beyond the remediation of PTSD symptoms by enhancing those qualities that will increase clients' quality of life and their ability to cope with future life challenges. Many of the components described in this treatment model—thinking, emotions, control, realistic beliefs, self-worth, friendship, love—are also important dimensions of wellness (Myers & Sweeney, 2005). Therefore, life areas targeted in recovery can serve to enhance a client's overall life wellness. Further, survivors who strengthen these qualities and skills in recovery will develop the ability to cope more effectively with life demands. In time, many clients may even become empowered to engage in advocacy and activism in working to reduce the prevalence of sexual violence (Robinson & Howard-Hamilton, 2000; Worell & Remer, 2002).

Modality Four: Anxiety Management

There are a variety of anxiety management techniques, but stress inoculation training (SIT) is one of the most researched and comprehensive anxiety management programs for survivors of sexual assault and rape (Meadows & Foa, 1998). The goal of SIT is to promote a set of coping skills that help to reduce general anxiety, hypervigilance, hyperarousal, sleep disturbances, and difficulty in concentration (Foa et al., 1999). These coping skills include muscle relaxation training, controlled breathing exercises, role playing, covert modeling, positive thinking and self-talk, assertiveness training, guided self-imagery and dialogue, and thought stopping.

Krakow et al. (2001) recently examined the use of an anxiety management technique in reducing PTSD-related sleep disturbance and nightmares. In a randomized, controlled study of women survivors of sexual assault who experienced nightmares and insomnia, participants were asked to consider their nightmares as learned habits that are influenced by what they think about during the day. Through the use of imagery rehearsal, women were asked to select one of their disturbing dreams, to change the dream, and to describe the new dream in writing. Over the course of three sessions, survivors were asked to describe the new dream using self-imagery and to rehearse the new dream throughout the week for at least 5 to 20 minutes. According to Krakow and colleagues, the survivors in the treatment group experienced a significant decrease in overall PTSD symptoms when compared with survivors in the control group. Further, as the survivors who learned to use self-imagery gained a greater sense of control over their nightmares, they also implemented these techniques as a successful method for coping with other problems in their lives. Clients are empowered as they develop these and other anxiety management techniques to facilitate recovery from rape-related trauma.

Case Study: Part 2

Review Part 1 of the case study of Alaina. Now that you have reviewed the treatment model, design a treatment approach based on the four phases described previously.

Phase One: Psychoeducation

1. What type of education or information might be particularly helpful to Alaina, and why do you think it might benefit her?

Phase Two: Exposure

1. What kind of explanation would you provide Alaina regarding your rationale for asking her to revisit and reexperience painful memories?
2. What type of imaginal exposure procedures would you use in helping her face her memories and to tolerate her painful emotions related to the rape?
3. Would there be a need for in vivo exposure techniques in this case?
4. How might exposure techniques need to be modified due to her lack of specific memories of the rape?

Phase Three: Cognitive Strategies

1. In exploring Alaina's maladaptive cognitions related to the rape around the five "stuck points" identified in the chapter, what issues might you focus on around each of the following areas:
   a. Self-blame
   b. Power and control
   c. Self-esteem
   d. Trust
   e. Intimacy

Phase Four: Anxiety Management

1. What are some specific symptoms Alaina experiences that might benefit from enhanced anxiety management skills?
2. What coping skills are particularly needed?

Conclusion

Counselors who wish to deliver quality services for women who experience rape-related trauma should be knowledgeable of best practice guidelines based on expert consensus and controlled outcome studies. The multimodal approach described here incorporates the use of four empirically supported treatment modalities specifically designed for the reduction of PTSD symptoms commonly experienced by survivors of rape. Awareness of these guidelines is particularly important in an era of accountability in which counselors are challenged to stay abreast of current mental health trends and standards of care (Marotta, 2000).

While the recommended strategies and methods described in this model are straightforward, the actual process of recovery from rape-related trauma is a difficult, lifelong process (Koss & Kilpatrick, 2001; Worell & Remer, 2002). Survivors are vulnerable to victim-blame, self-blame, unwillingness to disclose the rape to others, and an overall lack of support, in addition to PTSD symptoms and other significant negative

psychological and physiological outcomes. Survivors of rape need validation as they attempt to recover in the aftermath of rape, but they frequently
receive inadequate support and even skepticism from those systems des-
ignated to provide services to victims of trauma. It is, therefore, understandable that survivors may experience disruptions in trust and be
reluctant to seek mental health services until PTSD symptoms are chronic
or compounded. Unfortunately, many mental health professionals report a
lack of formal training in working with survivors of rape (Campbell et al.,
1999), and this inadequate preparation likely perpetuates survivors' reluctance to seek or continue treatment. With education and enhanced awareness, however, it is possible for counselors to serve an important role in
assisting survivors of rape, as mental health counselors' developmental,
wellness-focused approaches to treatment are particularly well-suited to
working with survivors of rape-related trauma (Marotta, 2000).

There are several areas for future research in rape-related treatment issues and interventions. First, studies can examine necessary modifica-
tions for practice guidelines that account for memory impairment and
other important treatment differences related to the specific nature of an
assault. Further, future research is needed to examine women's treatment
needs in the context of sociocultural variables such as ethnicity and class.
Finally, mental health counselor educators can examine the ways in which
they can effectively incorporate information into their programs regarding best practice guidelines and salient treatment issues.

Counselors can provide sensitive treatment for survivors of rape by
balancing their focus on PTSD symptom reduction with support, validation, and client empowerment (Draucker, 1999). By integrating the support that survivors need with a structured treatment approach for
rape-related trauma symptoms, counselors can best assist survivors of
rape in their journey toward resilience and recovery.

Activities for Further Exploration

1. What are your reactions to the use of prolonged exposure in working
   with survivors of sexual assault? How can counselors work collaboratively and empathically with clients during this process?
2. To enhance your comfort level in working with survivors of drug-
   facilitated sexual assault, review the following article: Hensley, L. G.
   (2003). GHB abuse trends and use in drug-facilitated sexual assault:
   Implications for prevention. *NASPA Journal, 40,* 17–28. As a counselor,
   what are some things you might need to explore to become more
   knowledgeable about GHB and other "date rape drugs"?
3. How can clients learn to view a rape experience as a traumatic but
   growth-enhancing experience? What can you do to promote survivors' resilience through the counseling process?
4. What are your opinions regarding the involvement of alcohol (by
   both the perpetrator and the survivor) in understanding date or ac-

quaintance rape? What would be your response to the opinion that if both a woman and man were intoxicated at the time that sexual activity took place, then a rape did not really occur? This is an area often debated by students and clients, and it is important for counselors to have processed their attitudes and beliefs around these issues.

5. Become familiar with the laws concerning sexual assault and rape in your state. Knowledge of these laws is helpful when providing education to girls and women about legal definitions of rape. This is particularly helpful for women who are uncomfortable in labeling their experience as rape (e.g., if she was intoxicated, has no memory of the event, or did not try to fight back). Further, it is important for counselors to explore their own attitudes regarding a client's decision to report a rape and to bring charges against the perpetrator. How difficult will it be for you to respect a client's decision not to report a rape, even when you believe it might be in her best interest?

Suggested Readings

Brener, N. D., McMahon, P. M., Warren, C. W., & Douglas, K. A. (1999). Forced sexual intercourse and associated health-risk behaviors among female college students in the United States. *Journal of Consulting and Clinical Psychology, 67*, 252–259.

Foa, E. B., Davidson, J. R. T., & Frances, A. (1999). Expert consensus guideline series: Treatment of posttraumatic stress disorder. *Journal of Clinical Psychiatry, 60*(Suppl. 16), 1–31.

Harris, M. (1998). *Trauma recovery and empowerment: A clinician's guide for working with women in groups.* New York: Free Press.

Marotta, S. A. (2000). Best practices for counselors who treat post-traumatic stress disorder. *Journal of Counseling & Development, 78*, 492–495.

Resick, P. A., & Schnicke, M. K. (1993). *Cognitive processing therapy for rape victims: A treatment manual.* Newbury Park, CA: Sage.

Tjaden, P., & Thoennes, N. (2006). *Extent, nature, and consequences of rape victimization: Findings From the National Violence Against Women Survey.* Retrieved July 5, 2007, from www.ojp.usdoj.gov/nij

Additional Resources

http://www.cdc.gov/ncipc/dvp/dvp.htm
   The National Center for Injury Prevention and Control (NCIPC) is the lead federal agency for violence prevention. The Web site provides information on intimate partner violence, sexual violence, suicide, and youth violence.

http://www.rainn.org
   The Rape, Abuse & Incest National Network is the nation's largest anti–sexual assault organization. It operates the National Sexual Assault Hotlines and carries out programs to prevent sexual assault, help victims, and ensure that rapists are brought to justice.

http://www.feminist.org/911
   The feminist majority online site provides links to sexual harassment resources, sexual assault resources, and domestic violence hotlines and information, as well as links to information on women's health.
http://www.kidshealth.org/teen
   This Web site provides answers and advice for teens regarding health, safety, and relationships. Articles on date rape and rape are provided under the safety and relationship tabs.
http://www.usdoj.gov/ovw
   The Department of Justice, Office on Violence Against Women Web site provides definitions and descriptions of sexual assault, domestic violence, and stalking, and offers helpful resources for victims.

References

American Psychiatric Association. (2000). *Diagnostic and statistical manual of mental disorders* (4th ed., text rev.). Washington, DC: Author.

Ahrens, C. E., & Campbell, R. (2000). Assisting rape victims as they recover from rape: The impact on friends. *Journal of Interpersonal Violence, 15,* 959–986.

Backos, A. K., & Pagon, B. E. (1999). Finding a voice: Art therapy with female adolescent sexual abuse survivors. *Art Therapy: Journal of the American Art Therapy Association, 16,* 126–132.

Bratton, M. (1999). *From surviving to thriving.* New York: Hawthorn Maltreatment and Trauma Press.

Breitenbecher, H. B., & Gidycz, C. A. (1998). An empirical evaluation of a program designed to reduce the risk of multiple sexual victimization. *Journal of Interpersonal Violence, 13,* 472–489.

Brener, N. D., McMahon, P. M., Warren, C. W., & Douglas, K. A. (1999). Forced sexual intercourse and associated health-risk behaviors among female college students in the United States. *Journal of Consulting and Clinical Psychology, 67,* 252–259.

Brownmiller, S. (1975). *Against our will: Men, women, and rape.* New York: Bantam Books.

Campbell, R., Raja, S., & Grining, P. L. (1999). Training mental health professionals on violence against women. *Journal of Interpersonal Violence, 14,* 1002–1013.

Carey, L. A. (1998). Illuminating the process of a rape survivors' support group. *Social Work With Groups, 21,* 103–116.

Clum, G. A., Nishith, P., & Resick, P. A. (2001). Trauma-related sleep disturbance and self-reported physical health symptoms in treatment-seeking female rape victims. *Journal of Nervous and Mental Disease, 189,* 618–622.

Cowan, G. (2000). Beliefs about the causes of four types of rape. *Sex Roles: A Journal of Research, May,* 807.

Donovan, J. W. (2000). Gamma-hydroxybutyrate, Gamma-Butyrolactone, and Butanediol: Abuse and effects. *Journal of Toxicology: Clinical Toxicology, 38*(2), 184.

Draucker, C. B. (1999). The psychotherapeutic needs of women who have been sexually assaulted. *Perspectives in Psychiatric Care, 35*, 18–29.

Dunn, P. C., Vail-Smith, K., & Knight, S. M. (1998). What date/acquaintance rape victims tell others: A study of college student recipients of disclosure. *Journal of American College Health, 47*, 213.

Easton, A., Summers, J., Tribble, J., Wallace, P. B., & Lock, R. S. (1997). College women's perceptions regarding resistance to sexual assault. *Journal of American College Health, 46*, 127.

Feldman, P. J., Ullman, J. B., & Dunkel-Schetter, C. (1998). Women's reactions to rape victims: Motivational processes associated with blame and social support. *Journal of Applied Social Psychology, 28*, 469–503.

Feldman, S. C., Johnson, D. R., & Ollayos, M. (1994). The use of writing in the treatment of PTSD. In M. B. Williams & J. F. Sommer (Eds.), *Handbook of post-traumatic therapy* (pp. 366–385). Westport, CT: Greenwood Press.

Foa, E. B., Davidson, J. R. T., & Frances, A. (1999). Expert consensus guideline series: Treatment of posttraumatic stress disorder. *Journal of Clinical Psychiatry, 60*(Suppl. 16), 1–31.

Foa, E. B., Hearst-Ikeda, D., & Perry, K. J. (1995). Evaluation of a brief cognitive–behavioral program for the prevention of chronic PTSD in recent assault victims. *Journal of Consulting and Clinical Psychology, 63*, 948–955.

Foa, E. B., Rothbaum, B. O., & Steketee, G. S. (1993). Treatment of rape victims. *Journal of Interpersonal Violence, 8*, 256–276.

Frazier, P. A., & Burnett, J. W. (1994). Immediate coping strategies among rape victims. *Journal of Counseling & Development, 72*, 633–639.

Hansen, L. S., Gama, E. M. P., & Harkins, A. K. (2002). Revisiting gender issues in multicultural counseling. In P. B. Pedersen, J. G. Draguns, W. J. Lonner, & J. E. Trimble (Eds.), *Counseling across cultures* (5th ed., pp. 163–184). Thousand Oaks, CA: Sage.

Hargrave-Nyakaza, K. (1994). An application of art therapy to the trauma of rape. *Art therapy: A Journal of the American Art Therapy Association, 11*, 53–57.

Harris, M. (1998). *Trauma recovery and empowerment: A clinician's guide for working with women in groups.* New York: Free Press.

Johnson, D. R. (2000). Creative therapies. In E. B. Foa et al. (Eds.), *Effective treatments for PTSD: Practice guidelines from the International Society for Traumatic Stress Studies* (pp. 302–314). New York: Guilford Press.

Johnson, D. R., & Lubin, H. (2000). Group psychotherapy for symptoms of PTSD. In R. H. Klein & V. Schermer (Eds.), *Group psychotherapy for psychological trauma* (pp. 141–169). New York: Guilford Press.

Kessler, B. L., & Bieschke, K. J. (1999). A retrospective analysis of shame, dissociation, and adult victimization in survivors of childhood sexual abuse. *Journal of Counseling Psychology, 46*, 335–341.

Kimerling, R., & Calhoun, K. S. (1994). Somatic symptoms, social support, and treatment seeking among sexual assault victims. *Journal of Consulting and Clinical Psychology, 62*, 333–340.

Koss, M. P., & Kilpatrick, D. G. (2001). Rape and sexual assault. In E. Gerrity, T. Keane, & F. Tuma (Eds.), *Mental health consequences of torture* (pp. 177–193). New York: Plenum.

Krakow, B., Hollifield, M., Johnston, L., Koss, M., Schrader, R., Warner, T. D., et al. (2001). Imagery rehearsal therapy for chronic nightmares in sexual assault survivors with posttraumatic stress disorder: A randomized controlled trial. *JAMA: Journal of the American Medical Association, 286,* 537.

Kubany, E. S. (1998). Cognitive therapy for trauma related guilt. In V. Follette, I. Ruzek, & F. Abueg (Eds.), *Cognitive–behavioral therapies for trauma* (pp. 124–161). New York: Guilford Press.

Littleton, H., Breitkopf, C. R., & Berenson, A. B. (2007). Rape scripts of low-income European American and Latina women. *Sex Roles, 56,* 509–516.

Low, G., & Organista, K. C. (2000). Latinas and sexual assault: Towards culturally sensitive assessment and intervention. *Journal of Multicultural Social Work, 8,* 131–157.

Lubin, H., & Johnson, D. R. (1997). Interactive psychoeducational group therapy for traumatized women. *International Journal of Group Psychotherapy, 47,* 271–288.

Marotta, S. A. (2000). Best practices for counselors who treat post-traumatic stress disorder. *Journal of Counseling & Development, 78,* 492–495.

Meadows, E. A., & Foa, E. B. (1998). Intrusion, arousal, and avoidance: Sexual trauma survivors. In V. Follette, I. Ruzek, & F. Abueg (Eds.), *Cognitive–behavioral therapies for trauma* (pp. 100–123). New York: Guilford Press.

Myers, J. E., & Sweeney, T. S. (2005). *Counseling for wellness: Theory, research, and practice.* Alexandria, VA: American Counseling Association Press.

Muran, E., & DiGiuseppe, R. (2000). Rape trauma. In F. M. Dattilio & A. Freeman (Eds.), *Cognitive behavioral strategies in crisis intervention* (2nd ed., pp. 150–165). New York: Guilford Press.

Nurius, P. S., Norris, J., Dimeff, L. A., & Graham, T. L. (1996). Expectations regarding acquaintance sexual aggression among sorority and fraternity members. *Sex Roles: A Journal of Research, 35,* 427–445.

Rauch, S. A. M., Hembree, E. A., & Foa, E. B. (2001). Acute psychosocial preventive interventions for post-traumatic stress disorder. *Advances in Mind-Body Medicine, 17,* 160–196.

Regehr, C., Cadell, S., & Jansen, K. (1999). Perceptions of control and long term recovery from rape. *American Journal of Orthopsychiatrty, 69,* 110–114.

Regehr, C., Marziali, E., & Jansen, K. (1999). A qualitative analysis of strengths and vulnerabilities in sexually assaulted women. *Clinical Social Work Journal, 27,* 171–184.

Resick, P. A., & Schnicke, M. K. (1993). *Cognitive processing therapy for rape victims: A treatment manual.* Newbury Park, CA: Sage.

Resnick, H., Acierno, R., Holmes, M., Dammeyer, M., & Kilpatrick, D. (2000). Emergency evaluation and intervention with female victims of rape and other violence. *Journal of Clinical Psychology, 56,* 1317–1333.

Resnick, H., Acierno, R., Holmes, M., Kilpatrick, D., & Jager, N. (1999). Prevention of post-rape psychopathology: Preliminary findings of a controlled acute rape treatment study. *Journal of Anxiety Disorders, 13,* 359–370.

Robinson, T., & Howard-Hamilton, M. (2000). *Convergence of race, ethnicity, and gender: Multiple identities in counseling.* Upper Saddle River, NJ: Prentice-Hall.

Sanders, B., & Moore, D. L. (1999). Childhood maltreatment and date rape. *Journal of Interpersonal Violence, 14,* 115–124.

Schwartz, M. D., & Leggett, M. S. (1999). Bad dates or emotional trauma? The aftermath of campus sexual assault. *Violence Against Women, 5,* 251–271.

Shapiro, B. L., & Schwartz, C. (1998). Date rape: Its relationship to trauma symptoms and sexual self-esteem. *Journal of Interpersonal Violence, 12,* 407–420.

Shwartz, R. H., Milteer, R., & LeBeau, M. A. (2000). Drug-facilitated sexual assault. *Southern Medical Journal, 93,* 558–561.

Spring, D. (1994). Art therapy as a visual dialogue. In M. B. Williams & J. F. Sommer (Eds.), *Handbook of post-traumatic therapy* (pp. 337–351). Westport, CT: Greenwood Press.

Stuhlmiller, C. M. (1994). Action-based therapy for PTSD. In M. B. Williams & J. F. Sommer (Eds.), *Handbook of post-traumatic therapy* (pp. 386–400). Westport, CT: Greenwood Press.

Tjaden, P., & Thoennes, N. (1998). *Prevalence, incidence, and consequences of violence against women: Findings from the national violence against women survey.* Atlanta, GA: Center for Disease Control and Prevention, Center for Injury Prevention and Control.

Tjaden, P., & Thoennes, N. (2006). *Extent, nature, and consequences of rape victimization: Findings from the National Violence Against Women Survey.* Retrieved July 5, 2007, from www.ojp.usdoj.gov/nij

Ullman, S. E., Filipas, H. H., Townsend, S. M., & Starzynski, L. L. (2006). The role of victim-offender relationship in women's sexual assault experiences. *Journal of Interpersonal Violence, 21,* 798–819.

Ullman, S. E., Karabatsos, G., & Koss, M. P. (1999). Alcohol and sexual assault in a national sample of college women. *Journal of Interpersonal Violence, 14,* 603–625.

Williams, M. B., & Sommer, J. F. (1994). Toward the development of a generic model of PTSD treatment. In M. B. Williams & J. F. Sommer (Eds.), *Handbook of post-traumatic therapy* (pp. 551–565). Westport, CT: Greenwood Press.

Worell, J., & Remer, P. (2002). *Feminist perspectives in therapy: Empowering diverse women* (2nd ed.). Hoboken, NJ: Wiley.

Young-Eisendrath, P. (1996). *The resilient spirit: Transforming suffering into meaning and purpose.* Cambridge, MA: Perseus Books.

Appendix
Prevention Focus: Strategies to Prevent Drug-Facilitated Rape

1. Women should avoid any drink that they didn't receive directly from the bar or that they didn't open themselves.
2. If someone offers a student a drink, women should walk with him or her to the bar, watch it being poured, and carry it themselves.
3. When at a bar or party, women should avoid trying new concoctions that they have never tasted. Shooters, shots, and drinks with multiple liquors may mask the slightly salty taste of GHB. Concoctions, such as margaritas, Long Island Iced Teas, fruity daiquiris, Goldschlager (a cinnamon-flavored liquor), and "fishbowl" drinks have all been used to drug women without their knowledge.
4. Women should not accept a drink poured from a punchbowl. Further, they should avoid sharing drinks that are passed from person to person.
5. Women should not leave their drinks unattended for any reason— they can carry drinks with them when going to the restroom, dancing, talking to someone across the room, and while using the phone. If their drinks have been left unattended for any reason, they should discard them immediately.
6. Women should use the buddy system. They should watch friends for signs of sudden intoxication such as slurred speech or having difficulty walking. If a friend is disproportionately intoxicated in relation to the amount of alcohol he or she has consumed, students should assist him or her in leaving the situation immediately.
7. If friends have passed out (particularly if disproportionately intoxicated in relation to the amount of alcohol the student knows they have consumed), women should not allow friends to "sleep it off." GHB-related deaths have occurred from friends deciding to put friends to bed rather than seeking immediate medical assistance. While waiting for medical intervention, women should make sure the victim is on his or her side to prevent aspiration. They should not leave friends unattended for any reason.

If students suspect they have ingested GHB, they should go to the emergency room immediately. Women should request a urine sample to screen for the presence of GHB within 12 hours of ingestion. This screen is not routinely done, as many medical professionals are not familiar with GHB symptoms.

Chapter 8

Dangerous Relationships in Adulthood: Women and Intimate Partner Violence

Intimate partner violence (IPV) is experienced by millions of women. Formerly termed *domestic violence* in the literature and in practice, the term IPV is now used as it best describes a particular type of family violence and is inclusive of any intimate relationship regardless of the marital status, age, or gender of the partners (National Center for Injury Prevention and Control [NCIPC], 2006). When including all types of abuse (physical, sexual, and psychological), 29% of U.S. women have been abused by a current or former intimate partner. While IPV affects both men and women, women are far more likely to be victims as 20–30% of women reported some type of physical abuse by a partner in their lifetimes versus 7.5% of men. Based on the frequency of the problem, it is likely that counselors will work with women who have experienced IPV.

With the high prevalence of IPV, it is noteworthy that most mental health training programs do not adequately prepare professionals to work in this area (Walker, 1994). This is alarming in that abused women are often reluctant to seek counseling, and when they do it is usually because they are in crisis. Even then, IPV can go undetected if the counselor is not trained to properly assess for it. This chapter (a) describes the various forms of IPV, (b) explores the cycle of abuse and how women often become entrapped in relationships characterized by this type of violence, and (c) presents a four-phase treatment approach for working with women who experience IPV.

Intimate Partner Violence

The Family Violence Prevention Fund (2004) defined IPV as a pattern of assaultive and coercive behaviors that may include inflicted physical injury, psychological abuse, sexual assault, progressive isolation, stalking, deprivation, intimidation, and threats. These behaviors are perpetrated by someone who is or was involved in an intimate or dating relationship with an adult or adolescent, and are aimed at establishing control by one partner over the other (Family Violence Prevention Fund, 2004, p. 3). The systematic pattern of abuse generally increases in frequency and in intensity over time (LaViolette & Barnett, 2000).

Women of all races/ethnicities, ages, and levels of socioeconomic status are affected by IPV, but women most at risk include African American women, American Indian/Alaskan women, and Hispanic women (NCIPC, 2006). Asian American women reported the lowest rates, although this might be related to underreporting by women in this population (Tjaden & Thoennes, 2006). Most surveys have found that American Indian women experienced the highest rates of IPV of any ethnic group, with 76% experiencing a history of domestic violence and 69% of children reporting some exposure to violence in their homes (Luna-Firebaugh, 2006). Tjaden and Thoennes (2006) also found that American Indian women reported the highest rates of victimization through physical assault (64.1%) compared to other racial/ethnic groups. While these rates are alarming, there are large intertribal differences in the American Indian population. Most of the available data are not tribe-specific, however, so these statistics cannot be generalized to women of any particular tribal group (Hamby, 2005).

Others at high risk for IPV include younger women, women who are separated or divorced, and those living below the poverty line. Further, women with a history of abuse in their families or who have witnessed IPV in their childhood homes are at highest risk (NCIPC, 2006). Researchers have examined how a woman's sexual orientation might influence her risk for IPV, and rates of IPV in lesbian relationships are roughly similar to those in heterosexual relationships (NCIPC, 2006).

Forms of Abusive Behaviors

IPV takes many forms, but abusive behaviors are generally categorized into four types: physical abuse, sexual abuse, stalking (Table 8.1), and psychological abuse (Table 8.2). Although counselors might believe physical abuse is the most damaging type of abuse a woman can experience, a large body of research indicates that the impact of psychological abuse is as great as that of physical abuse (Arias & Pape, 1999; Marshall, 1996; Shepard, 1992; Sutherland, 1999; Walker, 1994). Unlike the experience of physical abuse, psychological abuse is directly related to women's experience of PTSD symptoms (Arias & Pape, 1999). According to anecdotal evidence presented by Walker (1994), when women are asked to describe their worst incident of IPV, they almost always select an episode that is more humiliating or psychologically abusive than one that is physically abusive. This occurs because psychological abuse affects a woman's sense of self and has the potential to undermine her self-esteem and self-efficacy in all aspects of her life. As she begins to believe the abusers' insults and tactics used for humiliation ("You're no good! Who else would want you?"), the abuser is able to maintain control over her and she is more likely to stay in the abusive relationship (Marshall, 1996). Some women

Table 8.1
Forms of Abuse: Physical, Sexual, and Stalking/Harassment

Physical Abuse	Sexual Abuse	Stalking/Harassment
Slapping	Using sexual names	Following or stalking
Throwing the victim out	Degrading treatment	Refusing to leave when
of the car	Making her have sex	asked
Punching	when she doesn't	Embarrassing her in
Pushing	want to, is sick, or	public
Kicking	is under doctor's	Constantly checking up
Burning	orders not to	on her
Choking	Not telling her he has	
Beating	an STD or protecting	
Biting	her from an STD	
Raping	Refusing to wear a	
Cutting or stabbing	condom	
Shooting	Coercing sex	
Hitting with objects	Not letting her use birth	
Kidnapping	control	
Twisting arms, legs, skin	Forcing her to do sexual	
Smothering	things that make her	
Hitting	uncomfortable	
Holding tightly	Forcing her to wear	
Scratching	sexy or revealing	
Pulling hair	clothes she doesn't	
Strangling	feel comfortable in	
Shoving	Wanting to have sex	
	after hurting her	
	Making her watch	
	pornography against	
	her will	

might dismiss psychological abuse because it does not inflict physical harm, but it is important for counselors to recognize that physical abuse is almost always preceded by psychological abuse (O'Leary, 1999). Verbally abusive behavior in particular is the strongest predictor of other types of abuse such as physical assault, rape, or stalking (NCIPC, 2006).

The Cycle of Abuse

When I first started dating my partner, I thought I was in heaven. Constant attention, compliments, flowers, calls, e-mails . . . he seemed to be thinking about me all of the time. He seemed hurt when I wanted to spend time with friends or just to have a night with my family. At first I thought it was wonderful how he wanted to spend every waking minute with me, but sometimes I got a little frustrated when he didn't respect my decision to make other plans. When we started arguing regularly when I wanted to go

Table 8.2

Examples of Psychological Abuse

Abusing Trust	Economic Control	Verbal Abuse	Intimidation	Threats
Lying	Refusing to give her money	Mocking	Making it hard for her to see friends and family	Threatening to harm her, the children, family members, and pets
Breaking promises	Not allowing her to learn a skill	Yelling	Reading mail	Using physical size to intimidate
Being unfaithful	Prohibiting her from going to school	Swearing	Monitoring phone calls	Abusing pets
Being very jealous	Refusing to work and support the family	Name-calling	Controlling where she goes	Shouting
Blaming her for his faults and mistakes	Not letting her work	Making fun of her in a cruel or demeaning way	Destroying her passport	Keeping weapons and threatening to use them
Stealing from her	Interfering with her job	Constant criticism	Taking her car keys	Punishing children or others because he's angry at her
Withholding important information	Not paying bills	Making humiliating remarks	Checking mileage on her car	Breaking her things
Telling her about his affairs with other women			Ignoring her	

somewhere without him, I was alarmed, but then he would apologize and things would be great again. Little did I know that these were only warning signs of things to come.

—M.G., age 29

Women who experience IPV are caught in a pattern of behaviors that are cyclic in nature. A woman is not able to recognize the pattern developing while she is in the midst of it (DePorto, 2003). According to DePorto, these relationships rarely begin with abusive interactions, but are often described as ideal relationships in which a woman is showered with intense levels of attention and affection. Gradually, however, her partner's intense feelings translate into the use of jealous behaviors and even initial attempts at isolating the woman from her family and friends. Once she is established in the relationship, psychological abuse (yelling, criticism, tactics of humiliation) might begin on an intermittent basis. The abusive partner continues to isolate her from her existing support system, often encouraging her to quit her job and to limit her visits with others. The insults, yelling, and criticism seem so discrepant from her partner's usual loving behaviors that she tends to dismiss them as an aberration. Counselors should recognize that the intent of the psychological abuse is irrelevant; often a partner claims that comments, criticisms, or controlling behaviors are meant to "help" the woman ("I'm just looking out for you and trying to help you improve yourself."), yet they have an abusive effect over time (Marshall, 1996). Even when friends or family voice concerns about warning signs in the relationship, a woman in this type of relationship holds onto the good parts of the relationship. She makes every effort to give her partner what he or she wants, works hard to improve as a partner, and believes that the abuse is her fault (e.g., the abuse is caused by my personality flaws or by my failures to be a good partner). If she changes her behavior, she believes she can stop the abuse.

As the verbal abuse increases in frequency and intensity over time, she may begin to question it or even to protest. In retaliation, the partner may use manipulation, threats, and other means to let her know he or she could hurt her at any point. By creating an atmosphere of anticipated violence, the psychological abuse is enough to induce fear, even in the absence of physical violence. These messages can be conveyed through gestures, tone of voice, or expressions that may not be detected by others (Marshall, 1996). At this stage, a woman still is unlikely to identify herself as abused and will not reveal the abuse to others. She begins to recognize that the abuse is her partner's fault, not hers, but believes she can help her partner to change and that the abusive behavior is not the "real" person (e.g., "he's just under a lot of pressure at work"; Landenburger, 1998a).

When the other control strategies do not seem to be effective, her partner may start to use physical abuse. Eventually abuse becomes a larger part of the relationship. By this point, a woman begins to believe the abuser's negative perceptions of her, realizes that she can't change him or her, and starts to feel overwhelmed and entrapped. She can remain in this cycle for a long period of time, and in most cases it requires an escalation of abuse in terms of both frequency and intensity for a woman to recognize that she doesn't deserve to be abused, to become concerned about the level of violence, and to realize that the violence is unlikely to end while she remains in the relationship (Landenburger, 1998a). The process of leaving the relationship is complex and will likely involve several attempts at leaving and returning (DePorto, 2003; Landenburger, 1998b).

While this pattern emerges over a period of years, counselors should remember that the abusive partner also frequently is loving, attentive, and warm in the relationship. Walker (1994) described the cycle of violence as follows: (a) the tension building phase, in which the woman recognizes the cues that a violent episode is pending and may work especially hard to be "perfect" in an effort to prevent the violence; (b) the acute or battering phase; and (c) the honeymoon phase, characterized by contrition and an absence of violence in which the batterer makes every effort to ask for forgiveness and gives the victim reason to hope that he or she will change (Figure 8.1). According to traumatic bonding theory, a woman who has been physically abused is in need of affection and attention, which can

Figure 8.1
Cycle of Abuse

lead to an increased openness to her partner's contrition regarding the violence, and his loving behaviors during this phase reinforce her emotional bond with him (Dutton & Painter, 1993).

As part of this cycle, many women respond to violence with violence. In some cases, women can be just as violent as their partners, yet the myth of "mutual battering" (Walker, 1994) is rarely the best way to describe the dynamic of violence that occurs in the relationship. A woman can become entangled in a pattern of mutual violence, but she does not generally initiate or control the cycle. Her aggressive behaviors do not instill fear in her partner the way her partner's behaviors affect her life. Further, women typically don't use violence to obtain power in the relationship, and generally nothing changes in the relationship as a result of her use of violence. It is common for a woman to use violence as an act of self-defense or to act aggressively out of frustration (Miller & Meloy, 2006). These women do not need to be treated as perpetrators but need assistance in understanding the dynamics of this cycle and how to respond differently (see Leisring, Dowd, & Rosenbaum, 2002, for details regarding a treatment program for women who are violent in intimate relationships).

Whether or not a woman responds with violence can be culturally influenced. African American women may be more likely to respond to IPV with the use of violence (D. W. Campbell & Gary, 1998; Swan & Snow, 2002) than are women from other cultural groups. African American gender roles may not be as rigid and gender-related behaviors not as prescribed as they are for Caucasians or other groups. The power in male–female relationships may be relatively shared, and there is a cultural expectation that women will fight back if abused by their partner (Swan & Snow, 2002).

IPV is also present in lesbian relationships, and the ability to determine the perpetrator may become confusing when both partners are women and both engage in abusive behaviors toward one another. According to McClennen (2005), perpetrators may be distinguished from victims in that perpetrators intentionally initiate abusive behaviors, often blaming the victim for provoking the abuse. Victims, on the other hand, generally blame themselves and are distraught by the experience. Counselors can assess for each partner's motivations during a violent incident; generally one partner uses violence to gain control over her partner, and the other reacts in self-defense or out of frustration. McClennen reminded counselors that not all violent behavior in lesbian relationships is considered battering; rather, a behavior is considered to be battering when it creates fear and causes the perpetrator to become more powerful and controlling in the context of the relationship.

Why Doesn't She Just Leave?

Multiple persons in the client's life may wonder why a woman doesn't just leave, implying a bias against women who choose to stay in abusive relationships: "It must be her fault because she could leave if she wanted to." Instead, it is more helpful to view the decision to leave as a difficult and confusing choice. It is clear that the gradual and intermittent occurrence of the violence, paired with extensive efforts on behalf of abusers to win a woman back through attention and love, complicate a woman's decision.

Why Women Stay in Abusive Relationships

Here is a short list of some of the reasons women stay in abusive relationships.

1. Fear of retaliation, physical harm, or even death if she leaves
2. Fear of losing children: Partner may threaten to seek custody or to kidnap children.
3. Love for partner, large investment in the relationship, wanting to believe his/her promises of change
4. Does not want to disclose violence to law enforcement or the courts for fear of negative responses from friends, family, or community
5. Religious beliefs: Clergy might encourage her to preserve marriage and keep family together at all costs, or she holds the religious belief that divorce is not an option and that single parenthood is unacceptable; males may hold the religious belief that women are men's property and that they have the right to control their behavior.

6. Self-blame for perceived wrongdoings, shortcomings, and her own use of violence
7. Lack of financial resources: has no financial support other than from partner
8. Difficulty in accessing resources due to disability status, language barriers, proximity of services, or because of community attitudes of homophobia or racism
9. Threats by partner to report damaging information about her to family, friends, employers, or social agencies
10. Needs time to plan and prepare to leave, but can't plan when she is focused only on day-to-day survival
11. Feels she has nowhere else to turn due to extreme isolation created by the abuser
12. Fear of unknown or change: does not believe she can make it on her own
13. Low frequency or severity of abuse: During nonviolent phases the partner does fulfill her needs for affection.
14. Witnessing childhood abuse: If raised in a violent home, she is more likely to accept abuse as normal or tolerable.
15. Psychological abuse causes her to believe the abuser's insults and criticisms that she can't make it without him/her, or is unlovable.

Lesbian women who experience IPV in their relationships stay with their partners for many of the same reasons as heterosexual women; however, there are some important distinctions. First, the abusive partner might threaten to expose her partner's lesbian status to significant others (i. e., partner threatens to "out" her if she is closeted). Second, lesbian women might be more alienated from their families or other friends and tend to rely on their partners as their primary source of support. This over-reliance on their partners makes it even more difficult for them to leave. Third, lesbians have difficulty accessing formal services; many agencies are not prepared to offer services for lesbian IPV survivors. Fourth, lesbian women might be hesitant to reveal the abuse in their relationships because they fear it will create an even more negative image of same-sex relationships in society (McClennen, 2005; Rose, 2003).

Cultural beliefs also permeate women's decisions to stay in violent relationships. As mentioned previously, American Indian women as a group experience the highest levels of IPV, although historically there have been strong taboos against IPV in American Indian culture (Rivers, 2005). One cultural belief that might have served women well historically but now often serves to perpetuate IPV is the concept of balance. In most American Indian tribal cultures, a strong communal nature and interdependence within the tribe is more valued than personal happiness (Oetzel, Duran, Jiang, & Lucero, 2007). According to Rivers (2005), cultural teachings assert that balance is maintained only when male and female partners stay together and do their duty to their family and tribe. Therefore, women from certain American Indian tribal groups may stay in a violent relationship to help maintain balance within the community.

Additional Factors Influencing a Woman's Decision to Stay

Until recently, many mental health and other health care professionals likened women's tendency to stay in abusive relationships to learned helplessness. For example, it might be assumed that a woman experiencing IPV makes no attempts at making her situation better because her abuser has thwarted her previous attempts to leave or to make changes in the relationship. Observers may view the woman as passive and cannot understand her lack of willingness to take action, but research clearly indicates that women do not demonstrate learned helplessness but rather show resilience within the context of abuse. They make active decisions to make the situation more tolerable for themselves or their children, such as refraining from being assertive, declining to press charges, or staying in the relationship because these are the safest choices among her available alternatives. In other words, a woman's inaction does not represent learned helplessness but rather an assessment of risks and dangers (LaViolette & Barnett, 2000).

Further, there are cumulative effects of psychological and physical abuse on a woman's ability to make rational decisions and to think clearly. According to Chronister and McWhirter (2003), women experiencing IPV expend all of their energies trying to stop the violence. They try to anticipate the abuser's needs and wants or make efforts to change the abuser. While they are operating in survival mode, they are not able to make plans or think about the future as is illustrated in this quote reported by Petretic-Jackson and Jackson (1996):

> I got to the point I was only sleeping three or four hours a night. The rest of the time I was trying to figure out how to get the house and the kids perfect so that he wouldn't beat me again for something that was wrong at home. I was always alert. . . . All my energy went into planning every little detail so it would be perfect. I thought I could stop it (the abuse) by myself. (p. 205)

Women in relationships characterized by IPV also experience significant mental health symptoms that impair their ability to leave the relationship. The primary *DSM-IV-TR* diagnosis that best describes the constellation of symptoms resulting from IPV is posttraumatic stress disorder (PTSD). The PTSD diagnosis describes women's symptoms (such as high arousal, avoidance, intrusive memories, memory loss, cognitive confusion) as a consequence of experiencing prolonged trauma (Walker, 1994). Golding's (1999) meta-analysis of studies about women in abusive relationships reported rates of PTSD ranging from 31% to 84% of women (weighted mean prevalence estimate = 64%).

Other common mental health symptoms include depression (48% weighted mean prevalence estimate; Golding, 1999), somatization, anxiety disorders, phobias, sleep disorders, and social dysfunction (Family

Violence Prevention Fund, 2004; Jones, Hughes, & Unterstaller, 2001). Women in abusive relationships are also more likely to abuse alcohol and other drugs than are nonabused women (Family Violence Prevention Fund, 2004). Women who abuse substances might be using the substance as a method for coping with or for escaping from the reality of the violence, or because their partner also abuses substances.

Physical symptoms may impair a woman's ability to leave an abusive relationship. Women are likely to have long-term health problems during and after the physical abuse ends. They are at increased risk for chronic pain, central nervous problems, lower pain threshold, and gastrointestinal problems. Women who experience sexual abuse in their intimate relationships are significantly more likely to experience gynecological problems such as STDs and bleeding fibroids and to have higher rates of unplanned pregnancies than are nonabused women (Jones et al., 2001).

Finally, the most significant consequence of IPV that affects a woman's ability to leave the relationship is homicide. Women are most at risk for homicide when they leave their abusive partners. The majority (up to 80%) of women killed by an intimate partner had a long prior history of abuse and stalking by their partners. One third of all female murder victims in the United States were killed by a husband, ex-husband, or boyfriend (U.S. Bureau of Justice Statistics, 2004). As discussed more fully in the next section, counselors must consider a woman's safety when they help her plan to leave an abusive relationship. She has to evaluate whether or not leaving is the safest choice for her.

Treatment Strategies for Working With Women Who Experience IPV

Until recent years the battered women's movement recommended that women who experience IPV need community resources rather than counseling services. In addition, leaders in the movement were reluctant to refer women to counselors because it might imply that there is pathology in the woman that contributes to the abuse, or that it is the woman herself that provokes the abuse. Further, mental health professionals were seen as lacking the sensitivity needed for working with this population due to their lack of preparation and their tendency to ignore the power differential in the relationship and to blame the victim (Carlson, 1997). In contrast, current research supports the notion that counseling is needed to effectively prepare a woman for accessing community resources and for making clear decisions about leaving the relationship.

The treatment model described in this chapter draws from the empowerment feminist therapy model described in Chapter 1 and Walker's (1994) survivor therapy. The treatment modality can include either individual counseling or same-sex specific abuse groups, but couples or family counseling is not recommended once abuse has been detected in the couple (Morrow & Hawxhurst, 1989; Walker, 1994). Because couples therapy tends to assign equal responsibility for a problem to both partners in the relationship, this is not the preferred treatment for the woman or for the abuser (Walker, 1994). When at all possible, the woman and her abuser should not work with the same counselor.

Phase One: Prevention and Preparation

The first phase of treatment occurs before a counselor ever works with his or her first client experiencing IPV. Counselors need to prepare themselves by assessing their own attitudes in working with this issue. Walker (1994) recommended that counselors first address the discomfort they experience when thinking about IPV.

As part of this process, counselors can assess how they will address cultural differences in working with IPV. Counselors should respect and understand a client's cultural values, attitudes, and beliefs, but they must also know that certain culturally sanctioned abusive practices against women "should not be tolerated in the name of cultural differentness or adaptation" (Hansen, Gama & Harkins, 2002, p. 175). While counselors should advocate for their clients in questioning these cultural beliefs, counselors "must be extremely careful when challenging deeply accepted traditions, so as not to cause breakdowns in communication with clients or jeopardize client's well-being" (p. 175). The need to balance respect for specific cultural beliefs with respect for larger human values is a complex issue that counselors must prepare for in working with clients from a variety of cultural backgrounds.

Self-Exploration Exercise

1. What feelings emerged for you as you read about the cycle of violence? How open were you to staying with those feelings? Did they stir up any feelings regarding victimization experiences in your own past or in the lives of those close to you? How will you manage those feelings when working with clients?
2. How would you respond to the question, "Why doesn't she just leave?"
3. How will you monitor any tendencies to blame a woman for causing the violence in her life? How mindful are you of the cultural and situational variables that influence a woman's decision to stay with her abusive partner?
4. How aware are you of your attitudes toward a woman who might choose to stay in an abusive relationship? Or who is able to leave an abusive relationship only to return shortly thereafter?
5. How will you manage your feelings when your client decides she does not want to report the abuse to law enforcement? How will you convey respect for her right to make her own decisions about the relationship?

After examining their own attitudes, counselors can integrate an IPV prevention focus in their work with all women in an effort to help women recognize IPV before the cycle of violence begins. Prevention workshops or psychoeducational sessions can be provided to young women regarding strategies for evaluating their romantic relationships and warning signs that might alert them to the potential for IPV. The power and control wheel (see www.duluth-model.org for reproducible wheel handouts) is an extremely effective prevention tool for assisting clients in evaluating their current relationships against the qualities that are present in relationships based on equality.

Before working with women experiencing IPV, counselors should educate themselves about available resources. While counselors may prefer to work within the confines of their typical professional duties, working with battered women requires that we go outside of our traditional roles and work with professionals from other disciplines (DePorto, 2003). At minimum, this includes developing a list of referral sources for women experiencing IPV that can be made readily available to clients. A counselor's list should include the following resources:

- Medical care
- Crisis intervention
- Job bank
- IPV shelters
- Legal services
- Social service agencies
- Day-care programs
- Victim assistance programs
- Law enforcement and laws to protect women
- 24-hour crisis line for IPV
- Housing assistance
- Outreach/support programs

Not only should counselors be aware of the services in their area, they should become familiar with the attitudes of various service providers toward women in abusive relationships. For example, are certain agencies known to have racist, homophobic, or other negative attitudes toward women from certain sociocultural backgrounds? How adequate is your local IPV shelter? How quickly does law enforcement respond to IPV incidents? How do the courts typically handle IPV cases in your community? Being able to assist clients in anticipating what their interactions with other professionals might be like will help to reduce fears about accessing services (Petretic-Jackson & Jackson, 1996).

A third area of preparation is counselors' awareness of the influence of cultural context on a client's response to the abuse. Many factors influence the meaning a client assigns to the abuse and how she might choose to manage the abuse. One particular area of concern is her decision whether or not to report violent incidents to law enforcement. Reluctance to report is common in relationships with IPV. According Tjaden and Thoennes (1998), only one fourth of physical assaults, one fifth of rapes, and one half of stalkings are reported to the police. There are several reasons for this reluctance. Even though women might want the abuser to be punished, they don't necessarily want him or her to spend time in jail. Further, some women might not want to be seen as "betraying their communities" by reporting to police, and some African American women may fear that reporting violence will result in increased negative stereotypes about African American males (West, 1998). As mentioned previously, lesbian women might not want to report violence in their relationships so as not to worsen stereotypes about the lesbian community. Finally, women may be reluctant to press charges against their partner because they believe the police won't do anything to help (U.S. Bureau of Justice Statistics, 2005).

Phase Two: Engagement and Assessment

When counselors have made adequate preparation, the second treatment phase includes initial counseling sessions in which a working relationship is established and an appropriate assessment is conducted. Because of the nature of IPV, women might have difficulty developing an open, trusting relationship with a counselor. Counselors can use several strategies to help overcome the obstacles to a strong working alliance. In general, it is important for the client to be able to view counseling as a relationship in which the power is shared so that the counselor has "power with" rather than "power over" the client (Walker, 1994). Because of the preponderance of victim-blaming by significant others in her life, the client needs to know that her counselor believes her story and accepts her unconditionally regardless of whether or not she is ready to leave the relationship with her partner. Overall, because she might have lost the ability to view the world in an objective way, a client might perceive the counselor as either being "for her" or "against her"; therefore, counselors should be intentionally positive rather than neutral in the initial sessions (Walker, 1994).

Counselors should remain mindful of the following six areas that might interfere with the development of a working alliance (Carlson, 1997; Walker, 1994):

Denial and minimization. If a counselor observes denial or minimization of the abuse, it is often helpful to conceptualize these defenses as having a protective function in the client's life. Denial might even be encouraged in the client's culture to help her continue functioning in a productive manner. It is likely that suppressing her emotions is the only way she feels she can survive. Walker (1994) recommended that counselors refrain from using confrontational techniques that serve to break down a client's denial.

Self-blame. It is likely that the client believes she is at fault for the abuse and that the abuse will stop if she changes her behavior. It makes sense that she does not want to give up this illusion of control, so the client might be reluctant to work with a counselor in assigning blame to the abuser.

Shame and guilt. If she has internalized her abuser's critical and humiliating comments, the client is likely to feel that she does not deserve the counselor's help or that she can ever have the strength to leave the relationship.

Cognitive dysfunction. Her inability to think clearly because of the abuse might interfere with her understanding and progress in counseling.

Pleasing, overly compliant, or manipulative style. Because some women learn to become overly compliant in attempts to appease the abusive partner, the client might remain passive with the counselor. It is common for her to state that she agrees ("Yes, I'll try that this week") but fail to follow through with suggestions. She might have also learned to become manipulative in relationships as a way to maintain some sense of control. Sharing the power and developing a working alliance should help to reduce the client's need to manipulate in order to feel control in the counseling relationship.

Fear of punishment. The client might be reticent to talk openly in counseling due fears of retaliation by the abusive partner (Petretic-Jackson & Jackson, 1996).

An important part of establishing a strong working alliance is to assist the client in identifying treatment goals. A comprehensive assessment of the client's history and current life situation is needed to determine appropriate goals and strategies. The following guide, developed from suggestions by Carlson (1997), Petretic-Jackson and Jackson (1996), Walker (1994), and West (1998), can be used to structure the initial assessment.

Guide for Conducting Assessment With Women Experiencing IPV

1. Understand the client's story.
   a. Beginning the session: To increase her feelings of being in control of the session, allow her to initiate the session by asking, "Do you have any ideas about where it would be easier for you to start?" (Walker, 1994).
   b. Strategies for facilitating client disclosure:
      i. Acknowledge that this is difficult information for her to share. Reflect and validate her thoughts frequently and give her a rationale when you need to ask potentially embarrassing questions ("I need to know about this because . . ."; Petretic-Jackson & Jackson, 1996).
      ii. Clients may have difficulty articulating their stories in a clear, logical fashion. If this occurs, counselors should remain patient and refrain from any attempts to rush the client through the story, as she may interpret this as lack of understanding or interest (Walker, 1994).
      iii. Begin with more general questions and then move to a more specific focus when gathering information. Counselors can use open-ended questions to gently probe for additional details.

iv. Clients may talk of abusive incidents and emotionally charged events while using a monotone or conversational tone. They may also remember and "re-forget" incidents from week to week. Rather than becoming frustrated, counselors can remember that these behaviors are normal and expected ways survivors cope with trauma (Walker, 1994).

2. Determine the client's level of awareness and insight in terms of her perceptions of the abuse. For example, does she blame herself? Does she still believe she can change her partner?

3. Understand the abuse within her life context.
   a. Assess for child abuse history: Was she abused as a child? Did she witness violence as a child? These are important risk factors for further abuse (Walker, 1994).
   b. Assess for adult abuse history, as multiple victimizations are common occurrences for women who experience violence.

4. Assess for PTSD and other factors.
   a. In reviewing *DSM-IV-TR* criteria, focus especially on intrusive thoughts, memories, reexperiencing, flashbacks, arousal, and avoidance.
   b. Other disorders to consider: depression and other affective disorders, substance abuse, anxiety disorders, dissociative states and disorders.

5. Assess for physiological conditions such as sleeping, eating, and gastrointestinal problems.

6. Explore family relationship and friendship patterns: Who are her support systems? Who can she count on for help? Further, do her interpersonal skills interfere with her ability to establish relationships with potential sources of support?

7. Consider cultural factors: Race/ethnicity, economic status, family structure, level of acculturation, religious or spiritual beliefs, disability status, community reactions to IPV all affect a woman's responses to abuse (Chronister & McWhirter, 2003).

8. Identify coping skills: Help assess for the coping efforts she has made in the past. What has she already tried? What are things that get in the way?

9. Determine concurrent stressors such as financial, substance abuse, employment, family-of-origin conflicts, or parenting concerns (Carlson, 1997).

10. Conduct a safety assessment: It is essential that any assessment include assessment of suicidality. Is suicidal ideation present? Second, assessment should encompass level of lethality and a current risk assessment to determine the extent of danger to herself or to her children.

To determine how the abuse has escalated in frequency and intensity over time, ask the client to describe four types of IPV incidents: (a) the most recent incident, (b) the first incident, (c) the typical incident, and (d) the worst incident. Also assess for threats the abuser has made about her attempts to leave the relationship. Has she left the relationship before? What happened? What might she need to do differently next time?

Phase Three: Treatment Strategies for Women Currently Experiencing IPV

If IPV is ongoing, the first step after development of a strong working alliance is to create a crisis management plan. Safety is paramount, so the counselor should assist the client in developing a clear plan of action she can use when she feels that she is again in danger. To aid her in this process, refer to the Appendix at the end of this chapter for the Safety Plan Checklist for Women. Working with a client to develop this type of plan helps to accomplish three objectives: First, it gives the client hope that escape might be possible, even if she never uses the plan; second, it helps to reduce her denial that violent behavior won't happen again; and third, it helps her to think more clearly and logically (Walker, 1994).

The plan includes steps for identifying the abuser's cues or triggers that he or she typically displays before a violent episode. A woman is attuned to these cues but may not recognize them as helpful guides she can use for knowing when to implement her safety plan. It is important for the counselor to help the client mentally rehearse the plan in session so that the client can think through each step and anticipate any obstacles. At home the client can conduct an escape drill, walking through the plan with her children, if necessary (Petretic-Jackson & Jackson, 1996).

During this phase, clients also benefit from psychoeducation regarding the definitions of abuse (see Tables 8.1 and 8.2), the cycle of abuse (see Figure 8.1), and information about healthy versus controlling relationships (see www.duluth-model.org for helpful handouts about power and control in relationships and questions to assist her in evaluating the relationship). Most important, clients may need to hear the basic message that they are not responsible for and do not deserve to be abused, regardless of their actions or their own use of violence.

Clients also need information about resources and options available to them in their communities. As was emphasized in the preparation phase, counselors should have comprehensive lists of services and resources available for clients and should be aware of the best ways to access those services ("How do I access legal services?" "Who do I speak with first?")

A third area of psychoeducation includes information about the symptoms the client is likely to be experiencing. She needs to recognize that many of the physical or psychological difficulties she is experiencing are direct consequences of the abuse. It is helpful to label her reactions as normative responses to trauma so that she can begin to decrease the feeling that she is "going crazy." Here are some common characteristics women survivors of relationship violence might experience:

1. Intrusion
   - Reexperiencing of the trauma
   - Nightmares, flashbacks, recurrent thoughts
2. Avoidance
   - Avoiding trauma-related stimuli
   - Social withdrawal
   - Emotional numbing

- Hyperarousal
- Increased emotional arousal
- Exaggerated startle response
- Irritability

3. Mental confusion, inability to concentrate
4. Dissociative states
5. Avoidance of feelings
6. Sensitivity to potential danger (excellent ability to read danger cues)

Other areas of treatment during this phase recommended by Walker (1994) and Carlson (1997) include dealing with denial, coping, problem-solving and decision-making skills, breaking silence and isolation, obtaining cognitive clarity, expressing anger, and treating the trauma.

Dealing with denial. A woman experiencing IPV might use extensive denial and minimization as a way to cope with the abuse. She might minimize ("Its only a few bruises this time."), rationalize ("I yelled at him, so he got furious and went out of control when he punched my face."), or excuse the behavior ("He's going through a tough time at work right now."). Petretic-Jackson and Jackson (1996) suggested asking the client to keep a paper trail, logging the details of each violent incident, including the humiliating or harmful words used, using photographs to document injuries, and even saving voice messages containing threatening or psychologically abusive language. Maintaining and reviewing such documentation in session can serve as evidence to help the client see the discrepancies between her current description of the abuse and the actual events that have occurred.

Coping. After enduring IPV, a woman needs to be reminded of her strengths. Petretic-Jackson and Jackson (1996) noted that the coping skills a woman has used to survive the trauma of IPV are strengths she can use to reach her treatment goals. In examining coping skills, she can identify which ones have been effective, which ones have proven to be ineffective, and can brainstorm some new strategies to try. In initiating this discussion it is important that the counselor refrain from subtle forms of victim-blaming, such as questions like "What do you need to do so that he will stop abusing you?" (Ulrich, 1998), which puts the focus on the woman, rather than on her partner, and may cause her to feel even more responsible for stopping the abuse.

Because behavioral strategies for ending the violence are generally ineffective, it is important to address the client's maladaptive beliefs as a way to improve coping skills (Carlson, 1997). Assess for any of the following commonly held beliefs: "It's my fault, I deserved it." "I can work harder to control my partner's abusive behavior toward me." Or, "I'm a failure and can't make it on my own without my partner." She will benefit from thought stopping for interrupting such maladaptive cognitive patterns and by making conscious efforts to replace them with the truth: "I do not deserve the abuse, nor can I control my partner's behavior. I am a worthwhile person and I have a lot of qualities to offer in a relationship." She might also benefit from learning to view herself as a "survivor" (a person who makes active choices) rather than as a "victim" (a person who is acted upon). Adopting a survivor identity helps her progress toward taking action to make her situation better (Carlson, 1997). Other internal coping strategies might include a woman's spirituality. One study of low-income African American women experiencing IPV showed that the women cited prayer, spiritual beliefs, and their relationship with God as their preferred coping strategies. Women in the study were fearful of using public (behavioral) coping strategies, and only turned to these strategies when private ones failed (Mitchell et al., 2006).

Problem-solving and practical decision-making skills. A woman in an abusive relationship often has impaired decision-making skills, as all of her energies are devoted to daily survival rather than to longer-term decisions and because her partner has worked to undermine her sense of confidence in her abilities. She will therefore benefit from having assistance in accessing support, navigating resources and services, and in preparing a plan of action. Carlson (1997) recommended teaching clients the following general problem-solving strategies:

1. Define the problem.
2. Generate a range of possible solutions.
3. Critically evaluate the pros and cons of each possible solution.
4. Choose among the alternatives.
5. Put the solution into effect.
6. Evaluate the solution.

By implementing each step, she can learn to think more logically and evaluate consequences or outcomes of her actions and decisions. Finally, she will benefit from having small success experiences to increase self-efficacy (e.g., she contacts a local agency to obtain legal assistance, has a positive interaction with the staff, and feels more confident to set up a meeting with them in person) and from receiving encouragement for the positive decisions she is making.

Breaking silence and isolation. A hallmark of IPV is the abuser's use of tactics to isolate his or her partner from others. She may have learned to remain silent about the abuse for fear of negative reactions from others or fear of retaliation by the abuser. Counseling can be an initial outlet for discussing the abuse and for feeling supported. Connecting the client with support groups for women who are also survivors of IPV is recommended when possible. Overall, the client needs to be encouraged to develop resources and support outside of her relationship with her partner. A counselor and client can work together to find ways in which she can reach out to others for support even while recognizing that her partner may react negatively to these actions. As with any decision, she needs to evaluate the consequences of taking these steps (Carlson, 1997).

Obtaining cognitive clarity. Women who are abused often experience dissociation, a mild hypnotic or trancelike state in which a woman feels as if she is involuntarily focused on internal or external stimuli (Walker, 1994). These dissociative states affect a woman's ability to think clearly and to trust her perceptions. She may describe her dissociation as an "out of body" experience in which she feels she is watching herself being abused. Memory loss may result from severely abusive incidents, and women who were abused as children are particularly likely to develop dissociation. While she may feel as if she is losing control when she experiences an involuntary dissociative state, the client will benefit from understanding the protective function of these experiences. Dissociation can serve to buffer her from intense psychological or physical pain.

Recommended ways of controlling dissociative experiences include grounding techniques that help her stay focused on the present (such as deliberately focusing her attention on an object in the room), becoming more aware of the incidents as they are happening, and learning to report their occurrence in sessions. She can practice using body awareness techniques and physical exercise to help her become in touch with what she is feeling and experiencing in her body. Further, she can learn that while she may not be in control of the abuse itself, she is in control of how she thinks about the abuse. Through the use of guided imagery, she can actively change her intrusive memories of the abuse so that they affect her less negatively. For example, when memories of the abuse intrude upon her thoughts, she can instead choose to picture herself capturing her abusive partner in a cage and refusing to let him or her escape by throwing away the key (Walker, 1994).

Anger expression. A woman in an abusive relationship may have repressed her anger to the extent that she feels she needs to keep her emotions under tight control in order to function. She may feel that her anger will be explosive if expressed or that she may engage in violence herself if she allows herself to experience her anger. However, she can learn not to fear her anger and to express it in ways that are not harmful to herself or to others. Ideally, she can learn to use controlled anger to assist her in making important changes in her life (Walker, 1994). For example, the anger she feels toward her abusive partner can motivate her to take action in moving to a shelter so that her children will no longer have to witness violence in their home.

Treating the trauma. Rather than labeling the client with a mental disorder that might lead to victim-blaming (i. e., because of her pathology she somehow provokes or deserve the abuse), understanding her symptoms as PTSD helps to depathologize the client and clearly emphasizes the direct link between her symptoms and the IPV (Golding, 1999). Counselors can assist the client in reducing PTSD symptoms and in implementing symptom relief strategies. The recommended treatment phases of psychoeducation, exposure, cognitive–behavioral strategies, and anxiety management are explored fully in Chapter 7.

While working to reduce the symptoms of PTSD is important, recommended treatment strategies generally assume that the trauma has ended. Counselors should consider that when a woman remains in an abusive relationship, the trauma is ongoing and may continue even after the relationship has ended (DePorto, 2003). In these cases, addressing the PTSD symptoms will not be sufficient, and counselors should provide their clients with important safety planning, education, decision-making skills, coping strategies, and support.

With counseling and careful planning, a client can become better equipped to make a decision to leave the relationship. However, her decision to leave or not can be a long, complex process and should not be considered the outcome measure of counseling success. She will likely leave and return to the relationship many times (Petretic-Jackson & Jackson, 1996). J. C. Campbell and Kendall-Tackett (2005) as well as Walker (1994) noted that counselors should become comfortable with the goal of working toward nonviolence in the relationship, and not necessarily termination of the relationship. Even though it might be frustrating for counselors, we need to honor the client's right to make her own choices about leaving, and to be accepting of her if she decides to return to an abusive partner after she does manage to leave. It is helpful to remember that the greater the number of times a client leaves an abusive relationship, the less likely she will be to permanently return.

Consider your reaction to the client portrayed in the following case study, and answer the questions based on treatment phases one through three.

Case Study

K. G. is a 36-year-old married African American woman who has been in a violent relationship with her husband for 10 years. They have three children, ages 2, 6, and 7. At her husband's request, she does not work outside the home. The marriage did not start out as violent, but she describes their "fights" as becoming increasingly worse. She is an active participant in their physical alterations, always fighting back with kicks and slapping. According to her, she is usually the one that starts a fight because she becomes angry with his jealousy and name-calling. She also thinks she provokes the fights because she gives him a hard time about going out to bars at night with his friends. During their fights, he always tells her that she can never leave him because "If he can't have you, then no one can."

The latest incident (during which her shoulder was dislocated) was the impetus that brought her to counseling. After the latest incident she and her children moved in with her aunt for a few days, but they returned home after her husband apologized and told her that he would never hurt her again. She does not believe him because this has happened many times before, but she does not know how she could ever really leave the relationship permanently. She still loves him and wants her children to have a father, but she worries that because of all of the fighting that she is not a good mother to her children anymore. She spends a lot of energy trying to hide the abuse from her family and few remaining friends. Her relatives constantly tell her that she is lucky to have a husband who has a good job and who loves his children so much. She looks to you, her counselor, to help her become a "better person" so that she won't provoke him to get so angry with her.

1. As K. G.'s counselor, how do you work with her desired treatment goals?
2. Where would you need to start in terms of the issues outlined in phase one of this chapter? How would you prepare yourself in terms of your attitudes, knowledge of resources, and awareness of cultural context?
3. How would you establish a working alliance with this client? Which of the six issues that often impede working relationships might be factors in this case: denial, self-blame, shame and guilt, cognitive dysfunction, pleasing, and fear of punishment?
4. As you review the assessment guidelines in the chapter, how might this client answer some of these questions?
5. What are some safety planning issues that might be relevant with this client?
6. How might the treatment issues listed in phase three be pertinent to this case: denial, coping, problem solving, breaking silence, cognitive clarity, anger expression, treating the trauma?

Phase Four: Treatment Strategies for Postseparation Issues

If and when a woman experiencing IPV decides to leave the relationship, she needs to have a clear understanding of the potential for postseparation abuse. Abuse often doesn't stop when the relationship ends but instead increases in severity (Tjaden & Thoennes, 2006). One of the most frequent forms of postseparation abuse is stalking behavior in which the partner may follow her, show up at her place of employment, check up on her whereabouts, leave harassing messages, and threaten to follow through on previous threats to harm her. Women fear the threats their partners have made previously—"If you ever leave me, no one else can have you either. I will find you and hurt you."—and these fears are well founded. Statistics indicate that batterers do follow through on their long-standing threats (DePorto, 2003). Verbal threats like these are strong predictors of actual violent behavior, and women are more likely to be stalked and even killed following their decision to leave (DePorto, 2003). Women who experience postseparation IPV may wonder if the postseparation abuse is even worse than the IPV experienced while they remained in the relationship. As Mechanic, Weaver, and Resick (2000) pointed out, the important question is not "Why doesn't she leave?" but rather, "Why doesn't he let her go?"

Counselors should prioritize safety planning in their work with women who experience postseparation IPV. DePorto (2003) recommended that counselors assist women in assessing the potential for further abuse based on the abuser's past threats and behaviors. For example, what are some cues women can watch for in determining the likelihood of imminent danger? Women need to develop a specific safety plan for coping with postseparation violence, much as they did when planning to leave the relationship initially (see Safety Planning Checklist in the chapter Appendix).

During this time the client may be experiencing a variety of intense emotions, including self-blame, fear, and hopelessness. She may isolate herself from others due to her fear of retaliation by her partner and her shame about this pattern of violence. Counselors can work to normalize her feelings and can encourage her to seek necessary support. The counselor–client relationship can be an important first step in breaking her silence and in reducing shame and self-blame. The counselor can then assist her in carefully selecting people in her life who can help her to feel supported and to remain safe. DePorto (2003) noted that it is particularly important for a woman experiencing postseparation abuse to openly disclose the potential for abuse to others at her place of employment because the abuser has easy access to her at that location. If others know about the ex-partner's potential for violence, they can take actions such as screening calls and denying access into the work environment. DePorto also recommended that counselors engage in consultation with other professionals such as human resources personnel at her workplace, legal professionals, social services, and law enforcement to make it easier for her to access these services.

Another aspect in working with women who experience postseparation abuse is working with batterer management issues (DePorto, 2003). It may be confusing for a counselor when he or she learns that the client maintains close contact with and continues to interact with the abuser. These interactions are likely to be her attempts at alleviating some of her fears by talking with her ex-partner to get a sense of what he or she is thinking and feeling. While she was still in the relationship, she was able to read her ex-partner's cues and sense triggers for impending violence. Now that she is no longer with her partner, she feels she has less control because she isn't able to access these cues and triggers. Maintaining contact enables her to feel a sense of control. The problem with this coping strategy is that the more she interacts with her ex-partner the more he or she will try to find a way back into her life. Counselors can help her break out of this pattern by first validating her fears and normalizing her desire to monitor her ex-partner's thoughts and danger cues. However, the client needs to be aware that continued contact will make her problem worse in the long term. She needs assistance in developing new coping strategies that are based on her own best interest (DePorto, 2003).

In addition to postseparation abuse issues, a woman who has left an abusive intimate relationship may need to engage in the process of grieving. Counselors may assume that the woman feels relief at removing herself from the abuse, but the reality is that she might need considerable time to grieve the loss of her partner (and the father of her children), their mutual friends, her hopes and dreams for the relationship, her role as a wife or partner, and her security in knowing what to expect within those roles (Russell & Uhlemann, 1994). She might benefit from grief counseling techniques to help her understand the contradictions of her losses. She needs to be reassured that it is normal to experience sorrow and depression with the loss of the relationship and its associated roles. At this phase she might also need to work toward resolving her guilt for choosing to stay in the abusive relationship for as long as she did (Russell & Uhlemann, 1994).

Finally, when a woman has left an abusive relationship, counseling can begin to focus on fostering resilience and wellness. The client can begin to search for meaning from the IPV in the context of her life, and she can actively choose to begin viewing herself as a survivor with many strengths. As the energy that she spent on trying to survive the traumatic effects of the relationship is freed up, she can turn her energies toward healing, developing supportive relationships, and building a new self-concept (Senter & Caldwell, 2002). Survivors can begin to focus on all dimensions of wellness that will enhance their health and life satisfaction, particularly those that have been neglected during their time in the relationship. Instead of focusing on themselves, however, some women may want to spend time in planning how they can seek revenge against their abusive partners. When this occurs, it is helpful to remind clients that their time and resources are best spent on healing, creating positive life goals, and rebuilding their lives. As Walker (1994) noted, "Living well is the best revenge" (p. 323). Gradually, the power her partner has over her will diminish (Landenberger, 1998a) and she will begin to move on from the relationship, emerging as a stronger, more resilient woman.

Conclusion

Healing from the experience of intimate partner violence is a lengthy, often complex process for many women. Counselors should be as prepared as possible for working with women who seek assistance with relationships characterized by physical, sexual, psychological, or stalking abuse. As reviewed in this chapter, counselors can work to understand the typical cycle of violence and the multiple factors that influence a woman's decision to stay in an abusive relationship. Counselors must then step outside of their comfort zones by exploring their own biases in this area and by networking with local community agencies (medical, legal, law enforcement, housing assistance) that provide support for women in abusive relationships.

Above all, a client does not need a counselor who subtly encourages self-blame or who pressures her to leave her partner, but instead needs a counselor who can believe her story, value her perspective, respect her decisions regarding the relationship, and advocate for her safety. Most important, she needs a counselor who can instill the hope that she deserves to live in a violence-free environment, even though she may leave and return to her relationship many times before achieving this goal.

Activities for Further Exploration

1. Visit the Duluth Web site at www.duluth-model.org to review the Wheel Gallery. How might you use the Power and Control or the Equality wheels in your counseling work with women?
2. Contact a representative from your local IPV shelter to determine their services for women (e.g., temporary housing, crisis line, counseling programs, programs for children, advocacy services).
3. Develop a resource list for women clients experiencing IPV. What resources are available in your community? How can you go about developing relationships with specific individuals at these agencies?

Suggested Readings

Campbell, J. C., & Kendall-Tackett, K. A. (2005). Intimate partner violence: Implications for women's physical and mental health. In K. A. Kendall-Tackett (Ed.), *The handbook of women, stress, and trauma* (pp. 123–140). New York: Bruner-Routledge, Taylor & Francis Group.

DePorto, D. (2003). Battered women and separation abuse: A treatment approach based on "knowing." In M. Kopala & M. Keitel (Eds.), *Handbook of counseling women* (pp. 279–306). Thousand Oaks, CA: Sage.

Family Violence Prevention Fund. (2004). *National consensus guidelines on identifying and responding to domestic violence victimization in health care settings.* Retrieved November 15, 2006, from http://www.endabuse.org/programs/healthcare/files/Consensus.pdf

LaViolette, A. D., & Barnett, O. W. (2000). *It could happen to anyone: Why battered women stay* (2nd ed.). Thousand Oaks, CA: Sage.

Petretic-Jackson, P., & Jackson, T. (1996). Mental health interventions with battered women. In A. R. Roberts (Ed.), *Helping battered women: New perspectives & remedies* (pp. 188–221). New York: Oxford University Press.

Russell, B., & Uhlemann, M. R. (1994). Women surviving an abusive relationship: Grief and the process of change. *Journal of Counseling & Development, 72,* 362–367.

Walker, L. E. (1994). *Abused women and survivor therapy: A practical guide for the psychotherapist.* Washington, DC: American Psychological Association.

Additional Resources

http://www.break-the-cycle.org
This Web site contains information about domestic/dating violence and where/how to get help for adolescent females.

http://caepv.org
The Corporate Alliance to End Partner Violence Web site contains articles, research, statistics, related links, and tools for partner violence and information on dating violence and workplace issues.

www.ncadv.org
The National Coalition Against Domestic Violence Web site has information for victims on how they can protect themselves. The site also contains publications for counselors.
www.duluth-model.org
This Web site has information about the Duluth prevention model, including their wheel gallery illustrating the use of power and control in IPV relationships.

References

Arias, I., & Pape, K. (1999). Psychological abuse: Implications for adjustment and commitment to leave violent partners. *Violence & Victims, 14,* 55–67.

Campbell, D. W., & Gary, F. A. (1998). Providing effective interventions for African American battered women: Afrocentric perspectives. In J. C. Campbell (Ed.), *Empowering survivors of abuse: Health care for battered women and their children* (pp. 229–240). Thousand Oaks, CA: Sage.

Campbell, J. C., & Kendall-Tackett, K. A. (2005). Intimate partner violence: Implications for women's physical and mental health. In K. A. Kendall-Tackett (Ed.), *The handbook of women, stress, and trauma* (pp. 123–140). New York: Bruner-Routledge, Taylor & Francis Group.

Carlson, B. E. (1997). A stress and coping approach to intervention with abused women. *Family Relations, 46,* 291–298.

Chronister, K. M., & McWhirter, E. H. (2003). Applying social cognitive career theory to the empowerment of battered women. *Journal of Counseling & Development, 81,* 418–425.

DePorto, D. (2003). Battered women and separation abuse: A treatment approach based on "knowing." In M. Kopala & M. Keitel (Eds.), *Handbook of counseling women* (pp. 279–306). Thousand Oaks, CA: Sage.

Dutton, D. G., & Painter, S. (1993). Battered women syndrome. Effects of severity and intermittency of abuse. *American Journal of Orthopsychiatry, 63,* 614–627.

Family Violence Prevention Fund. (2004). *National consensus guidelines on identifying and responding to domestic violence victimization in health care settings.* Retrieved November 15, 2006, from http://www.endabuse.org/programs/healthcare/files/Consensus.pdf

Golding, J. M. (1999). Intimate partner violence as a risk factor for mental disorders: A meta-analysis. *Journal of Family Violence, 14*(2), 99–132.

Hamby, S. L. (2005). The importance of community in a feminist analysis of domestic violence among Native Americans. In N. J. Sokoloff & C. Pratt (Eds.), *Domestic violence at the margins: Readings on race, class, gender, and culture* (pp. 174–193). New Brunswick, NJ: Rutgers University Press.

Hansen, L. S., Gama, E. M., & Harkins, A. K. (2002). Revisiting gender issues in multicultural counseling. In P. B. Pederson, J. G. Draguns, W. J. Lonner, & J. E. Trimble (Eds.), *Counseling across cultures* (pp. 163–184). Thousand Oaks, CA: Sage.

Jones, L., Hughes, M., & Unterstaller, U. (2001). Post-traumatic stress disorder (PTSD) in victims of domestic violence: A review of the research. *Trauma, Violence, & Abuse, 2*(2), 99–119.

Landenburger, K. M. (1998a). The dynamics of leaving and recovering from an abusive relationship. *Journal of Obstetric, Gynecologic, and Neonatal Nursing, 27*(6), 700–706.

Landenburger, K. M. (1998b). Exploration of women's identity: Clinical approaches with abused women. In J. C. Campbell (Ed.), *Empowering survivors of abuse: Health care for battered women and their children* (pp. 61–69). Thousand Oaks, CA: Sage.

LaViolette, A. D., & Barnett, O. W. (2000). *It could happen to anyone: Why battered women stay* (2nd ed.). Thousand Oaks, CA: Sage.

Leisring, P. A., Dowd, L., & Rosenbaum, A. (2002). Treatment of partner aggressive women. *Journal of Aggression, Maltreatment, and Trauma, 7,* 257–277.

Luna-Firebaugh, E. M. (2006). Violence against American Indian women and the Services-Training-Officers-Prosecutors Violence Against Indian Women program. *Violence Against Women, 12,* 125–136.

Marshall, L. L. (1996). Psychological abuse of women: Six distinct clusters. *Journal of Family Violence, 11*(4), 379–409.

McClennen, J. C. (2005). Domestic violence between same-gender partners: Recent findings and future research. *Journal of Interpersonal Violence, 20*(2), 149–154.

Mechanic, M. B., Weaver, T. L., & Resick, P. A. (2000). Intimate partner violence and stalking behavior: Exploration of patterns and correlates in a sample of acutely battered women. *Violence and Victims, 15*(1), 55–72.

Miller, S. L., & Meloy, M. L. (2006). Women's use of force: Voice of women arrested for domestic violence. *Violence Against Women, 12*(1), 89–115.

Mitchell, M., Hargrove, G. L., Collins, M. H., Thompson, M. P., Reddick, T. L, & Kaslow, N. J. (2006). Coping variables that mediate the relationship between intimate partner violence and mental health outcomes among low-income, African American women. *Journal of Clinical Psychology, 62,* 1503–1520.

Morrow, S. L., & Hawxhurst, D. M. (1989). Lesbian partner abuse: Implications for therapists. *Journal of Counseling & Development, 68,* 58–62.

National Center for Injury Prevention and Control. (2006). *Intimate partner violence prevention, facts.* Retrieved May 5, 2006, from http://www.cdc.gov/ncipc/factsheets/ipvfacts.htm

The National Coalition Against Domestic Violence at www.ncadv.org

Oetzel, J., Duran, B., Jiang, Y., & Lucero, J. (2007). Social support and social undermining as correlates for alcohol, drug, and mental disorders in American Indian women presenting for primary care at an Indian Health Service Hospital. *Journal of Health Communication, 12,* 187–206.

O'Leary, K. D. (1999). Psychological abuse: A variable deserving critical attention in domestic violence. *Violence and Victims, 14,* 3–23.

Petretic-Jackson, P., & Jackson, T. (1996). Mental health interventions with battered women. In A. R. Roberts (Ed.), *Helping battered women:*

New perspectives & remedies (pp. 188–221). New York: Oxford University Press.

Rivers, M. J. (2005). Navajo women and abuse: The context for their troubled relationships. *Journal of Family Violence, 20,* 83–89.

Rose, S. M. (2003). Community interventions concerning homophobic violence and partner violence against lesbians. *Journal of Lesbian Studies, 4,* 125–139.

Russell, B., & Uhlemann, M. R. (1994). Women surviving an abusive relationship: Grief and the process of change. *Journal of Counseling & Development, 72,* 362–367.

Senter, K., & Caldwell, K. (2002). Spirituality and the maintenance of change: A phenomenological study of women who leave abusive relationships. *Contemporary Family Therapy: An International Journal, 24*(4), 543–565.

Shepard, M. (1992). Child-visiting and domestic abuse. *Child Welfare, 71*(4), 357–367.

Sutherland, C. A. (1999). Investigating the effects of intimate partner violence on women's health (physical abuse, suicide ideation, depression). *Dissertation Abstracts International, 60*(6-B), pp. 2642. (UMI No. AAI9936612)

Swan, S. C., & Snow, D. L. (2002). A typology of women's use of violence in intimate relationships. *Violence Against Women, 8*(3), 286–319.

Tjaden, P., & Thoennes, N. (1998). *Prevalence, incidence, and consequences of violence against women: Findings from the National Violence Against Women Survey.* Atlanta, GA: Centers for Disease Control and Prevention, Center for Injury Prevention.

Tjaden, P., & Thoennes, N. (2006). *Extent, nature, and consequences of rape victimization: Findings from the National Violence Against Women Survey.* Retrieved July 5, 2007, from www.ojp.usdoj.gov/nij

Ulrich, Y. C. (1998). What helped most in leaving spouse abuse: Implications for interventions. In J. C. Campbell (Ed.), *Empowering survivors of abuse: Health care for battered women and their children* (pp. 70–78). Thousand Oaks, CA: Sage.

U.S. Bureau of Justice Statistics. (2004, September 28). *Homicide trends in the U.S.* Washington, DC: Department of Justice, Office of Justice Programs. Retrieved May 5, 2006, from http://www.ojp.usdoj.gov/bjs/homicide/intimates.htm

U.S. Bureau of Justice Statistics. (2005, June 12). *Rate of family violence dropped by more than one-half from 1993 to 2002.* Washington, DC: Department of Justice, Office of Justice Programs. Retrieved November 15, 2006, from http://www.ojp.usdoj.gov/bjs/pub/press/fvspr.htm

Walker, L. E. (1994). *Abused women and survivor therapy: A practical guide for the psychotherapist.* Washington, DC: American Psychological Association.

West, C. M. (1998). Lifting the "political gag order": Breaking the silence around partner violence in ethnic minority families. In J. L. Jasinski & L. M. Williams (Eds.), *Partner violence: A comprehensive review of 20 years of research* (pp. 184–209). Thousand Oaks, CA: Sage.

Appendix
Safety Plan Checklist for Women Experiencing IPV

1. Determine triggers or cues for impending danger. During a recent incident:
   - What he said (curses, lies, stories)
   - How he said it
   - Tone of voice
   - Speed
   - Ability to listen
   - Effect of drugs or alcohol
   - Facial features (e.g., eyes)
   - Body posture
2. Where does the battering usually start?
   - Living room
   - Bedroom
   - Kitchen
   - Other room
3. Draw a floor plan map.
   - Doors, windows, exits
   - Baby or young children: What will you do to protect them?
   - Signal for older children: What will be the signal for them to leave immediately? Where will they go?
4. What do you need?
   - Money: cash, credit cards, ATM card, checkbook and bankbook with deposit slips
   - Keys: car, house, safety deposit or post office box
   - Way to communicate: cell phone, calling card, address book with important numbers (shelter, help line, etc.)
   - Clothes (keep a stash at your neighbor's house or at work)
   - Pets
   - Important papers: marriage certificate, divorce papers, custody orders, legal protection, health insurance papers/cards, medical records, children's school records, investment records and account numbers, work permits, immigration papers, rental/lease agreement or house deed, car title, registration, insurance information
   - Treasures: things you can sell if needed and other keepsakes to help you cope
   - Children's birth certificates and Social Security cards
   - Children's immunization records
   - Your Social Security card and your husband's Social Security card
   - Your identification
   - Prescription medications
   - Discuss with your children how you will handle an emergency situation and arrange to leave together

5. Location of a safe place
   - Police
   - Family
   - Friends
   - Shelter
6. Should you tell him you are leaving?
   - Options: Time out: "I need some time for you to cool off."
   - Conditions of possible return
   - Assess for possibility of stalking
   - Assess for lethality
7. Rehearse exit (two times or more).
   - Verbal: in session
   - Draw map: in session
   - Enact at home when abuser is not present

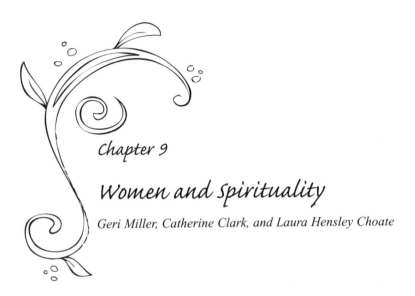

Chapter 9

Women and Spirituality

Geri Miller, Catherine Clark, and Laura Hensley Choate

Spirituality has been identified as the core of optimal wellness because it is involved with all aspects of a person (intellectual, physical, emotional, social, and occupational), facilitates connections with others, and provides a sense of hope, optimism, and purpose in life (Chandler, Holden, & Kolander, 1992; Myers & Sweeney, 2005; Myers, Sweeney, & Witmer, 2000). It is important for counselors to be knowledgeable about incorporating the spiritual dimension into their work with women clients because research indicates an association between spirituality and the health and well-being of women (Williams-Nickelson, 2006). Further, women are more likely than men to turn to spiritual practices to address life problems (Dudley-Grant & Daniel, 2003) and to incorporate spirituality as part of normal, everyday life (Ballou, 1995). It follows, then, that counselors should regularly assess the importance of the spiritual dimension in all of their women clients' lives (Harris, Thoresen, & Lopez, 2007). In this chapter we provide an overview of developmental theoretical models that can be used in understanding client spiritual issues, describe factors to consider in assessing client spiritual wellness, and present counseling techniques that facilitate the benefits of spirituality for women.

Self-exploration of a counselor's own spiritual perspective is an integral part of understanding client spiritual concerns, developmental models, assessment, and counseling techniques. Use the self-exploration exercise to assess the importance of spirituality in your own life.

Defining Spirituality

Spirituality (from the Latin word *spiritus*) is both universal and personal; it is difficult to define and can become limiting when defined in specific terms (Cashwell & Young, 2005). While noting these limitations, G. Miller (2003) defined spirituality as that which keeps our spirit alive, and Kelly

Spirituality Self-Exploration Exercise

As I looked at it I felt that all the sorrow humanity had ever had to endure was expressed in that face. I could almost feel the hot, stinging unshed tears behind the lowered eyelids. Yet in that expression there was something almost triumphant. There was a woman who had experienced every kind of pain, every kind of suffering . . . and had come out of it serene and compassionate. Whatever bitter unhappiness, whatever agony of body or soul the viewer might be going through that woman had known.

—Hickok Lorena response to the statue of *Grief* as she and Eleanor Roosevelt viewed it together (B.W. Cook, 1992, p. 492).

From a spiritual perspective, the woman's triumph over her pain and suffering in living may indicate her capacity to tap into the spiritual realm as a resource for resilience and wellness. To better understanding this interpretation of the statue and to frame spirituality from a developmental perspective, think of four times in your life when you experienced distress. If possible, think of one during childhood, one in adolescence, and two experiences from adulthood. Then answer these questions for each time frame:

- What were you facing?
- How did you cope with it?
- How did spiritual/religious factors fit into the development of the distress or into coping with the distress?

Framing a time of distress through a spiritual focus can be powerful for an individual. Use the thoughts and feelings that emerged through the exercise as an anchor for the following discussion regarding the integration of spirituality into the counseling of women.

Source: Adapted from an exercise presented at the American Psychological Association (2006) workshop on spirituality and counseling.

(1995) described it as a personal connection with the universe. The 1996 Summit on Spirituality, sponsored by the American Counseling Association's division of the Association of Spiritual, Ethical, and Religious Values in Counseling (n.d.), provided the following description:

Spirit may be defined as the animating life force, represented by such images as breath, wind, vigor, and courage. Spirituality is the drawing out and infusion of spirit in one's life. It is experienced as an active and passive process. Spirituality is also defined as a capacity and tendency that is innate and unique to all persons. This spiritual tendency moves the individual toward knowledge, love, meaning, peace, hope, transcendence, connectedness, compassion, wellness, and wholeness. Spirituality includes one's capacity for creativity, growth, and the development of a value system. Spirituality encompasses a variety of phenomena, including experiences, beliefs, and practices. Spirituality is approached from a variety of perspectives, including psychospiritual, religious, and transpersonal. While spirituality is usually expressed through culture, it both precedes and transcends culture. (para. 3)

In conceptualizing spirituality, it is critical to address what appear to be dichotomous definitions of spirituality and religion. In common language, we have a Western cultural tendency to think separately about religion and spirituality. In reality, "nuanced definitions of religion and spirituality abound, leading scholars struggling to clarify the 'fuzziness' of the language" (Zinbauer et al. as cited in Shafranske & Sperry, 2005, p. 14). Religion is viewed as the institutional practice of rituals and attendance at services, whereas spirituality is more commonly understood as one's ongoing search for meaning and understanding in life (Williams-Nickelson, 2006). This separate way of thinking about religion and spirituality may diminish the experience of clients whose personal stories blend religion and spirituality. When these concepts are interwoven within a client's experience, a client's spiritual quest may have religious undertones that are related to upbringing and the background of the client. It is prudent to allow the client to define these terms as existential themes arise, rather than the counselor labeling them.

Further, to fully understand the nature of a client's spiritual concerns, Cashwell and Young (2005) suggested that we examine the distinctions between spiritual beliefs, practices, and experiences. The authors defined *beliefs* as the "purely translative set of ideas and schemas that we hold," *practices* as the "behaviors that we use to experience and express our beliefs," and *experiences* as "any occurrences that occasion a deeper and more meaningful connection with the Truer or Higher Self" (p. 199). For example, a Christian woman may hold the *belief* of one true God and *practice* this belief by reading the Bible, which assists her in having an *experience* of being close to God. Cashwell and Young stated that these three areas may be connected, or they may not be connected. Assessment of these areas can assist the counselor in determining the individual's degree of wellness within the spiritual realm. This chapter incorporates these definitions and considerations when discussing spiritual concerns in counseling with women while recognizing the limitations of using a single perspective.

Developmental Theoretical Models of Spirituality

The counselor can use developmental theories of spiritual frameworks to assess the ways in which the client views spirituality as a strength as well as areas in which the client may be struggling with spiritual issues. Tisdell (2003) stated that humans develop spiritually in a spiral shape because of the tendency to return to old experiences and make new meaning of them as we accumulate different knowledge of self, others, our lives, and experiences. This new knowledge, gathered as we live in the world, affects our interpretation of our experiences (G. Miller, 2005b). Tisdell (2003) also stated that there is a fluidity to spiritual development because what we have learned in the past affects current living and future orientation. Finally, Tisdell reminded us that life transitions, such as birth and death, as well as dreams, experiential activities, and practices (stories, art, music, nature, meditation, and so forth), shape our thoughts and emotions. For example, experiences in life that involve role transitions can cause stress for the client because the old role has not been released or the new role has not been fully integrated into daily life (L. Miller, 2005). We encourage counselors to view the developmental models presented within this spiral perspective to avoid the tendency to view spiritual development as a linear or phase/stage development.

In the following example, we elucidate the spiral theory of spiritual development as it fits within a relationship-based client concern.

A woman who presents for counseling says she has difficulties dealing with her ex-husband regarding joint custody of their three children, ages 8, 12, and 15. On its face, this may appear to be solely a secular issue. However, if the counselor explores the story, the client may begin to talk about how she and her ex-husband have always strongly disagreed on how to raise the children because of their different values. Further exploration may reveal that the client is less tied to traditional religion than her ex-husband, who maintains a specific denominational religious perspective. Both parents have had concerns about the information and guidance being given to their children about values and living in the world, and these concerns underlie their general issues of joint custody. Finally, these issues have become more heightened recently because her ex-husband has been diagnosed as having terminal cancer and has only a few months to live. She has become increasingly concerned about her own decisions regarding the divorce, her role as an ex-wife during her ex-husband's final months, her ability to help her children grieve the potential loss of their father, and how she will function as a single parent.

G. Miller (2005b) provided a condensed summary of several life-span spiritual development theories that have an individual emphasis (Allport, Piaget, Rizzuto, Erikson, and Fowler) that are helpful for understanding a client's life history from a spiritual developmental perspective. This section is a brief version of that work and explores three theories that are particularly relevant to this case.

Piaget's Cognitive Development Stage Model
Worthington (1989) organized Piaget's cognitive development theory (object permanence, symbolic representation, logical thinking, and formal operational thought) within a spiritual development model according to

age. In *infancy,* object permanence is the presence of an unseen God, followed by *early childhood* in which symbolic representation focuses on symbolizing faith objects. In *late childhood,* logical thinking can be applied to an examination of religious questions, and, finally, in *adolescence,* when formal operational thought is emphasized, individuals explore the complex interactions between experiences in life and their religious faith.

For the woman in our example, this model can be helpful in the assessment and treatment process by gathering information about the evolution of her spiritual perspective through these different age stages. It is quite possible that her current struggles in her relationship are based in her being "stuck" at one of these developmental stages. For example, in adolescence she may have formed an answer to the meaning of life by believing that if one simply works hard on oneself and one's issues, then life circumstances will work out for the best. This perspective may have grounded her spiritually in the past, and even through the divorce, but may be called into question as she faces being the sole parent of her children upon the death of her ex-husband. She may question her role in the divorce and whether she made the right choices for her life, her marriage, and her children. She may become angry that her belief system ("If I'm a good person, then things will work out for me.") is no longer working as she had planned. This type of questioning can be processed in the counseling sessions.

Rizzuto's Object Relations

In object-relations theory, the objects (i.e., the primary caregivers) are viewed from how the needs of the baby or child are met. These views of the "objects," according to Rizzuto (1979), reflect one's perception of God and become primary introjects. An introject is the object when it is incorporated into the psyche of the person. These perceptions of God are changeable as individuals have new experiences or changed views of the attachment figures (G. Miller, 2005b). The relationship with God reflects the relationship of the person with others (Hall, Brokaw, Edwards, & Pike, 1998).

From this perspective, the counselor can explore how the client views her early caregivers/attachment figures. If she has had negative experiences, it is possible that her view of God has some aspects of being a punishing, critical God. In the example, while her God supported her through the divorce, she may view the recent news of her ex-husband's terminal illness as a punishment from God. The counselor can use this information to assist her in sorting out her current conception of God within this new transition she is facing. Through counseling, she can explore her early childhood relationships and how these might be influencing her current beliefs about the nature of God, how she currently expresses her spirituality, and how her early experiences influence her own parenting style.

Erikson's Psychosocial Stage Model

Worthington (1989) applied Erikson's theory to spiritual development. In the first year of life (trust vs. mistrust), the basis of faith occurs in terms of development of hope; in the years 1–3 (autonomy vs. shame and doubt), the child develops a healthy ego; from 3–6 years old (initiative vs. guilt) the child develops a sense of purpose; from 6–12 (industry vs. inferiority) a child develops a sense of adequacy; from 12–18 (identity vs. role confusion) the child makes a commitment to faith); from ages 18–35 (intimacy vs. isolation) the person faces self-imperfections and self-forgiveness; from 35–55 (generativity vs. stagnation) the individual has increased altruism as well as religious legacy; and from 65 until death (integrity vs. despair) life is focused on the present with hope for the future.

In addition, Kelly (1995) stated that Erikson's model can help counselors look at the strengths and weaknesses of a client's spiritual framework by examining the roles of faith, values, universality, and meaning in the client's life. The following questions may help the client clarify her spiritual strengths and areas for growth.

1. What are the strengths and weaknesses of her faith? In the case example, the client may discover that while she finds comfort in her individual expression of her spirituality, she doesn't feel connected with others and feels isolated from a spiritual community.
2. Does she express her values easily, and where does she struggle in applying them to her daily life? For example, the client adheres to her well-defined moral and value system yet often has difficulty explaining her life choices regarding the divorce to her children and currently struggles to explain the meaning of death to her children.
3. How connected or isolated does she feel in the world, and where is her sense of community? As discussed previously, the client may discover that she feels isolated from others, particularly after the divorce, and has no spiritual support system in place.
4. How does she make sense of the life she is living? For the client in the case example, this question poses a major source of confusion as she faces indecision about the future and her role as a single parent.

These themes may be emerging as she sorts through the transitional struggle she is currently experiencing.

Sociocultural Influences in Assessing Spiritual Development

Developmental models can assist the counselor in determining the general spiritual developmental stage of the client. To work effectively with women around these issues, it is important to consider a woman's spiritual development within her larger life context. Tisdell (2003) stated that spirituality is inherently embedded in a cultural context because affect, cognition, and unconscious processes are all connected to both spirituality and culture.

As noted throughout the chapter, gender is a primary influence on spiritual development. Women experience their lives in the context of relationships (J. B. Miller, 1976) and often come to counseling with relation-

ship concerns. Spiritual issues may be embedded in these relational problems, as spiritual issues of power, morality, and self–other understanding
are often amplified through connections with others (G. Miller, 2005a;
Surry, 1985). Further, depending on a woman's relationships with significant others throughout her life, she may experience religious or spiritual
practices as a potential source of confusion, guilt, or shame around her life
choices. Many women experience spirituality as a source of support, helping them to better cope with problems of everyday living. Counselors can
assist women in clarifying when their spiritual beliefs and practices are a
source of confusion and can work with them to reconceptualize spirituality as a source of support and strength.

Hill and Pargament (2003) noted the importance of gender and other
cultural factors in the assessment of spirituality as they discussed the
need for more culturally sensitive assessment instruments. In the interim
of improved assessment instruments, Hays (2001) suggested the following framework (ADDRESSING; the **R** section is automatically included in
a spiritual assessment), which can be used in a multicultural assessment
of spirituality.

Age and generational influences
Developmental and acquired **D**isabilities
Religion and spiritual orientation
Ethnicity
Socioeconomic status
Sexual orientation
Indigenous heritage
National origin
Gender

As G. Miller (2005b) indicated, this framework can assist both counselor and client in the organization and prioritization of cultural factors
on the client's life concerns. Miller provided a checklist that can be used
in the assessment process to ascertain the areas that need to be assessed.
Such a checklist can help the counselor determine strengths and weaknesses of the client's internal and external resources, thereby determining which areas can be drawn upon and which areas need to be
addressed and strengthened. A comprehensive exploration of these cultural influences is beyond the scope of this chapter but can be found in
Tisdell (2003). Religious and gender influences are integrated throughout
this chapter, so we briefly explore the remaining areas of the ADDRESS-
ING framework next.

With regard to *age and generational influences*, Tisdell (2003) pointed out
that people typically question their faith in adulthood, often leaving the
religion of their childhood on either a temporary or permanent basis.
Worthington (1989) further specified how spiritual issues may manifest in
adulthood. Young adulthood focuses on issues regarding work, partnership, and parenting. Middle adulthood draws out themes related to career

and power, family and care, and possibly a more personally reflective process that examines the places one has "fallen short" in relation to self and others. Older adulthood emphasizes concerns focused on death, autonomy, and retirement. Koenig, Larson, and Matthews (1995) reported that many older adults use religion as a coping resource for problems related to aging. For example, an older female client diagnosed with a terminal illness may find spirituality increasingly important in her life. Further, the ways in which death is understood from her particular cultural background may affect how she interprets the spiritual dimension.

Developmental and acquired disabilities cover a broad spectrum. Albrecht (1992) defined disability as an impairment affecting a person's performance in a limited manner that is physical, mental, or emotional in nature. Atkinson and Hackett (2004) reported that people with disabilities experience discrimination socially, educationally, economically, and environmentally. Therefore, it is important that a counselor consider the impact of a disability on the client's spiritual development as it relates to her current living problems as well as how a disability has or currently affects her spiritual views. G. Miller (2003) recommended that counselors encourage clients with disabilities to join spiritual communities that strengthen their faith and possibly result in a stronger mind–body–spirit connection, find people who have similar spiritual values who can be "spiritual buddies" in daily living, and find individuals who have learned to live with a similar disability by operating from a spiritual perspective.

Ethnicity and socioeconomic status are critical factors to consider when working with women. One's ethnicity can be linked to socioeconomic status as many oppressed individuals are in poverty. As Bell (2002) pointed out, those in poverty have less "margin for error" both emotionally and financially. This reduced error margin may result in clients feeling pressure to address situations perfectly or experience the harsh day-to-day burdens that poverty brings. As G. Miller (2005a) stated, factors of health care, housing, crime, family stability, and levels of employment/income/education need to be considered in working with clients. It is important to explore how clients interpret their poverty within their spiritual perspective.

Another aspect of how ethnicity may be related to spirituality has to do with specific cultural practices. This aspect can involve *indigenous heritage and national origin*. Fukuyama, Siahpoush and Sevig (2005) stated that there are interrelationships between religion, spirituality, and culture and suggested that we view them as circles that overlap. Four ethnic groups are discussed in this section: African Americans, Native Americans, Latinas, and Asian Americans.

African Americans

D. A. Cook and Wiley (2000) indicated that spirituality is typically integrated into daily life, coping strategies, and overall lifestyle for African American women. Therefore, Cook and Wiley recommended that the spiritual focus be used throughout counseling to assist clients in finding their identity. Further, African American churches have been core to this ethnic group's survival and can be a helpful resource to clients, especially in combination with Afrocentric spiritual traditions. For example, an African American client may be very connected to the Black Church, and this church affiliation can provide social support, release of pain, spiritual and political support, and a place to discuss intellectual concepts and develop self-identity (G. Miller, 2003).

Native Americans

Trujillo (2000) reported that trust between counselor and client is an essential core in working with Native American/American Indian women. The therapeutic relationship must include the aspects of respect and flexibility as mental health problems are addressed. This respect can be demonstrated through an awareness of the American Indian woman's spiritual pain resulting from tragic events that have occurred both in the past and in the present and that have affected American Indian women, their loved ones, and the communities in which they live (Olson, 2003).

Religion and spirituality are typically used to guide Native American clients through life development stages (Trujillo, 2000). Therefore, when working with American Indian women, the counselor should consider the extent to which traditional spiritual practices are enmeshed in a client's daily life. However, the counselor must understand that there may be limits to the amount of information the client can share about specific practices of Native American spirituality. For example, a female client who participates in sweat lodge rituals may talk about the impact of this ritual on her life but be unable to tell the counselor the specific components or meaning of the practice.

Latinas

It is critical that the counselor express openness to understanding the spiritual beliefs of Latina clients because they are often "ridiculed, stigmatized and pathologized" (Zea, Mason, & Murguila, 2000, p. 416). The counselor's respect for these beliefs will invite a sense of client empowerment. Historically, Latina spiritual beliefs "have been sources of empowerment for individuals and communities because the interplay between humans, spirits, and gods through ritual, sacrifice, and communication provides them with a strong sense of self-determination" (p. 416). For example, for a client who practices *Curanderismo,* a spiritual/folk healing system that looks at physical health as connected with mental or spiritual health, illness may be viewed as a disruption of this interconnectedness or an imbalance between the woman, her family, community, and environment. The counselor working with a Latina woman needs to understand how the client views her disease within this context of disruption or imbalance.

Asian Americans

As with other cultural groups, Tan and Dong (2000) cautioned against making generalizations about counseling Asian Americans because this population consists of numerous subgroups. Some general counseling recommendations are to understand how clients struggle with their religious faith and culture with respect to family elders who have different beliefs. Further, counselors can help clients negotiate between the spiritual beliefs of the dominant culture in which they live and their own spiritual value systems. When working with an Asian American female client, the counselor may need to assess the acculturation level of the client, her own spiritual development, and the specific religious background of her parents. For example, a single, highly educated, Catholic, Taiwanese woman living in the United States whose parents are Taoists may pose specific developmental concerns that need to be addressed in counseling.

In the area of *sexual orientation*, the counselor should to be sensitive to how sexual orientation may affect the spiritual views and practice of the female client. Gay, lesbian, bisexual, and transgendered (GLBT) clients experience discrimination in general (G. Miller, 2005a), and this discrimination can be present in the spiritual communities in which they were raised or that surround them. GLBT clients may desire a strong sense of spirituality to help them cope with the oppression they experience (Davidson, 2000). However, monotheistic religions such as Islam, Judaism, and Christianity traditionally have been closed to these individuals (Davidson, 2000). This paradox of having a "spiritual hunger" in the face of potential rejection by organized religion can be emotionally scarring and painful for the GLBT client.

Lesbian, bisexual, or transgender female clients need to be asked about their spiritual development as it relates to their sexual orientation. Counselors also can ask how this affects their current spiritual perspective and how they live with discrimination on a daily basis, especially with respect to their spiritual/religious orientation. The experience of being judged and condemned because of sexual orientation in both the past and present needs to be explored and processed in counseling. Such examination may draw out wounds that are closely related to the issues presented in counseling. Counselors need to carefully examine their countertransference issues in this area for moral and religious assumptions that may affect the counseling process in an implicit or explicit fashion (Davidson, 2000). For example, a counselor who views homosexuality as immoral or as a sin may implicitly or explicitly avoid exploring or addressing the spiritual views of GLBT clients.

Finally, another useful strategy may be to help the client find a spiritual/religious community of support that can meet the "spiritual hunger" and provide support for living with the oppression she experiences in daily life. Such a community can result in a sense of being affirmed for her basic goodness and an improved relationship with the God of her understanding (Davidson, 2000).

Counseling Strategies for Working With Women's Spiritual Concerns

Prior to working with spiritual issues in treatment, counselors need to prepare themselves for work in this area. First, counselors can become better informed about a variety of religious and spiritual practices (see the Web site resources at the end of this chapter for more information in this area). Eck (2001) stated that most individuals are aware of the religion in which they were raised but typically do not have much information about other religions or varieties of spiritual expression. This limited perspective on religious and spiritual concerns can limit the counselor's ability to accurately assess the presenting problem with regard to religious/spiritual issues.

Second, counselors need to become aware of their biases and increase their awareness of possible countertransference issues (see G. Miller, 2003, for a summary). Counselors tend not to be as religiously oriented as clients, and this tendency may result in a limited understanding of the issues presented in counseling (Worthington, 1989). Counselors also struggle with their own biases toward religious/spiritual concerns, which are anchored in the past or the present, such as professional experiences in education, training or supervision, and personal experiences (G. Miller, 2003, 2005b). Traditionally, there have been few opportunities for a counselor-in-training to explore the integration of the spiritual dimension in counseling. As a result, counselors may need additional training to become familiar with a variety of spiritual practices, to become aware of their own biases, and to learn how to set clear boundaries in their work with spiritual issues (Favier & Ingersoll, 2005).

Depending on one's setting (secular vs. nonsecular), spiritual concerns may emerge in the session to varying degrees. For example, if a counselor has a label of "Christian Counselor" within a Christian counseling agency, clients may enter counseling with a readiness to discuss religious concerns directly or as they relate to the presenting life issue. However, we focus here on women's concerns with spirituality as they are raised in a setting in which neither the agency nor the counselor may be specifically identified with a particular religious or spiritual affiliation.

Several counseling techniques can invite spiritual exploration. To initially probe into the spiritual realm, Harris, et. al. (2007) suggested asking questions such as, "How important is spirituality or religion in your daily life?" "In what ways has spirituality been important to you?" "Are there spiritual or religious practices you perform regularly?" and "What do you think gives life meaning or purpose?" (p. 10).

An assessment of client wellness using the Myers and Sweeney (2005) wellness model is another way to approach the spiritual dimension with clients. Using the informal assessment approach described in Chapter 1, clients can consider the spiritual dimension of wellness to ascertain strengths, areas for growth, and to develop a specific plan for improvement in this area. For example, a client can review the definition of spiritual wellness, rate herself as to how well she feels in this area, then rate herself regarding her level of satisfaction with that particular rating. Next she can identify the strengths and limitations of her spiritual wellness, and then design goals and objectives for improving wellness in this area (Myers & Sweeney, 2005).

As part of a wellness plan to facilitate client spiritual awareness and growth, one helpful strategy is to ask a woman about her conception of God: "What is God like?" (Griffith & Griffith, 2002, p. 76). This question tends to draw out broad public metaphors. A follow-up question is, "What human relationship in your life most reminds you of the one you have described with God?" (p. 76). This two-question technique may be helpful in clarifying a female client's perspective of the God of her understanding.

G. Miller (2003) also suggested the use of bibliotherapy (including but not limited to daily meditation books, hopeful stories of individuals' struggles, prayer books, and general books on spirituality), meditation/relaxation/imagery, and journal writing.

In one guided journal writing exercise, the client keeps a kindness journal over a few days, recorded in any form she likes (drawing, writing, and so forth). There are three parts to the journal: (1) the client tracks a kindness done to another (preferably anonymously); (2) the client records her thoughts and feeling in response to the kind action; and (3) the client records her thoughts, feelings, and behaviors related to leaving every place better than when entering it. Finally, the client shares the journal and her reactions with the counselor. This exercise can enhance spirituality within daily living by encouraging a sense of altruism, self-worth, community, and mindfulness.

Another possible technique is to incorporate rituals that can provide meaning, truth, and a sense of safety (G. Miller, 2003). Specific rituals may be used regarding grief, mourning, anger, and other painful feelings that require some type of cathartic release (G. Miller, 2003). Fukuyama and Sevig (1999) encouraged counselors to explore the use of rituals to assist with old wounds as well as to cope with current transitions. Counselors can assist clients in determining whether they want to experience these rituals alone or with others.

Counselors also can link women with supportive community groups. For example, self-help groups for women who deal with addiction in themselves or their loved ones may be very beneficial. These may be found in 12-step organizations or other groups that focus on addiction but that are not 12-step-based. Such self-help groups may be especially helpful for women who feel alone and have limited funds for resources or supports. In addition, particular religious groups may be supportive of their spiritual struggles (see Web site resources at the end of the chapter).

Finally, counselors can assist women to view spirituality as a potential coping resource and source of strength (Harris et al., 2007). In cultivating spiritual growth, many clients learn to better care for themselves, for others, and to enhance their resilience to life stressors. The American Psychological Association's (2002) brochure *Aftermath: The Road to Resilience* presents 10 ways individuals can build resilience in themselves, all of which are related to spiritual wellness:

1. Making connections with others
2. Avoiding the view of crises as insurmountable
3. Accepting change as a part of life

4. Moving toward one's goals
5. Taking decisive actions
6. Watching for self-discovery opportunities
7. Nurturing a positive view of self
8. Keeping situations in perspective
9. Maintaining a hopeful perspective
10. Caring for self

Counselors can work with women in prioritizing and practicing these resilience strategies in their lives. A focus on wellness and resilience can facilitate a woman's reduction of shame, guilt, and emotional pain and can result in a triumphant healing from wounds (as stated in the quote from the exercise near the beginning of the chapter). A resource that specifically explores aspects of women's resilience as well as providing exercises is *The Woman's Book of Resilience: 12 Qualities to Cultivate* (B. Miller, 2005).

To integrate the material presented in this chapter, consider your reactions to the client in the following case study and how you might implement assessment strategies and counseling techniques.

Case Study

Your client is a 70-year-old woman who recently has been widowed. She was referred to counseling by a local religious leader because her grief seems deep and lasting. When questioned about her spirituality as it relates to this life transition phase, she states she feels very alone in the world and questions why the God of her understanding punished her by taking her husband from her so suddenly and earlier in her life than she had expected.

1. Are there any aspects of this story that might make it difficult for you to work with this client? Easy to work with this client?
2. Which of the three life-span spiritual developmental theories seem to best fit this client's story? How might you use this theory to guide your work with her?
3. How might you incorporate the spiral spiritual development perspective in your work with her?
4. What counseling techniques might you use to facilitate her spiritual healing?
5. What cultural factors would you need to take into account or explore further with her to facilitate your understanding of her spiritual struggles?

Conclusion

This chapter has assessed spirituality within the context of gender. Developmental theoretical models, assessment factors, and counseling techniques were addressed. Counselors are encouraged to enter into the spiritual area with clients from the viewpoint that it can become an important and helpful resource in the daily lives of women.

Activities for Further Exploration

1. How might you incorporate a spiritual dimension more in your counseling practice with women?
2. What techniques might you use to facilitate exploration of the spiritual dimension with your female clients?
3. What countertransference issues regarding the spiritual dimension do you anticipate facing in the exploration of spiritual issues with clients?
4. How might you expand your own spiritual experiences and increase your knowledge base?
5. What are your strengths in working with clients' spiritual issues?

Suggested Readings

American Psychological Association. (2002). *Aftermath: The road to resilience.* Washington, DC: Author.

Cashwell, C. S., & Young, J. S. (2005). *Integrating spirituality and religion into counseling: A guide to competent practice.* Alexandria, VA: American Counseling Association.

Chandler, C. K., Holden, J. M., & Kolander, C. A. (1992). Counseling for spiritual wellness: Theory and practice. *Journal of Counseling & Development, 71,* 168–175.

Fukuyama, M. A., & Sevig, T. D. (1999). *Integrating spirituality into multicultural counseling.* London: Sage.

Miller, B. (2005). *The woman's book of resilience: 12 qualities to cultivate.* Boston, MA: Conari.

Miller, G. (2005a). Religious/spiritual life span development. In C. S. Cashwell & J. S. Young (Eds.), *Integrating spirituality and religion into counseling* (pp. 105–122). Alexandria, VA: American Counseling Association.

Miller, G. (2003). *Incorporating spirituality in counseling and psychotherapy.* Hoboken, NJ: Wiley.

Worthington, E. L. (1989). Religious faith across the life span: Implications for counseling and research. *The Counseling Psychologist, 17,* 555–612.

Additional Resources

Addiction-Related 12-Step Programs

Adult Children of Alcoholics
World Service Organization
P.O. Box 3216
Torrance, CA 90510
(310) 534-1815
www.adultchildren.org

Al-Anon Family Group Headquarters
1600 Corporate Landing Parkway
Virginia Beach, VA 23455
(757) 563-1600
(757) 563-1655 (fax)
www.al-anon.org (e-mail)

Alcoholics Anonymous World Services, Inc.
P.O. Box 459
Grand Central Station
New York, NY 10163
(212) 870-3400
www.aa.org

Cocaine Anonymous
CAWSO, Inc.
3740 Overland Avenue, Suite C
Los Angeles, CA 90034-6337
(310) 559-5833
www.ca.org

Co-Dependents Anonymous
P.O. Box 33577
Phoenix, AZ 85067-3577
(602) 277-7991
coda.usa.nsc.outreach@usa.net (e-mail)
www.codependents.org

Nar-Anon Family Group Headquarters
P.O. Box 2562
Palos Vendes Peninsula, CA 90274
(310) 547-5800
www.naranon.com

Narcotics Anonymous
World Service Office
P.O. Box 9999
Van Nuys, CA 91409
(818) 773-9999
(818) 700-0700 (fax)
www.na.org

Alternatives to 12-Step Programs

Rational Recovery Systems
P.O. Box 800
Lotus, CA 95651
(530) 621-4374 (8 a.m. to 4 p.m.)
(530) 621-2667
(530) 622-4296 (fax)
www.rational.org/recovery

Secular Organization for Sobriety (SOS)
4773 Hollywood Boulevard
Hollywood, CA 90027
(323) 666-4295
(323) 666-4271 (fax)
www.sossobriety.org

16 Steps
Many Roads, One Journey, Inc.
(406) 273-6080
(406) 273-0111 (fax)
P.O. Box 1302
Lolo, MT 59847
www.charlottekasl.com/16steps.html

SMART Recovery
7537 Mentor Avenue, Suite 306
Mentor, OH 44060
(440) 951-5357
(440) 951-5358 (fax)
www.smartrecovery.org
listserv@maelstrom.stjohns.edu
(List serve discussion group)

Women for Sobriety (WFS)
Men for Sobriety (MFS)
P.O. Box 618
Quakertown, PA 18957-0618
(215) 536-8026 (phone)
(215) 536-9026 (fax)
www.womenforsobriety.org

Counseling and Spiritual Web Sites

American Academy of Religion: www.aarweb.org
American Association of Pastoral Counselors: www.aapc.org

Association of Spiritual, Ethical and Religious Values in Counseling: www.aservic.org

Center of Spirituality, Theology and Health: www.dukespiritualityand health.org

Christian Association of Psychological Services: www.caps.net

Christian-Based Web Sites

www.christianitytoday.com

www.christianity.net.au

Religious-Related Web Sites

The following Web sites are provided for individuals interested in learning more about specific religions. This list is not meant to be all-inclusive.

African American Islamic: www.islam.org

African American Methodist Episcopal: www.ame-today.com

American Baptist: www.abc-use.org

Buddhism: www.tricycle.com; www.livingdharma.org/index.html; www.members.tripod.com/~lhamo

Catholicism: www.catholic.org

Christian Scientist: www.tfccs.com

Church of Christ: www.church-of-Christ.org

Church of God: www.churchofgod.cc

Church of Jesus Christ of Latter Day Saints: www.mormon.org

Confucianism: www.chineseculture.about.com

Episcopalian: www.episcopalian.org

Evangelical Lutheran: www.elco.org

Greek Orthodox: www.goarch.org

Hinduism: www.indiadivine.com

Islam: www.islamworld.net

Jainism: www.jainnet.com; www.jainsamaj.org; www.jainworld.com

Judaism: www.aish.com

Mennonite: www.mennoniteusa.org

Methodist: www.umc.org

Native American Religions: www.native-american-online.org

Pentecostal: www.upci.org

Presbyterian: www.pcuse.org

Quaker: www.quaker.org

Scientology: www.scientology,org

Seventh Day Adventist: www.adventist.org

Sikhism: www.sikhs.org; www.sikhnet.com

Shintoism: www.egroups.com/group/shintoml

Southern Baptist: www.sbc.net

Taoism: www.geocities.com/athens/aegean/7201/index:html; www. religiousworlds.com/taoism/index/html

Unitarian-Universalist: www.uua.org

Zoroastrianism: www.zoroastriansim.com

References

Albrecht, G. L. (1992). *The disability business: Rehabilitation in America.* Newbury Park, CA: Sage.

American Psychological Association. (2002). *Aftermath: The road to resilience.* Washington, DC: Author.

American Psychological Association. (2006, August). *Integrating spiritual and religious interventions in psychological treatment.* [Workshop]. New Orleans, LA.

Association for Spiritual, Ethical, and Religious Values in Counseling. (n.d.). *Position paper.* Retrieved November 30, 2001, from http://www.counseling.org/aservic/Spirituality.html

Atkinson, D. R., & Hackett, G. (2004). *Counseling diverse populations* (3rd ed.). Boston: McGraw-Hill.

Ballou, M. (1995). Women and spirit: Two nonfits in psychology. *Women and Therapy, 16,* 9–20.

Bell, P. (2002). *Chemical dependency and the African-American* (2nd ed.). Center City, MN: Hazelden.

Cashwell, C. S., & Young, J. S. (2005). *Integrating spirituality and religion into counseling: A guide to competent practice.* Alexandria, VA: American Counseling Association.

Chandler, C. K., Holden, J. M., & Kolander, C. A. (1992). Counseling for spiritual wellness: Theory and practice. *Journal of Counseling & Development, 71,* 168–175.

Cook, B. W. (1992). *Eleanor Roosevelt: Volume 1.* New York: Penguin.

Cook, D. A., & Wiley, C. Y. (2000). Psychotherapy with members of African American churches and spiritual traditions. In P. S. Richard & A. E. Bergin (Eds.), *Handbook of psychotherapy and religious diversity* (pp. 369–396). Washington, DC: American Psychological Association.

Davidson, M. G. (2000). Religion and spirituality. In R. M. Perez, K. A. DeBord, & K. J. Bleschke (Eds.), *Handbook of counseling and psychotherapy with lesbian, gay, and bisexual clients* (pp. 409–433). Washington, DC: American Psychological Association.

Dudley-Grant, G., & Daniel, J. H. (2003). Women and spirituality. In L. Slater, J. Daniel, & A. Banks (Eds.), *Complete guide to mental health for women* (pp. 379–382). Boston: Beacon Press.

Eck, D. (2001). *A new religious America.* San Francisco: Harper.

Faiver, C., & Ingersoll, R. E. (2005). Knowing one's limits. In C. S. Cashwell & J. S. Young (Eds.), *Integrating spirituality and religion into counseling: A guide to competent practice* (pp. 169–183). Alexandria, VA: American Counseling Association.

Fukuyama, M. A., & Sevig, T. D. (1999). *Integrating spirituality into multicultural counseling.* London: Sage.

Fukuyama, M. A., Siahpoush, F., & Sevig, T. D. (2005). Religion and spirituality in a cultural context. In C. S. Cashwell & J. S. Young (Eds.), *Integrating spirituality and religion into counseling: A guide to competent practice* (pp. 123–142). Alexandria, VA: American Counseling Association.

Griffith, J. L., & Griffith, M. S. (2002). *Encountering the sacred in psychotherapy.* New York: Guilford Press.

Hall, T. W., Brokaw, B. F., Edwards, K. J., & Pike, P. L. (1998). An empirical exploration of psychoanalysis and religion: Spiritual maturity and objects relations development. *Journal for the Scientific Study of Religion, 37*(2), 305–315.

Harris, A. H. S., Thoresen, C. E., & Lopez, S. J. (2007). Integrating positive psychology into counseling: Why and (when appropriate) how. *Journal of Counseling & Development, 85,* 3–13.

Hays, P. (2001). *Addressing cultural complexities in practice: A framework for clinicians and counselors.* Washington, DC: American Psychological Association.

Hill, P. C., & Pargament, K. I. (2003). Advances in the conceptualization and measurement of religion and spirituality: Implications for physical and mental health research. *American Psychologist, 58,* 64–74.

Kelly, E. W. (1995). *Spirituality and religion in counseling and psychotherapy: Diversity in theory and practice.* Alexandria, VA: American Counseling Association.

Koenig, H. D., Larson, D. B., & Matthews, D. A. (1995, March). *Religion and psychotherapy with older adults.* Paper presented at the Boston Society for Gerontologic Psychiatry, Boston.

Miller, B. (2005). *The woman's book of resilience: 12 qualities to cultivate.* Boston, MA: Conari.

Miller, G. (2003). *Incorporating spirituality in counseling and psychotherapy.* Hoboken, NJ: Wiley.

Miller, G. (2005a). *Learning the language of addiction counseling* (2nd ed.). Hoboken, NJ: Wiley.

Miller, G. (2005b). Religious/spiritual life span development. In C. S. Cashwell & J. S. Young (Eds.), *Integrating spirituality and religion into counseling* (pp. 105–122). Alexandria, VA: American Counseling Association.

Miller, J. B. (1976). *Toward a new psychology of women.* Boston: Beacon Press.

Miller, L. (2005). Interpersonal psychotherapy from a spiritual perspective. In L. Sperry & E. P. Shafranske (Eds.), *Spiritually oriented psychotherapy* (pp. 153–175). Washington, DC: American Psychological Association.

Myers, J. E., & Sweeney, T. J. (2005). *Counseling for wellness: Theory, research, and practice.* Alexandria, VA: American Counseling Association.

Myers, J. E., Sweeney, T. J., & Witmer, J. M. (2000). The wheel of wellness counseling for wellness: A holistic model for treatment planning. *Journal of Counseling & Development, 78,* 251–266.

Olson, M. J. (2003). Counselor understanding of Native American spiritual loss. *Counseling and Values, 47,* 109–117.

Rizzuto, A. M. (1979). *The birth of the living God.* Chicago: University of Chicago Press.

Shafranske, E. P., & Sperry L. (2005). Addressing the spiritual dimension in psychotherapy: Introduction and overview. In L. Sperry & E. P.

Shafrankse (Eds.), *Spiritually oriented psychotherapy.* Washington, DC: American Psychological Association.

Surry, J. (1985). The "self-in-relation": A theory of women's development. *Work in progress* (No. 13). Wellesley, MA: Stone Center Working Papers Series.

Tan, S. Y., & Dong, N. J. (2000). Psychotherapy with members of Asian American churches and spiritual traditions. In P. S. Richards & A. E. Bergin (Eds.), *Handbook of psychotherapy and religious diversity* (pp. 421–445). Washington, DC: American Psychological Association.

Tisdell, E. J. (2003). *Exploring spirituality and culture in adult and higher education.* San Francisco: Jossey-Bass.

Trujillo, A. (2000). Psychotherapy with Native Americans: A view into the role of religion and spirituality. In P. S. Richards & A. E. Bergin (Eds.), *Handbook of psychotherapy and religious diversity* (pp. 445–466). Washington, DC: American Psychological Association.

Williams-Nickelson, C. (2006). Balanced living through self-care. In J. Worell & C. D. Goodheart (Eds.), *Handbook of girls' and women's psychological health* (pp. 183–191). New York: Oxford University Press.

Worthington, E. L. (1989). Religious faith across the life span: Implications for counseling and research. *The Counseling Psychologist, 17,* 555–612.

Zea, M. C., Mason, M. A., & Murguila, A. (2000). Psychotherapy with members of Latino/Latina religions and spiritual traditions. In P. S. Richards & A. E. Bergin (Eds.), *Handbook of psychotherapy and religious diversity* (pp. 397–420). Washington, DC: American Psychological Association.

Chapter 10

Counseling Older Women for Vitality

Now that I am approaching old age myself (I am sixty-four) I begin to sense all this
in a new way, on my own pulse. For I am happier and more at ease with myself and
the world now than I have ever been. It is not a matter of having "arrived" but rather
that the journey itself is far more fun than it has ever been and I am more able to enjoy
it because there is less tension and less conflict. I have less energy than I used to . . .
but I get more done because I have learned not to waste time.
—May Sarton (1997, p. 230)

The older population is expected to increase to 20% of the total population by the year 2030 (National Council on Aging [NCOA], 2006). While
the older Caucasian population will increase by 77% between 2000 and
2030, the older minority population is expected to increase by 223%
during the same period (NCOA, 2006). As contemporary women approach midlife and beyond, they will become part of a diverse, rapidly
growing group.

Today's older women significantly outnumber older men, and the fem-
inization of the older population increases with age. For every 100 women
age 65 to 74, there are only 82 men, and for every 100 women age 85 and
older there are only 41 men (U.S. Census Bureau, 2001). Because of their
increasing numbers and the lack of information most counselors receive
regarding the specific issues women face as they age, it is important to
focus more attention on effective counseling with older women.

As has been emphasized throughout this book, when counselors approach their work with clients it is helpful to focus on women's wellness
rather than maintaining a pathology-driven perspective. Along these
lines, there has been a recent call for research and practice that addresses
the continued growth and development of older adults and ways in
which adults can age positively and successfully (Hill, 2006; Palmore,
2005). The majority of older adults adjust positively to the stressors and

transitions that occur in old age (Myers & Harper, 2004) and are satisfied with their lives (Myers, 1999). Among older adults ages 65–69, 49% agreed that "these are the best years of my life" (NCOA, 2006). In a Centers for Disease Control (CDC) report, women age 65 and older reported the lowest rates of emotional distress (e.g., sadness, hopelessness, feelings of worthlessness) when compared to younger groups of women (Pleis, Benson, & Schiller, 2003).

Although most women are satisfied with their lives during this time period, these women will face major transitions during midlife and beyond (Degges-White & Myers, 2006). The focus of this chapter is on counseling women to strengthen coping resources for managing the changes that many older women experience and working with them as they adjust to new life roles. First, I describe the life challenges to which older women must adapt in six general areas: (a) changes in appearance, (b) changes in role status, (c) adapting to the loss of significant others, (d) transitioning to menopause, (e) becoming a caregiver, and (f) becoming a grandmother. Second, I provide an overview of the primary mental health concerns of older women that often emerge as a consequence of the transitions of midlife. Finally, I conclude with a discussion of resilience: What are the qualities of women who age optimally, and how can counselors do more to promote these strengths in their older women clients?

Adjusting to Challenges in Midlife and Beyond

I look in the mirror each morning and can't believe what I see. I am not that old woman with wrinkled skin and bags under her eyes. On the inside I feel like I did when I was sixteen. I still look at the world that way, but that is not how people react to me. They either dismiss me or expect me to be their grandmother. Who is the real me—the inside or the outside?

—Mary, age 70

Most people know little about the aging process, and their lack of information and misconceptions lead to the formation of negative stereotypes about older people. Despite a movement in recent years to recognize the strengths of older adults, ageist attitudes continue to exist and are particularly negative toward women. Prevalent stereotypes include the following beliefs about older women:

- Less intelligent and less competent than younger women and older men
- Perceived of as reaching "old age" earlier than men
- Evaluated more negatively in terms of physical appearance than older men
- Asexual
- Nurturing grandmother
- Irritable, angry, bored, or miserable (Palmore, 2005)

Self-Exploration Exercise: How Do I Feel About Aging?

To help you examine your own attitudes and beliefs about aging, reflect on the following questions. How have your attitudes changed over time?

1. How do you feel about your current age?
2. Take a moment to visualize yourself as an older woman. Are you excited about the opportunities, or discouraged by the limitations?
3. How can your own attitudes toward aging affect your counseling relationships with older women?

Source: Adapted from Arcement (2005) and Etaugh & Bridges (2004).

Most of these stereotypes do not apply to older men, who are evaluated more positively than are older women. This gender difference is explained by what Sontag (1979, 1997) termed the *double standard of aging.* According to Sontag, the stigma of aging is far greater for women than it is for men. In a culture in which men are valued more for what they do and women are valued for how they look, and in which beauty is the primary criterion for women's success, older women are at a significant disadvantage (Saucier, 2004; Sontag, 1997). Traditionally masculine qualities such as competence, autonomy, and power are highly valued and only increase with age, so aging becomes a benefit to men. However, traditionally feminine qualities such as noncompetitiveness and gentleness remain stable over time and are not valued in our culture, so aging is viewed negatively for women. Further, Sontag posited that women are sexually ineligible much earlier than men because their primary value in our culture is related to their beauty and to the fertility of youth.

There is some empirical support for the double standard theory. Harris (1994) found that aging women were evaluated more negatively than were aging men. Further, men were more likely to evaluate the signs of aging as unattractive, particularly when evaluating women. In contrast, some men actually view the impact of aging as having a positive effect on their own appearance (Halliwell & Ditmar, 2003). For example, whereas gray hair and wrinkled skin are viewed as distinguished in a man (what has been termed the "Sean Connery effect"; Halliwell & Ditmar, 2003), they are viewed quite negatively in a woman. Consider how acceptable it is to see older men romantically paired with significantly younger women in recent films like *As Good as It Gets* (starring 61-year-old Jack Nicholson paired with 35-year-old Helen Hunt), whereas the converse is almost never true.

Older women are rarely present in advertising or in popular media, and when they are, they are praised for their ability to hide their age well. It is not surprising that women learn to fear aging and to conceal or prevent its effects at an early age. Many current advertising campaigns capitalize on this fear, arguing "Fight Aging Before It Begins" (which suggests aging is a "war" to be "fought" instead of a natural process that occurs to all people). The "war" has spawned an anti-aging industry, encouraging many younger women to spend large amounts of money on age-concealment techniques: anti-aging creams, cosmetics, diets, exercise regimens, and even surgeries. It remains to be seen whether the pressures for women to conceal signs of aging will become even more intensified as the aging population increases (Zerbe & Domnitei, 2004).

All of these anti-aging messages lead to pressure for a woman to attain an unrealistic beauty ideal, and many women internalize this cultural standard for themselves. They accept the "Myth of Eternal Beauty"; that is, women can and should maintain a youthful, thin appearance regardless of their age (Saucier, 2004). The myth implies that women should exert the energy needed to conceal signs of aging, and if they don't, then they are to blame. Unfortunately, this becomes a frustrating struggle for women as the signs of aging—weight gain, changing posture, skin changes (wrinkling, sagging, age spotting, dryness, yellowing), graying and thinning of hair, tooth loss or discoloration—inevitably appear (Fey-Yensan, McCormick, & English, 2002). Women worry about changes in weight, skin, and body functioning, but weight gain is their primary area of concern (Zerbe & Domnitei, 2004). Overall, most women gain 10 pounds per decade of life (Webster & Tiggemann, 2003; Zerbe & Domnitei, 2004). Furthermore, as women age, the body increasingly resists efforts to control weight and shape due to changes in body fat deposition after menopause paired with changes in basal metabolic rate, muscle tone, and strength (Johnston, Reilly, & Kremer, 2004).

It would make sense then that older women might have a more negative body image than any other group as their weight gains and changes move them further from the thin ideal espoused in our culture. On the other hand, the stereotype of older women as "asexual" and "sexually ineligible" might indicate that women would have a more positive body image as they age because they are less worried about being physically attractive to others. In attempts to answer this question, a vast body of research indicates that older women's level of body image dissatisfaction remains high and that women's body image satisfaction is remarkably stable across the life span (Allaz, Bernstein, Rouget, Archinard, & Morabia, 1998; Lewis & Cachelin, 2001; McLaren & Kuh, 2004; C. Stevens & Tiggemann, 1998; Tiggemann, 2004; Tiggemann & Lynch, 2001; Webster & Tiggemann, 2003). As an example, McLaren and Kuh (2004) found that in a national sample of 54-year-old women, 80% were dissatisfied with their weight, and 50% of normal weight women in the sample were dissatisfied. Women reported being most dissatisfied with their weight currently (in their 50s) as opposed to earlier years. Many of these women reported that their body dissatisfaction caused them to avoid daily activities, including physical activities, wearing bathing suits, changing clothes in front of others, physical intimacy, and social activities. In another study, Allaz et al. (1998)

found that of women age 65 and older, 62% wanted to lose weight and that most of these were currently dieting.

Interestingly, this does not seem to be the case for Black women. As is the case for younger Black women (see Chapter 2), older Black women are more likely to have a positive body image and to be accepting of their bodies. One study examining overweight older women (ages 66–105) found that Black women were less likely to feel guilty after overeating, less likely to diet, were more likely to be satisfied with their weight, and more likely to consider themselves attractive than were White women (J. Stevens, Kumanyika, & Keil, 1994). Older Black women also reported more contentment with their lives than White women, even though they were more disadvantaged financially and perceived their overall health as worse than that of Whites (Armstrong, 2001).

The women who are the most concerned with the effects of aging on their appearance tend to be more concerned about losing weight and to engage in excessive dieting (Gupta & Schork, 1993). Lewis and Cachelin (2001) found that older women who believed that losing weight will result in a more youthful appearance were the most likely to diet. Being worried about wrinkled skin also is related to a drive for thinness and dieting behavior (Gupta & Schork, 1993). Perhaps when women experience the inevitable signs of aging, they react by engaging in one behavior that they feel they can control—their food intake. While wrinkled or sagging skin may be uncontrollable, women feel that if they can lose weight they can maintain control of this one aspect of their changing appearance.

This belief and resulting behavior is of concern because dieting in older individuals can pose a serious health threat that significantly affects the aging process, particularly among normal-weight women (Allaz et al., 1998; Fey-Yensan et al., 2002; Hetherington & Burnett, 1994). Caloric restriction can result in more serious consequences for older women than for younger women, including neurological and functional problems such as nausea, dizziness, fluctuations in glucose levels, and osteoporosis. Contrary to women's beliefs, a low body mass index (BMI) is associated with higher mortality and morbidity in old age. Carrying some extra weight within a normal weight-for-height range is a protective factor to older women in times of acute and chronic illness (Fey-Yensan et al., 2002; Hetherington & Burnett, 1994;).

Even while older women experience a high level of body dissatisfaction, a closer examination of the research in this area reveals a more nuanced view of women's self-perceptions. There is evidence that the *importance* of physical appearance to women, in contrast with their *satisfaction* with it, seems to diminish with age (Tiggemann & Lynch, 2001). Older women are less likely to change their behaviors as a result of their body dissatisfaction (Lewis & Cachelin, 2001) and have lower levels of body monitoring and appearance anxiety than do younger women. Furthermore, they are more likely to have more realistic expectations regarding their ideal shape and size than do younger women (Tiggemann

& Lynch, 2001) Most important, research indicates that older women's negative body image is not as related to their overall self-concept and self-esteem as it is for younger women (Webster & Tiggemann, 2003). Webster and Tiggemann's findings demonstrate that women's perception of having cognitive control increases with age, so that older women are more likely to use strategies such as increasing their acceptance of their bodies and developing more realistic appearance-related expectations to maintain their self-concept and self-esteem.

Taken together, these findings have important implications for practice because they emphasize the futility of interventions that attempt to change a woman's evaluation of her body and appearance, given its stability across the life span. Instead, counselors should focus on helping a woman develop cognitive control strategies to prevent a negative evaluation of her body from pervading her overall sense of self (Webster & Tiggemann, 2003). To address these concerns, three cognitive control strategies are suggested: education, redefining beauty, and reconceptualizing identity.

Educate Women About Body Image

One way to prevent negative body image from causing distress is to educate women about ways to differentiate between body image evaluation (positive or negative self-evaluation of appearance), affect (resulting emotional distress), and investment (the measures a woman is willing to take as a result of the evaluation; Muth & Cash, 1997). While a woman's evaluation may remain negative, she can work to reduce negative affect and to question the time and energy she is willing to invest to meet unrealistic cultural standards of beauty.

Redefine Beauty

Another strategy is to help older women change their definition of beauty so that it is focused on health, remaining disease-free, improving physical fitness, and maintaining body functioning (Crose, 1999; Franzoi & Koehler, 1998; Hurd, 2000). Rather than a sole focus on appearance, women can learn to accept their bodies for the ways that they move and function. The benefits of midlife women's participation in physical activity to improve fitness and health are well documented (see NCOA, 2006), but some evidence indicates that older women's participation in exercise has a negative effect on their body image. Some studies found that midlife women exercisers had a more negative body image than did nonexercisers, presumably because the exercisers were engaging in exercise in an attempt to pursue the cultural standard of thinness (Fey-Yensan et al., 2002; Hallinan & Schuler, 1993). As indicated in Chapter 2, when women exercise to improve fitness and health (vs. trying to improve their appearance), they are more likely to experience satisfaction with their bodies. Therefore, older women who engage in exercise but who continue to compare themselves to unrealistic standards will remain dissatisfied. Counselors who work with women should encourage them to exercise but should first assess their motivations for engaging in physical activity.

Reconceptualize Identity

A third way to increase cognitive control is to help older women view their sense of self as stable and intact, even while their bodies are changing with age. In her interviews with midlife women, Clarke (2001) reported how the women distinguished between their "Inside" and "Outside" selves, referring to their bodies as masks, shells, or containers that hide their true selves. Women in mainstream U.S. culture are socialized to define themselves (and to judge their worth) solely in terms of their appearance. It may require considerable time and effort for a woman to reconceptualize her view of herself as encompassing more than her appearance and to learn to value all aspects of herself. She can learn to distinguish between outer beauty (which often changes with age) and inner beauty (which remains stable or even becomes enhanced with age). Counselors can be of great assistance in helping her to make this transition in her identity development.

Counseling Interventions for Adapting to Changes in Appearance

1. Women may need help in acknowledging and understanding physical changes that occur in their appearance at midlife. Counselors need to educate women about midlife transition changes that are genetically based. Women are born with more fat cells, have slower metabolic rates, and have different hormonal influences than males, all of which increase the likelihood of weight gain throughout the life cycle (Zerbe & Domnitei, 2004).
2. Counselors can assist women in recognizing the tension they experience between societal promotion of the idea that their body is within their ultimate control and the reality that much of the aging process is uncontrollable (Johnston et al., 2004). They can begin to question the anti-aging bias in our culture, challenging society's message that "younger is better." Women can learn to view media images they see with a more critical eye, questioning how these standards are unattainable for most women. It is helpful to ask, "Will my drastic efforts to maintain a youthful appearance fill the needs for love and connection for which I am searching?" (Saucier, 2004). Finally, women can develop an internally derived standard of beauty by exploring the question "What do I think is beautiful for myself?"
3. Counselors can provide women with a place to express their feelings and to develop resistance to negative societal messages about aging women. Support from other women facing similar issues helps reduce a sense of isolation during this time (Saucier, 2004).
4. Women can learn to develop a broader standard of beauty that encompasses both inner and appearance-based beauty. As part of cognitive restructuring, counselors can help women to create written positive affirmations to reframe their negative perceptions about

their bodies such as "My gray hair is a well-earned silver crown" (Saucier, 2004).

5. As emphasized in Chapter 2, women can view physical appearance as only one aspect of themselves and learn to develop other life domains.

Changes in Role Status

My husband is home on disability now and I have retired from my job. Our kids are grown—still ask us for money, but they are out of the house. So it's just us, and we are kind of lost. My husband and I get up every morning and do everything we can to avoid each other. When we were younger we were always working and taking care of other people, so I really don't think we've spent any real time together in almost 20 years. Sometimes it feels like living with a stranger.

—Linda, age 55

The importance of relationships in women's lives has been emphasized throughout this book. Women typically identify themselves as people in relation to others, often as a wife/spouse/partner, mother, daughter, friend, or relative. While connections with others have the potential to be growth enhancing for women, women can become overly reliant on the approval of others in order to feel a sense of self-worth. As stated earlier, this becomes problematic for women if they frequently suppress their own needs, values, and opinions to maintain the approval of significant others in their lives. If women define their identities in terms of their embeddedness in relationships, the loss of these roles as they age will have a significant impact on their lives. For example, when their adult children leave home, they become widowed or divorced, or an aging parent dies, many women develop a sense of role ambiguity (Crose, 1999). Some women in midlife, perhaps for the first time, have to evaluate their sense of self apart from their marital/partnered, parenting, or caretaking roles (Saucier, 2004). They may wonder, "Who am I apart from my role as mother? wife? partner? daughter?"

According to Petersen (2000), these types of struggles are less predominant in African American women than in Caucasian women. In her study, African American women did not feel they had to redefine themselves based on midlife changes in their relationships or circumstances. They maintained a stable sense of self (what Petersen termed an *internal anchor*) throughout their lifetimes. While the Caucasian women in the study struggled to free themselves from cultural standards that encourage them to be dependent upon others, the African American women did not report an internal conflict to maintain their sense of self.

All women can benefit from the attitudes exhibited by African American women when they refuse to conform to limiting cultural prescriptions for women (i.e., being overly reliant on others' approval). As noted throughout this book, this process may be more complex for women from other cultural groups. To heal, all women can learn to develop a more autonomous sense of self while maintaining a strong network of supportive relationships. For example, one study found that in a sample of older Korean Americans, those with the most positive mental health outcomes had achieved a balance between a sense of autonomy and mastery with the more traditional Asian values of familism and collectivism (Jang, Kim, & Chiriboga, 2006). In sum, counselors working with women who experience these developmental issues can help them view these types of role losses as an opportunity to define themselves on their own terms, within the context of their relationships, perhaps for the first time.

A problem with role ambiguity also occurs for women who are married or partnered in midlife, as significant shifts in their partnered relationship can occur in empty nest homes (i.e., when children move out of the home) and in the postretirement years (including retirement for either spouse). During the years of child rearing and career, mothers might place child rearing as their first priority, career or caretaking concerns second, followed by the relationship with her partner as the lowest priority. In midlife, couples must renegotiate the relationship, asking "What do we have in common?" and "How will we now balance individual and couple time?" (Qualls, 2002). This becomes difficult for couples who have spent many years focusing on others while neglecting their own relationship. For many women, caretaking for aging parents or relatives replaces their parenting responsibilities, and couples may postpone addressing relationship issues for an even longer period of time. Counselors working with women can encourage them to maintain a focus on their relationships with their partners, as a quality marital/partnered relationship is related to positive mental health for women and can help them to better negotiate all other life roles.

There is evidence that lesbian women are less conflicted during this time in their lives because they are more likely to have a partner with a similar life expectancy and therefore have a significant other with whom they can expect to grow older. Further, they are used to dealing with the stigma of being gay and are better able to deal with the negative stigma of aging in our culture. Finally, they may be less worried about changes in physical appearance than are heterosexual women and are more likely to have their own financial resources from which to draw in old age (Grossman, D'Augelli, & O'Connel, 2001).

Adapting to the Loss of Significant Others

A major loss that many women who are partnered with men will face in midlife is the loss of a partner. Loss of a spouse is an issue that disproportionately affects women. Women are more likely to become widowed than men because women have a longer life expectancy than men and tend to marry men older than themselves (Canetto, 2001; Etaugh & Bridges, 2004). According to the U.S. Census Bureau (2003), 23% of women ages 60 to 69 were widowed, compared to only 7.6% of men, and 56% of women ages 70 and older were widowed, compared to 23.1% of men.

Widows experience difficulties in adjusting to widowhood, with financial problems being a leading reason for the physical and mental health problems they experience following the death of a spouse. Poverty is a serious concern for older women, with women comprising two thirds of older adults who are classified in the poverty range. Women from diverse racial/ethnic groups are particularly vulnerable to issues of poverty (Myers & Harper, 2004). Due to their lower financial status, older women are less likely to have health insurance and are more likely than men to exhaust their limited financial resources on health-related expenses (Canetto, 2001). This is of concern because women experience a gender paradox when it comes to their physical health: Although they live longer than men, they live their lives in poorer overall health (Canetto, 2001; Etaugh & Bridges, 2004).

Most widows adjust to the death of their partner within 2 to 4 years, but 10 to 20% of widows experience more chronic problems such as substance abuse, depression, and vulnerability to physical illness. According to Canetto (2001), common acute symptoms include sleep problems, restlessness, depression, anger, and guilt. Even though women are more affected by the loss of a spouse (both in intensity and duration of grief), they seem to adjust better overall to this loss than do men. While both women and men experience high levels of distress, women experience fewer physical and mental health problems than men following the death of a spouse (Canetto, 2001). Overall, widowers experience more depression and other mental disorders, physical illness, death rates, and suicide rates than widows. Canetto asserted that this gender difference may be due to several factors. First, marriage is better for men's overall well-being and health (while it benefits women only if the quality of the relationship is good), so men are more affected by the aftermath of widowhood. Second, men often do not have well-developed support systems, including close relationships with their children, grandchildren, and friends. Finally, women are more likely to have prepared for widowhood and to have experience in completing the day-to-day duties required in running a household.

Following the loss of a partner, women's reliance on a broad support network is critical to recovery. Most older women don't remarry (partially due to the low female-to-male ratio in midlife) but find intimacy and support through friends and family (Crose, 1999). Because of the importance of a strong support network, counselors working with widows can begin by helping them to (re)establish relationships with friends and family. This might include psychoeducation regarding social skills necessary for making new friends or for reconnecting with important people in their lives. Jacobs (1997) recommended that older women cultivate friendships that meet the following needs: (a) inclusion, (b) connectedness, (c) affirmation of one's competence, (d) help during times of crisis overload, (e) intimacy, and (f) stimulation/challenge. Counselors can work with their clients in assessing their support networks to determine whether each of these needs is being met. As part of building support, counselors can also involve their clients in support groups. Mixed-gender support groups are particularly effective for this issue (Myers & Harper, 2004).

Clients might also need to be educated to broaden their conceptualization of intimacy to encompass more than sexual activity. Rice (2001) asserted that it is important for older women to learn that there are many ways to feel close to others. Some alternatives to suggest to clients include the following (adapted from S. Rice, 2001):

- Seek out others with whom you would like to be closer.
- Accept love and affection from children and grandchildren.
- Give yourself permission to accept your sexuality in whatever form it currently exists for you.
- Consider pets as a way to provide unconditional love and affection
- Consider sharing a home with other women.
- Feed "skin hunger" (Crose, 1999) by inviting and receiving regular touch from friends, family, grandchildren; ask for back rubs or foot massages.

While the specific treatment of bereavement following the loss of a spouse is beyond the scope of this chapter, there are some excellent resources available for counselors as well as for widows. (See the resources listed at the end of this chapter.)

Transitioning to Menopause

This time in my life is great for the most part—aside from the occasional hot flashes and mood swings, and signs of aging that I don't like. I mostly feel like I'm taking my body and my life back. No more periods!! No more pregnancy worries!! Finally I feel like I can live a little for myself.

—Angela, age 54

Menopause, a life transition for all women who live into their 50s, can be viewed as a rite of passage into later life (Robinson Kurpius & Nicpon, 2003). As a woman might live one third of her life in post menopause, counselors need to be knowledgeable about these changes and be willing to discuss them with clients (Huffman & Myers, 1999).

Menopause is defined as the cessation of menstrual periods for 12 consecutive months as a result of a loss of progesterone and estrogen produced in the ovaries. Although it is technically one point in time (i.e., one "reaches" menopause), menopause is an umbrella term that commonly includes perimenopause, menopause, and the postmenopausal years. In the United States women typically reach menopause between the ages of 44 and 55, with the average age being 51.4 (North American Menopause Society [NAMS], 2004).

Many women are not aware that changes related to menopause begin up to 10 years prior to the cessation of menstruation. Termed *perimenopause*, this stage can begin in a woman's late 30s and early 40s and is characterized by symptoms such as erratic menstrual cycles, hot flashes, headaches, dry skin, joint pain, forgetfulness, constipation, or dizzy spells. Women need education to become better prepared for these signs associated with changing hormonal levels (Huffman & Myers, 1999).

When a woman does reach menopause, she can experience the following symptoms (NAMS, 2003):

Hot flashes	Poor concentration
Headaches	Forgetfulness
Vaginal dryness	Thinning of vaginal lining
Reduced libido	Sleep disturbance
Irritability	Depression and anxiety
Palpitations	Tingling sensations
Joint and muscle pain	Urinary incontinence

Hot flashes are the most common symptom that women experience and are the reason most women give for seeking medical attention related to menopause. In one study of women ages 39 to 60, hot flashes were reported by only 41% of women who were premenopausal but by 85% of the women who had reached the onset of menopause (Oldenhave & Netelenbos, 1994).

It is difficult to isolate symptoms that are distinctly related to menopause because every woman experiences menopause differently based on biological factors, cultural factors, internalized attitudes, and life experiences (Defey, Storch, Cardozo, Diaz, & Fernandez, 1996; V. M. Rice, 2005; Sommer et al., 1999). For example, women in high social castes in India report few negative symptoms related to menopause, presumably because of the high social status conferred on older women (Feldman, 2000). In contrast, in the United States menopausal women are often viewed negatively as old, disease-ridden, emotionally unstable, and useless to society (Huffman & Myers, 1999; Warnke et al., 1993). These types of cultural attitudes and beliefs highly influence women, who often internalize them as their own personal values. This is important, as research indicates that a woman's attitudes about and expectations of menopause highly influence her experience. In other words, when women view menopause as a negative event, they experience more negative symptoms (Sommer et al., 1999).

Further, stressful midlife circumstances such as loss of a spouse, career changes, children leaving home, or caring for an aging parent affect a woman's experience of menopause. There is strong empirical support for the relationship between psychosocial stressors and menopausal symptoms (Huffman & Myers, 1999). Marital quality and sexual satisfaction are also directly related to the experience of menopausal symptoms (Robinson Kurpius & Nicpon, 2003).

It is important then for counselors to help women normalize menopause as a life transition so that they can reframe their expectations more positively. Women need to be aware that women adjust well to menopause and cope with the symptoms with few problems (NAMS, 2005;

Sommer et al., 1999). One cross-cultural study of more than 160,000 women found that women from all major racial/ethnic groups possessed attitudes toward menopause that ranged from neutral to positive. Black women had the most positive attitudes compared to Japanese American, Chinese American, Latina, and White women (V. M. Rice, 2005; Sommer et al., 1999). The authors explain these findings by concluding that for African American women menopause might be a minor stressor compared to the larger consequences of racism and sexism and that they might be less vulnerable to negative stereotypes because they directly observe the effects of menopause through spending considerable time with older female relatives.

Along with education to refute the stereotype that most women suffer a multitude of negative symptoms during the menopausal years, counselors can explore the many positive events associated with menopause, including the freedom from worries about pregnancy that may lead to heightened sexual interest and pleasure, especially within a quality spousal relationship (Etaugh & Bridges, 2004). One large-scale study of women in Uruguay found that women viewed the postmenopausal years as positive; they reported these years as a time to reflect on their lives and to give priority to their own needs (Defey et al., 1996). In the United States 51% of postmenopausal women in a recent national Gallup Poll reported that they were more fulfilled now compared to earlier years and that many areas of their lives improved after menopause, including family, home life, and focus on hobbies or interests. Further, menopause can be an impetus for positive life changes, as 75% of the women surveyed reported making a positive lifestyle change in nutrition, exercise, or reduced stress (NAMS, 2005).

To summarize, to assist women who are concerned about menopause, counselors need to work with women around two major themes. First, women benefit most from a conceptualization of menopause as a normative life transition, not a disease. It can be an important time of reevaluation and change, not a crisis to be dreaded. (Huffman & Myers, 1999). Second, women are both alike and different from other women in their experiences of menopause, and their experiences are highly influenced by biological, cultural, and psychosocial factors.

Prevention and Counseling Strategies for Assisting Women During the Menopausal Transition

To address the features described previously, the following seven-phase guide is presented for counselors to help their clients adapt to the transitions accompanying menopause (adapted from Huffman & Myers, 1999). The phases are summarized here; see Huffman and Myers (1999) for additional information.

Phase one: Education. Counselors can provide accurate biomedical information to increase client awareness of misconceptions and misinformation related to menopause. Recommendations regarding treatment of physical conditions is certainly beyond the scope of counselors' practice, but it is helpful for counselors to collect and maintain a resource file on menopause as well as on the major diseases that affect large numbers of postmenopausal women, including heart disease, breast cancer, and osteoporosis. Women report that they fear breast cancer more than any other condition, yet they are far more likely to die from heart disease. While heart disease is the number one killer among women, most surveys show that women lack information about its risks. Today's women are more aware of the risks of breast cancer due to massive national educational/awareness campaigns by organizations such as the Susan G. Komen Race for the Cure. Perhaps counselors can do more to increase awareness regarding heart disease, including the factors which are under our control to change: physical inactivity, smoking, being overweight, having a poor diet, and using certain hormones (Etaugh & Bridges, 2004).

Phase two: Recognize the importance of biomedical issues. Clients can schedule an appointment with their health care provider to receive accurate information and treatment recommendations. One controversial medical consideration for women is the use of hormone replacement therapy (HRT), which replaces the hormones whose levels drop after menopause. Weighing the benefits and risks of HRT can be frightening for women, as information related to HRT is often contradictory and confusing (Mayo Clinic, 2005).

HRT is effective for the relief of vasomotor symptoms, vaginal dryness, protects against osteoporosis, and improves psychological and cognitive functions. It is particularly effective for hot flashes that cause sleep disturbance (Mayo Clinic, 2005). However, women need to be aware of the risks of the use of HRT. A 2003 report in the *New England Journal of Medicine* concluded that HRT should not be initiated for the purpose of preventing disease, because even though the loss of hormones puts a woman at risk for several diseases, replacing these hormones puts her at risk for additional diseases including blood clots and stroke (Grodstein, Clarkson, & Manson, 2003). The use of HRT is also consistently linked to an increased risk of breast cancer with increasing duration of use. In a recent study of 55,000 menopausal women from all major racial groups, the use of HRT resulted in increased risk of breast cancer (Lee et al., 2006). The Susan G. Komen Breast Cancer Foundation issued a statement in 2004 recommending that any woman taking combination HRT (a combination of progesterone and estrogen) should discuss the benefits and risks with her health care provider. This statement was released after a 2004 HRT trial by the Women's Health Initiative was halted due to participants' increased rates of breast cancer, cardiovascular events, and blood clot formation (Komen Foundation, 2004).

Because of these reports, many women feared the use of HRT because they were told it increases the risks of breast cancer and cardiovascular disease. However, a 2006 study (funded by the Women's Health Initiative, NIH) reversed those warnings regarding heart disease, indicating that younger women who initiated HRT near menopause had a 30% lower risk for heart disease than did women who didn't take hormones, but older women who started HRT at least 10 years after menopause received no benefit (Grodstein, Manson, & Stampfer, 2006). The research in this area is advancing rapidly, and counselors should advise their clients to consult with a health care provider who is knowledgeable about current research before making any decisions about HRT.

Phase three: Self-assessment. Counselors can help clients ask themselves some of the following questions:

- How have sociocultural attitudes about aging and menopause affected my attitudes?
- What are my expectations and fears about menopause?
- What are my most immediate needs and concerns? Are they biomedical, cultural, psychosocial?
- How healthy is my lifestyle in terms of diet, exercise, smoking, excessive alcohol intake, use of over-the-counter or other drugs and medications?
- What is my family medical history of osteoporosis, heart disease, and breast cancer?
- What are the major stressors in my life, and what can I do to reduce the stressors?
- How much thought and effort have I put into taking care of myself lately?
- What symptoms have I noticed that may be related to perimenopause or menopause?
- What are my information gaps about menopause?

Phase four: Dialogue and definition. To help normalize their experiences, women need strong support systems during this phase of their lives. Some questions counselors can ask include the following:

- Who are my support people who will listen to me, talk with me, and help me make sense of my experience?
- Who can I talk to in my family?
- What are other women thinking and experiencing who are at the same stage in life?
- What was the experience of my mother? Older friends and relatives?
- How do I anticipate my life changing in terms of losses? Gains?
- How do I want to define menopause?
- Who is in charge of my menopause?

Phase five: Use resources and create a plan. While clients need to rely on their medical care providers for accurate medical information, clients have the power to create their own reaction to and experience of menopause. Rather than relying solely on professionals for advice, women today are far more likely to seek out information for themselves (NAMS, 2005). Counselors can facilitate their clients' abilities to be active agents in creating a plan of care by informing them of resources and options. It might be helpful for them to research alternative treatments for menopausal symptoms that are widely used in practice. The following is a partial list of recommended treatments:

Healthy eating (reduced caffeine and alcohol)	Relaxation techniques
	Deep breathing
Weight maintenance	Yoga
Exercise	Vaginal lubricants
Vitamins	Smoking cessation
Calcium	

Plant estrogens such as soy and red clover are also recommended, although clinical trials are equivocal in their results. A large-scale study is under way to determine the effectiveness of black cohosh, an herb marketed as a dietary supplement (Mayo Clinic, 2005).

It is especially helpful to explore the use of exercise as a highly recommended alternative treatment that has been found to relieve symptoms such as hot flashes, night sweats, vaginal dryness, depression, irritability, headache, and sleep disturbance (Li, Holm, Gulanik, Lanusa, & Penckofer, 1999). In the first years postmenopause, women are especially vulnerable to bone loss and osteoporosis as they transition to a postmenopausal stage. Exercise in general and weight training in particular have been shown to slow bone loss during these years (Pratt & Matthews, 2006). See additional resources at the end of this chapter for information on alternative treatments.

Phase six: Implement the plan. Women can assume responsibility for implementing their own care plans. Counselors may need to encourage clients to be assertive with medical service providers until they obtain satisfactory results (see the National Institute on Aging publication "Talking With My Doctor" at nih.gov/nia).

Phase seven: Reevaluation and adjustments. Counselors can reassure clients that menopause is a period characterized by variability and change; therefore, their plans must be continually updated and adjusted. Clients may need to be reminded that menopause is a time of transition that does have an end. Encouragement and social support throughout the process is important.

Adapting to the Caregiving Role

I just placed my mother in a retirement facility after taking care of her at my house for the last eight years. I don't know how to feel. Relief? No more round-the-clock chores and demands on me. Failure? I've let her down because I just can't do it myself anymore. Guilt? Yes, guilt. I should be willing to do more for her, and I'm not going to do it anymore. I didn't know this would be so hard.

—Benita, age 53

The most rapid growth in the elderly population is among those 85 and older, a 35% increase between the years 1990 and 2000 (U.S. Census Bureau, 2001). As the baby boomer generation, our nation's largest population segment, begins to reach retirement age, the need for caregivers for the oldest-old will increase. Given these demands, it is noteworthy that 73% of caregivers are women (NCOA, 2006).

Today's women in midlife are often referred to as the *sandwich generation*— women who are caught between caring for or launching their own children or grandchildren while simultaneously caring for their aging parents (Qualls, 2002). While assuming these roles, women also may be caring for a husband, friends, or other relatives, all while coping with their own age-related issues such as those highlighted throughout this chapter. Although older women might not feel prepared for these multiple caregiving roles, many feel a sense of obligation to take on these tasks. Single women (either never-married or newly single) are often assigned to the caregiver role by default because it is assumed that they have the time to devote to caring for their parents or loved ones (Kerson, 2001).

It is important for counselors to be aware of the issues that caretaking women may experience; the toll placed on these women interferes with their physical and mental health, including impediments to their personal development and self-care (Canetto, 2001). Caregivers are more at risk for depression than are noncaregivers (Qualls, 2002), especially when there is a conflict between their work and other family responsibilities. Caregiving wives have reported problems of isolation, loneliness, financial difficulties, and role overload (Kerson, 2001). The caregivers who have the most difficulty with these roles are those who accept the caregiving role out of obligation or loyalty but don't have the skills to establish clear boundaries or rights when negotiating with other family members. If they are unable to speak assertively about their rights, women may experience *role captivity* and feel trapped in the caregiving role (Qualls, 2002). For example, other family members might expect a woman to assume all the responsibilities for an ill parent, even though she has her immediate family to care for in addition to her own needs for self-care. If she does not communicate with them directly regarding her needs for breaks from caregiving or for help with certain tasks, they will continue to assign all duties to her. She, in turn, will feel frustrated and increasingly isolated in her role as caregiver.

As counselors work with women who are caregivers, it is helpful to match counseling strategies with the three broad stages of caregiving: initial stage, transition stage, and bereavement stage (Qualls, 2002). In the *initial stage*, education, prevention, and planning are recommended. The woman might need education regarding the illness of her loved one, and prevention, short- and long-term planning for legal needs, social services, and medical services. In the *transition stage*, the counselor might want to focus more on the emotional well-being of the client, addressing role captivity issues and the need for assertiveness skills. It is important that caregiving women are aware of the relationship between their own physical health and psychological well-being. One study of midlife caregivers found that their psychological health was largely dependent on their current state of physical health (Killian, Turner, & Cain, 2005). The authors recommended programs that integrate emotional support, stress management, and physical fitness along with regularly scheduled breaks from caregiving to increase both physical health and emotional well-being. One large-scale program funded by NIH is designed to develop and test new ways for helping caregivers manage the stresses of caring for people with Alzheimer's disease or related disorders. Additional information about the holistic program, Resources of Enhancing Alzheimer's Caregiver Health (REACH), is available at Reach.org. The Alzheimer's Disease Education and Referral (ADEAR) program through the National Institute on Aging is also helpful (see nia.nih.gov/Alzheimers).

At the *bereavement stage,* a caregiver needs to focus on closure and readjustment to help her disengage from the caregiving role. When a loved one dies, the grieving process may be more complicated as a caregiver may experience a sense of guilt and failure for not preventing the death. If institutionalization of her loved one occurs, she may feel that she has failed because preventing institutionalization is often the goal of caregiving (Kerson, 2001). At this stage, women might find it difficult to shift out of a caregiving role after assuming care for others for many years. If they become ill or incapacitated themselves as they age, women may experience problems with *role reversal* as they must learn to receive care from others (Crose, 1999). As discussed previously, counselors can help women recognize this period as an opportunity to define a new identity for themselves outside of the caregiving role.

Adapting to Grandmothering

My daughter is in rehab for drugs and can't take care of her baby. I'm willing to step in and take charge but I am just too old to be raising an infant! In between trying to keep my daughter clean and taking care of the baby night and day, I am worn out.

—Avery, age 66

The grandmother role often is a positive one for older women, with grandmothers being viewed as kinkeepers, the ties that bind families together (Trotman & Brody, 2002). About half of all adults over the age of 65 are grandparents (Etaugh & Bridges, 2004), and 50% of women experience this event by age 47. It is common for midlife women to provide care for their grandchildren, with nearly half of all grandparents providing support for their infant and preschool-age grandchildren on a regular basis. One third of all preschoolers whose mothers work are cared for by grandparents, usually grandmothers (Baydar & Brooks-Gunn, 1998). There are many benefits of regular interaction with grandchildren for midlife women, and many women report that it fulfills their need for staying active, feeling useful, and for being satisfied with their ability to provide quality care for the child (Reynolds, Wright, & Beale, 2003).

However, current trends indicate that increasing numbers of grandmothers are raising their grandchildren, which increases stress for older women. In *skipped generation households,* parents leave the responsibility for their children exclusively to their own parents, usually their mothers. Skipped generation households are more common among ethnic minority groups, particularly in African American families. Parents ask their own parents to raise their children due to teen pregnancy, divorce or remarriage, death, drug abuse, incarceration, or incompetence (Reynolds et al., 2003). It is understandable that serving as a custodial grandparent can cause increased anxiety, child-rearing strains, and financial burdens for older women. Grandparents serving in this role also face difficulty in obtaining resources; when grandparents are not given legal custody or are not appointed as foster parents, most existing laws give them no legal status or rights. They may have difficulty obtaining educational or medical records or in proving eligibility for medical or financial assistance (Reynolds et al., 2003).

Further, the social isolation inherent in raising young children may inhibit women from receiving the social support from other adults that they need. They also may experience frustration from unfulfilled expectations for what they thought they would be doing during the retirement years such as traveling, socializing with others, and relaxing. Many women feel responsible for the dysfunction of their own children and spend a lot of their time attempting to help their adult children regain stability so that they might resume their parenting duties. As stated earlier, it is common for women to be in the middle of caring for both grandchildren and elderly parents (Reynolds et al., 2003).

In today's culture in which divorces are common, another concern of grandparents involves grandparent rights when parents separate and divorce. Many grandparents are denied access to their grandchildren as a result of family dysfunction or remarriage. Even though grandparents can provide a sense of stability for children during this time of upheaval and disruption, they may be unable to serve as a resource if parents do not allow them to do so. Many grandparents experience grief over the loss of their grandchildren, feeling left out and forgotten during the transition (Myers & Schwiebert, 1999). It is especially difficult in cases in which grandmothers were serving as the primary caregiver, but then were forced to relinquish care back to the parent without having any further contact with the child. According to the Foundation for Grandparenting (2007), increasing numbers of grandparents have sued for better visitation rights and have called for more uniformity in state laws. As a result of these protests, most states now have laws allowing grandparents to petition the court to continue seeing their grandchildren after their child's marriage ends by death or divorce, but these laws vary from state to state (Etaugh & Bridges, 2004). While grandparents need to know that parental rights supercede grandparent rights and that they should only intervene when a child's safety is at risk, grandparents can be proactive by asking parents to put a provision in their separation agreement about visitation rights for grandparents (National Committee of Grandparents for Children's Rights, 2005). It is recommended that grandparents coping with these issues consult helpful online resources such as Grandtimes.com, Grandparentsunited.com, and Grandparents for Children.org.

Mental Health Concerns of Older Women

Despite the challenges described throughout this chapter, older women generally do well in coping with losses and adapting to new life roles, particularly when effective prevention and early interventions are in place. However, life stressors for women during this period can result in significant mental health problems for some women. The most common mental health concerns of older women are anxiety and depressive disorders.

Anxiety

Across all age groups, women experience higher rates of anxiety disorders than men (Glicken, 2005). Factors associated with the onset of anxiety in older women include health problems, loss of significant others, marital or family conflict, financial insecurities, lack of a support network, sense of isolation, lack of self-worth, and lack of control (Glicken, 2005; Kerson, 2001).

Anxiety manifests itself in older women in the following ways (Glicken, 2005; Richardson, 2001):

Chest pains	Essential hypertension
Heart palpitations	Headaches
Night sweats	Shortness of breath
Generalized pain	

Because these symptoms are experienced physically, physicians often misdiagnose anxiety disorders in older persons and leave the underlying emotional components untreated. Further, anxiety symptoms often coexist with physical conditions such as cardiac conditions, seizure disorders, and metabolic or respiratory disorders, and it is difficult to distinguish a physical origin from an emotional origin for the anxiety. Kerson (2001) offered the following guidelines for making this distinction.

A physical cause is more likely if:

- Onset of symptoms appears suddenly.
- Symptoms fluctuate in strength and duration.
- Fatigue is present before symptoms are first experienced.

An emotional cause of anxiety is more likely if:

- Symptoms have lasted 2 or more years.
- Long-lasting symptoms exist with little change in strength and severity.
- There are coexisting symptoms of emotional disturbance.

Recommended treatment for older women includes cognitive behavioral therapy (CBT) with relaxation training, particularly when presented in a small-group format (Myers & Harper, 2004; Stanley & Averill, 1999).

Treatment for Anxiety in Older Women

CBT with relaxation training presented in a small-group format is particularly effective in older adults (Myers & Harper, 2004; Stanley & Averill, 1999). It works especially well when it matches a client's religious beliefs and encourages her to engage in a life review. Before proceeding with treatment, it is important that counselors understand client reluctance to change their thinking about the ways they approach their lives. If they have viewed the world in a certain way throughout their adulthood, giving up this approach to life in favor of something new might increase anxiety levels. For this reason, many older adults prefer to think of their anxiety as physically based (Glicken, 2005).

Stanley and Averill (1999) presented a program to address anxiety in older adults. In the 15-week program, members meet weekly in a small-group format to increase their social contact and address symptoms of anxiety. The program includes the following components:

1. *Education and self-monitoring*: Education about anxiety in the form of reading material is provided. Clients are taught ways to monitor their anxiety throughout the week.
2. *Relaxation training*: Clients are taught progressive muscle relaxation and how to practice it throughout the week.
3. *Cognitive therapy*: Clients learn basic strategies for modifying thoughts and behaviors such as examination of logical errors, decastrophizing, and thought stopping.
4. *Behavioral therapy*: Clients engage in graduated behavioral practice using a hierarchy of anxiety-producing situations they have rated between 0 and 100. Starting with the least anxiety-provoking situation, clients practice using imaginal and in vivo desensitization (see Stanley & Averill, 1999, for more information).

Depression

It is estimated that up to 15% of older persons experience depression. While women are twice as likely as men to experience depression before the onset of menopause, sex differences in depression rates sharply decline by age 80. This shift occurs because men's depression rates greatly increase after they turn 60, whereas the rates for women remain stable or decrease (Etaugh & Bridges, 2004).

Women become vulnerable to depression when they accumulate a series of losses. For example, the loss of a spouse might result in a loss of financial security and a woman's support network, both risk factors for depression in older women (Kerson, 2001). Counselors should be aware that it is difficult to diagnose and treat depression in older women because they may not experience the classic symptoms of sleeplessness, fatigue, low energy, loss of appetite, depressed mood, and guilt. Instead, symptoms may manifest in the following ways:

Anxiety	Malaise
Confusion	Physical complaints
Eating disorders	Lethargy
Digestive problems	Insomnia
Sudden irritability	Fault-finding in self and others

Women's concerns may not be taken seriously by mental health or health care professionals, and their complaints may be dismissed as "typical" in old age. Women may have been socialized to remain silent about their life dissatisfaction and to view their complaints as normal (Kerson, 2001). Counselors can be alert to these symptoms in their older clients and encourage women to verbalize their concerns. When older adults are treated for depression, they improve at a rate of around 80%. Individual counseling, self-help bibliotherapy, cognitive therapy, reminiscence therapies (explained later in the chapter), and group therapies all have demonstrated effectiveness with this population (Myers & Harper, 2004).

Treatment for Depression in Older Women

Interpersonal psychotherapy is a promising area for the treatment of depression in older women (Hinrichsen, 1999). This approach helps clients to examine current and past relationships as they might be related to depressive symptoms, reviews the nature of current important relationships, and examines what changes clients would like to make. Counselors help clients identify a specific interpersonal problem area on which to focus. The interpersonal problem areas include the following:

Grief: The focus is on helping clients through the process of mourning and helping clients to reconnect with others.

Interpersonal disputes: The goal is to identify the nature of the dispute, establish a plan to deal with the dispute, and examine ways to improve communication strategies or develop more realistic expectations regarding the relationship.

Role transition: Counselors can emphasize helping the client to mourn and accept the loss of the previous life role, accept the new role in a more positive way, and develop a greater sense of mastery regarding the new role.

Interpersonal deficit: As they transition into new life roles, some older women need assistance in developing the social skills needed to maintain effective interpersonal relationships.

For more information about this approach, see Hinrichsen (1999).

Life Review Work

Reminiscence and life review work are important counseling strategies commonly used with older adults coping with multiple losses. As adult women age, they inevitably become more conscious of their past experiences and unresolved conflicts. As they realize that they cannot escape death, they may wonder, "How has my life made sense?" "How do I want to be remembered?" "What issues do I need to resolve?" Reminiscence work is a natural, adaptive response to aging and can take many forms: oral and written storytelling or journaling, autobiography, music, poetry, scrapbooks, pilgrimages, or reunions. Reminiscence can take place at a superficial level and may or may not be therapeutic in nature, but *life review* is a form of reminiscence with an evaluative component (Molinari, 1999). In contrast to reminiscence activities, life review is more structured and is aimed at helping older adults come to terms with unresolved issues, integrate parts of the self, assist with problem solving, and help them to decide upon the legacy they wish to leave to future generations. Gestalt techniques are often used during life review to help clients achieve new insight and to gain closure on past events. For example, by using the empty chair technique, clients can talk with someone who is no longer present in their lives to achieve closure around a specific conflict (Crose, 1999).

Molinari (1999) recommended that life review be conducted in a small-group setting and suggested the following possible group topics:

Early and important figures in my life	Relationships with parents, siblings, friends
School experiences	Work histories
Relationships with spouses and partners	Most significant life events
Accomplishments	Turning points
Unfulfilled desires and regrets	Major transitions
Experiences with death or dying	Spirituality and purpose in life

See Molinari (1999) for more information on leading life review groups.

Substance abuse, particularly the abuse of over-the-counter and prescription drugs, is a common problem in older women. In addition, counselors working closely with older adults need to become familiar with the symptoms of and interventions of dementia.

The promising news is that older women respond well in treatment for these concerns. In their review of the literature, Myers and Harper (2004) reported that older persons respond as well as or better to counseling than do younger adults, but they may need more sessions due to the complexity of their concerns. For example, due to the stigmatization of seeking mental health services that remains present in the older population, older adults might not seek counseling until they are in crisis. According to Myers and Harper, an older person's first contact with the mental health system might be a psychiatric emergency and resulting hospitalization. Counselors who work with older women on an outpatient basis, therefore, might not have contact with them until their conditions are severe. For this reason, Myers and Harper recommended improved community counseling with an emphasis on prevention.

Qualities of Women Who Age Well

Aging is a self-fulfilling prophecy. If we dread growing old, thinking of it as a time of forgetfulness and physical deterioration, then it is likely to be just that. On the other hand, if we expect it to be full of energy and anticipate that our lives will be rich with new adventures and insight, then that is the likely reality. We prescribe who we are. We prescribe what we are to become (Bortz, as cited in Maples & Abney, 2006).

Counselors can play an important role in helping older women age well and create a vital life. Instead of focusing on their problems and limitations, counselors can use a wellness perspective to help clients focus on qualities of resilience for aging well. Women who age successfully have the following qualities that counselors can strive to foster in their women clients:

- *Positive attitude toward aging*: As the benefits of CBT have been emphasized in older adults, it makes sense to encourage older women to modify their world view to encompass a more positive attitude toward the aging process, even if this means pushing against the prevailing ageist cultural tide. All women can learn from attitudes exemplified by African American women, who are better able to refrain from internalizing damaging societal stereotypes than are those from other cultural groups (Petersen, 2000). A sense of humor, being able to laugh, and not taking oneself too seriously are important for aging well (Myers & Sweeney, 2005).
- *Self-determination/empowerment*: Older women who take responsibility for their own choices and for the changes that occur in their lives, and who recognize their own ability to solve problems, are more successful in their later years. No matter her age, a client has the right to make decisions about her life (Garner & Mercer, 2001; Gaylord, 2001) and to maintain a sense of control.
- *Balance between agency and communion*: Women are more likely to possess the traditionally feminine qualities of communion (e.g., emotional expressivity, affection, compassion, kindness, gentleness) than are men, who generally possess agentic traits (e.g., independence, activity, competitiveness, self-confidence, assertiveness). Older women who are able to integrate the two qualities and maintain a positive gender identity have high levels of self-esteem when compared with those who show only communal traits (Hubbs-Tait, 1989). Counselors can help clients develop the optimal balance that helps them to function successfully.
- *Purpose-directed life*: Women who age well are more likely to believe that life is meaningful and has a purpose. The American Perceptions on Aging in the 21st Century study found that 67% of older adults felt that having a spiritual life is the key to a meaningful and vital life (NCOA, 2002). A serene and spiritual approach to life helps women place the aging process in perspective and to maintain hope in the face of adversity. It is helpful to ask clients "What meaning do you de-

rive from your life? What sources of power can you draw on to aid you in your life?" (Brody, 1999).

- *Remaining active and healthy*: Women who age well view themselves as healthy and strive to maintain the physical activities they participated in when they were younger. Pratt and Matthews (2006) emphasized the important health benefits of regular physical activity for older women, asserting that exercise may be the single most important habit people aged 65+ can adopt for improving their overall health and well-being. As they age, older women begin to experience a loss of muscle mass and physical deterioration, which are often preventable with regular exercise. Exercise can significantly lower the risk of cardiovascular disease, the number one killer of women. Those women who engage in resistance training are the most likely to experience these benefits. One helpful resource, Growing Stronger, Strength Training for Older Adults, is available at: www.nutrition.tufts.edu/growingstronger.

- *Strong support network*: Women who age well experience their friendships and interpersonal relationships as positive. A recent study conducted by the National Council on Aging (2002) found that 92% of women rated having family and friends as "very important" to having a meaningful and vital life. A woman does not have to have a great number of relationships to function well. In fact, Myers (1999) reported that it is a woman's *perception of support*, not the *quantity* of supportive relationships that is related to life satisfaction.

    The family is the preferred source of support for older women. According to Armstrong (2001), the multigenerational extended family is the ideal form of support, and people of color are more likely to experience these family constellations than Caucasians. Older minority women are more likely to perceive themselves as part of an accessible extended family and to rate it highly as a source of support (Armstrong, 2001). This family network can extend to both blood and "fictive" kinships, including neighbors, friends, and church members. Drawing upon these sources of support, older Black women are often revered in their communities and frequently are viewed as "wise women" and church "mothers" (Armstrong, 2001). Counselors can help all women to develop support networks that encompass family and build fictive kinships as a source of community support.

- *Participation in creative pursuits*: To maintain creativity, older women who age well have successfully developed leisure activities that nourish the following needs: physical, social, intellectual, volunteer, and creative (Vaillant & Mukamal, 2001). Clients who may have a strong work ethic and feel that leisure is a nonproductive use of time may need help in understanding the importance of developing leisure preferences (Myers, 1999). They may need to focus on the meaning they want to derive from life outside of work. Some helpful suggestions for creative pursuits are included in Jacobs's (1997) book, *Be an Outrageous Older Woman*.

One important leisure activity, participation in volunteer activities, is related to overall satisfaction in older adults. About one fourth of all people age 75 and older still volunteer (Etaugh & Bridges, 2004). To encourage a sense of empowerment, counselors can help their clients to serve as advocates by playing an active role in creating local or social change. Helpful references for involvement in advocacy issues include AARP, Gray Panthers, and the Older Women's League (Etaugh & Bridges, 2004).

- *Adaptive coping resources for handling multiple losses, including changes in physical appearance*: Women who age successfully have the ability to adapt and remain open to inevitable life changes. They are able to cope with losses by grieving the roles associated with earlier life stages. Further, they are able to develop a sense of involvement with new life roles by viewing them as new opportunities and possibilities.

Case Study

Mary, age 67, comes to counseling after being widowed for more than 2 years ago. She is physically healthy, but she is lonely and "wants a new husband." She is worried about how unattractive she feels and is concerned that she won't be able to attract a romantic partner at this age. She realizes that she has few friends because she and her husband spent most of their time as a couple, and she mostly catered to her husband's needs while they were married. Her children live in different states and do not visit her except for major holidays, and she has no real relationship with her grandchildren. She struggles financially and has much anxiety related to her financial future. She tells the counselor that she is reluctant to come to counseling because she doesn't like to ask for help, but her loneliness and anxiety have become too much for her to manage on her own.

1. Which of the six issues explored in this chapter are pertinent to Mary's case? How would you address them?
2. What counseling interventions are recommended based on her current concerns?
3. How would you work to instill qualities of resilience in Mary? How do these play a role in her treatment?

Conclusion

The number of older women is increasing rapidly, and counselors should be prepared to work effectively with this population. As with other topics explored in this book, older women benefit most when they are assisted in identifying their strengths and in learning to appreciate cultural influences on their experiences. They also benefit when counselors help them strengthen their coping strategies for facing the complex changes that occur during this time in their lives. It is clear that maintaining a positive attitude toward the aging process, including appearance-related changes and the menopausal transition, helps women to develop resilience for aging well and for living a strong and vital life.

Activities for Further Exploration

1. Look through newspapers and magazines for ads that include middle-aged and older adults. Are there differences in the appearances of women and men? What is your reaction to seeing older women in these advertisements?
2. Interview a woman from a more advanced generation than your own (e.g., if you are 30, interview a woman in her 50s) about some of the topics explored in this chapter. Do her experiences mirror those described in this chapter?
3. In reading the section on menopause, were there any surprises for you? What areas of this transition would you like to learn more about?
4. Review the qualities described for aging well and explore how you can work to instill these qualities both in yourself and in your clients.

Suggested Readings

Canetto, S. S. (2001). Older adult women: Issues, resources, & challenges. In R. K. Unger (Ed.), *Handbook of the psychology of women and gender* (pp.183–200). New York: Wiley.

Gaylord, S. (2001). Women and aging: A psychological perspective. In J. D. Garner & S. O. Mercer (Eds.), *Women as they age* (pp. 49–68). Binghamton, NY: Haworth Press.

Hill, R. D. (2006). *Positive aging: A guide for mental health professionals and consumers.* New York: Norton Professional Books.

Huffman, S. B., & Myers, J. E. (1999). Counseling women in midlife: An integrative approach to menopause. *Journal of Counseling & Development, 77*, 258–266.

Maples, M. F., & Abney, P. C. (2006). Baby boomers mature and gerontological counseling comes of age. *Journal of Counseling & Development, 84*, 3–9.

Myers, J. E., & Harper, M. C. (2004). Evidence-based effective practices with older adults. *Journal of Counseling & Development, 82*, 207–218.

Robinson Kurpius, S. E., & Nicpon, M. (2003). Menopause and the lives of midlife women. In M. Kopala & M. A. Keitel (Eds.), *Handbook of counseling women* (pp. 269–276). Thousand Oaks, CA: Sage.

Saucier, M. G. (2004). Midlife and beyond: Issues for aging women. *Journal of Counseling & Development, 82*, 420–425.

Sontag, S. (1997). The double standard of aging. In M. Pearsall (Ed.), *The other within us* (pp. 19–24). Boulder, CO: Westview Press.

Tiggemann, M. (2004). Body image across the lifespan: Stability and change. *Body Image, 1*, 29–41.

Additional Resources

Menopause and Women's Health

North American Menopause Society: www.menopause.org; www.americanmenopause.org
American Heart Association: www.amhrt.org
Susan G. Komen for the Cure: www.breastcancerinfo.com

Women and Aging

National Institute of Aging: www.nia.nih.gov
Administration on Aging: www.aoa.gov
Alliance for Aging Research: www.agingresearch.org
National Council on Aging: www.ncoa.org

Professional Associations

AARP: www.aarp.org
The Gray Panthers: www.graypanthers.org
Older Women's League (OWL): www.owl-national.org
National Family Caregivers Association: www.nfcacares.org
National Institute on Aging: www.nih.gov/nia

References

Allaz, A., Bernstein, M., Rouget, P., Archinard, M., & Morabia, A. (1998). Body weight preoccupation in middle-age and ageing women: A general population survey. *International Journal of Eating Disorders, 23*(3), 287–294.

Arcement, P. (2005). *Aging self-exploration exercises.* Unpublished manuscript.

Armstrong, M. J. (2001). Ethnic minority women as they age. In J. D. Garner & S. O. Mercer (Eds.), *Women as they age* (pp. 97–114). Binghamton, NY: Haworth Press.

Baydar, N., & Brooks-Gunn, J. (1998). Profiles of grandmothers who help care for their grandchildren in the United States. *Family Relations, 47,* 385–393.

Brody, C. M. (1999). Existential issues of hope and meaning in late life therapy. In M. Duffy (Ed.), *Handbook of counseling and psychotherapy with older adults* (pp. 91–106). New York: Wiley.

Canetto, S. S. (2001). Older adult women: Issues, resources, & challenges. In R. K. Unger (Ed.), *Handbook of the psychology of women and gender* (pp. 183–200). New York: Wiley.

Clarke, L. H. (2001). Older women's bodies and the self: The construction of identity in later life. *Canadian Review of Sociology & Anthropology, 38,* 441–465.

Crose, R. G. (1999). Addressing late life developmental issues for women: Body image, sexuality, and intimacy. In M. Duffy (Ed.), *Handbook of counseling and psychotherapy with older adults* (pp. 57–76). New York: Wiley.

Defey, D., Storch, E., Cardozo, S., Diaz, O., & Fernandez, G. (1996). The menopause: Women's psychology and health care. *Social Science and Medicine, 42*(10), 1447–1456.

Degges-White, S., & Myers, J. E. (2006). Transitions, wellness, and life satisfaction: Implications for counseling midlife women. *Journal of Mental Health Counseling, 28,* 133–150.

Etaugh, C. A., & Bridges, J. S. (2004). *The psychology of women: A lifestyle perspective.* Boston: Pearson Education.

Feldman, R. S. (2000). *Development across the lifespan* (2nd ed.) Upper Saddle River, NJ: Prentice-Hall.

Fey-Yensen, N., McCormick, L., & English, C. (2002). Body image and weight preoccupation in older women: A review. *Healthy Weight Journal, 16*(5), 68–71.

Foundation for Grandparenting. (2007). *The grandparent foundation.* Retrieved January 14, 2007, from http://www.grandparenting.org

Franzoi, S. L., & Koehler, V. (1998). Age and gender differences in body attitudes: A comparison of young and elderly adults. *International Journal of Aging and Human Development, 47*(1), 1–10.

Garner, J. D., & Mercer, S. O. (2001). Conclusion: Empowerment and self-determination. In J. D. Garner & S. O. Mercer (Eds.), *Women as they age* (235–238). Binghamton, NY: Haworth Press.

Gaylord, S. (2001). Women and aging: A psychological perspective. In J. D. Garner & S. O. Mercer (Eds.), *Women as they age* (pp. 49–68). Binghamton, NY: Haworth Press.

Gliken, M. D. (2005). *Improving the effectiveness of the helping professions: An evidence based approach to practice* (pp. 217–240). Thousand Oaks, CA: Sage.

Grodstein, F., Clarkson, T. B., & Manson, J. E. (2003). Understanding divergent data on postmenopausal hormone therapy. *New England Journal of Medicine, 348*(7), 645–650.

Grodstein, F., Manson, J. E., & Stampfer, M. J. (2006). Hormone therapy and coronary heart disease: The role of time since menopause and age at hormone initiation. *Journal of Women's Health, 15*(1), 35–44.

Grossman, A. H., D'Augelli, A. R., & O'Connel, T. S. (2001). Being lesbian, gay, bisexual, and 60 or older in North America. *Journal of Gay and Lesbian Social Services, 13,* 23–40.

Gupta, M. A., & Schork, N. J. (1993). Aging-related concerns and body image: Possible future implications for eating disorders. *International Journal of Eating Disorders, 14*(4), 481–486.

Hallinan, C. J., & Schuler, P. B. (1993). Body-shape perceptions of elderly women exercisers and nonexercisers. *Perpetual and Motor Skills, 77,* 451–456.

Halliwell, E., & Dittmar, H. (2003). A qualitative investigation of women's and men's body image concerns and their attitudes toward aging. *Sex Roles, 49*(11/12), 675–684.

Harris, M. B. (1994). Growing old gracefully: Age concealment and gender. *Journal of Gerontology, 49*(4), 149–158.

Hetherington, M. M., & Burnett, L. (1994). Ageing and the pursuit of slimness: Dietary restraint and weight satisfaction in elderly women. *British Journal of Clinical Psychology, 33,* 391–400.

Hill, R. D. (2006). *Positive aging: A guide for mental health professionals and consumers.* New York: Norton Professional Books.

Hinrichsen, G. A. (1999). Interpersonal psychotherapy for late-life depression. In M. Duffy (Ed.), *Handbook of counseling and psychotherapy with older adults* (pp. 470–486). New York: Wiley.

Hubbs-Tait, L. (1989). Coping patterns of aging women: A developmental perspective. In J. D. Garner & S. O. Mercer (Eds.), *Women as they age* (pp. 95–117). Binghamton, NY: Haworth Press.

Huffman, S. B., & Myers, J. E. (1999). Counseling women in midlife: An integrative approach to menopause. *Journal of Counseling & Development, 77,* 258–266.

Hurd, L. C. (2000). Older women's body image and embodied experience: An exploration. *Journal of Women and Aging, 12*(3/4), 77–97.

Jacobs, R. H. (1997). *Be an outrageous older woman.* New York: HarperCollins.

Jang, Y., Kim, G., & Chiriboga, D. (2006). Health perception and depressive symptoms among older Korean Americans. *Journal of Cross-Cultural Gerontology, 21,* 91–102.

Johnston, O., Reilly, J., & Kremer, J. (2004). Women's experiences of appearance concern and body control across the lifespan: Challenging accepted wisdom. *Journal of Health Psychology, 9*(3), 397–410.

Kerson, T. S. (2001). Social work practice with women as they age. In J. D. Garner & S. O. Mercer (Eds.), *Women as they age* (pp. 69–84). Binghamton, NY: Haworth Press.

Killian, T., Turner, J., & Cain, R. (2005). Depressive symptoms of caregiving women in midlife: The role of physical health. *Journal of Women & Aging, 17*(1/2), 115–126.

Komen Foundation. (2004). *Estrogen-progestin combination used in Women's Health Initiative study found to elevate risks for invasive breast cancer, heart disease, stroke.* Retrieved April 21, 2006, from http://www.komen.org/intradoc-cgi/idc_cgi_isapi.dll?IdcService=SS_GET_PAGE&ssDocName=s_004175

Lee, S., Kolonel, L., Wilkens, L., Wan, P., Henderson, B., & Pike, M. (2006). Postmenopausal hormone therapy and breast cancer risk: The multiethnic cohort. *International Journal of Cancer, 118*(5), 1285–1291.

Lewis, D. M., & Cachelin, F. M. (2001). Body image, body dissatisfaction, and eating attitudes in midlife and elderly women. *Eating Disorders, 9,* 29–39.

Li, S., Holm, K., Gulanik, M., Lanusa, D., & Penckofer, S. (1999). The relationship between physical activity and perimenopause. *Health Care for Women International, 20,* 163–178.

Maples, M. F., & Abney, P. C. (2006). Baby boomers mature and gerontological counseling comes of age. *Journal of Counseling & Development, 84,* 3–9.

Mayo Clinic. (2005). *Hot flashes: Ease the discomfort of menopause.* Retrieved April 21, 2006, from http://mayoclinic.com/health/hot-flashes/HQ01409

McLaren, L., & Kuh, D. (2004). Body dissatisfaction in midlife women. *Journal of Aging & Women, 16*(1/2), 35–53.

Molinari, V. (1999). Using reminiscence and life review as natural therapeutic strategies in group therapy. In M. Duffy (Ed.), *Handbook of counseling and psychotherapy with older adults* (pp. 154–165). New York: Wiley.

Muth, J. L., & Cash, T. F. (1997). Body image attitudes: What difference does gender make? *Journal of Applied Social Psychology, 27,* 1438–1452.

Myers, J. E. (1999). Adjusting to role loss and leisure in later life. In M. Duffy (Ed.), *Handbook of counseling and psychotherapy with older adults* (pp. 41–56). New York: Wiley.

Myers, J. E., & Harper, M. C. (2004). Evidence-based effective practices with older adults. *Journal of Counseling & Development, 82,* 207–218.

Myers, J. E., & Sweeney, T. S. (2005). *Counseling for wellness: Theory, research, and practice.* Alexandria, VA: American Counseling Association.

Myers, J. E., & Schwiebert, V. L. (1999). Grandparents and stepgrandparents: Challenges in counseling the extended-blended family. *Adultspan: Theory, Research, and Practice, 1,* 50–61.

National Council on Aging. (2002). *American perceptions of aging in the 21st century: The NCOA's continuing study of the myths and realities of aging.* Retrieved April 21, 2006, from http://www.ncoa.org/Downloads/study_aging.pdf.pdf

National Council on Aging. (2006). *Press room: Fact sheets.* Retrieved April 21, 2006, from http://www.ncoa.org/content.cfm?sectionID=103

National Committee of Grandparents for Children's Rights. (2005). *Mission statement.* Retrieved April 21, 2006, from http://www.grandparentsforchildren.org

North American Menopause Society. (2003). *Menopause guidebook.* Retrieved April 24, 2006, from http://www.menopause.org/edumaterials/guidebook/mgtoc.htm

North American Menopause Society. (2004). *Menopause practice: A clinician's guide.* Retrieved April 21, 2006, from http://www.menopause.org/aboutmeno/04A.pdf

North American Menopause Society. (2005). *1997 survey.* Retrieved April 21, 2006, from http://www.menopause.org/aboutmeno/97survey.htm

Oldenhave, A., & Netelenbos, C. (1994). Pathogenesis of climacteric complaints: Ready for change? *Lancet, 343,* 649, 653.

Palmore, E. (2005). Three decades of research on ageism. *Generation, 29*(3), 87–90.

Petersen, S. (2000). Multicultural perspective on middle-class women's identity development. *Journal of Counseling & Development, 78*(1), 63–71.

Pleis, J. R., Benson, V., & Schiller, J. S. (2003). *Summary of health statistics for U.S. adults: National health interview survey, 2000.* Retrieved April 21, 2006, from http://www.cdc.gov/nchs/data/series/sr_10/sr10_215.pdf

Pratt, S. G., & Matthews, K. (2006). *Superfoods healthstyle: Proven strategies for lifelong health*. New York: HarperCollins.

Qualls, S. H. (2002). Women in the middle: Caretaking issues in therapy. In F. K. Trotman & C. M. Brody (Eds.), *Psychotherapy and counseling with older women* (pp. 87–106). New York: Springer.

Reynolds, G. P., Wright, J., & Beale, B. (2003). The roles of grandparents in educating today's children. *Journal of Instructional Psychology, 30*(4), 316–325.

Rice, S. (2001). Sexuality and intimacy for aging women: A changing perspective. In J. D. Garner & S. O. Mercer (Eds.), *Women as they age* (pp. 147–164). Binghamton, NY: Haworth Press.

Rice, V. M. (2005). Strategies and issues for managing menopause-related symptoms in diverse populations: Ethnic and racial diversity. *American Journal of Medicine, 118*, 142–147.

Richardson, V. E. (2001). Mental health of elderly women. In J. D. Garner & S. O. Mercer (Eds.), *Women as they age* (pp. 85–96). Binghamton, NY: Haworth Press.

Robinson Kurpius, S. E., & Nicpon, M. (2003). Menopause and the lives of midlife women. In M. Kopala & M. A. Keitel (Eds.), *Handbook of counseling women* (pp. 269–276). Thousand Oaks, CA: Sage.

Sarton, M. (1997). Toward another dimension. In M. Pearsall (Ed.), *The other within us* (pp. 229–232). Boulder, CO: Westview Press.

Saucier, M. G. (2004). Midlife and beyond: Issues for aging women. *Journal of Counseling & Development, 82*, 420–425.

Sommer, B., Avis, N., Meyer, P., Ory, M., Madden, T., Kagawa-Singer, M., Mouton, C., Rasor, N. O., & Adler, S. (1999). Attitudes toward menopause and aging across ethnic/racial groups. *Psychosomatic Medicine, 61*, 868–875.

Sontag, S. (1979). The double standard of aging. In J. H. Williams (Ed.), *Psychology of women: Selected readings* (pp. 462–478). New York: Norton.

Sontag, S. (1997). The double standard of aging. In M. Pearsall (Ed.), *The other within us* (pp. 19–24). Boulder, CO: Westview Press.

Stanley, M. A., & Averill, P. M. (1999). Strategies for treating generalized anxiety in the elderly. In M. Duffy (Ed.), *Handbook of counseling and psychotherapy with older adults* (pp. 511–525). New York: Wiley.

Stevens, C., & Tiggemann, M. (1998). Women's body figure preferences across the life span. *Journal of Genetic Psychology, 159*(1), 94–102.

Stevens, J., Kumanyika, S. K., & Keil, J. E. (1994). Attitudes toward body size and dieting: Differences between elderly Black and White women. *American Journal of Public Health, 84*(8), 1322–1325.

Tiggemann, M. (2004). Body image across the lifespan: Stability and change. *Body Image, 1*, 29–41.

Tiggemann, M., & Lynch, J. E. (2001). Body image across the lifespan in adult women: The role of self-objectification. *Developmental Psychology, 47*, 243–253.

Trotman, F., & Brody, C. (2002). Cross-cultural perspectives: Grandmothers. In F. Trotman & C. Brody (Eds.), *Psychotherapy and counseling with older women* (pp. 41–57). New York: Springer.

U.S. Census Bureau. (2001). *The 65 years and over population: 2000: Census 2000 Brief.* Retrieved April 21, 2006, from www.census.gov/prod/2001pubs/c2kbr01-10.pdf

U.S. Census Bureau. (2003). *Marital status: 2000: Census 2000 Brief.* Retrieved April 24, 2006, from http://www.census.gov/prod/2003pubs/c2kbr-30.pdf

Vaillant, G. E., & Mukamal, K. (2001). Successful aging. *American Journal of Psychiatry, 158*(6), 839–847.

Warnke, M. A., Hedstrom, S., Cook, E., Armsworth, M., Smith, P., & Prosser, D. (1993). Women's reproductive life cycle issues. In E. P. Cook (Ed.), *Women, relationships, and power: Implications for counseling* (pp. 179–210). Alexandria, VA: American Counseling Association.

Webster, J., & Tiggemann, M. (2003). The relationship between women's body satisfaction and self-image across the lifespan: The role of cognitive control. *Journal of Genetic Psychology, 164*(2), 241–252.

Zerbe, K., & Domnitei, D. (2004). Eating disorders at middle age, part 1. *Eating Disorders Review, 15*(2), 1–3.

Index

older women and, 242,
262–263, 266
spirituality as, 228
in violent relationships, 207–208,
210, 212
Counseling approaches, xi–xii, 1–26
See also specific disorders
activities for further exploration, 22
case study, 19–20
client empowerment and, 7–11, 22
counselor-client relationships
and, 16–18
crossroads in development and,
4–6
female perspectives and, 18–19
gender-role development and,
2–4
intersecting personal and social
identities and, 11–13
personal is political, 6–7, 13–16
self-care and, 20–21
self-exploration exercise, 3
substance abuse and, 15–16
working with girls and women,
6–11
Counselor-client relationships, 16–18,
212
Couples therapy, 200–201
Cowan, G., 174
CPT, 180
Crick, N.R., 67, 70
Crisis management plan, 206
Critical thinking skills, 43–45, 48
Crothers, L.M., 73–74
Culross, Rita R., xiii, 143
Cultural influences
See also Race and ethnicity;
specific cultures
in assessing spirituality,
226–230, 233
cross-cultural views of body
image resilience, 34–37
norms, 74–75, 83
sexual assault and, 171–172
worldviews of ethnic groups, 19
Cummings, A.L., 80
Curanderismo, 229
Cyberbullying, 68
Cyberstalking, 126
Cycle of abuse, 193–197, 196f

D

Dating, 38, 39, 91, 96, 124–125, 132
See also Hook-ups

DeBard, R., 118
Delegation in work-life balance, 162
Dellasega, C., 71, 72, 75, 76, 79, 83
Denial and minimization of abuse,
203, 207
DePorto, D., 194, 211, 212
Depression
body image and, 28, 34, 128
caregivers and, 257
counseling approaches for
women with, 14–15
in older women, 250, 256,
261–262
PTSD and, 170, 181
self-esteem and, 93, 94
substance abuse and, 91
violent relationships and, 199,
205, 213
*Diagnostic and Statistical Manual of
Mental Disorders (DSM-IV-TR)*, 17,
169, 199, 205
Dieting. *See* Body image dissatisfaction
(BID); Body image resilience
Disabilities, 11, 227, 228
Dissociation, 208–209
Dissonance-based strategies, 46, 61–62,
130, 131, 140
Dixon Rayle, A.D., 6
Domestic violence. *See* Intimate part-
ner violence (IPV)
Dong, N.J., 229
Double bind, 1, 4, 18–19, 92
Double standard of aging, 243
Dove campaign for Real Beauty, 131
Drug abuse. *See* Substance abuse
*DSM-IV-TR. See Diagnostic and Statisti-
cal Manual of Mental Disorders*
Dual-earner couples
care-giving concerns of, 151–153
prevention strategies for dealing
with work-life issues, 153–155
role strain and, 156

E

Early childhood, 64, 76, 90, 225
Eating disorders
body image dissatisfaction influencing, 28, 29, 128
prevention strategies for, 43, 130
rates of, 35
self-esteem influencing, 91,
95–96
thinness and, 30
Eck, D., 231
Education, ix, 148–149